MW00477889

Advance Praise

"Arguably, the quality of U.S. nat. _____
and even democracy are a reflection of the all-volunteer force (AVF). Yet
we lack both a comprehensive history and analysis. This book fills that void
while not shying away from the debates, problems, and unresolved issues
that are part of the AVF. Practitioners and scholars are sure to find this
book a valuable resource."—SHARON K. WEINER, associate professor of international relations, School of International Service, American University

"*The All-Volunteer Force* is a must-read. It is the most comprehensive work
to date on the subject of who serves in the modern U.S. military. Taylor
brilliantly organizes a synthesis of works provided by leading scholars in
their respective fields. This will be the go-to source for a multitude of
topics relating to a system that has prevailed for fifty years."—JEREMY P.
MAXWELL, author of *Brotherhood in Combat: How African Americans Found
Equality in Korea and Vietnam*

"In one lively volume, a balanced and comprehensive assessment of the
all-volunteer force. Historical chapters recount how the AVF got started
and how it evolved. Leading scholars offer praise and skepticism in their
assessments of the AVF today and its future challenges. The wide-ranging
chapters offer keen insights into the consequences for U.S. civil-military
relations of relying on volunteers."—CHARLES A. STEVENSON, lecturer,
Advanced International Studies, Johns Hopkins University, and author of
Warriors and Politicians: U.S. Civil-Military Relations under Stress

"*The All-Volunteer Force* is a timely and important look at the history,
challenges, consequences, and significance of America's volunteer military.
William Taylor has assembled an impressive array of essays from veterans
and leading scholars in the fields of military, social, and economic history.
Overall, the book is a substantive, thought-provoking analysis that provides
insight into the triumphs, trials, and tribulations of the U.S. Armed Forces
over the last fifty years."—MARTIN G. CLEMIS, Department of Military
History, U.S. Army Command and General Staff College

"Arriving on the fiftieth anniversary of the end of the draft, and amid a
deepening recruiting crisis across the entire U.S. military, *The All-Volunteer
Force* could not be timelier. Delivering on its editor's promise to provide
'the most comprehensive assessment of the AVF since its advent in 1973,'
this volume contributes greatly to our understanding of the past, present,
and uncertain future of a largely ignored pillar of modern American life:
the all-recruited U.S. military. As the sustainability of the AVF becomes increasingly doubtful, *The All-Volunteer Force* will be a major resource on this

looming strategic and societal question."—GIL BARNDOLLAR, senior research fellow at the Center for the Study of Statesmanship and a senior fellow at Defense Priorities. He has written for the *Wall Street Journal, Los Angeles Times, USA Today, The National Interest, The American Conservative*, and *U.S. Naval Institute Proceedings*.

"Editor William Taylor has assembled a diverse group of contributors—diverse in position taken and diverse in professional background—to conduct a comprehensive assessment of the AVF on its fiftieth anniversary. The immediate implication of an all-volunteer force was lessening of political constraints on sending troops into harm's way. The many results include an increasingly militarized foreign policy, a smaller force operating at far higher tempo than during the Cold War, a reserve force to be mobilized once in a generation for wars of necessity transformed into a force constantly engaged in wars of choice for which they are ill suited, and a force that does not fairly represent the society it defends. *The All-Volunteer Force* is necessary reading for policy makers concerned with the use and production of military force, especially those responsible for raising an effective force for a future war of necessity."—D. ROBERT WORLEY, author of *Shaping U.S. Military Forces: Revolution or Relevance in a Post–Cold War World*

"For over fifty years, young men and women have chosen to join America's military service rather than either await a notice from a local draft board or join during the patriotic surges that accompany most conflicts. Year after year, month after month, recruiting officers administered the traditional oath of office to groups of enlistees before sending them off to their assigned training bases. This recruiting system has served the nation through three major conflicts, two in Iraq and another in Afghanistan, and a half dozen smaller operations. Meanwhile, American forces remained ready to counter a declining Soviet Union and, later, a militarily resurgent China and an expansionist Russia. Yet, in what appears to be a well-oiled bureaucracy, Americans volunteered to serve.

One of America's most prolific political historians, William A. Taylor, has assembled a prominent panel of distinguished scholars to investigate the origins, results, and challenges of the all-volunteer force. They explore its successes, failures, and challenges as it struggled to provide the human capital for the world's most technologically savvy military force. Their descriptions, analysis, and insights into this process represents the most comprehensive investigation of this system of recruitment to date. This book should be required reading for all who need to understand the modern American military establishment."—STEPHEN A. BOURQUE, professor emeritus, U.S. Army Command and General Staff College

THE ALL-VOLUNTEER FORCE

STUDIES IN **CMR**
CIVIL-MILITARY RELATIONS

William A. Taylor, Series Editor

THE ALL-VOLUNTEER FORCE

Fifty Years of Service

Edited by William A. Taylor
Foreword by David M. Kennedy

UNIVERSITY PRESS OF KANSAS

To my wife and children
Renee M. Taylor
Madison G. Taylor
Benjamin A. Taylor

© 2023 by the University Press of Kansas
All rights reserved

Published by the University Press of Kansas (Lawrence, Kansas 66045), which was organized
by the Kansas Board of Regents and is operated and funded by Emporia State University, Fort
Hays State University, Kansas State University, Pittsburg State University, the University of
Kansas, and Wichita State University.

Library of Congress Cataloging-in-Publication Data
Names: Taylor, William A., 1975– editor.
Title: The all-volunteer force : fifty years of service / edited by William A. Taylor.
Description: Lawrence, Kansas : University Press of Kansas, 2023. | Series:
    Studies in civil-military relations | Includes index.
Identifiers: LCCN 2022056012 (print) | LCCN 2022056013 (ebook)
    ISBN 9780700635382 (cloth)
    ISBN 9780700634811 (paperback)
    ISBN 9780700634828 (ebook)
Subjects: LCSH: Military service, Voluntary—United States—History—20th century.
    | Military service, Voluntary—United States—History—21st century. | United States—
    Armed Forces—Recruiting, enlistment, etc. | United States—Armed Forces—Reserves—
    Recruiting, enlistment, etc. Classification: LCC UB323 .A6488 2023 (print) | LCC UB323
    (ebook) | DDC 355.2/23620973--dc23/eng/20221123
LC record available at https://lccn.loc.gov/2022056012.
LC ebook record available at https://lccn.loc.gov/2022056013.

British Library Cataloguing-in-Publication Data is available.

Printed in the United States of America

10 9 8 7 6 5 4 3 2 1

The paper used in this publication is acid free and meets the minimum requirements of
the American National Standard for Permanence of Paper for Printed Library Materials
Z39.48-1992.

Contents

Illustrations

Foreword

David M. Kennedy

This timely volume offers the most comprehensive analysis to date of the U.S. all-volunteer force (AVF), which came into being a half century ago. Controversy has attended the AVF ever since its inception, as the essays that follow amply document.

For many citizens, civil and military alike, the end of conscription—the "draft"—in 1973 seemed like a dramatic repudiation of tradition, a bold though risky abandonment of the kind of military machine that the Selective Service System had mustered to wage World War II as well as the "hot" phases of the Cold War in Korea and Vietnam. But, in fact, over the previous two centuries of the republic's existence, the nation had relied on a conscript force on just four occasions for a total of only thirty-five years. So, while it is true that conscription was the norm through the World War II and early Cold War decades, the advent of the AVF in a sense marked less of a rupture with custom than a reembrace of a venerable practice.

Yet that historical reflection did not fully lay to rest, neither in 1973 nor later, a range of anxieties about the character of the AVF in a time of increasingly challenged U.S. global hegemony. *The Report of the President's Commission on an All-Volunteer Armed Force*, released on February 21, 1970, made that clear. Chaired by former Eisenhower-era secretary of defense Thomas Gates, the commission unanimously recommended the transition to the AVF even while anticipating some of the problems to which it could conceivably give rise.

The AVF, wrote the commission, might

- Become isolated from civil society;
- Be disproportionately recruited from minority communities, especially African American as well as low-income households more generally;
- Lead to a decline in popular engagement with issues of foreign policy;

- Encourage military adventurism; and
- Erode civilian respect for the military.

Even as it expressed those concerns, the Gates Commission rather cavalierly dismissed them as developments that would not be tolerated by an ever-vigilant citizenry.

Yet as the essays that follow richly illuminate, arguably all of those eventualities—intriguingly, save the last, concerning civilian attitudes about servicemembers—have in some degree come to pass. Added to this is the observation that while the AVF was touted as a cost-saving measure, over time the expense of recruiting and retaining sufficient numbers of qualified personnel has steadily mounted. As the chief of the U.S. Navy Recruiting Command put it in 2015, "We are pricing ourselves out of some kinds of warfare."[1]

Perhaps the most chronically troubling implication of our reliance on a volunteer military concerns the role of civil society when it comes to the fateful decision to resort to armed force as an instrument of policy. Compared with the first quarter century after World War II, when the United States maintained a draft force, the rate of military deployments has increased by a factor of five in the AVF era. Nothing brought the implications of those numbers home more forcefully to this writer than hearing the president of the United States tell a group of Oval Office visitors on March 21, 2006, "If I had to do this [invade Iraq] with a draft army, I would have been impeached by now."[2] Here was a stark acknowledgment that the type of force at his command, insulated as it was from the lives of the vast majority of citizens, largely comprising recruits from the least privileged sectors of society claiming a scant 3 percent of GDP, created political space for the decision to use force that would have been markedly more constricted in a previous (draft) era.

For all its admirable virtues—duly acknowledged in the pages that follow—this book serves as a powerful reminder that the AVF must continue to command the vigilance of all citizens if it is effectively to safeguard the nation's security as well as honor its dearest values.

Notes

1. Vice Admiral William Moran, Hoover Institution Symposium, Stanford University, May 19, 2015.
2. Notes, Oval Office meeting with President George W. Bush, March 21, 2006, in author's possession.

Series Editor's Foreword

William A. Taylor

On July 1, 2023, the U.S. all-volunteer force (AVF) marked its fiftieth anniversary. Such a momentous occasion presents an ideal time to reflect upon its half century of existence and ponder what those five decades indicate about the distinct institution of the AVF, its broader meaning for military service in modern America, and its larger connection to civil-military relations. This comprehensive volume by leading scholars, experienced practitioners, and expert analysts deeply delves into the AVF across four major parts, examining in great detail its history, results, challenges, and implications. In doing so, this book provides many insights into the particulars of the AVF, including valuable perspectives from a diverse team of accomplished authors on its past, present, and future. Equally important, this work as a whole illuminates three expansive themes: who serves, how they serve, and why it matters for civil-military relations.

Who serves in the U.S. military has always been a relevant and vital question. Since the advent of the AVF, it has become even more so. The historic transition from the draft to volunteer service opened some opportunities for previously marginalized groups, especially women and African Americans. At the same time, many substantial obstacles endured. While much progress has been made, more work must be done. Serious problems persist, especially the dearth of minorities and women in the most senior leadership positions and the abhorrent presence of sexual assault and sexual harassment in the military that leaders—civilian and military alike—have failed to eliminate. In addition, the palpable shift in attitudes of American youth away from military service, either because they have a declining interest in pursuing it or because they cannot qualify for various reasons, reinforces that the recruiting and retention difficulties accompanying the AVF at its creation linger in newfangled forms.

How individuals serve also matters a great deal and reveals much about both the armed forces and American society. Contentious debates pitting compulsion versus volunteerism animated the milieu from whence the

AVF arose. Today, all those willing and able to serve can do so. Beyond the dichotomy between the draft and the volunteer military, however, associated concepts surface. The perennial tension between individual liberty and national security that undergirded the transition to the AVF is relevant to American democracy in a plethora of other contested arenas, including service, spending, surveillance, and citizenship, among others. Finding the appropriate balance between freedom on the one hand and security on the other remains an extremely difficult yet supremely indispensable undertaking. The perceptions of many Americans regarding what the government owes to its people often stand in stark contrast to questions running in the opposite direction.

Military service generally and the AVF specifically also shape our understanding of civil-military relations. The traditional conception of civil-military relations has often focused on the two-dimensional interface between presidents and generals. The issue of civilian control continues to be an important, and indeed essential, line of inquiry for the field. The AVF and its fifty years of service offer a powerful reminder, however, that governments, militaries, and societies interact in much broader exchanges. As a result, civil-military relations form a three-dimensional crossroads that simultaneously flow in multiple directions and consequently result in myriad complexities. The nodes at which these three entities intersect are profoundly transformative, often morphing one another in intriguing ways at every point of interaction. The AVF illuminates one key part of that triangular interchange: the relationship between the armed forces and the society that they seek to protect and vice versa. Therefore, an enhanced grasp of the AVF over five decades also broadens our understanding of civil-military relations in meaningful ways. Overall, *The All-Volunteer Force: Fifty Years of Service* delivers wide-ranging coverage of the AVF across its main dimensions and offers meaningful knowledge about who serves, how they do so, and why it matters for civil-military relations as a whole.

Acknowledgments

It has been a great honor to complete this volume. Every book is a collaborative endeavor, and edited collections are even more so. Along the way, I have had the prodigious fortune to work with many wonderful people. All contributed to this book in their own significant way. I wish to acknowledge them here as a small yet sincere token of my appreciation for their influence on this work and, indeed, to their valuable support in all my endeavors.

At the University Press of Kansas, I have been most blessed to work with Joyce Harrison, editor in chief, and her entire team. Joyce has always been a stalwart supporter of my efforts and has become a dear friend over the years. I am most grateful for her gracious mentorship, wise counsel, and warm camaraderie. At the 2018 Society for Military History annual meeting in Louisville, Kentucky, Joyce and I contacted each other to say that we each had a new and exciting proposal for the other. We agreed to have lunch, where Joyce asked me to start a new book series, and I suggested to her that we complete a fiftieth-anniversary volume on the AVF. Both endeavors became mutually reinforcing, one culminating in this book and the other resulting in the series within which it resides. Along the way, Joyce and I have worked closely on these related endeavors, and I have always benefited from her cogent insights. Kelly Chrisman Jacques shepherded the manuscript through editing and production, while Karl Janssen produced the wonderful cover design. Derek Helms directed marketing efforts and ensured widespread publicity.

The contributors to this volume represent the absolute best from several important fields, including war and society scholars, traditional military historians, political scientists, policy analysts, and personnel economists, as well as both senior and junior military officers. They each provide unique and valuable perspectives on the AVF through their vast individual knowledge and collective experience. I have spent my entire academic career respecting the work of each one, and partnering with them on this volume has been a dream come true. They all took my basic guidance and produced substantial studies that inform our understanding of the AVF in new and profound ways. In addition, they persevered through a global pandemic, showing commitment and dedication to this project that is genuinely humbling. For their hard work and unwavering support, I am truly thankful. Other esteemed colleagues agreed to read this book, including William T. Allison, Gil Barndollar, Stephen A. Bourque, Martin Clemis, Gregory A. Daddis, Peter Feaver, Robert L. Goldich, David Kieran, Kyle Longley, Jeremy P. Maxwell, Charles A. Stevenson, Sharon K. Weiner, James H. Willbanks, and D. Robert Worley. I am most grateful for their very positive endorsements.

The broad contours of this project began with a major conference on the AVF that Angelo State University hosted in 2019. When Maj. Gen. Dennis Laich called me out of the blue and to ask about hosting this forum at my institution, I was most honored and humbled. The leadership team at Angelo State University immediately backed the effort with both enthusiastic support and significant resources, something for which I remain most grateful. The conference enabled nationally known experts on the AVF—including multiple contributors to this volume—to engage with members of the ASU family, including students, faculty, staff, administrators, and community members. Everyone benefited, and the event, from which this collection draws its original inspiration, was a huge success.

At Angelo State University, I have found my intellectual home and academic family. The university recruited me straight from graduate school to help start a brand-new program, and I now serve as the Lee Drain Endowed University Professor of Global Security Studies in the Kay Bailey Hutchison Center for Security Studies, which resulted from those inauspicious beginnings. The university has always invested in my potential, and I have constantly felt a keen sense of responsibility to demonstrate through my teaching, research, and service a genuine appreciation of their confidence and commitment. My sincere hope is that, in some small way, I reflect the excellence of the Angelo State University values—the Ram Fam as we like to say—in everything that I do. President Ronnie Hawkins Jr., along with Donald R. Topliff, provost and vice president for academic affairs; Clifton Jones, vice provost; Michael W. Salisbury, dean of the College of Graduate Studies and Research; John E. Klingemann, dean of the College of Arts and Sciences; and Joseph C. Rallo, chair of the Department of Security Studies and Criminal Justice, have all been stalwart supporters of my work and have provided ASU with keen vision and leadership. I am most grateful to work with them all and benefit from their gracious mentorship and steadfast support. My department colleagues, Bruce E. Bechtol Jr., Anthony Celso, Kenneth Heineman, Won-Jae Lee, and Randolph Hicks, have nurtured me from my first day as a tenure-track assistant professor, always providing wise counsel, good guidance, and true friendship. Likewise, my many graduate and undergraduate students always stimulate my thinking and remind me that teaching, research, and service are not discreet activities but interconnected parts of true lifelong learning, both for them and for me.

The most thanks go to my family, both immediate and extended. My parents, Richard A. Taylor and L. Diane Taylor, have always modeled lifelong learning for me. Some of my earliest memories as a child involve sneaking around and hiding under my dad's desk in his home office as he labored on his PhD dissertation at the Catholic University of America—in his case, a second doctorate. Likewise, my mom modeled leadership at every level of education in both public and private schools, spanning classroom teacher, reading specialist, school principal, curriculum coordinator, and assistant headmaster. They always encouraged me to pursue my dreams and helped me do so along the way. My wife and kids—Renee, Madison, and Benjamin—to whom I have dedicated this work, have always supported my limitless fascination with history and my endless pursuit to find meaningful linkages between the past and present. I am forever grateful for their steadfast backing and infinite love.

Abbreviations

AFQT	Armed Forces Qualification Test
AVF	all-volunteer force
AWOL	absent without leave
CBO	Congressional Budget Office
CENTCOM	Central Command
CNAS	Center for a New American Strategy
DOD	Department of Defense
ERA	Equal Rights Amendment
FY	fiscal year
ISIS/ISIL	Islamic State of Iraq and Syria / Islamic State of Iraq and the Levant
MOS	military occupational specialty
NATO	North Atlantic Treaty Organization
NCO	noncommissioned officer
PTSD	post-traumatic stress disorder
PX	post exchange
ROTC	Reserve Officer Training Corps
VA	Veterans Affairs

Of course, civil-military relations will never be uncontroversial. They have not been so in the past, whether manpower has been raised by conscription or voluntarily. The military have a distinct and separate set of responsibilities of fundamental importance to the survival of American society. Military leaders seek assurance that they will be able to accomplish successfully the tasks they may be called upon to do. Uncertainty about potential threats and our ability to cope with them leads to differing judgments about the size of forces required. These differences bring about conflict between the demands of the military and those of other groups in our society and will do so regardless of whether there is a draft.

— President's Commission on an All-Volunteer Armed Force
   (Gates Commission), December 24, 1969

Introduction
Advent of the All-Volunteer Force

William A. Taylor

It was both a normal and unusually significant day in Oakland, California, on June 30, 1973. Amid the hustle of the vibrant city, an event that had been routine for more than thirty years suddenly became unique. In Oakland's Armed Forces Entrance and Examination Station at 2 P.M. that day, twenty-four-year-old Sacramento resident Dwight Elliot Stone took one step forward to symbolize his induction into the army as the "last draftee." That move must have seemed to him to cover a gigantic chasm between his past civilian life and his future military one. It was a ritual that more than 17 million men had participated in throughout U.S. history.

That moment—at once quite anxious, highly personal, and very weighty—did not go unnoticed for newly minted Private Stone, nor for the nation that he now served. "I think of the other draftees, the ones who went before, since I am the last draftee," reflected a solemn Stone. His immediate thoughts were on practical questions: where would he be stationed, what unit would he be assigned to, and what would the food be like? Even so, the young man resigned himself to his fate and sought to put his best foot forward, both literally and figuratively. "The thing in my mind was to serve my time and get out with an honorable discharge," Stone resolved. "I'm certain that's what the other draftees thought of, too. I don't plan to make a career of it, but since I'm here, I might as well put forth my best effort."

The army assigned Private Stone to Company E, 2d Battalion, 2d Basic Combat Training Brigade at Fort Polk, Louisiana, where heat, humidity, and precipitation became constant companions, although certainly not welcome ones. There, he encountered many surprises. Once again, his thoughts turned to food. "I figured the food would be horrible, but it's quite good," Stone admitted. "It's better than a lot of restaurants I've been to where I've paid $7 or $8 for a steak and couldn't chew it." Other experiences were more meaningful. Stone provided leadership to his unit as the assistant platoon guide for Echo Company's 4th Platoon.

Still other revelations were not as pleasant. As a civilian plumber, Stone had made roughly $285 per week for a monthly pay around $1,140 after taxes. As a draftee, his pay would hover around "a grand total" of $307 per month before taxes. Despite the drastic pay cut, Stone showed much potential. Captain Robert H. Cooper, his commanding officer, boasted that the private had "the makings of a good soldier" and acknowledged that he was unique as the personification of the major shift from draftees to an all-volunteer force. "Pvt. Stone, being the last draftee, is going to get recognition from all over the nation," Cooper conceded. "How he does in the service will probably affect the many young people who will enlist."[1] Indeed it would.

This book is the most comprehensive assessment of the all-volunteer force (AVF) since its advent in 1973, examining its history, results, challenges, and implications, and argues that the AVF has been the most significant development in modern American military history. Throughout the vast majority of the twentieth century, the United States relied on a mixture of volunteers who chose to serve and conscripts provided through the Selective Service System, colloquially known as the draft, to mobilize for its wars, including World War I, World War II, the Korean War, and the Vietnam War. When the United States emerged as a world superpower in the aftermath of World War II, policymakers depended on the draft during peacetime as well.

First, the opening chapters outline the basic history of the AVF, including historical context, background on the conscription system that preceded it, analysis of the economics that undergirded its advent, evaluation of the Gates Commission that recommended it, and considerations of race within it. The draft operated continuously from 1940 to 1947, lapsed briefly from 1947 to 1948, and then functioned constantly from 1948 to 1973. Largely for political reasons, presidential candidate Richard M. Nixon ran for election with a pledge to end the draft. Economists became major supporters of the AVF, and many of their arguments formed the central rationale for ending the draft. Once elected, Nixon formed the Gates Commission, named after Thomas S. Gates Jr., its chair and former secretary of defense in the Dwight D. Eisenhower administration, to deliver on his campaign promise. The handpicked official group did just that, recommending an end to the draft and the creation of the AVF in 1973 amid significant angst from military leaders. Race was an omnipresent subject in debates about the AVF, and the heightened racial tensions in the U.S. armed forces at that time proved pivotal. Since its advent in 1973, the AVF has been the sole provider of military personnel during times of both peace and war.

Part two of this collection delineates the results of the AVF, including scrutiny of its transformation of gender within military service, exploration of its socioeconomics, and analysis of its consequences for military benefits and their relationship to the welfare state. At its core, the AVF shifted the concept of military service from an obligation of citizenship to one possible career path among many. In addition, it has held momentous sway on broader American society, changing fundamentally the representation of women within the armed forces. Prior to the AVF, the percentage of women in the services was less than 2 percent. Immediately upon its inception, policymakers recruited women as a necessary offset for the loss of male draftees. As a result, their numbers in uniform rose steadily, reaching 16 percent today. Such revolutions altered both the U.S. military and American society.

The chapters in the third part summarize the myriad challenges of the AVF, including an appraisal of its viability, scrutiny of its efficiency, and review of its use of reserve components. The AVF faced difficult questions from its creation. These trials, however, have increased significantly as a result of the Iraq and Afghanistan Wars in the twenty-first century. In the aftermath of these conflicts, it is appropriate—and indeed necessary—to reassess the AVF. The inability of it to win recent wars, the use of reserve components in an operational role versus a strategic one, and its vast human toll—including rising rates of divorce, post-traumatic stress disorder (PTSD), homelessness, and suicide among veterans—demand an unvarnished evaluation of the problems that it faces.

Finally, this compilation closes by considering the implications of the AVF, including appraisal of its influence on foreign policy, accounting of its relationship to military culture, consideration of its force structure, judgment of its contribution to the civil-military gap, and a conclusion that explores its overall legacy at fifty years of service. Several important trends have surfaced and present cautionary tales for the future of the AVF. It has militarized foreign policy, granting the executive branch carte blanche with respect to engaging in long and costly wars. Policymakers have deployed the AVF five times more often than the hybrid draft/volunteer force that preceded it. Finding the necessary personnel for the armed forces proves increasingly difficult as young Americans' propensity to join and ability to qualify for military service both have declined significantly in the recent past. Its existence has created a palpable divide between the less than 0.5 percent of the American population who serves in the military and the broader civilian society. In addition, more civilian capacity is necessary to augment the armed forces in such missions as stability operations and counterinsurgency, especially regarding such traditional civilian roles as economic development and postconflict resolution that policymakers have transferred recently to military personnel. Therefore, cogent and comprehensive scholarship on the AVF and its place in American society is vital. While this volume is crucial based on merit, relevance, and significance alone, it also benefits greatly from timing—there is no better occasion to read about and reflect upon the AVF than at its fifty-year anniversary.

The AVF has been a major institution of the U.S. military specifically and American society generally since its advent in 1973. Over the course of five decades, it has displayed notable successes and has experienced evident trials. In the wake of the Iraq and Afghanistan Wars, however, the AVF has attracted more attention than ever before. Officials have struggled to use it effectively, and the AVF's sustainability has become problematic. Several examples prove the point. The opening of combat roles to women in December 2015 has triggered debates on whether women will have to register for the draft. In September 2017, Congress created the National Commission on Military, National, and Public Service, which was the largest public reassessment of the AVF since its inception. Throughout 2018, the U.S. Army failed to meet its recruiting goals across all components, including the active force, reserves, and National Guard. This major shortfall has received widespread notice at the highest levels and triggered an army-wide reassessment of the AVF. In the 2019 defense budget, more than one-third of all spending went to personnel costs, and this proportion has risen rapidly, leading to extensive and crucial questions about sustainability and critical tradeoffs in maintenance, modernization, research, and development. In February 2019, a federal judge ruled that an all-male draft would be unconstitutional, setting up what will likely be a major Supreme Court ruling and attendant vigorous debate. The national commission concluded its work in 2020, sparking renewed public interest and wide-ranging dialogue.

Therefore, the AVF has become a critical national issue. In reflecting on the force after fifty years, this book employs a multidisciplinary approach, presenting the best scholarship on the AVF by eminent historians, political scientists, leading economists, military officers, and policy experts. It offers a balanced approach, assessing both the strengths and the weaknesses of the AVF, in an accessible format. Of the little recent writing existing on the AVF, much of it is polemical. In contrast, this anthology offers a ready resource for journalists, policymakers, and general readers looking for rigorous analysis as they grapple with the crescendo of issues relating to the AVF and consider the myriad options necessary to address them.

The President's Commission on an All-Volunteer Armed Force noted the meaningful and widespread implications of the advent of the AVF as it advocated for its creation. The group also explicitly understood that such a momentous move transcended military mobilization: at its core, the AVF epitomized civil-military relations. "Of course, civil-military relations will never be uncontroversial. . . . These differences bring about conflict between the demands of the military and those of other groups in our society and will do so regardless of whether there is a draft."[2]

As the epigraph to this book clearly demonstrates, the AVF—and armed services more broadly—at the very core reveals valuable insights into civil-military relations, which exist anytime policy, politics, and society interact. Therefore, it provides an excellent case study through which to examine such vital connections. Rarely has one topic involved so many crucial aspects to such an important overall theme. The AVF involves policy, specifically the initial decisions to end the draft and to rely exclusively on volunteers, the subsequent programs and initiatives that occurred over the next five decades to shape it, and the policies that remain necessary today and into the future to address its many challenges and implications. Likewise, politics have always been at the core of the AVF. Such considerations formed the crux of the Nixon administration's twin goals to end the war in Vietnam and to end the draft. And politics— or rather the lack of political engagement by Congress and the American public with the AVF—have allowed presidents repeatedly to use it with little public discourse over either the wisdom or costs of military action, whether in terms of money, lives, or social ramifications. Finally, the AVF relates directly to American society. Important debates about its implications in terms of race, gender, socioeconomics, foreign policy, and the civil-military gap have existed since its inception. They continue unresolved today, if anything in more pointed and significant ways.[3]

Existing works on the AVF generally fall into one of five main categories. First, there are books that examine the transition to the AVF.[4] Second, there are commemorative volumes analyzing it from the vantage point of its past anniversaries.[5] Third, there are accounts on alternatives to it, including the draft, universal military training, and the privatization of armed force, among others.[6] Fourth, there are general overviews of military service that touch on the AVF among such other related topics as integration based on race, gender, or sexual orientation; recruiting and retention; and the relationship between military service and citizenship.[7] Finally, there are the critiques, censuring it on a number of important grounds, including sustainability, the civil-military gap, fairness, effectiveness, or all the above.[8]

On the whole, these publications demonstrate two important dynamics: the AVF continues to attract great interest across multiple categories, and there is increasingly more attention focused on it in the aftermath of the Iraq and Afghanistan Wars and upon its fiftieth anniversary. While the AVF deserves extensive study for the five categories discussed above, its influence on America—historically, presently, and into the future—is far vaster. This will continue to increase in the future, encompassing the most significant issues of military history, defense policy, and war and society in modern American history.

The various chapters in this volume reveal a great deal regarding the AVF. In chapter 1, Amy J. Rutenberg provides exceptional context on conscription. She gives a useful overview of the draft in wartime throughout American history, including the Revolutionary War, the Civil War, and World War II. While many differences existed, Rutenberg expertly explains the main commonalities in the draft throughout the American experience: all were essentially wartime, quite unpopular, and eschewed universal male military service with various exemptions and deferments. From this, she shows how the Cold War draft was decidedly different in important ways, including its fundamental purpose to maintain a large standing army during general peacetime. Such other elements as its unpopularity, exemptions, and deferments remained. Her cogent analysis of manpower channeling gives remarkable insights into the inner workings of the Cold War draft.

Michael Gibbs and Timothy J. Perri explore in chapter 2 the complex yet vital relationship between economics and the AVF. In doing so, they uncover one of the earliest economic analyses of conscription by Gary Becker. They illustrate the major economic views of conscription and demonstrate the profound influence that both economics as a field and economists as a community had on ending the draft and creating the AVF. Becker's ideas predated more public views held by such towering figures as Milton Friedman and Walter Oi that later figured prominently in the advent of the AVF. While Gibbs and Perri admit that the lack of apparent influence of Becker's work is a quandary, their novel study demonstrates the interconnectedness of the economics community at the moment of decision for the AVF. Therefore, the group as a whole played a vital role in its creation.

In chapter 3, William A. Taylor explores the significance of the President's Commission on an All-Volunteer Armed Force, colloquially known as the Gates Commission after its chair, Thomas S. Gates Jr. He reveals how the heightened personnel requirements of the Vietnam War placed

the Selective Service System front and center in American society. Sensing a political opportunity and delivering on a campaign pledge, President
Richard Nixon convened this commission of prominent citizens to solidify the arguments for the AVF and to create a viable plan to implement it.

Beth Bailey reveals in chapter 4 the prominent place of race in the
debates regarding the AVF. In many ways, the AVF became a microcosm
for the racial divisions of the time. She also reveals how it subsequently
changed the racial demographics of the U.S. military. The AVF made
the armed forces more representative of American society and opened
more opportunities for previously marginalized groups, including African Americans. As a result, representation became a major component of
the AVF.

Kara Dixon Vuic demonstrates the important place of gender within
the AVF, both at its founding and beyond, in chapter 5. She clearly shows
how the advent of the AVF fundamentally redefined the historic linkages
between masculinity and military service, even if it did not completely
overturn them. Her study reveals the two central facets of debates regarding gender and the AVF, namely, conscription and combat. As a result,
Vuic reminds us that women were always an essential component of the
volunteer armed forces, even when their service was greatly conscribed.
With the advent of the AVF, opportunities for women in military service
expanded, even though many challenges remained.

In chapter 6, Jennifer Mittelstadt persuasively shows how the end of
the draft and the advent of the AVF fundamentally transformed military
benefits. Before committing themselves to the AVF, recruits expected
enhanced benefits, and the government provided them in an expanding
array of forms. Most notably, officials broadened who received benefits
to include all ranks and their families. Such a momentous shift had many
prominent consequences, most tangibly significant costs, and fundamentally revolutionized government benefits vis-à-vis the armed forces. In
part, such a shift contributed to the widening civil-military gap in the
sense that servicemembers now enjoyed expanded benefits at the same
time that civilian social-welfare benefits contracted, thereby making the
two divergent in both quantity and quality.

Titus Firmin explores in chapter 7 the socioeconomics of the AVF.
He counters persistent characterizations of the armed forces as predominately working class and instead persuasively shows its predominately
middle-class composition. Firmin interrogates the transition toward
high-technology weapons procurement, most notably the U.S. Army's
"Big Five." Such a move ensured that recruiting efforts attempted to find
young Americans capable of excelling at skilled training. The result was
an increasingly middle-class force with high educational attainment and

valuable technical skills. Firmin convincingly demonstrates how these technological changes drove additional alterations in force structure, thereby ensuring that the AVF became more representative of American society in socioeconomic terms.

In chapter 8, Major General Dennis Laich forcefully argues that the AVF has numerous challenges, most notably viability. He questions whether it is effective and considers if it will work in the future, touching on a range of challenges vis-à-vis the AVF, including fairness and sustainability. Laich reveals numerous mechanisms that policymakers have used—dwell time, psychotropic drugs, and stop-loss—to offset these myriad obstacles. His "AVF arithmetic" highlights some of the many issues confronting the AVF after fifty years of service. Perhaps most troubling, Laich divulges that both willingness and ability to serve have dramatically declined among American youth.

Lawrence B. Wilkerson, in chapter 9, evaluates the contested record of the AVF in terms of efficiency. He shows how the AVF has created a problematic imbalance: a force that keeps shrinking due to higher costs but tasked with responsibilities that keep growing at the behest of its civilian masters. Making important distinctions between major war and smaller actions, Wilkerson questions the track record of the AVF, comparing its apex in the Persian Gulf War to its nadir in the Iraq and Afghanistan Wars. Wilkerson also reflects on such global threats as Russia's aggressions in eastern Europe and China's provocations in the South China Sea and saber rattling against Taiwan. In his assessment, the AVF would prove woefully lacking in both, perhaps even either, scenario.

In chapter 10, Major General Jeffrey E. Phillips provides a detailed accounting of the reserve components and their close and essential relationship with the AVF. While the reserves and National Guard have a long and storied history all their own, the advent of the AVF proved critical in transforming their role in U.S. national security. Some of the changes were positive, while others proved more vexing. The Iraq and Afghanistan Wars heavily utilized the reserve components, as the attendant Total Force policy had indeed envisioned. Such unintended consequences as repeat deployments and shrinking dwell time have proved far more problematic. Overall, Phillips challenges Americans to ponder the numerous shifts in the reserve components engendered by the AVF and to consider more fully their significant consequences.

Adrian R. Lewis explores military culture and the AVF in chapter 11. He draws much needed attention to the contrast between two vital yet opposing notions: the nation and the state. Lewis argues that the AVF severed the intimate connection between citizens and their government, thereby emphasizing the *state* while minimizing the *nation*. With no obligation for any American to serve in the armed forces, that state was able to wage wars of choice in Iraq and Afghanistan while the nation increasingly fractured along various—and multiplying—identities. The overall result, Lewis contends, is a retreat from U.S. leadership of the very system that it intentionally created after World War II, largely because Americans are no longer willing to view military service as an essential obligation for a nation, a perspective most tangibly represented by the advent of the AVF.

In chapter 12, Mark F. Cancian explores the complicated yet undeniable connection between force structure and the AVF. He expertly describes how the advent of the AVF led to major adjustments to the force structure of the U.S. armed forces. Some of the changes were expected, including higher costs and a smaller force. Others, however, were unanticipated at the dawn of the AVF, including more reliance on reserves, government civilians, capital assets, and private contractors. In charting these substantial modifications to force structure, Cancian discloses the considerable variations that the advent of the AVF wrought on the U.S. military, both at that time and ever since. Ultimately, such fluctuations to force structure have had far-reaching repercussions, fundamentally altering how the United States wages war.

Finally, in chapter 13, Marybeth P. Ulrich explores the association between the civil-military gap and the AVF. She argues that the AVF has exacerbated the divide between the U.S. military and the society that it protects. Ulrich highlights several important factors that contribute to this divide, including demographic imbalances and differences in political attitudes between civilians and servicemembers. As a result, she demonstrates the critical linkages between a military and the society it seeks to defend and the vital importance of drawing them together in a closer bond.

These chapters provide a plethora of insights in and of themselves. Each stands on its own merits as a substantial contribution to our understanding of the AVF. Collectively, however, they illuminate three major themes related to the momentous influence of the AVF and its legacy after fifty years.

First, the AVF has fundamentally transformed the U.S. military. Firmin challenges the persistent perception regarding the U.S. military's socioeconomic composition. In doing so, he clearly establishes the predominantly middle-class makeup of the AVF. Firmin demonstrates how the AVF profoundly altered the military by focusing more on high-quality recruits, efforts ensuring that the armed forces became progressively more middle class over time. Major General Laich argues that the AVF presents enormous challenges and is both unfair and unsustainable. In doing so, he contends that the AVF has indeed altered the U.S. military, though not in positive ways, having undercut it by making it less fair, less efficient, and far more expensive. Wilkerson clearly shows how the AVF has limited the armed forces' efficiency, leading to massive costs in both blood and treasure with few tangible returns. By explaining how it has proven woefully lacking in terms of efficiency, he reveals how the AVF has resulted in a smaller and smaller force with larger and larger responsibilities. Major General Phillips describes how the advent of the AVF, especially the Total Force policy that accompanied it, changed the reserve components and the U.S. military as a result. The momentous shift from a strategic to an operational reserve was the most notable consequence. Such a transformation altered the U.S. armed forces as well as the American way of waging war, placing tremendous strain on the reserve components through repeated deployments and dwindling dwell time. Cancian explains how cost pressures associated with the AVF made the armed forces smaller, resulting in several unexpected yet quite important changes to the force structure of the U.S. military. This has placed an increased emphasis on reserves, civilians, capital assets, and private contractors. Such alterations also profoundly transformed how the United States wages war.

Second, the AVF has had major influences on the U.S. government. Gibbs and Perri demonstrate how military questions do not always focus exclusively on military issues. The decisive influence of economists in the advent of the AVF is one example of alternative factors—in this case, costs—and alternate sources of sway—in this case, economists. Taylor shows how politics infused the debates over the AVF. Capitalizing on the increasing unpopularity of the draft, presidential candidate Nixon seized a political opportunity by making ending the draft a major campaign promise. Once in office, he relied on a presidential commission to solidify the case for the AVF and to chart a viable path toward its enactment. Mittelstadt shows how the advent of the AVF greatly modified the benefits that the government provided for military service and who received them. This historic shift marked a significant departure in the way that the government supported military servicemembers and their families. Lewis demonstrates how the AVF vitally affected the relationship between the government and its citizens by arguing that it severed the connection between citizenship and military service, thereby making the emphasis on the government—that is, the state—rather than the broader nation itself. As a result, he contends, most Americans now emphasize the benefits of citizenship and eschew consideration of its attendant responsibilities. In this sense, then, the AVF has redefined their notions regarding obligations to government in a democracy.

Third, the AVF has essentially reshaped American society. Rutenberg uncovers the significance of manpower channeling and its rhetorical connection to American families through deferments for fathers and married men. She also explores how momentous rehabilitation efforts, most notably Project 100,000, attempted to reshape American society by eradicating poverty. Bailey illustrates how debates regarding the AVF have often centered on race. During a time of racial division and anger, it came to represent diverse racial interpretations to different audiences. Military leaders often envisioned race, especially internal racial strife among white and Black servicemembers, as a challenge to be managed. Other observers saw in the AVF a powerful opportunity to increase opportunities for African Americans. Still others protested that the armed forces would become unrepresentative of American society or, worse yet, exploit African Americans in the name of national security. Vuic demonstrates how the move to the AVF basically challenged, and in many ways transmuted, broader notions about gender and women's roles in military service. She also links gender and the AVF to broader developments in American society, most notably the Equal Rights Amendment. Ultimately, Vuic illustrates how the AVF altered the possibilities of women's military service, opening additional opportunities even if many hurdles persisted. Ulrich reveals how the AVF greatly affected the relationship between civilian and military spheres within American society, namely in the form of the civil-military gap, by presenting an array of factors, both demographic and political, that have exacerbated this critical divide. In doing so, she reminds us of the delicate yet supremely vital connections between the armed forces and the society they defend.

Taken together, these themes reinforce the critical importance of the AVF, not only to the U.S. military and more broadly the nation's security but also to American society writ large. The advent of the AVF was a critical moment in modern U.S. history, its results were wide ranging and far reaching, its challenges remain both significant and vexing, and its implications are profound, not only for today but also for the future.

While this august and varied group of contributors comprises many of the leading experts on the AVF today, it is important to remember that they do not agree on every aspect of the AVF, nor should they. The intent of this book is to reflect upon the importance of the AVF and to ruminate upon its history, results, challenges, and opportunities, not to approach it as a settled issue in any one of its many facets. The result is a collection of valuable yet diverse perspectives on the AVF. Each contributor makes his or her own observations and conclusions vis-à-vis the AVF. We hope readers will do the same.

When Private Stone took that momentous step signaling his transition from civilian to soldier as this nation's last draftee, he personified the seismic shift that simultaneously occurred as the United States ended the draft and moved to the AVF. Of course, nothing was certain, and many questions remained. Richard J. Levine, military-affairs correspondent for the *Wall Street Journal*, asked the most important one: "Will a Volunteer Army Work?" He pointed to both past accomplishments and future trials to provide guidance in answering it. Referring to the advent of the AVF on July 1, 1973, Levine pointed out, "the nation will be without a military draft law for the first time since April 1947, making the all-volunteer force a legal fact as well as an administration pledge." He considered it "an impressive accomplishment" but also admitted that the concurrent problems of inflation and the Watergate scandal meant that the Nixon administration was "quick to ballyhoo this success." Overall, Levine was not yet convinced, cataloging such potential obstacles for the AVF as viability, efficiency, and costs, among many others.[9]

After the fiftieth anniversary of the AVF, Levine's question and many others remain. *The All-Volunteer Force* explores both the strengths and weaknesses of this significant institution through a comprehensive assessment of its history, results, challenges, and implications since its inception and a serious consideration of its profound and momentous relationship to the military it composes, the government that it serves, and the society that it protects. It is our sincere hope that the insightful and perceptive chapters in this volume will foster serious reflection on and spur additional dialogue about the AVF and its broader significance in modern U.S. history, trigger further research into its many significant dimensions, and generate public dialogue about its past, its legacy, and its future.

Notes

1. M. Gene Mearns, "'Last Draftee' Doing Fine: Pvt. Stone, Who Long Sought Deferment, Changes Views," *Washington Post, Times Herald*, August 12, 1973.

2. Gates Commission, "Chapter XII," December 24, 1969, 23–24, box A31, folder Volunteer Army (2), Arthur F. Burns Papers, Gerald R. Ford Library, Ann Arbor, MI (hereafter cited as GRFL).

3. Gates Commission, "Chapter XII," 23–24.

4. See William A. Taylor, *The Advent of the All-Volunteer Force: Protecting Free Society* (New York: Routledge, 2023); Beth Bailey, *America's Army: Making the All-Volunteer Force* (Cambridge, MA: Belknap Press of Harvard University Press, 2009); and Robert K. Griffith Jr., *The U.S. Army's Transition to the All-Volunteer Force, 1968–1974* (Washington, DC: U.S. Army Center of Military History, 1997).

5. Examples include Bernard Rostker, *I Want You! The Evolution of the All-Volunteer Force* (Santa Monica, CA: RAND, 2006); and Barbara A. Bicksler, Curtis L. Gilroy,

and John T. Warner, eds., *The All-Volunteer Force: Thirty Years of Service* (Washington, DC: Brassey's, 2004).

6. For instance, Amy J. Rutenberg, *Rough Draft: Cold War Military Manpower Policy and the Origins of Vietnam-Era Draft Resistance* (Ithaca, NY: Cornell University Press, 2019); William A. Taylor, *Every Citizen a Soldier: The Campaign for Universal Military Training after World War II* (College Station: Texas A&M University Press, 2014); Sean McFate, *The Modern Mercenary: Private Armies and What They Mean for World Order* (Oxford: Oxford University Press, 2014); J. Garry Clifford and Samuel R. Spencer Jr., *The First Peacetime Draft* (Lawrence: University Press of Kansas, 1986); and James M. Gerhardt, *The Draft and Public Policy: Issues in Military Manpower Procurement, 1945–1970* (Columbus: Ohio State University Press, 1971).

7. See Douglas W. Bristol Jr. and Heather M. Stur, eds., *Integrating the US Military: Race, Gender, and Sexual Orientation since World War II* (Baltimore: Johns Hopkins University Press, 2017); William A. Taylor, *Military Service and American Democracy: From World War II to the Iraq and Afghanistan Wars* (Lawrence: University Press of Kansas, 2016); Nathaniel Frank, *Unfriendly Fire: How the Gay Ban Undermines the Military and Weakens America* (New York: Thomas Dunne, 2009); David R. Segal, *Recruiting for Uncle Sam: Citizenship and Military Manpower Policy* (Lawrence: University Press of Kansas, 1989); and Eliot A. Cohen, *Citizens and Soldiers: The Dilemmas of Military Service* (Ithaca, NY: Cornell University Press, 1985).

8. Examples include Andrew J. Bacevich, *Breach of Trust: How Americans Failed Their Soldiers and Their Country* (New York: Metropolitan, 2013); Dennis Laich, *Skin in the Game: Poor Kids and Patriots* (Bloomington, IN: iUniverse, 2013); and James Wright, *Those Who Have Borne the Battle: A History of America's Wars and Those Who Fought Them* (New York: PublicAffairs, 2012).

9. Richard J. Levine, "Goodbye Draft: Will a Volunteer Army Work?" *Wall Street Journal*, June 28, 1973.

History

1

Conscription

Amy J. Rutenberg

Although 2023 marks the fiftieth anniversary of the modern all-volunteer force in the United States, these five decades are hardly the first time the American military has depended on volunteers. In fact, it has done so for the majority of its existence. In relying on voluntary enlistments, the armed forces of the last fifty years could be framed similarly to those of the nation's first fifty years. Of course, as this volume as a whole makes clear, that type of long view would be overly simplistic. Comparing the modern AVF to the miniscule, provincial force of the early national period is the manpower equivalent of comparing apples to oranges.[1] The modern AVF only makes sense when juxtaposed against the decades of conscription that preceded its advent in 1973.

Understanding how and why conscription has been used in American history provides the context for both the Cold War draft and for the AVF that followed. Through the majority of the nation's existence, the military has used the apparatus of conscription only in wartime. But the exigencies of the Cold War changed planners' calculus for manpower procurement. Except for a brief fourteen-month window in 1947–1948, young men faced the prospect of the draft continuously from 1940 until 1973 through both peacetime and wartime. This shift away from relying on conscription only during times of war broke with longstanding American tradition, but it created a new normal for generations of young men. It also provided a stable base of manpower on which the Department of Defense and each service branch planned. Peacetime conscription, instituted in 1940 and reinstated in 1948, marked a sea change in the way the United States conceived of military service. By 1973, the move back to an AVF marked an equally monumental transformation. The decades of conscription in between, combined with the expanded U.S. role in the world, ensured that the modern AVF bore little resemblance to the peacetime force of 1939.

The AVF's proponents used the excesses of the extended period of peacetime conscription as their starting point for change. Some centered their policy recommendations on philosophical opposition to a draft. Others suggested that a modern, technologically driven military required fewer, more committed people with longer terms of service and better training than draftees. Still others identified structures of inequity within the Selective Service's policies and procedures as the main problem with a conscripted force. Virtually all of these arguments pushed back against an entrenched manpower system created over decades in response to the emergence of the Cold War. The Vietnam War, with its high draft calls, badly exacerbated the system's problems and led to mass opposition to the draft. The political will to reinstate a voluntary system grew directly from that war, but the transition to the AVF was a reaction to the system of peacetime conscription that preceded American military involvement in Vietnam.

A Brief History of the American Wartime Draft

Conscription exists at two levels. The first is conceptual, encompassing the principles used by the state to compel military service from its subjects or citizens. Within the United States, a nation founded on the rhetorical promise of individual liberty from tyrannical power, the specter of government coercion historically sat heavily.[2]

The relationship between the state and its citizens, as potential soldiers, was contested ideological ground from the time of the Revolution. To liberal political theorists, standing armies, even those consisting of volunteers, posed a threat to the polity. They believed that all rulers had the potential to misuse armed force in order to bolster their own power at the expense of citizens' rights. On the other hand, those who lauded civic republicanism stressed the responsibility of the citizen to defend the nation. Fulfillment of military obligation tied the citizen to the state and provided a justification for civic participation.[3] The question was—and remains—how to balance the rights and responsibilities of citizens.[4]

To answer this question, the founders of the United States pulled from both ideological traditions as they built a political structure to undergird the nascent American military. The Constitution placed the U.S. armed forces under civilian control, and the Militia Act of 1792 codified the importance of the citizen-soldier.[5] The law required free, able-bodied, white male inhabitants to enroll in and drill with local militia units that were organized at the state level. Its authors intended universal white, free, male militia service to foster civic virtue, keep defense local, prevent the development of a warrior elite, and ensure a small standing force. Militiamen would remain civilians when not actively engaged in the defense of their homes and property. They served at the discretion of governors in the hopes of eliminating the potential abuse of presidential power. Yet, because the law empowered the president to bring state militias under federal control in certain circumstances, it also provided for the national defense.[6] Theoretically, this meant the nation's standing army and navy could be kept small. And for most of U.S. history, this compromise formula worked well enough despite common problems and inconsistencies. Public militia service was never universal, and it trailed off significantly during the nineteenth century. In the early national period, states routinely ignored federal orders while funding for equipment, training, and law enforcement dwindled until the service requirement was finally repealed in 1903.[7] Nevertheless, the general philosophy of a small standing national force remained salient until World War II.

There were times in American history, however, when the federal government deemed conditions dire enough to require coercion. At these moments, expedience trumped philosophy. The second level at which conscription exists, therefore, is the nuts-and-bolts reality of justifying, administering, and experiencing a draft.

The Revolutionary War set the precedent. Despite their emphasis on the political philosophy of liberty, the new nation's leaders needed manpower to win their war for independence. General George Washington found state militias unreliable, and volunteers for the Continental Army proved hard to come by. National survival required conscription. The convoluted system that emerged placed the onus of procuring men on individual states, but even so, 1778 marked the first time Congress authorized a draft in order to man a national military.[8]

Almost a century passed before Americans again faced conscription, as the manpower needs of the Civil War forced both the Union and the Confederacy to turn to the draft. In the North, Congress and the War Department once again tried to raise men through state militias, including by compulsion. But local opposition, inconsistent regulations, and lack of political will from individual governors ensured inadequate results. Under pressure from Secretary of War Edwin Stanton and the states themselves, Congress passed the Enrollment Act of 1863 to institute a national draft. In the South, where the population of men deemed eligible to bear arms—that is, white men—was smaller, the Confederate Congress turned to conscription a year earlier. It approved the First Conscription Act in 1862 by a margin of two to one. The ease and speed with which the law passed indicates how quickly Confederate lawmakers could abandon their commitment to state sovereignty when necessity dictated, even as state governors and some individuals objected. In both cases, legislatures

combined conscription with provisions that allowed men to provide substitutes or pay commutation fees, while a variety of actors, from local
communities to national governments, offered enlistment bounties. The
Union and the Confederacy both used the combined carrot-and-stick approach to encourage voluntary enlistment, ensuring that the majority of
both forces consisted of volunteers rather than draftees.[9]

The American military began the work of reorganizing and profes-
sionalizing itself as part of the Progressive project to rationalize and cen-
tralize during the late nineteenth and early twentieth centuries.[10] As a
result, America's World War I draft functioned differently from those
that had come before. The combined local-state-federal models of the
previous centuries gave way to what John Whiteclay Chambers II termed
the nation-state model, in which the nationwide Selective Service agency
shepherded a "wartime national mass mobilization." Between April 1917,
when President Woodrow Wilson signed the Selective Draft Act, and the
armistice at the end of 1918, local draft boards oversaw the expansion of
the U.S. armed forces from fewer than 150,000 men to almost 4 million,
the majority of whom were conscripts.[11]

The United States once again turned to conscription just prior to its
entrance into World War II. Although the Selective Training and Service Act of 1940 was technically the nation's first peacetime draft, the
designation is a slippery one.[12] If, as Mary Dudziak has argued, wartime
"is the calibration of an era," the United States had already begun to cali-
brate for war by the time President Franklin Roosevelt signed the bill into
law. The Neutrality Acts of the 1930s had been pushed to the side as the
United States increased its own production of war matériel and provided
financial aid and arms to the United Kingdom and China.[13] Such nuance
became moot after Japan's attack on Pearl Harbor in December 1941.
By war's end in 1945, just under 16 million American men had served in
uniform, a number that would have been impossible without widespread
conscription.[14]

Each of these experiences with the draft was unique to its own historical moment. Questions about how to administer conscription, who
should be deferred or exempted, and how coercive the laws should be
were answered differently depending on each period's prevailing political currents and manpower needs. The long view, for example, shows
a diminishing role for states over time, a shift from military to civilian
administration, and the greater manpower requirements of industrialized
warfare. Where the Revolutionary and Civil War drafts were primarily
designed to encourage voluntary enlistment, the world wars needed the
mass armies that only broad-based conscription could provide.

Yet the various drafts had several characteristics in common. Most importantly, with the nominal exception of World War II, the laws that authorized conscription passed Congress only after it had declared war and expired when an armistice was signed. The size of America's standing forces remained tightly constrained during times of peace and limited conflict. The combined U.S. armed forces did not exceed 335,000 personnel in peacetime until after World War II.[15]

Second, each draft faced significant pushback from politicians and private citizens. Even though conscription in a democracy only functions when the majority of the people accept the government's right to draft, the measure is rarely popular. During the Revolution, fearing popular backlash, some governors simply failed to comply with the manpower quotas established by Congress.[16] New York City's 1863 draft riots are probably the best-known example of pre–Vietnam era protest, but for all their destructive fury, they were only the tip of the iceberg.[17] The Union alone saw spontaneous antidraft protests erupt in New Hampshire, Ohio, Wisconsin, Pennsylvania, and Iowa.[18] An estimated 160,000 northern men registered their discontent by refusing to enroll with authorities as the law required.[19] Although armed uprisings remained small and sporadic during World War I, federal, state, and local governments put considerable resources into crushing printed and spoken objections to the draft.[20] Up to 3 million men, from common laborers to professional baseball players, avoided the draft between 1917 and 1918 through both legal and illegal means.[21] Ultimately, the United States raised the manpower it needed to fill the ranks during each war but only with tremendous effort.

Part of that effort went into making conscription palatable to the people. Civilian populations rescind their political support of a conflict when perceived inconveniences outweigh expected benefits. Inconvenience defines forced military service. One way of minimizing the coercion of a draft, therefore, is to increase voluntary enlistment, which was the rationale behind the bounties and substitutes of the Revolutionary and Civil Wars. Whether substitutes or bounty seekers enlisted for ideological reasons or for monetary gain, the thinking went, at least they fought out of choice.[22] As historian Christopher Capozzola has observed of the World War I draft, it was "crucial both for the draft's political legitimacy and for its operation on the ground" that the "coercive claim" of conscription be masked in the fiction of mass voluntarism.[23]

Planners also offered deferments and exemptions from military service in each of the above wars. Men deemed physically, mentally, or morally incapable of service could be excused. So were men labeled "essential" to the war effort or civilian economy. At various times, farmers, industrial workers, teachers, doctors, political officeholders, and civil servants received special consideration. Deferments and exemptions also supported

American social and moral values. The U.S. commitment to freedom of religion, for example, led to regulations deferring conscientious objectors from military service.[24] At times, fathers and even married men without children also received deferments. Such dependency deferments assumed that men were breadwinners and anchored the moral lives of their families. As such, they were needed at home more than they were needed in uniform, even if the military paid as well as their civilian jobs.[25] In other words, the third thing that linked all American drafts between the Revolution and World War II is that none required universal male military service. By design, the laws compelled some men to serve and allowed others to avoid similar service.

Realistically, however, political, economic, social, and military needs conflicted with one another during each of these wars, particularly since "essentiality" is hard to define and consistency almost impossible to achieve. During World War II, President Roosevelt called competing manpower interests a "jigsaw puzzle," as Congress, the Selective Service, the War Department, and lobbyists from the industrial, agricultural, and educational sectors squabbled over who needed America's men most. *Time* magazine called the problem "a vast, sticky pudding which the Administration stirred and stirred, hoping that something in the way of a solution would come to the top."[26] Examples of competing interests abound in all American wars. During the Civil War, for example, the Confederacy's infamous "Twenty Negro" law caused lawmakers significant trouble. This measure exempted from military service one white man on every farm that enslaved more than twenty people. White male overseers were considered essential in an economy based on enslaved labor and in a social system based on white patriarchal authority. Viewed through that specific lens, the law made sense. Rank-and-file soldiers and their wives, however, disagreed. These constituents forced changes to the law, but the Confederacy's dependence on enslaved labor meant that protestors could not compel its repeal amid a food shortage.[27] Southern officials believed that exempting white overseers of enslaved labor was the only way to feed Confederate forces.

Thus, the final element linking all American drafts prior to 1945 is that, at the end of the day, military need overrode political and civilian pushback. In each war, deferments and exemptions became harder to get as available manpower dwindled. The Confederacy ended substitution in 1863. The Union ended commutation in 1864. Because the World War I draft existed for such a short time, policymakers were able to avoid curtailing deferments by deepening the manpower pool. They extended the age range of eligibility and made noncitizen nationals, including Native Americans and Puerto Ricans, liable for conscription.[28] Through the last third of World War II, however, deferments became almost impossible for men in the prime age group, as there was no other way to maintain a fighting force in excess of 10 million men.[29]

Ultimately, every American draft required tremendous effort and expenditure in order to function. But within the context of wartime, when the state needed men more than virtually any other resource, planners were willing to spend what was necessary to raise their armies. When war ended, however, large armies once again became too expensive and dangerous to maintain. Between the end of the Revolution in 1783 and the start of the World War II draft in 1940, the U.S. armed forces depended on volunteers during peacetime.

Militarized Peace and the Cold War Draft

The U.S. commitment to a peacetime volunteer military waned with the end of World War II and the rapid growth of tensions with the Soviet Union. As the war wound to its conclusion, Americans demanded demobilization. Active-duty personnel and their families had no stomach for extending terms of service beyond the congressionally mandated duration of the war plus six months. Maintaining two far-flung occupation forces, however, required manpower. So, although U.S. forces demobilized rapidly, dropping from approximately 12 million to 3 million men within one year, the military needed a steady influx of replacements.[30] Amid fierce congressional and public debate, President Harry S. Truman signed legislation extending the Selective Service System's power to conscript three times between the spring of 1945 and the fall of 1946.[31] With the backing of the War Department, Truman finally allowed that authorization to expire in 1947 in the hopes of getting a bill for universal military training (UMT) through Congress.[32] But by the spring of 1948, proposed legislation had not passed, Czechoslovakia had "fallen" to communism, tensions with the Soviet Union continued to ratchet up in Germany, and the U.S. military was, according to Secretary of State George C. Marshall, "a hollow shell, over-deployed."[33] Truman reluctantly but successfully called for a reinstatement of the draft, arguing that the United States needed a large and ready military to protect the nation's interests against the growing communist threat. Peacetime conscription had come to America.

On its surface, the Cold War draft looked similar to that of World War II. Men registered with the Selective Service System on their eighteenth birthdays and received their draft classifications through local boards. Board members, all of whom were unpaid volunteers, based their decisions on their own personal priorities, prejudices, and biases as well as on regulations written at the Selective Service's headquarters in Washington, D.C. Lewis B. Hershey, the director of Selective Service from 1941 to 1970, doggedly defended local control, arguing that board members understood their own communities' needs better than any Washington bureaucrat ever could.[34] Theoretically, only local officials knew whether a man genuinely supported his family, worked diligently in a job essential to the local populace, or was simply a shirker. When this "little group of neighbors" granted a deferment, they reviewed it annually to make sure the extenuating circumstance still existed.[35] Men declared eligible for service were called as needed, starting with the oldest available man first and leaving the threat of conscription hanging over most men's lives until they turned twenty-six.[36]

Although the system functioned much as it had during World War II, its justification was decidedly different. After 1948, conscription was used to maintain a large standing force at the ready in case hostilities escalated rather than to fight a war that had already started. Planners demanded armed forces large enough to fight a major war with the Soviet Union or the People's Republic of China, to prosecute proxy wars elsewhere around the world, and to fill a civil-defense role domestically in the event of nuclear war.[37] Despite interservice rivalries that led the size of the army, in particular, to fluctuate significantly in the years between World War II and the Vietnam War, total active-duty-force strength stabilized at approximately 1.5 million in the years before the Korean War and at approximately 2.5 million following the Korean armistice.[38] The majority of these men enlisted voluntarily, but surveys indicated that at least half of them joined up under the threat of the draft. Officials pointed to such draft-motivated enlistments as one of the main benefits of maintaining Selective Service, arguing that enlistment rates had plummeted in 1947 and 1948 when the War Department had agreed to suspend inductions.[39] Coercion, maintained most planners, was the most effective way to raise a military large enough to defend U.S. interests at home and abroad.[40]

Maintaining conscription, however, created a number of problems for the Selective Service, particularly in the years following the Korean War. With no active conflict, the army became the only branch of the armed forces that regularly required draftees, even as President Dwight Eisenhower's New Look policy slashed its size by almost half.[41] Meanwhile, demographic pressures that had forced the Selective Service to scrape the bottom of the manpower barrel during the Korean War began to ease once the baby boom generation started to come of age. In the decade between 1955 and 1965, the number of men available to draft grew while the army's need for numbers dropped. Draft calls dipped so low that the Selective Service seemed to delegitimate its own existence. Newspaper

Director of Selective Service Major General Lewis B. Hershey (*middle*), Georgia Neese Clark, and Secretary of the Interior Oscar Chapman at the Washington Hotel for a meeting, September 6, 1950. (Courtesy Harry S. Truman Library)

articles highlighted the low odds of being called, placing them anywhere between one in four and one in fifteen.[42] Media coverage framed conscription as something that happened to "suckers," while smarter or luckier men avoided military service all together.[43] New Hampshire's state director of Selective Service complained that such news items fostered "callous disrespect" for the system among the young men who were supposed to register.[44] Other state directors wrote Hershey in Washington, begging to know what to do with their excess men.[45]

Hershey and his staff settled on a solution that seemed counterintuitive. They could not increase draft calls unless the DOD indicated a need for more men. So, beginning in 1955, they went in the other direction, looking for ways to limit the number of persons classified as I-A, or available for service.[46] Offering more deferments ensured a smaller I-A pool, which, ironically, guaranteed that a higher proportion of those in it received draft notices, thus undercutting the negative media coverage. A smaller I-A pool also spurred enlistment by younger men who preferred to get their service out of the way at age eighteen rather than wait to be drafted at twenty-four or twenty-five.[47] By 1961, with enlistments and reenlistments on the rise, inductees constituted just 9 percent of new accessions across the service branches.[48]

The expansion of deferments, however, was not just a cynical move on Hershey's part to protect his agency's existence in times of low draft calls. It grew out of his sincere belief that citizens had an obligation to serve their country in whatever way they could and in whatever ways the nation required.[49] Unlike a conventional conflict, he reasoned, the political, economic, and technological tensions that characterized the Cold War demanded many types of public service, of which a stint in the military was only one. Men who developed new weapons systems, computer-programming languages, or antibiotics could all be seen as performing essential service to the nation. Throughout the decade, the Selective Service regularly revised regulations governing deferments in the fields of science, technology, and education as well as guidelines for dependency deferments, making all of them easier to get. These changes were designed to guide men's professional and family choices in order to "channel" them into jobs or family arrangements deemed important for national security.[50] In the Selective Service's own words, "the club of induction" could be used to "drive" individuals "out of areas considered to be less important" and into "areas of greater importance."[51] Fear of losing those deferments, Hershey hoped, would keep men in deferred fields until they were too old to easily change professions.

Hershey and other Selective Service officials made no secret of this new role for the agency. He first used the term "manpower channeling" in congressional testimony in 1958 but clearly viewed the policy as a continuation of work the Selective Service had been doing since at least the Korean War, when it had first regularized deferments for college students.[52] During that conflict and even World War II, he explained in an article for its in-house newspaper, the agency had worked tirelessly "to make people think they [had] volunteered when they [were] actually being channeled through a process. . . . The only reason the Nation is not short 40,000 or 50,000 engineers today is because they were deferred in 1951, 1952, and 1953."[53] Hershey talked and wrote about the practice of channeling regularly. A few journalists picked up on its existence, but, in general, it was considered too unremarkable to bother saying much about.[54] Most Americans remained unaware of it, and those who did know about it did not much care.

The Selective Service System's literature on channeling mainly focused on occupational deferments, a classification that expanded by 650 percent between 1955 and 1963.[55] Jobs in engineering, scientific fields, research and development, the social sciences, and teaching were all thought essential to beating communism, particularly after the Soviets' successful launch of *Sputnik* in 1957 stoked American fears of falling behind.[56] During the militarized peace of the Cold War, it was easy to frame men in STEM (science, technology, engineering, and mathematics) fields as citizens doing their duty to defend the nation. But dependency deferments were also part of the channeling equation.

Family structure was an integral part of the multifaceted discourse Americans developed to distinguish their society from that of the Soviets. According to the narrative, Americans lived the good life thanks to their consumer-capitalist economy. They had access to homeownership, cars, labor-saving appliances, an array of convenience foods, beauty products, and abundant leisure time, while Soviets stood in lines to bring limited quantities of limited goods back to their sad, drab apartment blocks. Moreover, where communist women slaved away at the factory and farm labor demanded by their government, American women had the freedom to raise their children in comfort and style, or so the story went. And the whole gendered, consumerist system depended on an independent male breadwinner who provided for his wife and children.[57] Regardless of the accuracy or inclusivity of this discourse, the rhetoric had real power. While looking for ways to decrease the size of the I-A manpower pool, the Selective Service repeatedly expanded deferments for fathers and even married men without children. Although he did not elaborate further, Hershey described Eisenhower's 1956 executive order moving all fathers to a lower order of call than nonfathers as a measure "designed to strengthen the Nation's civilian economy."[58]

Official focus on masculine breadwinners as a source of national strength led to another set of military manpower policies in the 1960s intended to use the military apparatus, including the Selective Service, to "rehabilitate" men deemed unable to meet their domestic responsibilities. A few months before President John F. Kennedy's assassination, Secretary of Labor W. Willard Wirtz sent the president a memo explaining that almost half of draftees failed the Armed Forces Qualification Test before induction. To Wirtz, such a high rate of failure was a "national disgrace." He pointed to the Selective Service as an "incomparable asset" in locating the "25% or more" of the population that would, as he put it, "unquestionably cause 75% or more" of the nation's "social and economic problems."[59] Kennedy quickly established the President's Task Force on Manpower Conservation to study the problem and propose solutions.

The task force published its report, *One-Third of a Nation: A Report on Young Men Found Unqualified for Military Service*, just months into Lyndon Johnson's presidency. Its findings were damning. Selective Service rejectees were overwhelmingly born into poverty and likely to pass that poverty on to their children. Black draftees, who faced systemic racism in all facets of their lives, including in their schools, access to health care, and ability to accumulate wealth, were significantly more likely to be rejected from military service than their white counterparts.[60] Johnson quickly mobilized the Selective Service and the Departments of the Army, Labor, and Health, Education, and Welfare to establish counseling programs, job-referral services, and literacy-skills training for men who failed the AFQT. The hope was to use the manpower-procurement apparatus to help underprivileged men become responsible breadwinners, thus lifting all their family members out of poverty.

Wirtz called the effort "the most important human salvage program" in the history of the United States, but it proved an abject failure.[61] Rehabilitation would have made men eligible for the draft just as the Vietnam War was escalating. As a result, many chose not to participate in the programs. Secretary of Defense Robert McNamara, convinced that "poverty and social injustice . . . endanger[ed] . . . national security as much as any military threat," began looking for a less voluntary way to combat poverty *within* the military.[62]

In August 1966, McNamara announced the DOD's intention to bring up to 100,000 previously ineligible men into the armed forces each year in order to "salvage" them. Project 100,000, as it came to be known, would "rescue" poor men, especially minority men, from the "poverty-encrusted environments" in which they had been raised.[63] These "New Standards" men—those who were otherwise ineligible for military service—would be admitted into all branches of the armed forces, both voluntarily through enlistment and involuntarily through the draft. All branches of service ultimately added a combined total of 354,000 New Standards men to their active-duty rosters between 1966 and 1971, when the program ended. Forty percent of them were Black men at a time when the entire military was only 9 percent African American. That it provided manpower during an active war is likely one of the reasons the project lasted as long as it did; officers throughout the armed forces, including the Joint Chiefs of Staff, hated what they called "McNamara's Moron Corps."[64]

Together, these two sets of policies—those governing manpower channeling and those governing rehabilitation efforts—created a vastly inequitable system of conscription. Elite and middle-class men were able to leverage their privilege much more easily than white working-class men and all men of color in order to obtain deferments. Those who could access private health-care options were significantly more likely to receive medical deferments. Those with solid schooling and financial resources could gain deferments as college students. The channeling process advantaged jobs that required college degrees. Occupational deferments expanded as a whole, but those for agricultural and industrial jobs declined.[65] Enlistment in the National Guard, an option theoretically open to anyone, became the province of the privileged. Even dependency deferments, which were supposedly available to any man with a willing partner, became harder to access for those with fewer means since Selective Service regulations required the father to financially support his children.[66] Meanwhile, voluntary rehabilitation programs and then Project 100,000 specifically targeted white working-class men and all men of color for military service. Every New Standards man drafted into the armed forces was one fewer conscripted middle-class man. The racial inequities are particularly stark, considering that only 5 percent of Black men attended college in the early 1960s but 40 percent of New Standards men were African American.[67]

And yet very few people complained. By 1966, when McNamara launched Project 100,000, the Cold War draft was well established as necessary in times of either active mobilization or militarized peace. The Selective Service had become an institution. Congress had reliably renewed its authority to conscript every four years between 1951 and 1963 with little to no pushback from the defense or political establishments or even the public at large. Organized opposition came mostly from pacifist and antimilitarist organizations whose reach was limited.[68]

In general, Selective Service was a political unicorn. Its coercive—and potentially life-altering—powers reached into almost every U.S. home in the two decades between the end of World War II and the escalation of the Vietnam War. And Americans, for the most part, accepted the system. Registration and preinduction exams became a rite of passage. Through widespread deferments, voluntary enlistment, or simply being lucky in times of low draft calls, most men's contact with the Selective Service ended with the draft card in their wallets. Most of those who did receive Uncle Sam's greetings grudgingly accepted them. In the words of historian Loren Baritz, those men caught in the draft thought of it as "an event like measles, a graduation, the weather, something that happened to people."[69] It just was.

The Vietnam War Era and the AVF

It was the Vietnam War that pushed many more people to question the necessity of the draft and the federal government's right to conduct it, even as many elements of the wartime draft were similar to those of the wars that preceded it. Men behaved during the Vietnam War much as they had during every other American experience with the draft. In the aggregate, they avoided conscription however they could. Like those who paid commutation fees or hired substitutes during the Revolutionary and Civil Wars, men of the Vietnam era took advantage of every legal option available. Like those who simply never registered during World War I, somewhere between two and three million men did the same during the Vietnam era.[70] Similarly, regulations established a class-based system of coercion primarily designed to spur enlistments, just as they had during earlier periods.

Yet conscription during the militarized peace considerably changed Americans' relationship with the draft from what it had been in the past. Increased draft calls after 1965 shined a bright light on the inequities that had been baked into the system over the previous two decades, highlighting just how much the mission of the Selective Service had changed over the years. By design, the peacetime draft had become more a tool of social engineering than manpower procurement. Manpower channeling purposefully defined the occupational and domestic choices of elite and middle-class men as public service in the name of national defense. For this group, deferments became increasingly easier to obtain. While never guaranteed, their broad availability allowed these men to see military service as a choice rather than an obligation. The burden of service fell squarely on the white working class and all men of color, who were being forced to fight an increasingly unpopular war within the context of a mass movement for racial justice and a "War on Poverty." It is no wonder that civil rights activists, the burgeoning New Left, and then liberals more generally attacked the draft along with the war.

But the libertarian Right also took issue with Selective Service. The Vietnam War's manpower needs were not the source of channeling or rehabilitation efforts, including Project 100,000.[71] Both sets of policies grew out of Cold War definitions of strength, national security, and public service. Like the regulations that governed America's previous experiences with the draft, those that defined these sets of policies worked together to meet the nation's defense needs in the moment. They were designed to ensure a fully staffed military, maintain essential civilian roles, and support important social values. But within the peacetime context, even that of a militarized peace, such goals necessarily focused more heavily on domestic security than military mobilization. The social-engineering element eclipsed the military need for conscription and became a clear example of government overreach to those who objected to increased federal power.

Opposition from both ends of the political spectrum combined with significant ambivalence from the majority of American men created an untenable situation. When manpower needs increased, policymakers tried to contract the availability of deferments, just as they had during every previous use of conscription. But where in past wars the public eventually, if grudgingly, acquiesced to those rollbacks under government pressure, this time officials could not overcome opposition to coercive manpower policies. Military service had become an unappealing choice that too many men were unwilling to make. A system of conscription only functions if it has broad public and political support, both of which Selective Service lost by 1969.

At base, systems of selective service rest on citizens' obligations to serve and defend the nation. In the United States, that obligation was tenuous from the beginning, but it remained strong enough to function during times of war. In the militarized peace of the Cold War, when the armed forces did not require the service of most men, the Selective Service defined civilian occupations and domestic roles as the equivalent of military service in order to justify its existence and support the domestic security needs of the nation. But its actions unintentionally weakened the already thin connection between citizenship and military responsibility to the point that it snapped during an unpopular war. The shift to an all-volunteer force removed obligation from the equation, in reality if not in rhetoric. It codified a relationship between military service and citizenship that, ironically enough, the Selective Service itself had created by the time of the Vietnam War.

Notes

1. For more on the U.S. military in the early national period, see Lawrence Cress, *Citizens in Arms: The Army and Militia in American Society to the War of 1812* (Chapel Hill: University of North Carolina Press, 1982).

2. Bernard Bailyn, *The Ideological Origins of the American Revolution*, enlarged ed. (Cambridge, MA: Belknap Press of Harvard University Press, 1992), chap. 3, 112–117, 354–358.

3. For more on the ideological differences between civic republican and liberal conceptions of citizenship, see Eliot A. Cohen, *Citizens and Soldiers: The Dilemmas of Military Service* (Ithaca, NY: Cornell University Press, 1985), chaps. 5–6; R. Claire Snyder, *Citizen-Soldiers and Manly Warriors: Military Service and Gender in the Civic Republican Tradition* (New York: Rowman and Littlefield, 1999), 1–2; and Isaac Kramnick, "The 'Great National Discussion': The Discourse of Politics in 1787," *William and Mary Quarterly* 45, no. 1 (January 1988): 3–32.

4. The most recent manifestation of this question is the congressional appointment and final report of the National Commission on Military, National, and Public Service. See *Inspired to Serve: The Final Report of the National Commission on Military, National, and Public Service*, March 2020, Homeland Security Digital Library, https://www.hsdl.org/?view&did=841630.

5. For more on how liberal and civic-republican ideologies affected the ideal of the citizen-soldier in the United States, see Snyder, *Citizen-Soldiers and Manly Warriors*, chap. 4; Peter Karsten, "The US Citizen-Soldier's Past, Present, and Likely Future," *Parameters* (Summer 2001): 61–73; Ronald R. Krebs, *Fighting for Rights: Military Service and the Politics of Citizenship* (Ithaca, NY: Cornell University Press, 2006), chaps. 1–2; and Cress, *Citizens in Arms*, esp. 42–46, chaps. 7–8.

6. John K. Mahon, *History of the Militia and the National Guard* (New York: Macmillan, 1983), 52–53.

7. Mahon, *History of the Militia and the National Guard*, 62, 67–69, 79, 83, 127–129.

8. There is some debate over whether the system of manpower procurement that developed for the Continental Army constitutes national conscription, as decisions about who to send into service were made within state militia units at the behest of state governments. The states, however, acted as a result of congressional mandate. See Meyer Kestnbaum, "Citizenship and Compulsory Military Service: The Revolutionary Origins of Conscription in the United States," *Armed Forces and Society* 27, no. 1 (Fall 2000): 7–36. For more on the hybrid system of conscription that emerged during the Revolutionary War, see Mark Edward Lender, "The Conscripted Line: The Draft in Revolutionary New Jersey," *New Jersey History* 103, nos. 1–2 (1983): 23–45; and Arthur Alexander, "How Maryland Tried to Raise Her Continental Quotas," *Maryland Historical Magazine* 42 (September 1947): 184–196.

9. The definitive book-length histories of conscription during the Civil War are James W. Geary, *We Need Men: The Union Draft in the Civil War* (Dekalb: Northern Illinois University Press, 1991), and John M. Sacher, *Confederate Conscription and the Struggle for Southern Soldiers* (Baton Rouge: Louisiana State University Press, 2021).

10. See James L. Abrahamson, *America Arms for a New Century: The Making of a Great Military Power* (New York: Free Press, 1981), esp. chap. 6.

11. For more on America's World War I draft, see John Whiteclay Chambers II, *To Raise an Army: The Draft Comes to Modern America* (New York: Free Press, 1987), 6 (quote); and Joshua E. Kastenberg, *To Raise and Discipline an Army: Major General Enoch Crowder, the Judge Advocate General's Office, and the Realignment of Civil and Military Relations in World War I* (DeKalb: Northern Illinois University Press, 2017), 7.

12. J. Gary Clifford and Samuel R. Spencer Jr., *The First Peacetime Draft* (Lawrence: University Press of Kansas, 1986).

13. Mary L. Dudziak, *WarTime: An Idea, Its History, Its Consequences* (New York: Oxford University Press, 2012), 15 (quote), 40–52.

14. For more on the World War II draft, see George Q. Flynn, *The Draft, 1940–1973* (Lawrence: University Press of Kansas, 1993), chaps. 2–4.

15. Department of Defense, *Selected Manpower Statistics: Fiscal Year 1990* (Washington, DC: Government Printing Office, 1990), 62–68.

16. New Jersey, for example, ignored Congress's 1779 call for troops. See Lender, "Conscripted Line," 37.

17. For more on the New York Draft Riots, see Iver Bernstein, *The New York City Draft Riots: Their Significance for American Society and Politics in the Age of the Civil War* (New York: Oxford University Press, 1990).

18. James W. Geary, "Civil War Conscription in the North: A Historiographical Review," *Civil War History* 32, no. 3 (September 1986): 218–219.

19. Peter Levine, "Draft Evasion in the North during the Civil War, 1863–1865," *Journal of American History* 67, no. 4 (March 1981): 817.

20. Chambers, *To Raise an Army*, 205–210; Erik M. Zissu, "Conscription, Sovereignty, and Land: American Indian Resistance during World War I," *Pacific Historical Review* 64, no. 4 (November 1995): 537–566; Jeanette Keith, "The Politics of Southern Draft Resistance, 1917–1918: Class, Race, and Conscription in the Rural South," *Journal of American History* 87, no. 4 (March 2001): 1335–1361.

21. Christopher Capozzola, *Uncle Sam Wants You: World War I and the Making of the Modern American Citizen* (New York: Oxford University Press, 2008), 30; Lindsay John Bell, "Reconstructing Baseball's Image: Landis, Cobb, and the Baseball Hero Ethos (PhD diss., Iowa State University, 2020), 52–66.

22. See Lender, "Conscripted Line," 34–35; Matthew J. Gallman, *Defining Duty in the Civil War: Personal Choice, Popular Culture, and the Union Home Front* (Chapel Hill: University of North Carolina Press, 2015), 163; and Patrick J. Doyle, "Replacement Rebels: Confederate Substitution and the Issue of Citizenship," *Journal of the Civil War Era* 8, no. 1 (March 2018): 3–31.

23. Capozzola, *Uncle Sam Wants You*, 27.

24. See Charles C. Moskos and John Whiteclay Chambers II, eds., *The New Conscientious Objection: From Sacred to Secular Resistance* (New York: Oxford University Press, 1993), esp. part 2.

25. See, for example, Dorit Geva, "Different and Unequal?: Breadwinning, Dependency Deferments, and the Gendered Origins of the U.S. Selective Service System," *Armed Forces and Society* 37, no. 4 (2011): 589–618.

26. "Army & Navy—Pudding," *Time*, March 27, 1944, quoted in Dean J. Kotlowski, *Paul V. McNutt and the Age of FDR* (Bloomington: Indiana University Press, 2015), 341, 364.

27. John M. Sacher, "'Twenty-Negro' or Overseer Law: A Reconsideration," *Journal of the Civil War Era* 7, no. 2 (June 2017): 269–292.

28. Chambers, *To Raise an Army*, 231–232.

29. See Amy J. Rutenberg, *Rough Draft: Cold War Military Manpower Policy and the Origins of Vietnam-Era Draft Resistance* (Ithaca, NY: Cornell University Press, 2019), 34–36.

30. Department of Defense, *Selected Manpower Statistics*, 58.

31. Flynn, *Draft*, 88–97.

32. For more on UMT, see William A. Taylor, *Every Citizen a Soldier: The Campaign for Universal Military Training after World War II* (College Station: Texas A&M University Press, 2014).

33. Quoted in "Secretary Is Firm," *New York Times*, March 19, 1948.

34. For more on Lewis B. Hershey, see George Q. Flynn, *Lewis B. Hershey: Mr. Selective Service* (Chapel Hill: University of North Carolina Press, 1985).

35. James W. Davis and Kenneth M. Dolbeare, *Little Groups of Neighbors: The Selective Service System* (Chicago: Markham, 1968).

36. Men who had taken certain deferments extended their draft liability to age thirty-five, although few older men were ever inducted.

37. Brian McAllister Linn, *Elvis's Army: Cold War GIs and the Atomic Bomb* (Cambridge, MA: Harvard University Press, 2016), 2, 75–77.

38. James M. Gerhardt, *The Draft and Public Policy: Issues in Military Manpower Procurement, 1945–1970* (Columbus: Ohio State University Press, 1971), 192.

39. See, for example, the statements of Charles E. Wilson and Arthur Bradford, Senate Committee on Armed Services, *1955 Amendments to the Universal Military Training and Service Act, Hearings before the Committee on Armed Services, United States Senate on H.R. 3005, H.R. 6057, and S. 1467*, 84th Cong., 1st sess., June 1955, 182–185.

40. Between 1948 and 1965, none of the service branches and very few politicians advocated the end of the draft. Adlai Stevenson and Barry Goldwater were the notable exceptions. See Flynn, *Draft*, 209; and Gerhardt, *Draft and Public Policy*, 229.

41. Linn, *Elvis's Army*, 85–86.

42. See, for example, "Legion Head Says Draft Is Unfair," *Baltimore Sun*, March 28, 1955; and David Lawrence, "Young Men Can Relax Again," *U.S. News and World Report*, January 6, 1956, 52–53.

43. See Rutenberg, *Rough Draft*, 99–101.

44. John H. Greenaway to General Hershey, January 6, 1955 [*sic*], attached to Bernard T. Frank III to Mr. Greenaway, January 30, 1956, 127 General N.H. 1963–1948, box 48, Central Files, Records of the Selective Service System, RG 147, National Archives and Records Administration, College Park, MD (hereafter cited as NACP).

45. See, for example, Commencement of Classification, August 1, 1955, attached to R. T. Finks to Major General Lewis B. Hershey, August 8, 1955, 300 Classification-Gen. & Ala.–Nev. 1963–1948, box 61; Chester A. Furbish to General Hershey, March 29, 1955, attached to Bernard T. Franck III to Colonel Furbish, April 26, 1955, 127 General Mass. 1963–1955, box 47; and Lewis B. Hershey to Colonel Armstrong, January 5, 1956, and attachments, 127 General Ill. 1963–1953, box 46, all in Central Files, RG 147, NACP.

46. John E. Walsh to Maj. Gen. Lewis B. Hershey, July 13, 1955, attached to Dee Ingold to General Walsh, July 26, 1955, 127 General Idaho, 1955–1948, box 46, Central Files, RG 147, NACP.

47. "Proposal to Ease Draft Is Offered," *New York Times*, September 23, 1955. See also Gerhardt, *The Draft and Public Policy*, 228–229.

48. Gerhardt, *The Draft and Public Policy*, 218.

49. Flynn, *Lewis B. Hershey*, 70.

50. See Rutenberg, *Rough Draft*, 117–126.

51. U.S. Selective Service System, "Channeling," *Orientation Kit*, 1965, 3, 6, 8.

52. Subcommittee on Independent Offices, House Appropriations Committee, *Independent Offices Appropriations for 1959: Hearings before the Subcommittee of the Committee on Appropriations, House of Representatives*, 85th Cong., 2d sess., January 1958, 200.

53. Lewis B. Hershey, "Altered Role, Continuing Need for Draft Stressed," *Selective Service*, March 1958, 1–2.

54. See, for example, "Manpower for Defense," *Indianapolis Star*, November 10, 1958; and "Draft Seen to Guide Science, Teaching," *Washington Post*, April 23, 1958.

55. See U.S. Selective Service System, *Annual Report of the Director of Selective Service for the Fiscal Year 1953 to the Congress of the United States Pursuant to the Universal Military Training and Service Act as Amended* (Washington, DC: Government Printing Office, 1955), 22 (hereafter cited as *Annual Report*, [year]); *Annual Report*, 1963, 11.

56. See Aaron L. Friedberg, "Science, the Cold War, and the American State," review essay, *Diplomatic History* 20, no. 1 (1996): 107–118. See also "U.S. Tries Hard to Catch Up," *Life*, November 4, 1957; and David C. Greenwood, *Solving the Scientist Shortage* (Washington, DC: Public Affairs, 1958).

57. See, for example, Lizabeth Cohen, *A Consumers' Republic: The Politics of Mass Consumption in Postwar America* (New York: Vintage, 2003), 144–150; and Elaine Tyler May, *Homeward Bound: American Families in the Cold War Era* (New York: Basic, 1988), chap. 1.

58. *Annual Report*, 1956, 28.

59. Memorandum to the President, September 10, 1963, attached to Secretary Wirtz's Proposal to Work with the Selective Service System in Identifying and Training a Large Group of Young Men Rejected for Military Service because of "Mental Reasons," September 23, 1963, Selective Service Rejectees, box 2, entry UD-UP 3, Records of the Department of Health, Education, and Welfare, RG 235, NACP.

60. President's Task Force on Manpower Conservation, *One-Third of a Nation: A Report on Young Men Found Unqualified for Military Service* (Washington, DC: Government Printing Office, 1964).

61. "Salvaging Young Americans," *Washington Daily News*, January 15, 1964.

62. Robert McNamara, *The Essence of Security: Reflections in Office* (New York: Harper & Row, 1968), xi, 123.

63. "Excerpts from Address by McNamara," *New York Times*, August 24, 1966; "McNamara Plans to 'Salvage' 40,000 Rejected in Draft," *New York Times*, August 24, 1966.

64. See, for example, Ted Sell, "Can Draft Rejects Be Upgraded," *Louisville (KY) Courier-Journal*, September 4, 1966.

65. Gerhardt, *The Draft and Public Policy*, 187, 222.

66. See Rutenberg, *Rough Draft*, 173–177.

67. James E. Westheider, *The African American Experience in Vietnam: Brothers in Arms* (New York: Rowman & Littlefield, 2008), 26.

68. Flynn, *The Draft*, 162–163, 167–169.

69. Loren Baritz, *Backfire: Vietnam—The Myths That Made Us Fight, the Illusions That Helped Us Lose, the Legacy That Haunts Us Today* (New York: Ballantine, 1985), 278.

70. Lawrence M. Baskir and William Strauss, *Chance and Circumstance: The Draft, the War, and the Vietnam Generation* (New York: Vintage, 1978), 86–87.

71. Even though Project 100,000 began in 1966, its roots were clearly in the War on Poverty, not the war in Vietnam. McNamara had first tried a rehabilitation program within the army in 1964. See Senate Subcommittee of the Committee on Appropriations, *Department of Defense Reprogramming, 1965: Hearings before the Subcommittee of the Committee on Appropriations, United States Senate, on the Department of the Army Special Training Enlistment Program (STEP)*, 89th Cong., 1st sess., January 1965.

2

Economics

Michael Gibbs and Timothy J. Perri

Gary Becker was one of the most influential economists of the twentieth century. Throughout his career, he pioneered economic analyses of topics previously considered beyond the realm of the field. These included racial discrimination, investments in human capital, marriage and divorce, fertility, household production, crime and punishment, and addiction. He received many awards over his career, including the Nobel Prize in 1992.

Becker earned his PhD in economics at the University of Chicago, studying with many luminaries, including Milton Friedman. Toward the end of his studies, he joined the faculty of the Department of Economics at Chicago, then, in 1957, moved to Columbia University. Between those two positions, Becker spent the summer of 1957 at the RAND Corporation in Santa Monica, California. While there, he wrote two papers, one of which may be the first economic analysis of conscription. Less than a decade later, economists played a key role in an important public-policy debate during the Vietnam War, which eventually led to the abolishment of the military draft. Becker had connections to many of those scholars who studied the economics of conscription, and his paper foreshadowed many of the ideas in that literature. Despite this, none cited his paper on conscription. In this chapter we discuss this history and speculate on this puzzle.[1]

Experts on military manpower issues, conscription, and the all-volunteer force have recognized the importance of Becker's contribution. "Becker's paper is relatively short, but his brilliance comes through. In cursory fashion, it contains much if not most of the ideas and arguments contained in the Gates Commission final report as well as the more detailed reports by Gates Commission staff (including Walter Oi, Harry Gilman, and others)," remarked John Warner, professor emeritus of economics at Clemson University. "If that paper had seen the light of day in 1957, research on conscription and the AVF would probably have proceeded much faster."[2] In a similar vein, Bernard Rostker, eminent expert on the AVF, commented, "Becker's ideas flowing from the paper would have made a real contribution to the debate."[3]

While at the RAND Corporation in the summer of 1957, Becker wrote two papers. The first, recently discovered by Timothy J. Perri in 2019, contained his initial thinking about on-the-job training and evolved into his famous *Journal of Political Economy* article on that subject in 1962.[4] The second was an analysis of the economics of conscription.[5] It was apparently forgotten for fifty years.[6] We assess the relationship of Becker's lost paper to the literature on the economics of conscription and to the important policy debate about abolishing the draft that occurred a few years later during the Vietnam War. In doing so, two main arguments emerge. First, it appears that Becker's was the first formal economic analysis of conscription. Second, Becker knew many of the economists who analyzed conscription, but there is little evidence that his paper influenced that literature or the policy debate. Our conclusions speculate on why this may have occurred.

How Economists Helped End Conscription

One can appreciate the potential value of Becker's lost paper on conscription by understanding the arguments of economists against the draft and the role of economists in ending it. In the late 1960s, economists had five basic arguments against conscription.[7] First, the opportunity cost of an AVF would generally be lower and never exceed that of a mixed force of the same size. Second, there are evasion costs of a draft that are absent with an AVF. Third, turnover cost is lower with an AVF than with a mixed force. Fourth, performance incentives are greater with an AVF than with a mixed force because of market-based pay with the former. Fifth, paying below market wages with conscription induces the military to employ too much labor relative to capital (that is, machinery).

Economists Milton Friedman and Walter Oi each noted the distinction between the *budget cost* and the true *opportunity cost* of the military.[8] By keeping military wages low and conscripting individuals, the budget cost was lower than the opportunity cost because of the hidden tax on conscripts. This fact, along with the other costs listed above, suggests that a mixed force was more costly than an AVF. In addition to other arguments against conscription, such as the appropriateness of compelling some to serve, the cost factors were the reasons economists opposed the draft.

An important reason conscription ended in the United States is that economists in the 1960s demonstrated its disadvantages (as outlined above).[9] Popular writing and a large number of research papers were important in illustrating its problems.[10] The beginning of the end for the draft may have been the 1964–1965 study by the Department of Defense conducted at the request of President Lyndon B. Johnson. It proved to be a "training ground for those, mainly economists, who worked on the study."[11] Oi headed the economic analysis of the DOD report, which advocated an AVF but was only released to the public in summary form a year after its completion.

In December 1966, a conference was held at the University of Chicago, attended by seventy-four invited participants, including many academics (Friedman and Oi attended; Becker did not) and some elected officials. The presentations made during the meeting were later published.[12] A poll taken at the beginning of the four-day conference showed that two-thirds of attendees supported conscription. Another taken at the end of the meeting showed that two-thirds now opposed the draft.[13]

Bernard Rostker claims that Friedman, a University of Chicago economics professor, was the father of the intellectual argument for an AVF.[14] Besides attending the Chicago conference and later serving on the President's Commission on an All-Volunteer Armed Force (also known as the Gates Commission), Friedman's popular writing was instrumental in ending the draft.

In 1967, Martin Anderson, a young economist at Columbia University, became an advisor to former vice president Richard Nixon, who contemplated running for president in 1968. Anderson had read a paper by Friedman (which he presumably presented at the 1966 conference) that advocated an AVF.[15] He then wrote memos to Nixon in support of an AVF.[16] With Anderson's influence, Nixon publicly advocated an AVF. Without the influence of Anderson, the Gates Commission, whose membership he helped select, might not have occurred.[17]

Between Nixon's election as president in November 1968 and his inauguration the following January, the president of the University of Rochester, Allen Wallis, visited Arthur Burns, head of Nixon's transition team, and reminded Burns of the president-elect's promise to end conscription. Although a practicing statistician, Wallis had been a graduate student in economics at the University of Chicago with Friedman. Burns asked for a brief analysis of the budget costs of an AVF versus the existing force. Wallis put together a team of economists at Rochester to write up a quick report. The team consisted of Martin Bailey, Harry Gilman, and Walter Oi. A commission on an AVF was already being considered at that time.[18]

When it was formed in 1969, the Gates Commission had three economists among its fifteen members: Friedman, Allan Greenspan, and Wallis. The staff was drawn from those who had worked on the Rochester

Richard M. Nixon as president, January 6, 1972. (Courtesy Richard M. Nixon Library)

memorandum and the DOD study of 1964–1965. The commission largely accepted the arguments of its economists that conscription was a tax on those called to service that was both inequitable and regressive, devoting an entire chapter of its report to this issue. It further agreed with the economists that military labor was inefficiently used because of artificially low wages.[19] At the beginning of the Gates Commission's deliberations, Friedman believed that the members were about evenly split, with five each in favor of, opposed to, or uncertain about an AVF. At the end, the commission unanimously supported an AVF—one member who had been ill and missed many meetings abstained.[20]

Friedman and Oi both attended the 1966 conference at the University of Chicago and presented influential papers. Both played important roles on the Gates Commission, with Oi also working on the DOD AVF study and the memorandum to Burns on ending the draft. It is likely not a coincidence that conscription soon ended. Friedman and Oi, along with many other economists, were instrumental in bringing the AVF to the United States.

Becker's Forgotten Paper on Conscription

Returning to the work of Becker, the second paper he produced at RAND in the summer of 1957 was titled "The Case against Conscription." In a video interview with Friedman conducted by Becker, the latter mentioned this paper and expressed disappointment that RAND had not published it.[21] A few years after this, it was located, perhaps at Becker's request. Becker published an abridged version online in the *Hoover Digest*. In a preface, he notes:

> The following argument against the military draft was written while I was at the RAND Corporation during the summer of 1957. It was never published, and I had lost any copies until recently, when Charles Wolf of RAND found it on microfiche in the files. I had submitted it as a working paper. It was rejected. Fifty years ago, the Air Force provided most of the financial support to RAND, and Air Force leaders were convinced that they benefited from the draft—that many high-quality potential draftees volunteered for the Air Force only because they preferred serving there to serving in the Army. As I recall, I was told informally that the Air Force's attitude toward the draft was why RAND had turned down this paper.[22]

Becker's paper was probably the first formal economic analysis of conscription.[23] Like many of his works, it is remarkable for the depth and breadth of ideas packed into a mere thirteen pages, along with one supply and demand figure. His analyses foresee much of the future literature on the economics of conscription. He discusses many topics, including the misallocation of resources with a draft, the budget cost versus the social cost of the military, lower effort provided by those conscripted, the pay that might be necessary to attract enough volunteers, and the role of substitutes in the American Civil War. All but the last would soon be central issues in a new economic literature and important policy debate during the Vietnam War.

In 1963, before the escalation of the conflict in Vietnam by the United States, members of Congress raised the issue of abolishing conscription.[24]

This led to a DOD study of the draft, begun in 1964 and headed by Oi. Completed in 1965, it concluded that the United States should move to an all-volunteer military. With the escalation in Vietnam, however, defense officials worried about filling the manpower requirements without a draft and thus withheld the study from Congress for one year.[25] In 1967, Sol Tax published a book collecting some of the papers presented at the 1966 University of Chicago conference that focused on reform of the Selective Service System (that is, conscription). Subsequently, many studies of the relative costs of a draft and a volunteer military have appeared.

Thus, although the growing unpopularity of the war in Vietnam in the late 1960s was critical in abolishing conscription, there was consideration of ending the draft in Congress several years earlier. As Professor Warner suggested, had Becker's 1957 paper been widely distributed, it may very well have stimulated studies on topics that were analyzed over a decade later by the Gates Commission. Additionally, Rostker has noted that some issues discussed by Becker—such as the difference in labor quality and reenlistment rates between an all-volunteer military and one with draftees—were not covered in detail in the Gates Commission's report.[26] Therefore, knowledge of Becker's paper might have affected the scope of the debate about ending conscription.

Becker's Connections to Conscription Researchers

By the time others began analyzing conscription for the DOD in 1964, Becker was a well-known economist. He had published seminal work on investment in human capital, education, training, and discrimination.[27] If those working on the economics of military manpower had known of his conscription paper, they likely would have acknowledged it. Moreover, Becker was connected to many of the individuals involved with the internal DOD study of the feasibility of ending the draft (1964–1965), the Gates Commission (1969–1970), or in writing papers related to conscription. Despite these facts, it seems that his conscription paper was never cited prior to 2008 and 2015.[28] We investigated these connections between Becker and those working on the economics of conscription but discovered only scant evidence that any but H. Gregg Lewis, Becker's thesis chair, was aware of his RAND working paper.

CHICAGO
The first published paper on the economics of conscription appears to be by Edward Renshaw.[29] Having earned his PhD degree at the University of Chicago in 1958, Renshaw probably knew Becker there. It is unlikely

that they communicated after Becker left for RAND and Columbia in 1957, and Renshaw does not mention him or cite his conscription paper. He does thank Roland McKean of RAND, who also earned his PhD degree at Chicago in 1948, for comments on his paper. Three years earlier, Becker had thanked McKean for comments on *his* conscription paper. It is possible that he influenced Renshaw's work on conscription indirectly, via McKean, who certainly had Becker's paper. Yet Renshaw's work is quite different from Becker's, presenting a public-finance perspective and treating conscription as a tax. He cites an earlier draft from 1959, suggesting that he worked on conscription only after both he and Becker had left Chicago.

Correspondence exists between Becker and his dissertation advisor, H. Gregg Lewis, from 1957 to 1979.[30] Yet none after 1957 comments on any issues concerning the military. On July 21, 1957, Becker mentioned that he was at RAND working on papers on conscription and on training and pay for military personnel.[31] Lewis replied on August 1: "I would like very much to see the papers you have prepared. . . . I know that you have had this general topic on your mind for quite a long time and have done work on it both here and at RAND."[32] He suggests that Becker had such topics in mind for some time and had done preliminary analysis on the topic before leaving Chicago. We are unaware of any written work by Becker on conscription or other military topics before his RAND papers, but he may have had informal conversations with Lewis, and possibly other colleagues and students, about the economics of the draft.[33] In a second letter to Lewis on October 8, 1957, Becker enclosed those two papers and discusses some of the issues considered in both.[34] Lewis acknowledged their receipt in a letter dated October 16.[35]

In 1964, Deputy Assistant Secretary of Defense William Gorham was asked to lead a study on the budgetary cost of replacing conscription with a volunteer military.[36] Gorham contacted Lewis to ask him to serve as director of the Economic Analysis Division of the study. Lewis had a previous commitment and suggested Oi for the job.[37] Having received Becker's paper on conscription seven years before, he may not have contacted him in 1964 about the DOD study realizing that Becker, like himself, was too busy to spend a year on the project.[38] Oi had worked on fixed labor costs and transportation issues but had done no work that we can find on military issues.[39] It is curious that Lewis apparently did not mention Becker's paper to Oi.

Friedman also served on Becker's dissertation committee, and they remained close friends and colleagues until Friedman's death. Friedman was a famous advocate for the AVF. His interest in the possibility of replacing conscription may have stemmed from 1940, when the first peacetime draft was debated.[40] In his joint autobiography with his wife, Rose, Friedman says he had publicly favored ending the draft "beginning with the Wabash lectures and *Capitalism and Freedom*."[41] While he did give some lectures at Wabash College in the mid-1950s, Friedman seems to have been mistaken about their content since those lectures make no mention of conscription. In *Capitalism and Freedom* (1962), he briefly suggests that conscription should be replaced. His first written work solely focused on a volunteer military appeared in 1966, but he does not cite Becker's paper.[42] The correspondence between Becker and Friedman from 1953 to 1983 also makes no mention of the conscription paper.[43] In the video interview of Friedman, Becker mentions his conscription paper and expresses disappointment that RAND had not published it, although Friedman appears to be unaware of the study.

COLUMBIA

Becker continued to be interested in conscription and military-manpower issues when he was a faculty member at Columbia University from 1957 to 1969. For example, one of four questions on his microeconomic-theory exam in 1965 involved the tax burden and composition of the military with conscription and a volunteer military and how the answer changed if those conscripted could hire a substitute.[44] Becker's 1971 textbook, *Economic Theory*, was based on his graduate price-theory lectures at Columbia from 1967 to 1968. In lecture thirty-four, he discusses the level of military pay required for an AVF and cites Oi's work on estimating the supply of individuals to the military.

William Landes, Becker's teaching assistant at Columbia from 1964 to 1965, recalls Becker discussing a volunteer military in class and mentioning the RAND papers in their conversations. Upon reviewing a draft of this chapter, Landes remarked, "[Becker] must have also discussed his work [on conscription] with several of the economists mentioned here."[45]

At Columbia, Becker advised students on at least two doctoral dissertations that involved military manpower. Gorman Smith, an active-duty U.S. Army officer, wrote a study that he supervised on occupational pay differences.[46] Smith's dissertation was closer in content to Becker's other RAND paper on training and pay in the military, but it also considered conscription. Smith's main concern was the optimal compensation package required to retain trained individuals in the military.

Anthony Fisher wrote a 1968 dissertation, supervised by Becker and Jacob Mincer, on the costs of conscription and of ending the draft, which was published in part the following year.[47] Fisher's study is strongly related to Becker's RAND paper on conscription. He estimated a labor-supply schedule and calculated how much pay would have to increase if the draft were eliminated. Becker had discussed both issues in his working paper. Given the close relationship in content between the two studies, it seems likely that Becker discussed his ideas with Fisher, though he might not have shared (and might have already misplaced) the RAND conscription paper. We contacted Fisher in April 2020; he did not recall seeing that paper. Neither Fisher nor Smith cite Becker's RAND papers nor indicate in their dissertations any familiarity with them.

Martin Anderson was a finance professor at Columbia when he became an advisor to Nixon's 1968 presidential campaign. He was an early proponent of a volunteer military.[48] In 1964, the year in which Anderson joined the Columbia faculty, Friedman began an academic year visiting Columbia, and Anderson cultivated a relationship with him. In 1967, he read the comments Friedman and Oi made at the 1966 University of Chicago conference on conscription. Already an advisor to the Nixon campaign, Anderson wrote a memorandum on moving toward a volunteer army, which piqued the curiosity of Nixon.[49] At that time, Becker was an economics professor at Columbia. We did not find any evidence indicating that Becker and Anderson knew each other then or knew their work on a volunteer military. Later, both were affiliated with the Hoover Institution, with Anderson beginning in 1971 and Becker in 1973. Both served on a policy advisory board for the DOD beginning in 2001.[50] But the draft was not likely a topic for that board, given that a volunteer military had existed for almost thirty years at that time.

ROCHESTER

A group of economists at the University of Rochester became heavily involved in analyses of a volunteer military in the late 1960s. Allen Wallis, the president of Rochester, was opposed to conscription. In December 1968, he met with his friend Arthur Burns, a domestic-policy advisor to president-elect Nixon. Wallis then called William Meckling, dean of the Rochester Graduate School of Management, who assembled a team to prepare a report for Burns on the budget cost of eliminating conscription. The team consisted of Martin Bailey, Harry Gilman, and Walter Oi, the latter having joined Rochester's faculty in 1967.[51] Wallis became a member of the President's Commission on an All-Volunteer Armed Force that Nixon formed in 1969. Subsequently, Meckling served as the Gates Commission's executive director for research, supervising four research directors: Gilman, Oi, Stuart Altman, and David Kassing.[52] He was one of five individuals thanked by Becker for his comments on the RAND conscription paper, but we found no mention of that paper by Meckling. Perhaps he had forgotten it ten years later.

Oi and Becker each had Lewis as his dissertation supervisor at Chicago.

Oi became a graduate student at Chicago in 1954, the year Becker transitioned from student to assistant professor. We do not know if Becker taught any classes in which Oi was a student, though they certainly knew each other and would have attended some of the same workshops.[53] Lewis sent Becker a letter dated August 1, 1957, stating that Oi would try to see him before he left RAND for Columbia.[54] According to Lewis's letter, he had told Oi that Becker had some ideas about his dissertation. If they did meet, it seems plausible that Becker discussed what he was working on at RAND. But we have no evidence that the two actually met at that time.

In Oi's 1962 paper in the *Journal of Political Economy* on quasi-fixed labor costs, which he based on his 1961 dissertation, he thanked Becker for sharing two unpublished papers.[55] Presumably, one of these became Becker's 1962 article on training in the *Journal of Political Economy*.[56] We do not know what the other one was.

BECKER AND OI

Oi was arguably the foremost economist researching the possible move to the AVF. He and Becker had strong connections from being in the Economics Department at Chicago at the same time and from having the same dissertation advisor. To further explore any possible influence of Becker's conscription paper on subsequent research, we considered the analysis in Becker's work and three early papers of Oi's on conscription and an AVF.[57] The Oi papers are his chapter in the volume of papers presented at the 1966 conference at the University of Chicago, his paper in the American Economic Association Papers and Proceedings, and his coauthored paper in the studies prepared for the Gates Commission.[58] It is important to note that the second item is essentially a shorter version of the first.

Becker's paper on conscription begins by discussing how a draft with the hiring of substitutes compares to an AVF. Because substitutes had not been allowed in the United States since the Civil War, this part of his paper is not relevant for the future analysis that compared conscription and an AVF. He then turns to issues that are pertinent for that time. Becker argues that fewer enlistees would be demanded as the private cost of conscription increased to equal the social cost with an AVF. He guesses that military pay would have to increase by about 30 percent to attract a force of the (then) current size. Yet he undertakes no empirical analysis to estimate labor supply to the military. Becker contends that effort would be lower with a conscript than with a volunteer because the latter would have more incentive to keep his job (all draftees being male). This would imply less of a *budgetary cost* increase with an AVF. Also, with the military paying for training cost, it recouped some of this outlay with reenlistments, which would be greater with an AVF.[59] Becker also discusses the notion of a duty to serve and that patriotism should drive enlistments. He points out that, if patriotism were sufficient to induce enough individuals to enlist at low wages, then a draft would not be necessary. An AVF, he argues, always attracts those who are the most patriotic (that is, those willing to forfeit income in order to serve in the military). With conscription, the armed forces tend to enlist those with the average amount of patriotism. Other arguments he makes against conscription are that involuntary servitude is immoral, that conscription misallocates resources (too many are drafted with skills little used in the military, while too few are drafted with skills greatly used in the military), and that it is inequitable (similarly situated individuals are treated differently, some drafted and others not). Finally, Becker considers how to get more volunteers. Suggesting that bonuses encourage desertion and insincere enlistment, he instead advocates for higher money wages, better pensions, and the like.[60]

In contrast to Becker's theoretical paper, Oi's work is mainly empirical, although he discusses theoretical issues. Oi argues that conscription imposes at least three costs on those forced to serve.[61] More enlistees are required to serve due to higher turnover. Further, those conscripted are not compensated for the disutility they had from military service, and they are denied the higher wages that would exist with an AVF.

Oi estimated a military supply schedule and determines that an AVF would require a 68-percent pay increase for first-term enlistees.[62] During the transition to an AVF, the pay increase for first-term enlistees is estimated to be 94 percent. Oi's only reference to Becker is to his book *Human Capital* when discussing how training on the job shapes age-earnings profiles.[63]

An argument similar to Becker's analysis involves training. Oi and Brian E. Forst, his coauthor, discuss the value of increased lateral entry into the military.[64] Becker has suggested that a wide range of training activities should be obtained outside the military, at universities and other institutions, with enlistees then provided with training in purely military subjects. But this analysis is not contained in his conscription paper, rather, it is found in a companion paper on military training he wrote while at RAND.[65] But, in general, there is little overlap between the Becker and Oi papers. The fact that Oi and Forst do not mention the Becker training paper suggests that they were unaware of it. Both Becker and Oi discuss the necessity of increased pay and reduced turnover with an AVF, but these observations are obvious to any economist comparing conscription and a volunteer military. Finally, Oi's correspondence with

Becker, which began in 1975, does not mention anything involving conscription.[66]

Why No Apparent Influence?

We are left with a curiosity for the history of economic thought. Gary Becker famously pioneered many new and creative applications of microeconomics over his career. One of those was what seems to be the first formal economic analysis of conscription. That paper is characteristically Beckerian in how so many economic ideas are packed into a short first draft. His analysis raised many issues later considered in the literature. Yet it was not cited in that literature, and Becker does not seem to have participated in or influenced that important economic and policy debate over the draft, though he knew many of the key figures. Fifty years later, he expressed pride in the working paper he produced at RAND and conveyed regret that it had been unpublished and forgotten.[67]

While Becker may have provided the first formal analysis of conscription, he probably did not come up with this topic on his own. Walter Oi reported hearing that Milton Friedman and his former University of Chicago classmates discussed the draft in 1940 in the context of the debate about whether the United States should enter World War II. Friedman was probably Becker's most important influence at Chicago and throughout his subsequent career. He taught the doctorate-level microeconomics class in the era when Becker was a student. It would not be surprising if his interest in conscription was inspired by Friedman via conversations, lectures, or homework and exam questions.

It is possible that Becker's analysis influenced the most important work on conscription, that produced by Oi. When Oi arrived at Chicago as a graduate student, Becker was a new professor and might have taught him. Both were doctoral students of H. Gregg Lewis, and Becker may have provided some advice to Oi at the early stages of his dissertation. We do not know if he visited Becker at RAND, but Oi later thanked him for providing access to two working papers. One of them could have been Becker's RAND report on training.

Beyond Oi, we found no evidence that Becker played any role in the efforts to study the economics of conscription initiated by the DOD. He did not work on or advise the resulting commissions, is not cited in any of the research, and did not attend any of the major conferences. The two Columbia students he advised on dissertations related to military manpower also were not part of that DOD effort and policy debate. Given his connections to many of these economists and the strength of the ideas in his RAND report, why was this the case? There are several possible explanations, which are not mutually exclusive. First, Becker may have lost the paper at some point after his move to Columbia. He might have felt it was either too late to ask RAND to search for a copy when the topic became important some years later, or perhaps it was inappropriate to ask RAND since they had rejected it. Becker may have been too busy with other topics and work at Columbia. He also might have felt that the DOD-inspired efforts were already well advanced and would not benefit from his old working paper.

Becker may have been reluctant to interject himself and his old ideas into the new debate out of a combination of reluctance and disappointment. In his introductory remarks in the *Hoover Digest* post in 2007, Becker states:

> I was discouraged by the RAND rejection. I also felt that the opposition to a fully voluntary military was so powerful that the United States would never abandon the draft. Naturally, I did not anticipate the Vietnam War and the enormous reaction against it, especially by young people subject to the draft. This reaction and opposition led then-president Nixon to set up the Gates Commission in 1969 to consider whether to keep the draft. Fortunately, Nixon asked Milton Friedman to serve on the commission, and he was a persuasive advocate of fully voluntary armed forces, turning an initially divided commission into one that unanimously supported ending the draft. The draft ended in 1973. Since then, other countries—France and Germany, for example—have been persuaded by the US example to end conscription.[68]

This helps explain why he did not circulate the paper, other than to Lewis, or work further on the topic.[69] As a RAND consultant, Becker was bound by the terms of the DOD contract that funded his research. RAND contracts generally state that it will not publish work without clearance by the funder, in this case the U.S. Air Force.[70] It is possible that he could have worked on the topic and published it after leaving the corporation. But the air force was the primary source of funding for RAND at that time. If they were (not surprisingly) unhappy with a working paper titled "The Case against Conscription" and rejected it for further consideration or publication, Becker may have felt that he was not allowed to pursue it further or should not do so out of consideration for RAND's relationship with the air force. He also may have decided that it would be best to refrain from mentioning this work to others.[71]

Finally, Becker might not have been interested in attempting to shape public policy. He may have believed that economists should examine problems using the best economic analysis they could without considering how public policy would be affected.[72] He may have felt that politicians were unlikely to eliminate conscription.[73] Regarding Becker's conscription paper, a *Wall Street Journal* interviewer said that he was "discouraged from publishing it because . . . the popular view was that the military draft could never be abolished."[74] Furthermore, Becker had already moved into human-capital research by 1957 and had other research interests by the 1960s, including crime and punishment, self-insurance, and marriage.

Becker's early work on conscription apparently influenced him throughout his career. In discussing the limits to using prices and markets to organize the economy, he noted that opponents of a volunteer army thought such soldiers would be mercenaries.[75] He argued that the then almost thirty years of experience in the United States with a volunteer military disproved such arguments. Additionally, when he and Julio J. Elias considered the market for organs, they compared arguments against paying organ donors to those against paying market wages with a volunteer military.[76]

But before this, at the beginning of his career, Becker had conceived another creative application of microeconomics that he dropped, even though it became a major public-policy question seven years afterward. Finally, fifty years after writing it, he published an abridged version of his conscription paper online. In doing so, he remarked: "This experience taught me that ideas and policies that are politically impossible at one time can come to fruition later if events and circumstances change. Analyzing defects in public policies can create intellectual ammunition, if you will, for dramatic policy changes not yet on the horizon." Indeed.

Notes

1. We thank Diana Sykes at the Hoover Institution Library and Archives for duplicating and sending us correspondence between Gary Becker and Milton Friedman; Megan O'Connell and Kate Collins at the David M. Rubenstein Rare Book and Manuscript Library at Duke University for duplicating and sending us correspondence between Becker and H. Gregg Lewis; Melissa Mead at the Rare Books, Special Collections, and Preservation, River Campus Libraries, University of Rochester for duplicating and sending us correspondence between Becker and Walter Oi; and Cara McCormick at the RAND Corporation archives for information on Becker's RAND consultancy. We are grateful for comments from Beth Asch, Guity Nashat Becker, Julio Elias, Ron Hansen, Kathryn Ierulli, Christopher Jehn, Bill Landes, Bob Michael, Steve Millsaps, Casey Mulligan, Marjorie Oi, Don Parsons, Bernard Rostker, and John Warner.

2. John Warner, personal communication with authors, 2020.

3. Bernard Rostker, personal communication with authors, 2020.

4. Gary S. Becker, "Should the Military Pay for Training of Skilled Personnel?," working paper D-4508, RAND Corporation, August 1957, in *The Power of the Economic Approach: Unpublished Manuscripts of Gary Becker*, ed. Julio J. Elias, Casey B. Mulligan, and Kevin M. Murphy (Chicago: University of Chicago Press, forthcoming); Timothy J. Perri, "Gary Becker's Neglected Early Research on Training on the Job," working paper, Department of Economics, Appalachian State University, November 2019; Gary S. Becker, "Investment in Human Capital: A Theoretical Analysis," *Journal of Political Economy* 70 (October 1962, pt. 2): 9–49.

5. Gary S. Becker, "The Case against Conscription," working paper D-4514, RAND Corporation, August 1957.

6. Gary S. Becker, "The Case against the Draft," *Hoover Digest* 3, June 19, 2007, https://www.hoover.org/research/case-against-draft.

7. Beth J. Asch, James C. Miller, and John T. Warner, "Economics and the All-Volunteer Military Force," in *Better Living through Economics*, ed. John J. Siegfried (Cambridge, MA: Harvard University Press, 2010), 253–269.

8. Milton Friedman, "Why Not a Volunteer Army?," *New Individualist Review* 4 (Spring 1967): 3–9; Walter Y. Oi, "The Costs and Implications of an All-Volunteer Force," in *The Draft: A Handbook of Facts and Alternatives*, ed. Sol Tax (Chicago: University of Chicago Press, 1967), 221–251.

9. David R. Henderson, "The Role of Economists in Ending the Draft," *Economic Journal Watch* 2 (August 2005): 362–376.

10. On popular writing, see Milton Friedman, *Capitalism and Freedom* (Chicago: University of Chicago Press, 1962); Friedman, "A Volunteer Army," *Newsweek*, December 19, 1966, 100; Friedman, "Why Not a Volunteer Army?," 3–9; and Friedman, "The Case for Abolishing the Draft—and Substituting for It an All-Volunteer Army," *Newsweek*, May 14, 1967, 23, 114–119. On research reports, see Bernard Rostker, *I Want You!: The Evolution of the All-Volunteer Force* (Santa Monica, CA: RAND Corporation, 2006).

11. Rostker, *I Want You!*, 29.

12. Sol Tax, ed., *The Draft: A Handbook of Facts and Alternatives* (Chicago: University of Chicago Press, 1967).

13. Milton Friedman and Rose D. Friedman, *Two Lucky People* (Chicago: University of Chicago Press, 1998), 378.

14. Rostker, *I Want You!*, 15. Bernard Rostker held many positions in the DOD and wrote the definitive study of the evolution of the AVF. In it, he argues that there were five reasons why the United States was ready to move to an AVF in the early 1970s. One of these was the "rational and intellectual basis" offered by Friedman for ending the draft. Nixon Legacy Forum, "Ending the Draft: The Creation of the All-Volunteer Force," January 19, 2012, 5, Richard Nixon Foundation, https://www.nixonfoundation.org/wp-content/uploads/2012/01/Nixon-Legacy-Forum-Nixon-Ends-the-Draft.pdf. Gary Becker's paper on the draft preceded Friedman's extensive writing on that subject by almost a decade.

15. Friedman, "Why Not a Volunteer Army?," 3–9.

16. Martin Anderson, "An Outline of the Factors Involved in Establishing an All-Volunteer Armed Force," memorandum to Richard Nixon, April 1967, Richard Nixon Foundation, Yorba Linda, CA; Martin Anderson, "An Analysis of the Factors Involved in Moving to an All-Volunteer Armed Force," Columbia University working paper, July 10, 1967.

17. Henderson, "Role of Economists in Ending the Draft," 370.

18. Rostker, *I Want You!*, 62. Outgoing assistant secretary of defense Alfred Fitt warned incoming secretary of defense Melvin Laird that economists at the Council of Economic Advisors, who presumably were outgoing as well, were strongly opposed to conscription. See Alfred B. Fitt, "Arguments against a Special Commission," memorandum to Melvin R. Laird, Washington, DC, January 29, 1969, in Rostker, *I Want You!*, accompanying CD. This is more evidence of the widespread opposition of economists to conscription.

19. Rostker, *I Want You!*, 78.

20. Friedman and Friedman, *Two Lucky People*, 379.

21. Liberty Fund, *A Conversation with Milton Friedman*, Intellectual Portrait Series, video, 2003.

22. Becker, "Case against the Draft."

23. For a discussion of the end of conscription in the United States and a list of many of the papers written on the economics of the draft, see John T. Warner and Paul F. Hogan, "Walter Oi and His Contributions to the All-Volunteer Force— Theory, Evidence, Persuasion," *Defence and Peace Economics* 27, no. 2 (2016): 161–171.

24. Rostker, *I Want You!*

25. Rostker, *I Want You!*

26. Bernard Rostker, personal communication with the authors, 2020.

27. Gary S. Becker, *The Economics of Discrimination* (Chicago: University of Chicago Press, 1957); Becker, "Investment in Human Capital," 9–49; Becker, *Human Capital: A Theoretical and Empirical Analysis, with Special Reference to Education* (New York: Columbia University Press, 1964).

28. Timothy J. Perri, "The Economics of US Civil War Conscription," *American Law and Economics Review* 10 (Fall 2008): 424–453; Casey B. Mulligan, "In-Kind Taxes, Behavior, and Comparative Advantage," National Bureau of Economic Research working paper 21586, September 2015.

29. Edward F. Renshaw, "The Economics of Conscription," *Southern Economic Journal* 27 (October 1960): 111–117.

30. Correspondence Series, Gary Becker, 1957–1979, box 10, H. Gregg Lewis Papers, 1939–1990, David M. Rubenstein Rare Book and Manuscript Library, Duke University, Durham, NC (hereafter cited as Lewis Papers, DU).

31. Gary S. Becker to H. Gregg Lewis, July 21, 1957, Correspondence Series, Gary Becker, 1957–1979, box 10, Lewis Papers, DU; Becker, "Should the Military Pay for Training of Skilled Personnel?"

32. H. Gregg Lewis to Gary Becker, August 1, 1957, Correspondence Series, Gary Becker, 1957–1979, box 10, Lewis Papers, DU.

33. As Michael Gibbs, a former student of and teaching assistant for Becker, painfully but fondly remembers, Becker regularly wrote homework, test, or doctoral core

exam questions on new ideas that he was considering working on, often unsure as to what the correct answer would be.

34. Gary S. Becker to H. Gregg Lewis, October 8, 1957, Correspondence Series, Gary Becker, 1957–1979, box 10, Lewis Papers, DU.

35. H. Gregg Lewis to Gary Becker, October 16, 1957, Correspondence Series, Gary Becker, 1957–1979, box 10, Lewis Papers, DU.

36. Rostker, *I Want You!*, 29.

37. Walter Y. Oi, "A View from the Midway," *American Economist* 43 (Fall 1999): 18n14.

38. Becker was heavily involved in the Labor Economics Workshop at Columbia at that time. See Shoshana Grossbard-Shechtman, "The New Home Economics at Columbia and Chicago," *Feminist Economics* 7 (November 2001): 103–130.

39. Walter Y. Oi, "Labor as a Quasi-Fixed Factor," *Journal of Political Economy* 70 (December 1962): 538–555; Walter Y. Oi and Paul W. Shuldiner, *An Analysis of Urban Travel Demands* (Evanston, IL: Northwestern University Press, 1962).

40. Allen Wallis was president of the University of Rochester when he was appointed to the Gates Commission in 1969. He had been a graduate student in the 1930s at the University of Chicago with Milton Friedman, and they remained friends. See Friedman and Friedman, *Two Lucky People*. Wallis told Walter Oi that he, Friedman, Aaron Director, and other former Chicago classmates discussed the draft in 1940. See Walter Y. Oi, "Historical Perspectives on the All-Volunteer Force: The Rochester Connection," in *Professionals on the Front Line: Two Decades of the All-Volunteer Force*, ed. J. Eric Fredland, Curtis L. Gilroy, Roger D. Little, and W. S. Sellman (Washington, DC: Brassey's, 1996), 53n23.

41. Friedman and Friedman, *Two Lucky People*, 377. In *Capitalism and Freedom*, Milton Friedman says the book is based on the Wabash lectures and others. It is possible he discussed ending conscription in those other lectures.

42. Binyamin Appelbaum says that Friedman first condemned conscription in his Wabash College lecture, but his source is *Capitalism and Freedom*. See Appelbaum, *The Economists' Hour* (Boston: Little, Brown, 2019), 29; 343n27. For other examples of Friedman's writings on the draft, see Friedman, "Why Not a Volunteer Army?," 3–9; and Friedman, "Case for Abolishing the Draft," 23, 114–119.

43. Collected Works of Milton Friedman, folder 30, box 20, Milton Friedman Papers, Hoover Institution Library and Archives, Stanford, CA.

44. Irwin Collier, "Columbia, Microeconomic Theory Exam, Becker, 1965," *Economics in the Rear-View Mirror: Archival Artifacts from the History of Economics* (blog), August 30, 2018, http://www.irwincollier.com/columbia-microeconomic-theory-exam-becker-1965/.

45. William Landes, personal communication with authors, 2020.

46. Gorman C. Smith, "Occupational Pay Differentials for Military Technicians" (PhD diss., Columbia University, 1964).

47. Anthony C. Fisher, "The Cost of the Draft and the Cost of Ending the Draft," *American Economic Review* 59 (June 1969): 239–254.

48. Martin Anderson provides more detailed analysis in his Columbia working paper than in his earlier memo to Nixon. Compare Anderson, "Analysis of the Factors

Involved in Moving to an All-Volunteer Armed Force"; and Anderson, "Outline of the Factors Involved in Establishing an All-Volunteer Armed Force."

49. Appelbaum, *Economists' Hour*.

50. Hoover Institution, "Eight Hoover Fellows Appointed to the US Defense Policy Board Advisory Committee," press release, November 29, 2001, https://www.hoover.org/press-releases/eight-hoover-fellows-appointed-us-defense-policy-board-advisory-committee; Stephen F. Knott and Allison Asher, "Interview with Martin Anderson," 2001, Ronald Reagan Oral History Project, Miller Center of Public Affairs, Charlottesville, VA.

51. Oi, "Historical Perspectives on the All-Volunteer Force," 44–45.

52. John D. Singleton, "Slaves or Mercenaries? Milton Friedman and the Institution of the All-Volunteer Military," in *Milton Friedman: Contributions to Economics and Public Policy*, ed. Robert A. Cord and J. Daniel Hammond (Oxford: Oxford University Press, 2016), 516–517.

53. Becker attended Oi's presentation of his work on labor as a quasi-fixed cost in a Chicago workshop in 1956. See Oi, "View from the Midway," 15.

54. H. Gregg Lewis to Gary Becker, August 1, 1957, Correspondence Series, Gary Becker, 1957–1979, box 10, Lewis Papers, DU.

55. Oi, "Labor as a Quasi-Fixed Factor," 538.

56. Becker's work on training at RAND contained the seeds of his later work on general and specific training, but it was quite preliminary. See Becker, "Should the Military Pay for Training of Skilled Personnel?"; and Perri, "Gary Becker's Neglected Early Research." Becker sent part of a chapter to his reading committee at the National Bureau of Economic Research (for whom *Human Capital* was published) on August 31, 1959. See Gary S. Becker, "Memorandum to Milton Friedman, George Stigler, and Richard Easterlin," 1959, Collected Works of Milton Friedman, folder 30, box 20, Milton Friedman Papers, Hoover Institution Library and Archives, Stanford, CA. This material formed the theoretical core of his 1962 *Journal of Political Economy* article and his 1964 book, *Human Capital*. The unpublished papers that Oi mentions are likely based on Becker's work on human capital at Columbia and the National Bureau of Economic Research after he had left RAND in 1957.

57. Becker, "Case against Conscription."

58. Oi, "Costs and Implications of an All-Volunteer Force," 221–251; Oi, "The Economic Cost of the Draft," *American Economic Review* 57 (May 1967): 39–62; Walter Y. Oi and Brian E. Forst, "Manpower and Budgetary Implications of Ending Conscription," study 1, vol. 1, *Studies Prepared for the President's Commission on an All-Volunteer Force* (Washington, DC: Government Printing Office, 1970), I-1-1–I-1-90.

59. But as his analysis published five years later suggests, this would only be true if training provided skills specific to the military. See Becker, "Investment in Human Capital," 9–49.

60. Becker's arguments were likely shaped by his knowledge of the problems with bonuses during the Civil War. See Perri, "Economics of US Civil War Conscription," 424–453.

61. Oi, "Costs and Implications of an All-Volunteer Force," 221–251.

62. Oi, "Economic Cost of the Draft," 39–62.

63. Oi, "Economic Cost of the Draft," 39–62; Becker, *Human Capital*.

64. Oi and Forst, "Manpower and Budgetary Implications of Ending Conscription," I-1-1–I-1-90.

65. Becker, "Should the Military Pay for Training of Skilled Personnel?"

66. Walter Y. Oi Papers, Rare Books, Special Collections, and Preservation, River Campus Libraries, University of Rochester, Rochester, NY.

67. Guity Nashat Becker, personal communication with authors, 2020; Liberty Fund, *Conversation with Milton Friedman*.

68. Becker, "Case against the Draft."

69. If this is the case, then why did Becker share the paper with Lewis? As the latter indicated, they had been discussing conscription previously, and Lewis was a close advisor. Moreover, Becker sent him the papers in October 1957, just after arriving at Columbia. The study might have still been under review at RAND for working-paper status. Alternatively, he might have decided after sharing it with Lewis that wider dissemination might not be wise, given the reaction to it by the air force.

70. We thank Beth Asch for helping us understand these contractual issues for RAND projects and external consultants.

71. Moreover, in 1957, Becker faced "strong opposition" to the publication of his PhD thesis, eventually released as *The Economics of Discrimination* (Chicago: University of Chicago Press, 1957).

72. We thank Casey Mulligan for insight on this argument.

73. Casey B. Mulligan, "Ideas, Costs, and the All-Volunteer Army," *New York Times*, January 15, 2014, https://economix.blogs.nytimes.com/2014/01/15/ideas-costs-and-the-all-volunteer-army/.

74. Mary Anastasia O'Grady, "Now Is No Time to Give Up on Markets," *Wall Street Journal*, March 21, 2009.

75. Gary S. Becker, "What Limits to Using Money Prices to Buy and Sell?" *Becker-Posner Blog*, October 21, 2012, https://www.becker-posner-blog.com/2012/10/what-limits-to-using-money-prices-to-buy-and-sell-becker.html.

76. Gary S. Becker and Julio J. Elias, "Introducing Incentives in the Market for Live and Cadaveric Organ Donations," *Journal of Economic Perspectives* 21 (Summer 2007): 3–24; Becker and Elias, "Cash for Kidneys: The Case for a Market for Organs," *Wall Street Journal*, January 17, 2014, http://www.lkdn.org/LKDN_WSJ_Cash_for_Kidneys.pdf.

3

Gates Commission

William A. Taylor

In order to have an informed understanding of the all-volunteer force, one must first understand the commission that launched its advent. The President's Commission on an All-Volunteer Armed Force, colloquially known as the Gates Commission after its chair, Thomas S. Gates Jr., was a major milestone leading to the AVF. This chapter details the Gates Commission, explores its examination of both the draft and the AVF, and considers the results and implications of its momentous efforts.[1]

"One of the serious problems troubling our country today, and, in particular, our young men, is compulsory military service," newly inaugurated president Richard M. Nixon complained.[2] While debates regarding the draft had long existed, they had risen in furor since the mid-1960s, largely in direct proportion to increasing U.S. involvement in the Vietnam War.[3] In fact, the mid-1960s marked the high-water mark for the draft during the Cold War. "From the time of its inception in 1948, the current operation of the Selective Service System in the United States has passed through some exceptionally active periods," admitted Lewis Hershey in his official history of the system that he oversaw as director. "None has been more active, however, than the 1963–1969 period."[4] Hershey characterized Selective Service during the Lyndon B. Johnson administration as its most active period since 1948.

Indeed, it was a time of great change for both the U.S. armed forces and American society. Military requirements for personnel significantly rose, and the Selective Service System had to fill them in the absence of sufficient volunteers. Such augmented reliance on the draft to sustain a heightened engagement in the Vietnam War also led to renewed attention on the inequities of conscription and the war, thereby triggering intensified resistance and amplified protest against them both.

As a result of deepened immersion in Vietnam and an enlarged demand for armed forces personnel that routinely eclipsed the number of volunteers, military service garnered enhanced attention nationwide. Hershey

President Nixon and Pat Nixon pose for an official state portrait by the stair-
way with General Lewis B. Hershey and Mrs. Hershey before attending a state
dinner honoring General Hershey on February 17, 1970. (Courtesy Richard M.
Nixon Library)

admitted, "The years of the Johnson Administration may also be characterized as an era of intensive analysis and re-evaluation of the Nation's
military manpower procurement policies and programs."[5] Military service, specifically in reference to the draft and questions of its equity—or
lack thereof—become a major theme during the Johnson years. Before-
hand, during John F. Kennedy's presidency, military personnel requirements had been quite small, so the draft was not extensively used. This
situation began to change in 1965.

"The President's announcement on July 28, 1965, of plans to increase
the military forces, to use Selective Service for this buildup and the maintenance of these armed forces, directed the System, of course, to the
immediate necessity of gearing its operations to the new requirements,"
Hershey divulged. He further explained, "The radically changed posture
of American military forces and the dramatization of the vital necessity
of a functioning and effective Selective Service diverted, at least for the
time being, the draft interest of the Congress into other channels."[6]

Therefore, this situation was the catalyst that changed everything related to the draft and the AVF. Significantly ramping up the personnel

requirements due to the Vietnam War and directly placing the onus on Selective Service ensured that the reach of the draft dramatically grew throughout the 1960s. At the same time and compounding matters, population growth in the United States meant that even as the draft claimed more personnel, those men represented a smaller percentage of the population, resulting in expanded deferments. Within this context, the inequity argument amplified, ultimately leading to support for the AVF.

Until early 1965, draft calls remained quite low. In January 1965, only 5,400 men were drafted, with even fewer draft calls—only 3,000—occurring in February. For the entire year of 1965, draft calls totaled 233,200—mostly in the second half of that year. They started to rise in April to 13,700 and spiked in September at 27,400. They then remained very high throughout 1966, ranging from 12,000 to 50,000 per month for a total of 364,600. In 1967, draft calls tapered off somewhat, varying from 10,000 to 30,000 per month for a total of 218,700. Draft calls spiked again in 1968, fluctuating from 10,000 to 50,000 per month, with March (41,000), April (48,000), and May (45,900) especially high, for an annual total of 299,000. They remained steady in 1969, ranging from 10,000 to 30,000 for a yearly total of 289,900. In 1970, draft calls fell, ranging from 10,000 to 20,000 per month. As these numbers indicate, the Vietnam War fundamentally changed the nature of the draft. Its personnel requirements significantly spiked draft calls, resulting in over 1.5 million call ups between 1965 and 1970. As a result of these greatly amplified numbers and the lengthy involvement in Vietnam, the draft came to dominate the American social conscious, especially affecting the lives of the young men who existed in its shadow and their many loved ones.[7]

The draft also caused the newly inaugurated Nixon administration serious problems by the end of the 1960s. Even before he became president, however, Nixon saw ending the draft as a possible coup de grâce. Doing this, therefore, became an early priority, both for his administration and personally for Nixon. His predecessor had chosen a different path, and the draft had negatively affected the Johnson administration throughout President Johnson's time in the White House. Sensing the shifting political winds and hoping to seize a political opportunity, Nixon wanted to reduce the draft's importance to the Vietnam War specifically and American society generally, thereby creating political maneuvering room for his other major priorities, including his administration's conduct in concluding the war. Such was the political side of the transition to the AVF, centered on avoiding the negative political consequences of reliance on the draft.

As a result, Nixon sought to move away from Selective Service toward a completely volunteer military. He achieved his first goal with the creation of the Gates Commission and his second with the advent of the AVF. "After careful consideration of this problem I have reached the conclusion that our national interest requires that we explore at once the specific steps that will need to be taken to enable us, once expenditures on Vietnam are substantially reduced, to move to an all-volunteer armed force," Nixon concluded. "Consequently, I have decided to appoint an Advisory Commission on an All-Volunteer Armed Force to develop and present to me a detailed plan of action for moving toward this objective."[8] In one fell swoop, Nixon moved beyond simply making rhetorical campaign promises to end the draft during his successful bid to defeat Hubert H. Humphrey Jr., his Democratic rival for the presidency and incumbent vice president, to embarking on a major study to enact such a significant policy change. He proved that he was fully committed to the AVF at this early point in his tenure, even though it would be some time before the AVF became a reality. Arthur F. Burns, counselor to the president, on March 17, 1969, provided Nixon a draft letter to prospective members of the commission and suggested that the new president personally telephone each to discuss the matter. He confided to Nixon, "This gives the essentials," referring to the draft letter.[9] Thus began an essential move toward the AVF, establishing the Gates Commission.

There were numerous precedents to the Gates Commission during the mid-1960s. In fact, in just the five years prior to its creation, there had been four major external studies of Selective Service: the Pentagon's Gorham Group (1964), President Johnson's Marshall Commission (1966), the Clark Panel (1966), and the Magruder Task Force (1967). All four substantiated the need for the draft and made only minor recommendations for change, if any at all. The Gorham Group argued that the draft was "generally quite satisfactory but espoused the adoption of a lottery," something Hershey characterized as a "procedural nebulosity." The Marshall Commission also advocated for a lottery system but added the removal of local boards in favor of a more centralized and automated process to its recommendations. The Clark Panel only critiqued the draft on two counts—college deferments and poor communication—while the Magruder report called for increased funding to allow the draft to operate more effectively. When Congress again renewed the draft, this time through the Military Selective Service Act of 1967, student deferments became the "only real change of moment," allowing Hershey to claim with both pride and characteristic hyperbole, "The System had been put through the fire of investigation and had not been found wanting in any respect."[10] Therefore, the draft was under constant and rigorous evaluation throughout Johnson's presidency; four separate groups analyzed it in great detail. While they differed on particulars, they all contended for the necessity—and therefore continuation—of conscription. The fact that Congress enacted the Selective Service Act of 1967 with only the change to student deferments illustrates that there was relatively broad consensus among policymakers that the draft was essential during the mid-1960s.

Among the four precedents, the most important one was the Marshall Commission, the only other presidential commission, which had made a strong case that the draft was indispensable. President Johnson had tasked its members to "consider the past, present and prospective functioning of selective service and other systems of national service," accounting for a myriad of factors in a specified order of importance: "fairness to all citizens"; "military manpower requirements"; "minimizing uncertainty and interference with individual careers and education"; "social, economic and employment conditions and goals"; "budgetary and administrative considerations"; and "any other factors that the Commission may deem relevant."[11] It reviewed the Selective Service System with an emphasis on equity, a function its members listed first before military-manpower requirements. The fact that the Marshall Commission titled its final report *In Pursuit of Equity: Who Serves When Not All Serve?* reinforced its primary emphasis. Selective Service had become more and more unpopular, primarily due to its many inequities. As a result, President Johnson wanted to improve this aspect of the draft even though he still desperately needed conscription to prosecute the Vietnam War. As a result, he doubled down on the war, unable to get rid of the draft without curtailing or even ending it. Therefore, the Marshall Commission recommended several reforms to Selective Service, primarily to combat its well-earned reputation for inequality.

But Congress largely opted for the status quo. "Despite pressure for major reform, Congress instituted only four major changes in the new draft law: the undergraduate student deferment was made a matter of right; the President was forbidden to institute a system of induction by lottery; changes with uncertain legal effect were made in the conscientious objector provisions of the law; and provisions were added to improve criminal enforcement." The Marshall Commission had highlighted many inequities, but when lawmakers passed the new draft law in the summer of 1967, they enacted only these four minor alterations. Much of the unfairness remained, and Congress simply deferred action as the unpopularity of the draft continued to mount. Congressional inaction, therefore, set the stage for the AVF. A 1967 article in the *Columbia Journal of Law and Social Problems* argued: "The Marshall Commission concluded that the Selective Service System structure was in dire need of overhauling. Congress, however, failed to provide in the new Act for changes in the method by which draft registrants are advised of their rights, or changes in the existing systems of local board discretion, appellate review, and quota imposition, the System's three greatest sources of inequity."[12]

It was within this milieu that Nixon sensed a potential opportunity. President Johnson exuded confidence about the draft's necessity and importance to the American people, publicly affirmed that he had thoroughly vetted the draft, and remained personally convinced that he needed Selective Service to prosecute the increasingly unpopular Vietnam War. "The knowledge that military service must sometimes be borne by—and imposed on—free men so their freedom may be preserved is woven deeply into the fabric of the American experience," the president claimed.[13] He also made the case that military service was an obligation, without conceding the corollary that the draft was also necessary for continuing the Vietnam War. Johnson also had a long history of advocating for the draft. He was directly involved in the 1940 draft law, the 1948 draft law, and especially the 1951 Universal Military Training and Service Act, all of which enacted or extended conscription. His position was consistently one of general support for the concept of military service as an obligation and of advocacy for the draft as a legitimate way to meet personnel requirements.

In stark contrast, undeclared presidential candidate Nixon campaigned to end two rather longstanding but increasingly objectionable endeavors by the United States: the Vietnam War and Selective Service. Speaking to the Student Bar Association at the University of Wisconsin in Madison on November 17, 1967, he boldly declared: "A change in the Selective Service System at this time is not likely and would probably not be wise. It would be a stop-gap—and the wrong kind of change—in a system that needs a complete reappraisal." Instead of either steadfastly relying on the draft to prosecute the Vietnam War, as President Johnson had done at significant human, financial, and political costs, or simply seeking to reform the draft to remove some of its most glaring inequities, Nixon contended that, if elected president, he would pursue "an entirely new approach . . . when we achieve peace in Vietnam." He further elaborated to the engaged audience about the types of wars likely in the future and advocated for the most appropriate force structure necessary to wage them, concluding, "What is needed is not a broad-based draft but a professional military corps." A necessary first step toward recruiting such a voluntary military was a significant pay increase for servicemembers, as it had long languished far behind anything similar in the civilian sector. Therefore, Nixon determined that the United States had to "move toward a volunteer army by compensating those who go into the military on a basis comparable to those in civilian careers."[14] Thus began the movement to end the draft and replace it with the AVF.

Nixon continued to campaign throughout the remainder of the 1968 presidential election on his twin promises to end both the Vietnam War and the draft, officially making the AVF part of his platform.[15] On October 17 while in Pennsylvania, Nixon made his first policy speech on ending the draft and replacing it with the AVF, which aired nationwide on the CBS Radio Network. He confidently proposed, "I say it's time we took a new look at the draft—at the question of permanent conscription in a free society."[16] His dual campaign promises unmistakably juxtaposed Nixon with his Democratic opponent, Vice President Humphrey. Indeed, Humphrey assailed the Republican's call to end the draft and transition to a volunteer military as "highly irresponsible." In great detail that filled nine pages of text, Humphrey vigorously contended that reforming Selective Service would eliminate its most severe inequities, while any envisioned volunteer force would prove prohibitively expensive, adding anywhere from $8 billion to $17 billion annually to military spending during a decade when defense budgets had consistently hovered between $40 billion and $50 billion. "No responsible candidate for high public office can, in my opinion, legitimately hold out the promise of ending the need for draft calls in the foreseeable future," Humphrey insisted.[17]

On Tuesday, November 5, 1968, Nixon defeated Humphrey in a very close election. The Republican garnered 43.4 percent of the popular vote compared to 42.7 percent for the Democrat, but Nixon performed more convincingly in the Electoral College, securing 301 electoral votes to Humphrey's tally of 191. George C. Wallace Jr., segregationist third-party challenger and former governor of Alabama, carried five states, gathered 46 electoral votes, and garnered nearly 10 million popular votes.[18] Martin Anderson, one of Nixon's leading advisors on the AVF, later recalled that, as a result of Nixon's victory: "The all-volunteer force was no longer simply an issue for debate among intellectuals. It was now a major commitment of a newly elected president."[19]

President Nixon's first hurdle, ironically, was Melvin R. Laird, his own secretary of defense. Upon assuming office, Nixon sought to move quickly to form a presidential commission, similar to the previous Marshall Commission but that would argue for ending the draft and replacing it with an AVF. Laird was not so sure. In his own memoranda, he argued that such a new commission "would encumber and delay" the Pentagon's efforts to evaluate the draft, advocating instead that the Department of Defense should take the lead in any such study. Tom Cole, an administration insider, analyzed the secretary's position for the president and countered

"Not so" and "I don't like this," arguing that a presidential commission would be far more preferable than a Pentagon study because "present DOD higher echelon officials (many of whom have stayed on) are, in my opinion, opposed generally to the all volunteer army concept. Those DOD people that have stayed on, of course, have great influence over new appointees." When Laird proposed that any potential commission only follow when the Pentagon's study was complete, Cole countered: "No! New Commission, which would be influenced greatly by DOD anyway, would be evaluating only those findings and recommendations that DOD laid out. We want *new* commission to look at *new* things in a *new* way." He concluded:

> The depth and bearing of some of Laird's memo shows a great deal of thought and study has already gone into the volunteer army concept. This is good. New commission can make use of such thought and study. Laird here almost defeats his own purpose. In showing what he thinks needs to be done—in lieu of our immediate commission approach, he shows what's needed is not more study, but steps toward implementation. Decision to move towards volunteer army has already been made. Let's get on with doing it![20]

This early and testy reaction from February 3, 1969, to Secretary Laird's position from the president's advisors illustrates that the Nixon administration came into office already committed to the AVF and wanted to move swiftly, not through the Pentagon but rather through its own appointed commission. Laird pushed back in some of his initial memos to Nixon, indicating that DOD was studying the matter and should take the lead on determining whether to move to an AVF. Presidential advisors, including Cole, Burns, and Anderson, in contrast, all reinforced that the decision was already made and sought ways to control the evolving path forward. The Gates Commission was the primary way that the Nixon administration seized control from DOD and ensured that its goal of an AVF was realized. Appointing the commission, therefore, became a chess move to wrest control of the debate away from the Pentagon. It illustrated that politics, not national security, was primarily driving the move toward an AVF.

Soon after assuming office, Nixon created on March 27, 1969, the President's Commission on an All-Volunteer Armed Force, which over time would be known as the Gates Commission after its chair, Thomas S. Gates Jr. Acknowledging that he sought to reform the draft in the short term, Nixon reinforced that his ultimate goal was the AVF. "Ideally, of course, minimum interference means no draft at all," the president conceded. "I continue to believe that under more stable world conditions and with an armed force that is more attractive to volunteers, that ideal can be realized in practice." Nixon emphasized that he eagerly anticipated the group's report and hoped to receive it by November 1969. He also left little doubt as to what their conclusions should be. "I asked that group to develop a comprehensive plan which will attract more volunteers to military service, utilize military manpower in a more efficient way, and eliminate conscription as soon as that is feasible," admitted Nixon.[21]

Even when announcing his intermediate draft reforms, the president immediately turned to the Gates Commission. Any Selective Service reforms were simply a stopgap measure because, even under the most favorable circumstances, the move to the AVF would take some time. In Nixon's best estimation, it would require a couple of years, hence the original plan for establishing the AVF in 1971. As events unfolded, however, the momentous shift did not occur until 1973. But Nixon could not wait that long before having some tangible proof of progress of ending the draft's most contentious features. His reforms achieved this midway result.

In addition to its chair, a former secretary of defense during the Eisenhower administration, the Gates Commission members were former representative Thomas Curtis (R-MO), vice president of Encyclopaedia Britannica; Frederick Dent, president of Mayfair Mills; Milton Friedman, professor of economics at the University of Chicago; Crawford Greenewalt, finance chair of E. I. duPont de Nemours and Company; Alan Greenspan, economic consultant; Gen. Alfred Gruenther, former supreme allied commander in Europe; Stephen Herbits, a student at Georgetown University Law Center; Rev. Theodore Hesburgh, president of Notre Dame University; Jerome Holland, president of Hampton Institute; John Kemper, headmaster of Phillips Academy; Jeanne Noble, vice president of the National Council of Negro Women and professor of educational psychology and counseling at New York University; Gen. Lauris Norstad, former supreme allied commander in Europe; W. Allen Wallis, president of the University of Rochester; and Roy Wilkins, executive director of the National Association for the Advancement of Colored People.[22]

President Nixon sent similar letters to each member of the commission outlining his vision and inviting them to serve.[23] These personal letters, however, did not reveal that the administration had previously identified specific groups that it sought to have represented by one or more commission members, including "Former Military," represented by Gates, Gruenther, and Norstad; "University Administrator," represented by Hesburgh, Holland, Kemper, and Wallis; "Professor," represented by

Friedman and Noble; "Business," represented by Dent, Greenewalt, and Greenspan; "Former Congressman," represented by Curtis; and "Student," represented by Herbits.[24] Therefore, the Nixon administration specifically assembled the Gates Commission membership to represent certain groups in American society. Although the student group was initially absent, Herbits was later added as its sole representative to appeal to young Americans who were most affected by the draft.

Even though the Nixon administration carefully crafted the composition of the Gates Commission, advisors quickly realized that they had made a significant, and obvious, omission in their original appointments. On April 9, Charles B. Wilkinson relayed to John Ehrlichman, "The Commission has 15 members including a former Congressman, five from private enterprise, five educators, two former military personnel, and two representing ethnic groups." Such a composition achieved Nixon's goal of having a representative body except in one vital category. Wilkinson pointed out, "*No* students were appointed, and no group is more concerned, involved, or aware of the system's inadequacies. The President could quite clearly express *his* interest in young people by giving them a voice and some representation through *supplemental* appointments to the Gates Commission and have students on the staff this summer."

The composition of the commission targeted specific constituencies, involving politics, business, education, military, and minorities. The Nixon administration carefully crafted the commission membership, although Wilkinson pointed out a serious shortcoming, no student representation. Wilkinson suggested two student representatives: Bruce Chapman, a "noted author in this field and National Director of The Ripon Society" and John Shattuck from Yale Law school, a "brilliant and respected draft counselor."[25] In actuality, Stephen Herbits became the student representative. He was a twenty-six-year-old law student at Georgetown University Law Center.[26]

Once assembled, the Gates Commission wasted little time to commence its work. The group assembled in the Roosevelt Room on May 15, 1969, at 9:30 A.M. to hold its first meeting. Members exchanged pleasantries, made introductions, and got situated. President Nixon joined the group forty-five minutes later to deliver his rationale for the AVF and his initial charge for the group.[27] Holding this first meeting in the Roosevelt Room perhaps served to symbolize volunteer military service, and the president's attendance gave it momentum and official sanction from his administration and his office. In addition to the commission's members and staff, Anderson and Burns attended, illustrating their importance to the AVF. The minutes of the meeting reveal a great deal:

Mr. Gates briefly described his initial meeting with the President, at which the President expressed his hope that an all-volunteer armed force would prove to be the ultimate solution to the draft problem, although intermediate reforms would also be necessary. The President had observed that he had both the desire and a commitment to do something about this problem, as indicated by his proposal of an alternative to the draft during the campaign. The President believes that no alternative to the draft could be considered if it weakened national security. Mr. Gates said that the President realized that the present partially conscript system could not be eliminated immediately and that a complete transition to an all-volunteer force might involve a phased program which would take some time.[28]

From this first meeting, it was clear to all involved that Nixon wanted to move toward an AVF. It was his "hope" and "ultimate solution." He considered Selective Service a "problem" and wanted nothing more than for it to go away as soon as possible. Nixon also tied the AVF to his campaign promises, which he planned to deliver on. The president understood that this was no simple transition and might take some time, although he wanted to proceed as fast as possible.

Even so, the task before Gates and the others was clear: "The Commission's recommendations must include specific plans for moving toward an all-volunteer force. Requirements for appropriations and legislation must be spelled out in detail."[29] At every turn, it was obvious that the Gates Commission must not only recommend an AVF but also craft a detailed plan on how to achieve it. There was some talk among members about being willing to consider critiques of the AVF, which they eventually took great care to counter. But the commission was never going to recommend anything but an AVF from the very start. The group's actual planning assumptions always included the AVF as the logical outcome.

On July 12, the group held its third meeting, this time at 299 Park Avenue in New York City. There, William H. Meckling, staff director, reviewed initial reports completed by the commission staff and highlighted a pivotal question for the group. "Does the Commission have a responsibility beyond that of developing a plan to move towards an all-volunteer armed force; e.g., should the staff develop an estimate of the hidden tax imposed by the draft on conscripts, or should it avoid such research which is oriented more towards supporting arguments in favor of an all-volunteer armed force than towards developing the plan itself."[30] From the outset, the Gates Commission considered its primary task as crafting the plan to implement the AVF. Members were curious whether they even needed to make arguments in favor of the AVF because it was evident that formulating the proposal for it was the fundamental task at hand. The group ended up spending a lot of time and discussion fleshing out their arguments in favor, including many of these in its final report, even though early on there was a question whether such an approach was even necessary.

As the commission continued its work throughout the summer, members considered everything from complex economic statistics to human-interest anecdotes. In one of the more poignant examples of the latter, Friedman presented a typed excerpt from a letter written by the draftee son of one of his friends, a young man the economist considered "a person of both ability and integrity" who was stationed at Fort Meade, Maryland.[31] The draftee's account portrayed some of the drawbacks of conscription at the individual level:

> The atmosphere of my new unit is truly depressing. There is no one here who has a kind word or thought for the Army—everyone hates his work, his officers, and his obligation to wake up every morning. All of this hatred is pretty well justified, so far as I can tell. It seems that most of the work done by my unit could be left undone, or be done by civilian policemen working under civilian conditions and for civilian wages. The feeling of resentment is probably inevitable in view of the fact that the country is not visibly in danger—there is no apparent necessity for the sacrifices that people *do* make here. When I was a civilian I didn't think that the sacrifice was great enough to justify all the griping—but now, having had a taste of the sacrifice, I am more sympathetic.[32]

While this was only one individual's perspective, its sentiments encapsulated many of the widespread critiques of the draft during the late 1960s. It led to low morale, created antagonism toward the military writ large, caused tension between enlisted servicemembers and their officers, generated resentment at military order (that is, "chicken shit"), was unnecessary during peacetime (although this concept of "peacetime" was problematic at best during the Cold War and especially during the Vietnam War), fostered inequality between civilian and military personnel in terms of pay and benefits, and did not address a direct threat to the United States.

The Gates Commission ultimately analyzed many of the arguments against the AVF, acknowledging that "the relationship between the military and society is at the heart of most objections to volunteer forces." Among the many criticisms at that time, members determined that most centered on civilian control of the military, one of the most fundamental aspects of U.S. civil-military relations. The commission highlighted four specific concerns related to this theme: civilian policymakers might find it challenging "to exert control over a 'professional' military"; the AVF might reinforce the "military-industrial complex" and make it "even more powerful" in U.S. society; the AVF could become "a threat to our democratic way of life"; and leaders might find it "easier . . . to get into and stay in (unpopular) foreign wars" with a volunteer rather than a conscripted military.[33] Such was the Gates Commission's analysis of objections to the AVF. The last of the four points seemed especially compelling: it alluded to the fact that the AVF decoupled military service and use of force from significant debate in American society.

Civil-military relations were not the only arguments against the AVF that the Gates Commission considered. Race was also a heated topic of conversation. Many critics at that time made the claim that the AVF would become unrepresentative of society, either racially or economically. "In the course of discussing this argument, the Commission again considered the claim that an all-volunteer army would be disproportionately composed of blacks." The staff estimated that with an AVF of 2.6 million personnel, African Americans would compose approximately 20 percent of the total, "even if all eligible blacks were to enlist." The commission revealed that concerns regarding the racial composition of the AVF derived from two very divergent perspectives from far different corners of society: "(1) that it was unfair for blacks to bear an undue proportion of the defense burden, and (2) that it was dangerous for that many blacks to have had military training."[34] For many African Americans and progressives, the underlying concern was fairness. They did not want Black men to be disproportionately used by the military, especially during the Vietnam War and in combat positions leading to higher casualties, due to structural racism. In juxtaposition, there were segregationists and racists who also did not want to see too many African Americans serve, but this was because either they would be armed, have military training, become more assertive, or have increased economic and social benefits.

Another issue dominating deliberations was military pay. From the start, it was clear that any move toward the AVF would require significant pay increases. Even more interesting, the Gates Commission had to navigate whether it could address this issue differently among the various military services. Members considered how "to adjust for differences among the four Services in their ability to attract sufficient manpower under an all-volunteer force." The commission considered not just across-the-board pay increases—especially for first-term enlisted servicemembers in their first two years—but also other more controversial ideas, including "explicit inter-service pay differentials," a "variable enlistment bonus," and "differing minimum length of service contracts."

In response to these suggestions, Roger T. Kelley, assistant secretary of defense (manpower and reserve affairs), clarified that the Pentagon opposed the first two proposals but supported the third one. "The establishment of explicit inter-service pay differentials in an attempt to make the four Military Services equally attractive to the average recruit appears undesirable," Kelley maintained. "It would result in numerous situations in which individuals of the same rank, performing similar duties, would be compensated at different pay rates simply because of their Service affiliation."[35]

Such a situation revealed that the Gates Commission had to work with multiple audiences: the Nixon administration, the Pentagon, the public, and Congress. It had to vet its ideas and proposals through all these audiences, and these various stakeholders each had different ideas and various conceptions, even regarding the same topic. For example, the commission simply concluded that the military could just pay more for service in areas where there were fewer volunteers, but DOD strongly disagreed. It was a difficult course for the group to navigate.

There were other thorny issues that the Gates Commission addressed. One was the ramifications of the AVF on reserve forces. The group concluded two major findings in this pivotal relationship: the AVF would make recruiting for the reserves more challenging and, paradoxically, would also require much more reliance on the reserves. Assistant Secretary Kelley admitted to William Meckling that the group's research "correctly recognizes that recruitment for the reserve forces would be difficult in a draft-free environment." He also characterized the commission's leanings toward "closer association between active and reserve components" as a "useful approach." Kelley concluded that the Pentagon envisioned that "strategic, economic, and political considerations in the post–Viet Nam era are likely to lead us, with the passage of time, to greater rather than lesser reliance on the reserve components."[36] Yet he further revealed that the DOD was not sure that it could sustain the reserves under the AVF. There was significant doubt among military leaders about whether the AVF was even feasible for a number of other reasons beyond the reserves, let alone agreement on whether it was even desirable. In addition, the growing reliance on the reserves would continue to be an important implication after the AVF's advent.

Another challenge for the Gates Commission was timing. Even before assuming office, Nixon had made ending the draft and creating the AVF a major political objective. As soon as he assumed the presidency, he pressed for quick progress toward that goal. As the group worked through the summer of 1969, it was clear that the administration wanted a definitive framework for moving toward the AVF by that fall. Martin Anderson, one of the president's primary advisors on the AVF, "had urged that the Commission submit some proposal by November on the theory that any Vietnam de-escalation and general reduction in manpower should be coupled with a pay increase as a first step in moving towards an all-volunteer armed force, and that a pay increase should be included in the President's budget message for fiscal year 1971."[37]

As evident, there was a sense of urgency from the very start. The Nixon administration wanted the entire AVF plan completed in far less than one year. They were in a rush. Still, they did not want withdrawal from Vietnam to get ahead of the transition from the draft. If this happened, it might prove difficult or even impossible to move toward an AVF afterward. These twin objectives—withdrawal from Vietnam and ending the draft—were linked in the administration's plans. Withdrawal from Vietnam permitted a smaller military and thus enabled ending conscription. In turn, the AVF countenanced the end of the draft and removed one of the biggest political liabilities, along with the Vietnam War, that the Nixon administration had inherited. These two issues were therefore intertwined, with the AVF intimately related to both.

No one personified the Pentagon's uncertainty regarding the AVF more than Secretary of Defense Laird. Indeed, Laird, the individual who would have to implement the actual transition from the draft to the AVF, exhibited initial angst about doing so, both in private and in public. While the Gates Commission was finalizing its report and recommendations, he presented the AVF to a group of students and explained some of the problems of switching to it from Selective Service, including the need to cut force levels to approximately 2 million, which was 1.3 million less than 1970 levels and 700,000 less than pre-Vietnam levels. The AVF also increased costs, $4 billion even at lower estimates. "All of these factors, and particularly the predicted cost, would seem to dim the prospects for an all-volunteer force," according to one newspaper report. "Secretary Laird certainly was far from optimistic. He even suggested to his young audience that if an all-volunteer system doesn't work, it may be worth while to look at some plan for universal service that would involve peace corps type duty as well as military. . . . He will be lucky if he ever sees the creation of a strictly volunteer force for all the services."[38] Even elsewhere within the Nixon administration, there was great uncertainty with the AVF. People at the time, including senior policymakers, were not sure that it would work. Ending Selective Service was going to result in a much smaller and more expensive military, they feared.

With little surprise, based on their mandate, the Gates Commission quickly concluded its work and recommended the AVF. "Starting with the basic premise that the national security of the country is paramount," Anderson explained to National Security Advisor Henry Kissinger, the commission "examined the pros and cons of an all-volunteer armed force and concluded that the armed forces, including reserve forces, can and should be raised by voluntary means." He provided Kissinger a good synopsis from within the Nixon administration of the findings prior to the public release of its report. The commission strongly supported voluntary means, along with three main recommendations. First, the group concluded, "raise basic pay for military personnel in the first two years of service from an average level of $180 a month to $315 a month, the increase to become effective on July 1, 1970. The basic pay of officers in the first two years should be raised from an average level of $428 a month to $578 a month. The estimated annual cost is $3.24 billion." The second was to "make comprehensive improvements in conditions of military service." Third, the commission urged the administration to "establish an effective standby draft." Of these three main recommendations , creating a standby draft was important and was often overlooked both at that time and later.[39]

The Gates Commission publicly released its final report on February 21, 1970. In it, the members unanimously recommended replacing the draft with an all-volunteer military by July 1, 1971, the date when the Military Selective Service Act of 1967 was set to expire. Because the administration had already submitted its 1971 budget, however, President Nixon ordered the commission's recommendations "carefully studied" and assigned Anderson to lead that review. "Given the President's interest in the issue and the commission's unanimous recommendation, the chief question regarding the administration's position now seems to be one of timing," reported Carroll Kilpatrick, staff writer for the *Washington Post*.[40]

Once the Gates Commission concluded its work and released its report, the Nixon administration spent the spring of 1970 garnering support for its recommendations and preparing plans to implement them. In his message to Congress on April 23, President Nixon called for action. "The draft has been with us now for many years. It was started as a temporary, emergency measure just before World War II. We have lived with the draft so long, and relied on it through such serious crises, that too many of us now accept it as a normal part of American life," Nixon explained. His solution was clear and consisted of two interrelated parts. First, Nixon advocated that the United States end Selective Service and move toward the AVF. Second, he sought in the short term to reform the draft to remove its most pernicious inequities while never hedging that he would end it very soon. "It is now time to embrace a new approach to meeting our military manpower requirements. I have two basic proposals," the president declared. "The first deals with the fundamental way this nation should raise the armed force necessary to defend the lives and the rights of its people, and to fulfill its existing commitments abroad. The second deals with reforming the present recruitment system—part volunteer, part drafted—which, in the immediate future, will be needed to maintain our armed strength."[41] Nixon laid down the gauntlet at this point. He was fully invested in the AVF and completely committed to making it a reality in the near term. His plan, however, had two related aspects. First, he made clear to all involved that he would move toward the AVF as the ultimate end. Second, he would take tangible steps to reform Selective Service and reduce draft calls to zero until he accomplished his primary goal.

Nixon centered both goals on the work of the Gates Commission. The president was able to use it as the foundation for the proposals that he already had in mind prior to appointing the commission. "On February 21," Nixon informed Congress, "I received the report of the Commission on an All-Volunteer Armed Force, headed by former Defense Secretary Thomas S. Gates. The Commission members concluded unanimously that the interests of the nation will be better served by an all-volunteer force than by a mixed force of volunteers and draftees, and that steps should be taken in this direction." He went even further, however, and disingenuously claimed that the work of the Gates Commission had led him to support the AVF rather than the other way around. "After careful consideration of the factors involved, I support the basic conclusion of the Commission," Nixon declared. "I agree that we should now move toward ending the draft."[42]

There was no surprise that Nixon endorsed the Gates Commission's recommendation to end the draft and move toward an AVF. What was surprising was that he did not support its recommendation to effect the transition in 1971 but delayed it until 1973. This was a calculated move. Ending the draft prematurely and then not having enough soldiers would have been disastrous for the prospects of the AVF and likely would have triggered strong recriminations against it as well as heightened calls for an immediate return to conscription. Nixon wanted to make sure that, when he made the transition, the AVF would be sustainable and therefore lasting. By waiting until 1973, he also allowed his plan for Vietnamization to lower U.S. force levels and thereby lessen reliance on the draft.[43]

Of course, Nixon was not content to rely on Vietnamization alone to reduce reliance on Selective Service. He immediately sought draft reforms that ameliorated the most glaring inequities of conscription and reduced call-ups toward his ultimate goal of none. "From now on, the objective of this Administration is to reduce draft calls to zero, subject to the overriding considerations of national security," Nixon boldly declared. Even so, he admitted that there were three "cautions" that were necessary as the nation moved toward the AVF. First, Nixon admitted that "the draft cannot be ended all at once. It must be phased out." Second, the president acknowledged that Congress would have to lengthen temporarily the induction authority because it was set to expire on July 1, 1971, too soon to enact the pay raises that were central to transition to the AVF. Third, he admitted, "as we move away from reliance on the draft, we must make provisions to establish a standby draft system that can be used in case of emergency."[44]

Timing was the only matter where President Nixon differed from the Gates Commission. Whereas the commission saw no reason to wait to make the switch, Nixon was much more cautious, arguing for a phased approach. He wanted more time to draw down U.S. forces in Vietnam, a major hedge aimed at the ultimate success of the AVF. For him, the worst possible scenario would be to move toward an AVF and then not have sufficient forces available. As noted, such a situation could lead to fear and doubt about the ultimate sustainability of the AVF and a hasty and unwanted return to the draft.

Nixon also made clear that he would not hesitate to make major reforms to the draft. "It is my judgment, and that of the National Security Council, that future occupational, agricultural and student deferments are no longer dictated by the national interest," the president declared. As a result, he used his executive authority to make fundamental changes to Selective Service. "I am issuing today an Executive Order to direct that no future deferments shall be granted on the basis of employment. . . . This same Executive Order will also eliminate all future paternity deferments."[45] This significant change was another example of Nixon reforming the draft on the way toward the AVF. He had already removed graduate-student deferments and now removed occupational and paternity deferments. Nixon was trying to eliminate the inequities of conscription—perhaps out of principle; conceivably out of a political calculation to fuel opposition to the draft so as to accelerate support for ending it, which he planned to do anyway; or possibly some combination of the two.

The president's final reforms sought to end undergraduate-student deferments and to create a draft lottery, both part of his effort to reduce the most obvious and increasingly contentious inequities. "I am also asking the Congress today to make some changes in the Military Selective Service Act of 1967. The first would restore to the President discretionary authority on the deferment of students seeking baccalaureate degrees. If the Congress restores this authority," Nixon avowed, "I shall promptly issue a second Executive Order that would bar all undergraduate deferments, except for young men who are undergraduate students prior to today." Such a move sought to address criticism that those with means and access to college were able to limit their liability to the draft in a way that others without such advantages sorely lacked. Nixon thus phased out these deferments, but those who already had them kept them; such deferments would no longer be applied moving forward.

Nixon also proposed a draft lottery for much the same reason. "My second legislative proposal would establish a direct national call, by lottery sequence numbers each month, to improve the operation of the random selection system," he confirmed. "We need to ensure that men throughout the country with the same lottery number have equal liability to induction."[46] The localized nature of Selective Service had meant that the lottery system was not truly a random-selection device across the nation. For example, a young man with the same lottery number could be called up by one draft board but not by another due to differing circumstances at each locality. In other words, if one draft board only had a few low numbers, then it had to fill its quota with higher numbers, meaning that the lottery system was not nationally standardized. Nixon attempted to address this inequity by ensuring the standardization of selected lottery numbers throughout the country.

Using the Gates Commission's work and report as the basis for his recommendations, President Nixon reinforced that ending Selective Service and moving toward the AVF would augment liberty, both for the individual and collectively for American society. "With an end to the draft, we will demonstrate to the world the responsiveness of republican government—and our continuing commitment to the maximum freedom for the individual, enshrined in our earliest traditions and founding documents," he maintained. "By upholding the cause of freedom without conscription we will have demonstrated in one more area the superiority of a society based upon belief in the dignity of man over a society based on the supremacy of the State."[47] Nixon encapsulated the libertarian ideological motivation for the AVF: the idea that a free society must be based on individual liberty. For him, that individual liberty was sacrosanct. There were times when national security trumped individual liberty, but those times must be few and far between and only when existential threats imperiled the republic. Otherwise, individual liberty must be paramount. This logic was the ideological basis for the AVF.

It is also notable that in the Cold War context, such language was meant to contrast the individual liberty of the United States with the state domination of the Soviet Union. Within this ideological milieu and contest between systems, the AVF became another argument for capitalism against communism, another way to differentiate them. That was one reason why economics made up such a large part of the justification for the AVF. It was not only about military personnel but also about what the United States represented, free-market capitalism and individual liberty—and therefore the AVF, according to Nixon. That was why in discussing the AVF he used such language as "in one more area" in relation to the U.S.–U.S.S.R. rivalry. The AVF versus conscription became another in a series of dichotomies Nixon and others saw as emblematic of the broader Cold War distinctions.

Still, the initial reaction to the Gates Commission's report was mixed, although many observers granted that the end of the draft was nigh. Less than one week after the report's release, the *Christian Science Monitor* presciently concluded that Selective Service "is most certainly on the way out." Sensing that "a national consensus favoring the all-volunteer force is strongly building," the newspaper concluded that the commission's report "should be helpful in persuading doubters."[48] Not all the feedback was positive, however. Secretary of Defense Laird critiqued the findings on several grounds, including whether increased pay would attract sufficient volunteers, what the actual costs would be, and the optimal timing of the shift from the draft to the AVF. Speaking at a dinner for the Reserve Officers Association and addressing the recommendation to end the draft by June 30, 1971, Laird concluded: "The most difficult question is the timing of the shift to an all-volunteer force. I believe it is premature to set a specific date for such a shift at this time."[49]

In Congress, there was a broad and diverse consensus for the AVF. This was not surprising given that the draft had gone from widely tolerated and largely accepted from World War II until the early 1960s to highly unpopular by 1970. The major change in support occurred as increased commitment to the Vietnam War required heightened draft calls, which allowed its many inequities to come into sharper focus. As public support for Selective Service waned, members of Congress felt more comfortable either significantly reforming it or abolishing it altogether. Representative Frank T. Bow (R-OH) relayed to his constituents:

> The list of sponsors for the new voluntary army legislation in both House and Senate indicate how widespread is the support for this proposal. The Congressmen who co-sponsored the House bill include liberal Alfred Lowenstein of New York, conservative George Bush of Texas, and 57 others representing every shade of political position and every section of the country. Similarly, in the Senate the co-sponsors

include Goldwater of Arizona and McGovern of South Dakota who have seldom been in agreement on any issue.[50]

The Hatfield-Goldwater-McGovern bill sought to implement the recommendations of the Gates Commission and end the draft in 1971.

Encouragement for the transition came from numerous corners of American society as well. The Nixon administration received feedback on the Gates Commission recommendations from a wide variety of sources, including the Peace Workshop Youth Camp held at Camp Mack in Milford, Indiana. Its members declared, "We the undersigned support the Gates Commission Report. . . . We feel that all militarism is an outdated mode for settling world disputes. As a transitional step from the present system to nonviolence we favor the voluntary system of enlistment to man the armed forces."[51]

Not all the feedback was positive, however. Robert E. Hunter, a freelance reporter writing for the *Washington Post, Times Herald*, leveled a scathing critique of the Gates Commission and the overall concept of the AVF that it advocated. He declared, "This decision to phase out the draft is undoubtedly good politics in Middle America; but it is almost as surely bad policy. Nor is this merely a question of the added expense. The extra few billion dollars diverted from domestic needs would be dwarfed by the grave social and moral costs of an all-volunteer army." Hunter attacked the AVF along several fronts, including its militarization of society, its promoting a civil-military divide, and its socioeconomic inequity. He argued that the AVF would vastly augment the sway of the Pentagon, would increasingly insulate the military from broader American society, and would disproportionately rely on racial minorities and the poor. "There is a moral question here that has been played down by most draft opponents," Hunter warned. "Can a society that tolerates vast differences in income ask the poor to bear a disproportionate part of the burden of society's defense?" He contended that the Gates Commission conveniently "sidestepped this moral issue" by caving to the vocal—and self-interested, in his assessment—protests emanating from college campuses and middle-class suburbs. "Reduced to essentials," Hunter concluded, "defending society, even in war, should either be something that is sufficiently worthy for everyone potentially to be involved, or it should involve no one."[52]

Overall, the Gates Commission converted the AVF from theory to reality. It fulfilled President Nixon's initial campaign promise to end the draft, gave it official sanction through a presidential commission, and charted a path forward for ending Selective Service and creating the AVF. Along the way, its members engaged with the major objections to the

AVF, although they never wavered from their original tasking to find the best way to end the draft, not to decide whether to end it. As a result, the Gates Commission ensured that the many implications and challenges of the AVF would go largely unresolved at the time of its creation.

Notes

1. On the Gates Commission, see Jomana Amara, "Revisiting the Justification for an All-Volunteer Force," *Defense and Security Analysis* 35, no. 3 (September 2019): 326–342; Louis G. Yuengert, "America's All Volunteer Force: A Success?," *Parameters* 45, no. 4 (Winter 2015): 53–64; and Matthew Ivey, "The Broken Promises of an All-Volunteer Military," *Temple Law Review* 86, no. 3 (Spring 2014): 525–576.

2. Richard M. Nixon, "Draft Letter to Prospective Members of the President's *Advisory Commission on an All-Volunteer Armed Force*," March 11, 1969, p. 1, box 1, folder WHCF: Subject Categories EX FG 249 Commission on an All-Volunteer Armed Force [1969–1970] [1 of 2], WHCF, Subject Files, FG 249 Commission on an All-Volunteer Armed Force, Richard M. Nixon Presidential Library and Museum, Yorba Linda, CA (hereafter cited as RMNL).

3. On previous debates over the draft, see Amy J. Rutenberg, *Rough Draft: Cold War Military Manpower Policy and the Origins of Vietnam-Era Draft Resistance* (Ithaca, NY: Cornell University Press, 2019); William A. Taylor, *Military Service and American Democracy: From World War II to the Iraq and Afghanistan Wars* (Lawrence: University Press of Kansas, 2016), 12–20, 23–24, 49, 53, 62, 86–89, 96–107, 108–109; and George Q. Flynn, *The Draft, 1940–1973* (Lawrence: University Press of Kansas, 1993). For protest during the Vietnam War, see Michael S. Foley, *Confronting the War Machine: Draft Resistance during the Vietnam War* (Chapel Hill: University of North Carolina Press, 2003).

4. Lewis B. Hershey, "The Selective Service System during the Administration of President Lyndon B. Johnson, November 1963–January 1969, Volume I Administrative History," 1969, p. 1, box 1 Selective Service System, Volume I, Volume II, Parts I & II, folder Vol. 1—Narrative History, Preface–Chapter II, Administrative History, Lyndon B. Johnson Presidential Library and Museum, Austin, TX (hereafter cited as LBJL).

5. Hershey, "Selective Service System during the Administration of President Lyndon B. Johnson," 12.

6. Hershey, "Selective Service System during the Administration of President Lyndon B. Johnson," 22–23.

7. "Draft Calls," July 1, 1970, p. 1, box 49, folder Draft, Robert T. Hartmann Papers, Gerald R. Ford Presidential Library, Ann Arbor, MI (hereafter cited as GRFL).

8. Nixon, "Draft Letter to Prospective Members of the President's *Advisory Commission on an All-Volunteer Armed Force*," 1.

9. Arthur F. Burns, "Memorandum for the President," March 17, 1969, p. 1, box 1, folder WHCF: Subject Categories EX FG 249 Commission on an All-Volunteer

Armed Force [1969–1970] [1 of 2], WHCF, Subject Files, FG 249 Commission on an All-Volunteer Armed Force, RMNL.

10. Lewis B. Hershey, "The Selective Service System during the Administration of President Lyndon B. Johnson, November 1963–January 1969, Volume I Administrative History," 1969, pp. 227–228, box 1, Selective Service System, Volume I, Volume II, Parts I & II, folder Vol. I—Narrative History, Chapters X–XIII, Administrative History, LBJL.

11. Lyndon B. Johnson, "Executive Order 11289: National Advisory Commission on Selective Service," July 2, 1966, p. 1, box 1, folder WHCF: Subject Categories EX FG 249 Commission on an All-Volunteer Armed Force [1969–1970] [2 of 2], WHCF, Subject Files, FG 249 Commission on an All-Volunteer Armed Force, RMNL.

12. "Changes in the Draft: The Military Selective Service Act of 1967," *Columbia Journal of Law and Social Problems* 4, no. 2 (December 1967): 3, copy in box 14, folder WHCF: SMOF Martin Anderson Military Draft Misc. 1968, White House Central Files, Staff Member and Office Files, Martin Anderson Files, RMNL.

13. Lyndon B. Johnson, "To the Congress of the United States: Message on Selective Service," March 6, 1967, p. 1, box 303, folder FG 282 Selective Service System 2/22/66–6/18/67, Lyndon B. Johnson Papers, President, 1963–1969, EX FG 282 11/23/63, LBJL.

14. Robert B. Semple Jr., "Nixon Backs Eventual End of Draft," *New York Times*, November 18, 1967.

15. Melvin R. Laird, "Introduction," in *The All-Volunteer Force: Thirty Years of Service*, ed. Barbara A. Bicksler, Curtis L. Gilroy, and John T. Warner (Washington, DC: Brassey's, 2004), 4.

16. Quoted in Martin Anderson, "The Making of the All-Volunteer Force," in Bicksler, Gilroy, and Warner, *All-Volunteer Force*, 18.

17. "HHH Calls Nixon Irresponsible on Draft," *Washington Post, Times Herald*, August 18, 1968. On defense budgets during the 1960s, see *Congress and the Nation: A Review of Government and Politics*, vol. 3, *1969–1972* (Washington, DC: Congressional Quarterly Service, 1973), 198.

18. On the 1968 presidential election, see Aram Goudsouzian, *The Men and the Moment: The Election of 1968 and the Rise of Partisan Politics in America* (Chapel Hill: University of North Carolina Press, 2019); Michael Schumacher, *The Contest: The 1968 Election and the War for America's Soul* (Minneapolis: University of Minnesota Press, 2018); and Michael Nelson, *Resilient America: Electing Nixon in 1968, Channeling Dissent, and Dividing Government* (Lawrence: University Press of Kansas, 2014).

19. Anderson, "Making of the All-Volunteer Force," 18.

20. Tom Cole, "Comments Re: Laird Response to Volunteer Army Directive," February 3, 1969, pp. 1–2, box A31, folder Volunteer Army (8), Arthur F. Burns Papers, GRFL. It is important to note that this was not a conversation between Laird and Cole. The Laird references are points made in Laird's memos, and Cole was simply countering those points for administration officials.

21. Office of the White House Press Secretary, "The White House: To the Congress of the United States," May 13, 1969, p. 1, box A31, folder Volunteer Army (8), Arthur F. Burns Papers, GRFL.

22. Carroll Kilpatrick, "1971 End to Draft Is Urged: All-Volunteer Force Backed by Nixon Unit," *Washington Post*, February 22, 1970.

23. Richard M. Nixon to Thomas S. Gates Jr., March 28, 1969, p. 1, box 1, folder WHCF: Subject Categories EX FG 249 Commission on an All-Volunteer Armed Forces 1969, WHCF, Subject Files, FG 249 Commission on an All-Volunteer Armed Force, RMNL. President Nixon sent similar letters to each member of the Gates Commission.

24. Martin Anderson, "Memorandum for the President, Subject: Meeting with Commission on an All-Volunteer Armed Force," February 21, 1970, p. 1, box 1, folder WHCF: Subject Categories EX FG 249 Commission on an All-Volunteer Armed Force [1969–1970] [1 of 2], WHCF, Subject Files, FG 249 Commission on an All-Volunteer Armed Force, RMNL.

25. Charles B. Wilkinson, "Memorandum for John Ehrlichman," April 9, 1969, p. 1, box 1, folder WHCF: Subject Categories EX FG 249 Commission on an All-Volunteer Armed Force [1969–1970] [1 of 2], WHCF, Subject Files, FG 249 Commission on an All-Volunteer Armed Force, RMNL.

26. Stephen Herbits to Richard M. Nixon, October 1, 1969, p. 1, box 1, folder WHCF: Subject Categories EX FG 249 Commission on an All-Volunteer Armed Force [1969–1970] [1 of 2], WHCF, Subject Files, FG 249 Commission on an All-Volunteer Armed Force, RMNL.

27. Dwight L. Chapin, "Memorandum for Mr. Martin Anderson," April 30, 1969, p. 1, box 1, folder WHCF: Subject Categories EX FG 249 Commission on an All-Volunteer Armed Force [1969–1970] [1 of 2], WHCF, Subject Files, FG 249 Commission on an All-Volunteer Armed Force, RMNL.

28. Gates Commission, "Minutes of the Meeting of the President's Commission on an All-Volunteer Armed Force," May 15, 1969, pp. 1–2, box A31, folder Volunteer Army (7), Arthur F. Burns Papers, GRFL.

29. Gates Commission, "Discussion Paper and Preliminary Outline for the All-Voluntary Army Study," p. 13, box A31, folder Volunteer Army (7), Arthur F. Burns Papers, GRFL.

30. Gates Commission, "Minutes," July 12–13, 1969, 1.

31. David J. Callard to Gates Commission Members, August 28, 1969, p. 1, box A31, folder Volunteer Army (6), Arthur F. Burns Papers, GRFL. The excerpt of the draftee's letter appeared with Callard's letter as an attachment.

32. Typed excerpt from a letter written by an unnamed draftee stationed at Fort Meade, MD, attached to David J. Callard to Gates Commission Members, August 28, 1969, p. 1, box A31, folder Volunteer Army (6), Arthur F. Burns Papers, GRFL.

33. Gates Commission, "Discussion Paper and Preliminary Outline for the All-Voluntary Army Study," pp. 11–12, box 11, folder WHCF: SMOF Martin Anderson All Volunteer Armed Force [3 of 4], White House Central Files, Staff Member and Office Files, Martin Anderson Files, RMNL.

34. Gates Commission, "Minutes," July 12–13, 1969, 6.

35. Roger T. Kelley, Assistant Secretary of Defense (Manpower and Reserve Affairs), to Dr. Harry J. Gilman, Director of Military Manpower Supply and Compensation Studies, President's Commission on an All-Volunteer Force, August 29, 1969, pp. 1–2, box A31, folder Volunteer Army (6), Arthur F. Burns Papers, GRFL.

36. Roger T. Kelley to William H. Meckling, August 29, 1969, pp. 1–2, box A31, folder Volunteer Army (6), Arthur F. Burns Papers, GRFL.

37. Gates Commission, "Minutes," July 12–13, 1969, 7.

38. Walter Trohan, "Ending the Draft," *Chicago Tribune*, February 5, 1970, clipping in box 4, folder WHCF: Subject Categories GEN ND 4 Defense Mobilization Begin–12/31/1970, White House Central Files, Subject Files, ND National Security—Defense, RMNL.

39. Martin Anderson, "Memorandum for Henry Kissinger, Subject: Summary of Report of the President's Commission on an All-Volunteer Armed Force," February 17, 1970, p. 1, box 1, folder WHCF: Subject Categories EX FG 249 Commission on an All-Volunteer Armed Force [1969–1970] [1 of 2], WHCF, Subject Files, FG 249 Commission on an All-Volunteer Armed Force, RMNL.

40. Kilpatrick, "1971 End to Draft Is Urged."

41. Office of the White House Press Secretary, "Message to the Congress of the United States," April 23, 1970, p. 1, box D74, folder Draft, Gerald R. Ford Congressional Papers, GRFL.

42. Office of the White House Press Secretary, "Message to the Congress," 1.

43. On Vietnamization, see David L. Anderson, *Vietnamization: Politics, Strategy, Legacy* (Lanham, MD: Rowman & Littlefield, 2020). For a case study on the limits of Vietnamization on the ground, see Kevin M. Boylan, *Losing Binh Dinh: The Failure of Pacification and Vietnamization, 1969–1971* (Lawrence: University Press of Kansas, 2016).

44. Office of the White House Press Secretary, "Message to the Congress," 2.

45. Office of the White House Press Secretary, "Message to the Congress," 3.

46. Office of the White House Press Secretary, "Message to the Congress," 4.

47. Office of the White House Press Secretary, "Message to the Congress," 5.

48. "Closing Out the Draft," *Christian Science Monitor*, February 26, 1970.

49. "Laird Faults Volunteer Army Report," *Washington Post, Times Herald*, February 28, 1970. The Gates Commission estimated the costs of the AVF from $3 billion to $4 billion, while other assessments placed the costs as high as $17 billion.

50. Frank T. Bow, "Your Congressman Reports from Washington," July 27, 1970, p. 30, copy in box D74, folder Draft, Gerald R. Ford Congressional Papers, GRFL.

51. Peace Workshop Youth Camp attendees to Richard M. Nixon, August 23, 1970, p. 1, box 1, folder WHCF: Subject Categories EX FG 249 Commission on an All-Volunteer Armed Forces 1969–1970, WHCF, Subject Files, FG 249 Commission on an All-Volunteer Armed Force, RMNL.

52. Robert E. Hunter, "The Moral Question of an All-Volunteer Army," *Washington Post, Times Herald*, May 2, 1970.

4

Race

Beth Bailey

The current all-volunteer force was proposed and created during a period of great racial division and anger in the United States. During those years, public debates over race—particularly over the role of African Americans in the military—threatened to undermine the initial move to an AVF, and they remained profoundly destabilizing through its first decade. At the same time, as the armed forces planned for what many feared would be a difficult transition, many leaders had grown convinced that internal Black-white racial conflict undermined the military's ability to provide for the national defense. Thus, as they managed the final months of ground combat in Vietnam and planned for the end of conscription, the Department of Defense and the individual services were also creating an interlocking series of initiatives to manage the military's racial crisis. The coincidence of the internal racial crisis—"the war in the barracks"—with highly public anxieties about how struggles over race would affect the AVF meant that the nation's new volunteer force would remain at the center of American discussions of race during the 1970s.

The post–Vietnam War AVF also influenced race relations and racial outcomes in American society at large. By the 1960s, the U.S. armed forces required racial integration in ways that went far beyond the boundaries of classrooms, workplaces, or neighborhoods. People of all races and ethnicities, regardless of their individual attitudes, backgrounds, and preferences, were put into close contact twenty-four hours a day. Such forced interaction had different results, sometimes reinforcing anti-Black prejudice or an existing suspicion of whites, sometimes creating strong relationships across racial lines, sometimes simply demonstrating that people of different backgrounds could work effectively together. As the proportion of minority servicemembers grew over time, many Americans had their fullest experience of the racial and ethnic diversity of U.S. society during the years they spent in uniform.

When those who served returned to civilian society, they carried such individual experiences into their postservice life. Their subsequent lives were also shaped by military programs developed to foster racial equity and to manage tensions among a diverse cohort of servicemembers. Whether those programs were training units on racial diversity, efforts to develop more Black and brown leaders, or race-conscious attention to job assignments and career paths, the successes and failures of military programs helped determine what options the roughly 12 million veterans of the AVF found when they returned to civilian society.

Finally, the demographic composition of the AVF has shifted over time, generally in alignment with the changing demographics of the United States but with some marked departures. Like the nation it serves, the U.S. military is becoming less white. Nonetheless, its racial composition does not neatly mirror changing national demographics. In the enlisted ranks, Black women serve in almost double the proportion of Black men; Asian Americans serve in disproportionately low numbers service-wide, but particularly in the marine corps; and Hispanics are overrepresented in the marine corps and underrepresented in the other service branches. The U.S. military is, overall, more diverse than the nation as a whole, though senior leadership is still highly disproportionately (non-Hispanic) white. In enlistment and subsequent service, however, race is not fully determinative; overlapping categories of gender, class, region, culture, and family history also shape the individual decisions that produce each new crop of recruits.[1]

These facts, however, leave us with a question that has remained constant throughout the history of the AVF. Should the nation's military be representative? In other words, should the U.S. armed forces look like the U.S. citizenry? Here, the nation confronts the limits of an AVF, of its decision to base military service on principles of individual liberty. When a military comprises the results of millions of individual decisions, which the institution itself can only affect through the persuasive tools of the consumer market and the (federally funded) job benefits of a labor market, there is no mechanism to ensure that the AVF looks like the nation it defends.

Initial Concerns about Race

When Republican candidate Richard Nixon spoke live on the CBS Radio Network two and a half weeks before the 1968 presidential election and—at the height of America's commitment to its war in Vietnam—pledged to end the draft, he saw that promise as a winning political move. He was more right than wrong. By 1968, the war had created a political perfect storm. The draft was widely unpopular, with Americans who otherwise agreed on little else finding common ground in opposition.

Nixon, in his radio speech, portrayed conscription as "an infringement on [the] liberty" of youth. Many Americans, however, understood that such "infringement" was not imposed equally, that the burden of war fell heavily on some young Americans while others escaped its force. As in so much of American life, class and race played a significant role. The system by which men were selected to serve undermined the credibility of the draft, as in 1966, African Americans made up only 1.3 percent of draft-board members in the nation as a whole, with the states of Alabama, Arkansas, Louisiana, and Mississippi counting none among those officials who decided young men's fate. And while, in the end, African American combat deaths were roughly proportionate to their portion of the civilian population, that was not initially the case. Though African Americans made up only 11 percent of the U.S. population, it was widely reported that they accounted for almost 25 percent of combat deaths in that initial year.[2]

These shocking figures prompted action. The DOD dramatically cut the percentage of African American men serving in combat forces, essentially halving Black assignments from 1965's 31 percent to 16 percent in 1966, and then cutting further to 9 percent in 1970. In the end, African Americans would account for 12.5 percent of deaths. But no matter the later statistics, the damage had been done. Black support for the draft plummeted as the initial statistics became public. In 1966, three-quarters of African Americans believed the draft was fair; by the next year, support lay at just over 50 percent. (For comparison, 93 percent of Americans overall believed the World War II draft fair in 1942; support hit a *nadir* of 75 percent in May 1945.)[3] The New York *Amsterdam News*, in early January 1966, had already begun to argue that young Black men were made "prime cannon fodder" precisely because they were "denied equal opportunity at home." The *Chicago Defender* joined in the following year. As "white America is engaged in the sordid business of denying the Negro his full citizenship rights," an editorial claimed, "the war in Vietnam is taking an unprecedented toll of American black soldiers." Racial inequity was central to one strand of argument against the draft.[4]

Many military leaders and politicians had discounted Nixon's initial proposal. He had secured no sign-ons from major stakeholders, and politicians say all sorts of things during preelection Octobers. But it was only nine days after his inauguration as president that Nixon drafted a memo to his new secretary of defense, Melvin R. Laird, requesting that he "immediately" begin to plan for a commission that could develop "a detailed plan of action for ending the draft." The President's Commis-

Thomas S. Gates Jr. meets with President Gerald R. Ford while seated by the fireplace in the Oval Office on March 19, 1976. (Courtesy Gerald R. Ford Library)

sion on the All-Volunteer Force, brought into existence on March 27, 1969, was chaired by former secretary of defense Thomas S. Gates Jr., and its fifteen distinguished members represented a range of perspectives on the subject. The Gates Commission's staff, however, overwhelmingly and publicly supported the move to an AVF. Distinguished economists in their own right, they saw the move in the context of free-market economics and sought to provide commission members with clear data and quantifiable proof.[5]

To make their case, the commission staff first dealt with common objections to the AVF. They generated a list of thirty-five items, which they sorted into five major categories of concern, from a potential civil-military divide to a decline in military efficacy and morale. When commission members pointed out that the staff had neglected to include the frequently voiced concern that an AVF would be "all-black," staff members rejected the possibility. Convinced that admissions standards made such overrepresentation nearly impossible, they had not registered the depth and extent of that concern.[6] From all points on the political spectrum, opponents of the AVF were pointing to the issue of race.

Just eight days after Nixon's speech, *Washington Post* reporter Joseph

Alsop warned of "subtle dangers" that "lurk in Nixon's plan to end [the] draft." Noting that, despite popular misconceptions, African Americans did not currently serve in disproportionate numbers, he argued that the proposed AVF might well change that fact, yielding infantry units that were up to 40-percent "Negro." Nixon's fiscal policies, Alsop explained, would slightly increase unemployment, affecting African Americans disproportionately. Combined with the higher pay needed to attract young men to the military, the president would thus provide both a stick and a carrot, creating a "recipe" for a military with a very large percentage drawn from "the black minority." Alsop was less concerned with the potential exploitation of Black Americans than with the dangers he saw in offering weapons training to large numbers of Black men. Pointing to African American leaders who had endorsed "guerilla action" and raising the likelihood of a heavily Black infantry, he asked: "Is this, then social and politically desirable, particularly in the present frightening climate in America?"[7] In contrast, Senator Edward Kennedy (D-MA) warned that an AVF could create a "Negro Army" fighting "white middle-class wars," a concern that one African American newspaper headlined as "Volunteer Army means 'More Negro Cannon Fodder.'"[8]

Both claims—of exploitation and of threat—gained power from context. Even as casualty rates for Black servicemembers fell, the suspicion borne of those initial numbers and rooted in the long history of American racism remained. Speaking in Los Angeles in February 1967, Martin Luther King surveyed "The Casualties of the War in Vietnam." He told his audience:

> We arm Negro soldiers to kill on foreign battlefields, but offer little protection for their relatives from beatings and killings in our own south. We are willing to make the Negro 100% of a citizen in warfare, but reduce him to 50% of a citizen on American soil. . . . There are twice as many Negroes in combat in Viet Nam at the beginning of 1967 and twice as many died in action (20.6%) in proportion to their numbers in the population as whites.[9]

By 1968, Black nationalists had taken up Stokely Carmichael's claim that by waging war in Vietnam, "the [white] man is moving to get rid of black people in the ghettos."[10]

The *Report of the President's Commission on an All-Volunteer Force*, when made public in February 1970, confronted (in the words of a *New York Times* reporter) "virtually every objection raised against an all-volunteer force, including that it would constitute a risk to national security and consist largely of poor blacks."[11] A segment entitled "An Army of the

Black?" acknowledged publicly voiced concerns, both that Black and impoverished Americans would bear a "disproportionate share of the burden of defense" and of the potential "dangers of having in the community a large number of blacks who have had military training" who might participate in "domestic disorder and riots." Such questions and concerns, the authors suggested, "cannot be answered rationally," as "racial attitudes and fears are emotionally based," and "solid facts and sound judgements are seldom cures for prejudice." Nonetheless, the following pages offered the "solid facts" of statistical data, incorporating factors ranging from the numbers (versus proportions) of poor Black and poor white Americans, racial differences in civilian earnings, projected demographic changes in the nation, and preinduction acceptance rates by race, to project the proportion of Black servicemembers in an AVF a decade hence. The conclusion: a projected AVF in 1980 would appear very similar to a mixed volunteer-draftee force, with Black servicemembers accounting for 12.8–16 percent of the active force.[12]

Such reassurances were simply that—reassurances. Even had the Gates Commission concluded that the future held an all-Black force, the AVF was a done deal. Thus, well before the commission issued its report, the military was confronting the enormous challenge of figuring out how to manage the transition. This task fell disproportionately on the U.S. Army as the largest and least specialized of the services. Army leaders understood that the service would need—in the wake of a very difficult and unpopular war, and without a draft or draft-induced volunteers—to convince twenty thousand to thirty thousand young Americans every month to join an institution that even its most devoted leaders believed was struggling and near-broken, at a moment when public respect for the military was at an all-time low, from a youth culture that appeared much more comfortable with the phrase "question authority" than with an automatic "yes, sir," and at a time of great social division within American society. They had a reprieve until combat troops were withdrawn from Vietnam, but that reprieve was devoted to planning.[13] As with much else in that era, that process was complicated by the racial struggles of the day.

Race relations had been a point of pride for the U.S. Army in the early 1960s, and that pride was put on public display in the first war fought, from its beginning, with a purposely integrated force. "I see only one color and that's o.d. [olive drab]," said officers. "Same mud, same blood," said the grunts (at least to journalists). Mainstream Black leaders had overwhelmingly agreed, praising the military—despite its obvious shortcomings—as an institution where color did not determine opportunity. Such claims gained legitimacy as cities erupted into violence, the racial uprising in Harlem during the summer of 1964 presaging continued unrest throughout the country. By September 1966, at least 170 U.S. cities had experienced the mass violence of racial uprisings. The military, in contrast, seemed a model of racial calm.[14]

But that calm would not hold. By mid-1968, what had been widely heralded as the best-qualified, best-trained army in U.S. history was descending into crisis. Morale was tanking. Absentee and desertion rates were rising. Enlisted men had begun to refuse lawful orders. "Fragging" of officers was no longer abnormal; the army recorded more than forty instances (leaving five dead, thirty injured) in 1968 alone. Rumors of war crimes were becoming impossible to ignore. And as the U.S. death toll in Vietnam approached 35,000 servicemembers, combat was no longer restricted to a foreign enemy.[15]

In August 1968 at Vietnam's Long Binh Jail, a group of Black soldiers seized control of the much-hated stockade, burned buildings to smoldering ruins, and beat a white inmate to death with a shovel. Such racial strife—what some called "the war within the war"—was not limited to the Republic of Vietnam. It also unsettled military installations in West Germany, in Okinawa, in Thailand, and in the Republic of Korea, as well as within the United States itself. Black discontent was palpable, often accompanied by specific and well-grounded demands for equal standing and treatment. But violence was also escalating, and it often spilled into the streets of the surrounding towns and cities, both at home and abroad.

Something fundamental had changed. Within the army, by the late sixties, a new generation of Black Americans was no longer willing to accept the individual slights and institutional racism their fathers had endured. The rage and frustration that left American cities in flames was exacerbated in the barracks, as large numbers of young men, many of them poor and working class, were forced together in an environment that required integration of racial groups in ways that went far beyond the workplace, the classroom, or even the neighborhood. This was true, to a greater and lesser extent, of all the military services. In the late 1960s, the U.S. military was forced to confront, perhaps more directly than any other American institution, the racial struggles that were tearing the nation apart.

In late 1969, both the secretary of the army and the army chief of staff defined race as the service's central challenge, second only to the war in Vietnam.[16] (Just two years before, a top-secret briefing on army morale had not even mentioned race.)[17] They, along with many senior officers, had come to believe that racial conflict compromised the internal stability of the army and undermined its ability to defend the nation. At a time when escalating Cold War tensions and growing instability in the Middle East were making worse an already dangerous and volatile strategic environment, military leaders believed that the problem of race demanded immediate attention and practical solutions.[18] If racial conflict threatened the institution's very reason for being, their logic went, then "the problem of race" had to be addressed.

From 1969 forward, the U.S. Army developed and instituted a range of programs and initiatives intended to calm racial conflict and to "affirmatively" address racial inequities within the service. Their effectiveness varied. In the end, much good came of them: efforts to address racial discrepancies in assignments and the lack of visible Black and minority leadership; a review of the military-justice system and its racial disparities; and a fundamental rethinking of what goods and services were offered by PXs across the world. The U.S. Navy, U.S. Marine Corps, and U.S. Air Force also launched their own initiatives, with the DOD often leading the way. But there was no immediate magic. Conflict continued. And in any case, the military was not—could not be—wholly separated from the continuing racial crisis in the nation from which its members were drawn. That meant that the army made its transition to an AVF amid a racial crisis of its own.[19]

The Initial Years

The members of the Gates Commission had concluded that "the mental, physical, and moral standards for enlistment will ensure" that the AVF will not recruit "an undue proportion from minority groups or the poor."[20] They were wrong.

The numbers changed quickly. The increase military-wide was significant, as the percentage of African Americans serving rose from 1970's 11 percent to 16 percent in 1974—an increase of more than 30 percent in the space of four years. (African Americans between the ages of seventeen and forty-four made up 11 percent of the U.S. population at the time.) The army was on the high end of the scale, moving from 14 percent to 21 percent African American. But in 1974, more than 30 percent of army *recruits* were African American. And Black reenlistment was rising as well. These numbers set off alarms. Manpower analysts feared that the army was approaching a "tipping point" from which, no matter what incentives were offered, white men would no longer be willing to join what was perceived as a low-status, "all-black" army.[21]

In response, Secretary of the Army Bo Callaway had begun to move recruiters from the relatively easy territory of poor urban neighborhoods, where employment opportunities were scarce, to the more difficult terrain of middle-class white suburbs and small towns. But as Black accessions dropped sharply in the first months of 1975 even as civilian unemployment rates were rising, rumors began to circulate in the Black press that the army was using its admissions tests to "weed out" Black volunteers. The *Amsterdam News*, a Black newspaper based in New York City, reported that, although a disproportionate number of African Americans test in the "lowest category" on military-admissions tests, many might well succeed in the armed forces if given the opportunity. But the services accepted no recruits who scored in the lowest quintile and were restricted to 18 percent from "Category IV." (For reference, the army considered a score in the top half of "CAT IV," falling between twenty-one and thirty, to be roughly equivalent to an IQ of eighty-two to ninety-one on the Stanford-Binet test; scores between ten and fifteen, the bottom half of the quintile, correlated with IQ scores of seventy-one to eighty-one.)[22] Such scores were critical both in army admissions and in determining what assignments individuals received.

As debates over the disproportionate enlistment of Black Americans grew more heated, these admissions scores and notions of "quality" came to play an ever-more central role. Discussions of quality were not solely linked to race; the "quality" of recruits (with "high quality" defined for military purposes as someone who held an earned high school diploma and scored in the top half of the admissions tests) had become a major point of discussion as Americans confronted the new reality of the AVF. Was "quality" declining in the absence of a draft that could capture those whose skills and education gave them other options? And did "quality" matter, in any case, or was military manpower simply about filling enough boots? Advocates for the AVF charged those who worried about "quality" with attempting to scuttle the volunteer force. "How many Viet Cong riflemen had Ph.D.s?" was one contemptuous phrasing.[23]

Nonetheless, concerns about race were frequently linked to "quality." Congressman Ron Dellums, former mayor of Oakland and a member of the Congressional Black Caucus, confronted Army Secretary Callaway in 1975 after the army cut back its CAT IV accessions from 18 percent to 6 percent—a move that seemed clearly tied to Callaway's efforts to achieve (in his words) "a representative Army."[24]

Dellums's suspicions had a history. In October 1973, the congressman had written the deputy secretary of defense for equal opportunity to ask about stories that the marine corps was using racial quotas in recruiting. It turned out that the stories were true: in an attempt to limit the number of Black CAT IV recruits, the corps had instructed recruiters that "minorities" could account for no more than 15 percent of CAT IV accessions each year.[25] That action also had a history: the deaths of young Black men brought into the military through Project 100,000. Project

100,000 was initially conceived as part of the Johnson administration's antipoverty drive. It had been founded on the arguably paternalistic and certainly misplaced belief that, by accepting men otherwise mentally disqualified from military service, the (peacetime) military could "salvag[e]" tens of thousands of young men from "poverty-encrusted" backgrounds and prepare them for "productive roles" in society. Instead, this program had coincided with rapidly escalating U.S. engagement in Vietnam. Project 100,000 put 350,000 "New Standards" men into the military. The majority of them—66 percent—went into the army, but the share for the marine corps was substantial, given its much smaller size. More than a third of the formerly rejected inductees were assigned to the infantry— not an unreasonable use of unskilled men in wartime, but certainly not the sort of training that prepared them for "productive roles" in civilian society. Thirty-eight percent of the New Standards men were African American. And their median Armed Forces Qualification Test score was 13 out of 100.[26]

The marine corps recruiting instructions were quickly overruled by the DOD; there would be no race-based limits. The corps then tried another tactic: a 10-percent limit on both "minority" and white recruits from CAT IV. That, too, was rejected by the general counsel, who banned any form of race-based limits even if applied similarly to all racial categories. The next step was a "computer based mathematical methodology" that promised to yield "fair-share proportionate distribution" without relying on racial quotas.[27]

Marine corps leaders were insistent because they recognized a looming problem. Black men had made up 43 percent of CAT IV recruits in the 1973 fiscal year; none of them qualified for "hard skill" or technical positions.[28] Marine rifle companies thus were becoming heavily African American. This virtually guaranteed that, should the corps be sent into combat, a highly disproportionate number of Black marines would be killed.[29] Charges of Black "genocide" in the U.S. war in Vietnam were still powerful, and it was clear that if combat units were disproportionately African American, so too would be combat casualties.

When Dellums brought his concerns to the army two years later, he well understood the logic of military claims. He was a former Marine who had been elected to Congress on an antiwar platform in 1970; he had initiated a series of hearings on both U.S. war crimes and on racism in the armed forces (both of which remained unofficial, as the House refused to endorse them). He needed no reminder of Black servicemembers' deaths in the U.S. war in Vietnam, nor of the still-fresh charges of "genocide" from African Americans. But he also saw military service in the new AVF as stable employment that offered excellent benefits and decent pay. That was, after all, the army's key recruiting claim. And Dellums did not intend for African Americans to be excluded from those jobs as they had been excluded from so many other arenas of American life. It was a strong argument, but Callaway countered it with an avalanche of statistical data, all centered on aggregate results of the AFQT.[30]

In 1977, the newly elected president, Jimmy Carter, appointed Clifford Alexander secretary of the army. Just as Callaway was adamant that military measures of "quality" were essential, Alexander was adamant that they were irrelevant and prejudicial. And as Callaway worried about the (racial) representativeness of combat units, Alexander saw those measures as "immaterial." He insisted that all that mattered was how well an individual performed his or her job; manpower analysts repeatedly explained that they were concerned with how well "predictive" factors worked in aggregate. These analysts explained that, for example, their data demonstrated that 1,400 high school dropouts yielded 940 soldiers at the end of six months, while 1,000 recruits with earned high school diplomas yielded approximately the same 940 soldiers. "Trainability," likewise, correlated closely with exam results, though only *in aggregate*. Alexander found such arguments unpersuasive and saw no reason why a single test should rule out a potentially good soldier. He clearly understood the ways that such exams affected not only individual careers but also aggregate opportunities for African American youth. Alexander, like many, had come to recognize the exams as culturally biased, built around assumptions of white, middle-class experience. And he believed that much opposition to the AVF—criticisms were growing as the military struggled with recruiting and training in the years following the 1973 transition—was due to racism, pure and simple.[31]

By the late 1970s, however, the AVF seemed to be in crisis. Stories of its failures filled the press. In 1978, ABC aired a television special entitled, *The American Army: A Shocking Case of Incompetence*. It offered a litany of alarming statistics; one of the more widely noted (and distressing) pullout lines was "too dumb, too black, too costly." The running theme in this negative coverage was the growing mismatch between low-skill recruits (of unspecified race) and the increasingly complex machinery of war.[32] As the international situation worsened at the end of the decade, with the Soviet Union invading Afghanistan and Iranian protesters overrunning the U.S. embassy in Tehran, concerns about the mismatch rose. Following reports that 90 percent of nuclear-weapons maintenance specialists failed their qualifications tests, and as the army lowered its passing level for skills qualifications tests from 80 percent to 60 percent, Senator Sam Nunn (D-GA) called a news conference. "Our Army is not an armed WPA and we must not permit it to become a jobs corps equipped with tanks and nuclear missiles," he declared. And while Nunn said nothing of race, many heard that subtext. Was the senator's concern about the Russians, asked *Black Enterprise*, or was it instead "fear of giving blacks good opportunities in American society?"[33]

Whether or not race was Nunn's subtext, the "quality" debate had centered around race, and it did not stop at the nation's borders. Soon after Ronald Reagan's election, Moshe Dyan, the former defense minister of Israel, demonstrated the international influence of American discussions of race, "quality," and the AVF. More U.S. troops would be welcome in the Middle East, he said, but he had concerns about the quality of the new military. The U.S. Army, he informed an Israeli television audience, "is composed only of volunteers, of those who have to make a living out of the army's payment. Therefore, up to the rank of sergeants, most of the soldiers are Black who have a lower education and intelligence." Dyan suggested that the United States reinstate the draft, thus providing "better blood and brains" to its military. Alarmingly, Dyan was not alone in his analysis. In 1982, a top DOD official acknowledged that NATO leaders had asked the Pentagon to limit the number of Black troops deployed overseas; West Germany, in particular, had expressed concern about "cultural differences," while others had raised questions about the "readiness" of heavily Black forces. The Pentagon, the DOD official noted, had denied the request.[34]

The debate over quality, central to the larger discussion over the sustainability of an AVF that consumed much of its first decade, reveals both anti-Black prejudices and the difficulties of maintaining individual opportunity in an institution that—perhaps necessarily—relied on aggregate data to set recruiting goals. Such debates, however, did not fully define the role of race in the transition to the AVF. What of the experience of servicemembers? What of the services' own programs and policies?

The AVF and Its Legacy

As the United States ended conscription, the services were still struggling with internal racial conflict. Many leaders believed that such strife was exacerbated by the end of the draft, as the ranks were initially filled by those with few other options. It was white men, in fact, who in aggregate had less-desirable backgrounds in comparison to Black men in the ranks; by the beginning of the 1980s, 90.6 percent of Black army recruits had earned a high school diploma compared to 76.3 percent of white recruits.[35] The recruiting command saw the high school diploma as a sign of discipline (at least in aggregate) and its lack as the opposite, an assumption that seemed to bear out: by 1983, Black soldiers received 20 percent more Honorable Discharges, proportionally, than did whites.[36] While studies suggested that increasing "quality" would decrease racial tensions, in the first decade of the AVF, a high percentage of recruits came from poorly educated, unskilled backgrounds.

Thus, even as the draft no longer delivered unwilling men to compelled service, the military created and implemented programs to address racial conflict and disorder. Chief among them were education and training. Basic training included a unit on race relations, which emphasized cross-race communication and highlighted the long history of African American contributions to the nation's defense, from the all-Black militias and the Black volunteers in southern guerilla forces during the American Revolution through the multitude of small conflicts and mass warfare composing the military's—and the nation's—history. That training, and subsequent educational efforts, also taught a broader history of the United States, of slavery and its lasting consequences, and of the civil rights movement and the bravery of those who fought for equal rights, along with some mention of Hispanics, Asian Americans, and even Appalachian whites.[37] Black and other "minority" volunteers found their experiences recognized and validated; white volunteers were exposed to a history many had not before encountered.

Policies also shifted. The armed services had been confronted with demands for change in a wide range of policies that linked to race, whether the willingness of post commanders both within and outside the United States to treat off-post racial discrimination as beyond their remit or the disproportionate number of Black men who received nonjudicial punishment and pretrial incarceration. They had, both individually and under the direction of the Pentagon, begun reforms on these issues and others; the move to an AVF, which required them to attract "high quality" recruits, only emphasized that need for change. The military would not attract skilled Black men if it did not offer them equal opportunity and attractive conditions, and it would certainly not keep them (an equivalent problem, as an AVF relies on a much higher reenlistment rate than does a conscripted force). Under Pentagon pressure, military leaders used their off-limits power to pressure integration of civilian housing in communities surrounding military bases. And all focused on making certain that Black recruits were not consigned entirely to the infantry and soft-skill positions.

Thus, by 1983, Black enlisted men were no longer overrepresented in the army's infantry, medical and dental specialists, and service and supply handlers; they instead made up a disproportionate share of administrative specialists and clerks (positions that transferred to the civilian job market). African Americans constituted a strikingly small share of senior officers, but an affirmative-action plan acknowledged and addressed institutional discrimination and laid out procedures for redressing discrimination in promotions and selection.[38] The move to a volunteer force made such reforms more urgent.

Finally, the move to an AVF changed the demographics of the U.S. military—and of the army, in particular, as it had the largest number of positions to fill. Manpower experts tracked the changing demographics of the United States, aware of the declining birthrate among non-Hispanic whites and the growing numbers of "minority" youth. Recruiting commands began attempting to create a positive association among the fastest-growing populations. For example, the army began airing advertisements in Spanish. "Unete a la gente que está en el Army" appeared in the late 1970s, and by the early 1980s, the army's advertising agency, N. W. Ayer, was subcontracting with Sosa & Associates for Latino-focused ads.[39] But the U.S. Hispanic population was still small—up from about 5 percent in 1976 to 6.4 percent in 1983—and remained underrepresented both in the army and in the armed forces as a whole, making up only 3.8 percent of the U.S. Army in 1983. Yet the propensity of Hispanic youth to enlist now surpasses that of youth from other ethnic groups, and the percentage of Hispanics in the armed services doubled between 2007 and 2017, growing from 9 percent to 18 percent.[40]

The move to the AVF also jumpstarted the integration of women, who represented all American races and ethnicities, in the Armed Forces. Almost unimaginably, the Gates Commission did not even discuss using women to help make up the recruiting shortfall left by the end of conscription, but the army, in particular, considered the possibilities—especially as it seemed almost certain that the Equal Rights Amendment would be quickly ratified by the states and invalidate current military gender restrictions. In 1971, women made up 1.3 percent of the armed forces' enlisted ranks; by 1979, they accounted for 7.6 percent—in the army, 8.4 percent. As of 2019, women composed over 14 percent in total, ranging from a high of 20 percent in the U.S. Air Force down to 9 percent in the marine corps.[41]

But from early days, Black women enlisted at much higher rates than their share of the population. In the U.S. Army in 2000, they served in higher absolute numbers than did non-Hispanic white women, with Black women composing 46.4 percent of female enlisted soldiers compared to white women's 37.8 percent. That striking level of African American service was only true of women; while Black men enlisted in disproportionately high numbers, they never approached the absolute numbers of non-Hispanic white men. In 2018, military data revealed that nonwhite women from all racial and ethnic categories served at higher rates than men from the same group, even as Black women no longer served in quite such disproportionate numbers.[42] In recognizing the changing demographics of the U.S. military, it is critical to note that today's AVF is much more selective (and considerably smaller) than its initial incarnation. Only approximately one in seven people among U.S. youth qualifies for induction into the armed forces.

Conclusions

From the initial discussions of the move to AVF, Americans worried that the resulting U.S. armed forces would not be representative of the wider population—and, concurrently, about whether it was either necessary or desirable to have a military that mirrors the nation it defends. The significance of such representation shifts with context. In times of war, a military that does not "look like" the nation means that some groups bear a disproportionate burden. In times of peace, unrepresentativeness may mean some are denied access to "good jobs" and excellent benefits. Most agree that, on some level, representativeness matters. But the bottom line remains—the purpose of the military is to defend the nation. And most military leaders today believe that purpose is best accomplished by an AVF.

The argument that the AVF creates inequity has continued, from initial worries about whether a formal system of conscription was being replaced with what was essentially a "poverty draft" of poor Black youth on through contemporary critiques that focus less heavily on race than on class, while still disproportionately affecting members of minority groups. But at same time, the AVF has offered more choice. Unlike in Vietnam, when qualified Black men were drafted at higher percentages than whites and assigned disproportionately to the infantry, Black men and women more recently select roles in the armed forces that best translate into civilian jobs; African Americans are proportionately *under*represented in the combat arms. There is also the choice of whether to enlist. As the wars in Iraq and Afghanistan continued, enlistment of women overall and of African American men declined.

In the end, when it comes to race, the U.S. military is not representative of the nation—though it is perhaps better when it comes to race and ethnicity than to region, socioeconomic status, and gender. The U.S. military is likely the institution in which Americans of different races and ethnicities work most closely together. It is the institution where, as Charles Moskos and John Butler argue in their 1996 tribute to the racial significance of the U.S. Army, a white man is most likely to take orders from a Black man.[43] And as the armed forces follow the emerging demographic trends, seeking the "minority" young people who will outnumber their white peers by the middle of the 2020s, U.S. military services are once again shaped both earlier and more fundamentally by these demographic shifts than are other institutions in American society.

Notes

1. Table, "Race and Ethnicity of Enlisted Recruits by Service and Gender, 2018," in Council on Foreign Relations, "Demographics of the U.S. Military," https://www.cfr.org/backgrounder/demographics-us-military (it also compares representation in the armed forces to civilian labor pools); table, "Race and Ethnicity by Rank, 2018," https://www.cfr.org/backgrounder/demographics-us-military; Kristy N. Kamarck, "Diversity, Inclusion, and Equal Opportunity in the Armed Services: Background and Issues for Congress," report R44321, Congressional Research Service, updated June 5, 2019, https://crsreports.congress.gov/product/pdf/R/R44321.

2. Richard Nixon, "The All-Volunteer Armed Force," address on CBS Radio Network, October 17, 1968, All-Volunteer Army—Misc., Center of Military History, Fort McNair, Washington, DC (hereafter cited as CMH); Daniel Lucks, "African American Soldiers and the Vietnam War: No More Vietnams," *The Sixties*, vol. 10, no. 2 (2017): 202; Christian G. Appy, *Working-Class War: American Combat Soldiers & Vietnam* (Chapel Hill: University of North Carolina Press, 1984), 19; Gerald Goodwin, "Race in the Crucible of War: African American Soldiers and Race Relations in the 'Nam'" (PhD diss., Ohio University, 2014), 131; Goodwin, "Black and White in Vietnam" (editorial), *New York Times*, July 18, 2017. Appy states that African Americans composed 20 percent of deaths, while Goodwin cites the "near 25 percent of all combat deaths" figure in his editorial.

3. Lucks, "African American Soldiers," 202; Beth Bailey, *America's Army: Making the All-Volunteer Force* (Cambridge, MA: Belknap Press of Harvard University Press, 2009), 10.

4. Lawrence Allen Eldridge, *Chronicles of a Two-Front War: Civil Rights and Vietnam in the African American Press* (Columbia: University of Missouri Press, 2011), 51, 60, 63. For general discussions of race and the transition to the AVF, see Bailey, *America's Army*, esp. chap. 4.

5. For a detailed account of the origins of the Gates Commission, see Bernard Rostker, *I Want You!: The Evolution of the All-Volunteer Force* (Santa Monica, CA: RAND, 2006), 62–67; and Bailey, *America's Army*, 24–32.

6. Gates Commission, Minutes, July 12–13, 1969, pp. 3, 6, folder 4, box 1, Alfred M. Gruenther Papers, Dwight D. Eisenhower Presidential Library and Museum, Abilene, KS.

7. Joseph Alsop, "Some Subtle Dangers Lurk in Nixon's Plan to End Draft," *Washington Post*, October 25, 1968, A25.

8. "Volunteer Army Means 'More Negro Cannon Fodder,'" *Rockford (IL) Crusader*,

March 21, 1969, 8.

9. Martin Luther King Jr., "The Casualties of the War in Vietnam" speech, February 25, 1967, Investigating U.S. History, American Social History Project, https://investigatinghistory.ashp.cuny.edu/module11D.php.

10. Carmichael quoted in Sol Stern, "When the Black G.I. Comes Back from Vietnam," *New York Times Magazine*, March 24, 1968.

11. Robert B. Semple Jr., "Nixon Panel Asks Volunteer Army by Middle of '71," *New York Times*, February 22, 1970, 1.

12. President's Commission on an All-Volunteer Armed Force, *The Report of the President's Commission on an All-Volunteer Armed Force* (Washington, DC: Government Printing Office, 1970), chap. 12, esp. 142, 149.

13. See Bailey, *America's Army*, chap. 2.

14. On mainstream Black responses, see, for example, "Integration in the Military," *Los Angeles Sentinel*, March 24, 1966; report on CBS special with Walter Cronkite reporting; "Military Leads the Way in Race Relations," *Los Angeles Sentinel*, December 28, 1967, A7; "Negroes in Vietnam: 'We, Too, are Americans,'" *Ebony*, August 1968, 90; Malcolm McLaughlin, *The Long, Hot Summer of 1967: Urban Rebellion in America* (New York: Palgrave Macmillan, 2014), 6.

15. On the rising discontent, see Beth Bailey, *An Army Afire: How the US Army Confronted Its Racial Crisis in the Vietnam Era* (Chapel Hill: University of North Carolina Press, 2023). Fragging statistics from George Lepre, *Fragging: Why U.S. Soldiers Assaulted Their Officers in Vietnam* (Lubbock: Texas Tech University Press, 2011), 22.

16. Secretary of the Army Stanley R. Resor, Keynote Address, Annual Meeting of the Association of the U.S. Army, October 13, 1969, 1, in Historical Reference Collection, Speeches: Stanley R. Resor, CMH.

17. "MACV J-1 U.S. Forces Morale," from briefings given the Secretary of Defense, Saigon, South Vietnam, July 7, 8, 1967, quotes from 1 on this topic (morale), 280 in sequence, SEA-RS-300a, CMH.

18. See "After Action Report—Department of the Army Race Relations Conference," 15, Fort Monroe Conference, Army Heritage and Education Center, Carlisle, PA.

19. Bailey, *Army Afire*.

20. President's Commission, *Report*, 16.

21. John W. Finney, "Very Soon Now, the Army Will Be R.A., All the War," *New York Times*, November 3, 1973, C3. See also Bailey, *America's Army*, chap. 4.

22. Army Personnel Research Office, Fact Sheet, 1965, sent by A. J. Martin to Richard Danzig, September 4, 1980. This document notes that the correlation between the AFQT and individually administered intelligence tests is "high"—"about .8"—but that they do not directly correspond.

23. See Bailey, *America's Army*, 99.

24. For Dellums and Callaway, see Bailey, *America's Army*, 115–117. For a detailed analysis of the debates over race and quality, see ibid., chap. 4.

25. Ron Dellums to Milton Francis, Deputy Assistant Secretary of Defense (Equal Opportunity), October 11, 1973; Assistant Secretary of Defense (M&RA), proposed reply to Dellums, January 31, 1974; and memorandum, Brehm to Deputy Secretary

of Defense, "Marine Corps Minority Procurement Policy," February 14, 1974, all in Rostker, *I Want You!*, accompanying CD, G054.pdf (hereafter cited as Rostker CD).

26. Homer Bigart, "M'Namara Plans to 'Salvage' 400,000 Rejected in Draft," *New York Times*, August 24, 1966; Janice H. Laurence and Peter F. Ramsberger, *Low-Aptitude Men in the Military: Who Profits, Who Pays?* (Westport, CT: Praeger, 1991), 36–43. See also Appy, *Working-Class War*, 31–33.

27. Ron Dellums to Milton Francis, Deputy Assistant Secretary of Defense (Equal Opportunity), October 11, 1973; Assistant Secretary of Defense (M&RA), proposed reply to Dellums, January 31, 1974; and memorandum, Brehm to Deputy Secretary of Defense, "Marine Corps Minority Procurement Policy," February 14, 1974, all in Rostker CD, G054.pdf.

28. Dellums to Milton Francis, Deputy Assistant Secretary of Defense (Equal Opportunity), October 11, 1973; Assistant Secretary of Defense (M&RA), proposed reply to Dellums, January 31, 1974; and memorandum, Brehm to Deputy Secretary of Defense, "Marine Corps Minority Procurement Policy," February 14, 1974, all in Rostker CD, G054.pdf.

29. Department of the Navy, proposed reply to Dellums, February 4, 1974, Rostker CD, G0548.pdf.

30. Memorandum Howard H. Callaway to Deputy Secretary of Defense, "Response to Congressman Dellums on Quality Standards and Discrimination," May 31, 1975; and Callaway to Dellums, May 22, 1975, both in Rostker CD, G0665.pdf.

31. John M. Swomley Jr., "Too Many Blacks? The All-Volunteer Force," *The Christian Century*, October 1, 1980, 903; Robert L. Goldich, "Recruiting, Retention, and Quality in the All-Volunteer Force," Congressional Research Service, 26–27; Robert B. Pirie testimony, Subcommittee on Manpower and Personnel, Senate Armed Services Committee, *Department of Defense Authorization for Appropriations for FY81, Part 3: Manpower and Personnel*, March 10, 1980, 96th Cong., 2d sess., 1290, Rostker CD, S0567.pdf.

32. Michael Specter, "Too Dumb, Too Black, Too Costly: Is the Volunteer Force a Failure?" *The Nation*, June 19, 1982, 743–745.

33. "Army Secretary Alexander under Attack by Nunn," *Atlanta Daily World*, June 29, 1980; George Davis, "Blacks in the Military: Opportunity or Refuge?," *Black Enterprise*, July 1980, 30.

34. Carl Rowan, "Moshe Dyan Insults Black Gis [*sic*]," *Amsterdam News* (New York), December 20, 1980; Winston Williams, "U.S. Aide Says Allies Criticize Blacks in Army," *New York Times*, June 6, 1982.

35. Williams, "U.S. Aide Says Allies Criticize Blacks in Army."

36. James A. Thomas, "Institutional Discrimination in the U.S. Army: Black Personnel (1962–1982)," in *Race Relations Research in the U.S. Army in the 1970s: A Collection of Selected Readings*, ed. James A. Thomas (Washington, DC: U.S. Army Research Institute for the Behavioral and Social Sciences, 1988), 468.

37. U.S. Army Research Institute for the Behavioral and Social Sciences, *Race Relations and Equal Opportunity in the Army: A Resource Book for Personnel with Race Relations/ Equal Opportunity Responsibility* (December 1973), 82–83; "Army Sets Up Race Relations Courses," *Fergus Falls (MN) Daily Journal*, 1 (grab); Thomas A. Johnson, "200 Trainees

at Ft. Dix Get Course in Race Relations," *New York Times*, February 5, 1971, 33.

38. For more on off-base housing, see Bailey, *Army Afire*, chapter 7. On occupational assignments, see Thomas, "Institutional Discrimination," 468–472.

39. "Unete a la gente"/"Join the people" advertisements, 1978, folder 4, box 4, Ayer Collection; John Hall, "Armies Seeking Hispanic-Americans," *Richmond (VA) Times-Dispatch*, August 17, 1986, 21; John H. Cushman Jr., "Minorities and the Ad Budget," *New York Times*, August 21, 1986.

40. James A. Thomas, "Institutional Discrimination in the U.S. Army: Hispanic Personnel (1976–83)," in Thomas, *Race Relations Research*, 474; Kamarck, "Diversity, Inclusion, and Equal Opportunity in the Armed Services," 19.

41. Figures for 1971 and 1979 calculated from tables 2-13 and 2-19, "Selected Manpower Statistics," Department of Defense, http://siadapp.dmdc.osd.mil/personnel /M01/fy95/SMSTOP.HTM, accessed November 21, 2008 (items removed). Percentages are for enlisted active-duty personnel. DOD Figures for 2019 from Mary Dever, "With Historic Number of Women in Uniform, the Vet Community Is about to Change," Military.com, March 11, 2019, https://www.military.com/daily-news/20 19/03/11/historic-number-women-uniform-vet-community-about-change.html.   See also Erin Duffin, "Distribution of Active-Duty Enlisted Women and Men in the U.S. Military in 2019, by Race and Ethnicity," Statista.com, https://www.statista.com/st atistics/214869/share-of-active-duty-enlisted-women-and-men-in-the-us-military/. Note that all percentages are not directly comparable because data is not standardized but as available.

42. W. Blair Haworth Jr., Department of the Army Historical Summary, FY 2000 (Washington, DC: Center of Military History, U.S. Army, 2011), 25; table, "Race and Ethnicity of Enlisted Recruits by Service and Gender, 2018," in Council on Foreign Relations, "Demographics of the U.S. Military."

43. Charles C. Moskos and John Sibley Butler, *All That We Can Be: Black Leadership and Racial Integration the Army Way* (New York: Twentieth Century Fund Books / Basic Books, 1996), 2.

II

Results

5

Gender

Kara Dixon Vuic

The U.S. military has always been an all-volunteer force for women. Although Congress has on occasion considered drafting women, they have never been compelled to serve and even today are prohibited from registering with the Selective Service System. In many ways, then, the military's switch from conscription to an AVF in 1973 changed little, if anything, in terms of women's reasons for joining and serving in the armed forces. But, in other ways, the AVF changed everything. The return to a volunteer force after three decades of nearly uninterrupted male conscription fundamentally altered the ways that military officials thought about women, men, and gender. The military's increasing reliance on women in the years that followed merged with contemporaneous political debates about women's place in society to raise questions about the nature, extent, terms, and meaning of their service. As they more fully integrated into the armed forces, women challenged longstanding associations between martial service and masculinity. Ultimately, the AVF weakened—though did not sever—the historic ties between masculinity and military service, opening the door to broader, more fluid understandings of the gendered nature of martial service.

Even before the military ended conscription, it was experiencing a kind of gender crisis. When Congress voted in 1971 to end the draft, the military was about to suffer its first large-scale defeat. A force that prided itself on technological advancement and that had expended wildly disproportionate amounts of weapons lost nearly sixty thousand Americans in a country with very little foreign-policy significance to the United States or the broader Cold War. Impending loss, low morale, and declining public support combined to pose significant challenges to long-cherished notions of martial vigor and victory. The era's swiftly changing gender norms added fuel to the fire. Women were pressing for and winning many progressive social, cultural, and legal changes. Increasing numbers of wives and mothers worked outside the home, challenged conventions

and laws that had constrained their educational and employment opportunities, and upturned longstanding sexual restrictions. As women moved
into jury boxes and corporate offices, they also fought to expand their
place in the military.

By the early 1970s, women occupied a stable position in the military.
They were serving in Vietnam, most as nurses but also in administrative, clerical, and intelligence positions. Wartime personnel needs and
the growing feminist movement had forced an increase in opportunities for women and had slowly but steadily removed historical restrictions on their service. Recruitment materials celebrated the military as
a place where women could find unparalleled equal opportunities, and
many indeed did. But many decision makers also believed that women
had a distinct place and specific roles that reflected their feminine gender.
Women were important members of the team, and their contributions
were valued, but they were fundamentally different than men.

Although the terms and nature of female military service had changed
dramatically throughout U.S. history, that basic understanding of women
as both important and different had always structured their relationship
with the armed forces. From the earliest days of an organized U.S. military, women provided essential labor. They laundered uniforms and
bandages, cooked, nursed, spied, and sometimes disguised themselves to
fight battles. But until the twentieth century, they held no formal position. The growing professionalization of nursing in the late nineteenth
and early twentieth centuries, along with its deepening ties to popular
understandings of femininity, solidified women's formal entrance to the
military. Thousands of them worked as contract nurses in the Civil War
and in the Spanish-American War, and their services convinced the U.S.
Army and U.S. Navy to establish formal, permanent nursing corps in the
early 1900s. These women held no formal rank or authority, but they
began a long process of integrating women into the U.S. armed forces.

Personnel and technological demands during World War I brought
women into new military roles outside of the medical corps. Secretary
of the Navy Josephus Daniels found a loophole in the Naval Act of 1916
that allowed him to enlist eleven thousand women into the Naval Reserve as Yeoman F (for "female") to work as stenographers, radio and
telephone operators, mechanics, chauffeurs, and munitions makers. The
army also needed women but chose to hire civilians to fill critical positions instead of enlisting women into the ranks. Some served in France—
most famously, the Signal Corps operators known as "Hello Girls"—but
because they were not formally enlisted in the army, they did not receive
veteran benefits at the war's end. Whatever the terms of their service, the

military released all women from their duties soon after the Armistice, leaving only a small number of nurses in uniform.

World War II brought women into temporary, sex-segregated positions within the military. Fittingly enough, Representative Edith Nourse Rogers, who had worked as a nurse in Europe during World War I, proposed the creation of an auxiliary corps of women for the army. Rogers had forecast the necessity of a women's corps months before the United States entered the conflict, but only the demands of the war proved pressing enough to push the measure through Congress. Even then, some congressmen characterized women soldiers as a sign of the failure of American manhood and a fundamental threat to the family. Military commanders soon appreciated their work, however, and by war's end, 350,000 women were serving around the world.

The almost immediate beginning of the Cold War moved the armed forces and Congress to permanently integrate the women's corps. Although women had held "relative rank" during World War II, the 1947 Army-Navy Nurses Act and the 1948 Women's Armed Services Integration Act formalized equal rank and pay for women, capped the number of female servicemembers at 2 percent of the active forces, and limited the rank they could achieve. By the Vietnam War era, servicewomen were pressing against these restrictions. Many began to advocate for the freedom to combine their career aspirations with their family plans, and many chafed against regulations and unwritten expectations that reflected old-fashioned ideas of how women should look and behave. They made much progress, even as limitations remained. In 1967, owing both to the legal strides of the women's movement and the personnel demands of the Vietnam War, Congress removed restrictions on the number of women who could serve and the ranks they could achieve. More and more women received waivers that allowed them to remain on active duty after having children. And, in 1970, U.S. Army Chief of Staff William C. Westmoreland pinned stars on the shoulders of the armed forces' first female generals. He also kissed them on the mouth, beginning what he called "a new protocol for congratulating lady generals."[1]

This odd mix of progress and fixedness framed women's experiences in the AVF. In the absence of a ready supply of conscripted (or at least draft-motivated) men, the military depended on women's service to meet personnel demands, keep recruitment costs low, and raise average scores on standardized enlistment exams. Each of the services increased the number of women in uniform, and they expanded the ways in which women could serve. Women in uniform became more common, more recognized, and more expected. This expansion raised questions about what did, or perhaps what should, distinguish male and female service. Without a compulsory obligation for men to serve, military service could no longer be characterized as a masculine duty. So what, if anything, differentiated the service of men and women in a volunteer force?

Military officials, Congress, the Supreme Court, and the American public all considered these questions in an era marked by broad—and quickly changing—discussions of equality, woman's rights, and gender change. This chapter focuses primarily on the first decade of the AVF and places discussions about women, gender, and the armed forces in the context of larger national conversations about the Equal Rights Amendment, the revival of registration for Selective Service, and evolving combat restrictions on women. These debates exposed radically different views of women's martial service as well as radically different understandings of gender as either socially and culturally determined or as biologically and divinely ordained. Combat, in particular, emerged as a pronounced issue, especially as it became the focal point and rallying cry of opponents to women's expanding roles and of the political Right as it coalesced around opposition to the ERA.

Military studies and plans for the transition recognized that women would be essential to meeting personnel needs in a volunteer force, and they pitched the armed forces as an equal-opportunity employer. Even before President Richard M. Nixon had committed the nation to a volunteer force, one army study posited that women could be "essential" to meeting personnel demands, in particular, by reducing the number of unhappily drafted male soldiers.[2] Even after the AVF became a reality and the military planned to increase dramatically the number of women in uniform, it needed relatively few of the nation's women. Reports suggested that recruiters should be able easily to recruit the highest-quality women who would be drawn to the military's comparatively higher pay.[3] The army's focused study of how it could transition to a volunteer force similarly suggested that women would be critical to meeting personnel needs and recommended doubling the size of the Women's Army Corps by 1977. To meet that goal, the report suggested that recruiters pitch the army as an equal-opportunity employer; a way for women to combine service with travel, education, job training, and independence; and as a place where women "do not take a back seat to men in regard to pay, promotion opportunity, and benefits."[4]

Overall, the studies adopted a mixed stance toward women. One army study adopted a somewhat progressive stance by suggesting that changing technologies would "erode the barriers of sexual prejudice" before indicating that they would also mitigate women's "innate" emotional and intellectual inferiority. Yet understandings of gender as biologically fixed and part of women's unique military contribution still had a place, even an important one. "Womanly charms and virtues," the same study insisted, could further the army's mission and add a feminine touch to its culture.[5] Another army report decried "traditionalism" as a hindrance to women's service but nonetheless insisted that they needed reassurance that military labor would not undermine their femininity. Moreover, it maintained that women's "social and biological limitations" ultimately precluded them from many roles in "an all-male atmosphere," including "the rigors of field duty" and "maneuver elements in tactical operations."[6] A broader Department of Defense study projected that any personnel shortage could be "practically eliminated by substituting more Servicewomen for Servicemen." As an added bonus, it suggested that adding women to the ranks would draw more men who otherwise would have been turned off by the military's sex-segregated nature.[7] As the military planned to radically transform the way it recruited and enlisted personnel, it continued a long history of seeing women as critically important. It acknowledged some erosion of conventional gender norms but continued to see gender difference as fundamental to women's service.

In anticipation of the ending of conscription, in March 1972, the Secretary of Defense's Central All-Volunteer Task Force directed each of the services to develop plans to increase the number of women serving outside of the medical field. The army, navy, and air force were asked to double their number of women, while the marine corps was tasked with an increase of 40 percent, all by the end of 1977.[8] The services also began to remove the restrictions on the jobs women could perform. In the summer of 1972, a year before the AVF began and a few months after Congress approved the ERA, the army opened to women all military occupational specialties (MOSs) except for those in the combat arms. Enlisted women could now serve in all but 48 of the army's 484 MOSs. The other services similarly expanded the available assignment options, and servicewomen began to enter previously closed occupations and to command mixed-sex units. They also began naval aviator training, served in ship's companies, and entered ROTC programs. In itself, this expansion of opportunities was a bold move, but it did not immediately transform the sexual division of the military. Rotational policies meant that many noncombat jobs were reserved for men returning from combat duty; several individual slots remained designated for men, women, or "interchangeable"; and the military struggled both to attract and retain women in nontraditional jobs.[9] Still, on the eve of the AVF, military officials understood that women were key to its success.

The AVF's plans to expand the number and roles of women intersected with broader national discussions and debates about the changing legal, social, and cultural status of women. The combination of personnel demands in a volunteer force and social pressures brought on by the prospect of the ERA forced the armed forces to enact a number of progressive changes. As many historical barriers fell, the remaining distinctions between the extent and terms of women's and men's service came under increased attack. Ultimately, discussions about the effects of the ERA merged with debates over the potential revival of the Selective Service System to expose the last remaining fault lines of women's military service: conscription and combat. Those debates highlighted deep divisions about the meaning of that service. Congress, the Supreme Court, women's organizations, legal scholars, and military leaders expressed conflicting, and often changing, opinions on the matter. Perhaps ironically, women, who gained much ground in the AVF, ultimately found their progress limited by debates about compulsory service.

In congressional debates about the ERA during the early 1970s, both proponents and opponents expected that the amendment would make women subject to conscription. There was, of course, no precedent for this, as women had never been drafted. But as they steadily gained legal rights and as courts struck down statutes and laws treating men and women differently, most analysts concluded that a constitutional amendment prohibiting sexual discrimination would require women to register for compulsory military service. By the time Congress passed the ERA in March 1972, it was clear that the nation's representatives fully intended it to require military service regardless of sex.

Representative Martha Griffiths (D-MI) knew her way around the House Judiciary Committee. She had successfully outwitted political opponents in 1964 to add sexual discrimination to the Civil Rights Act, and in 1970, she utilized a rare parliamentary procedure to force the ERA out of committee, where it had stalled. For nearly two years, the House and Senate debated the amendment. Opponents had previously tried to undermine and defeat the ERA by proposing changes that would limit its effect. In the 1950s, for example, opponents unsuccessfully sought to pass the Hayden Rider, which would have prevented the ERA from limiting any "rights, benefits, or exemptions" granted to women. By the early 1970s, opponents focused their efforts on the military. They cited the danger that conscription would have on women and on the family, a tactic that failed initially but would be repeated with greater success a decade later.

As members of Congress debated the ERA in 1970, 1971, and 1972, they agreed that it would make women subject to military conscription. Proponents insisted that this requirement would remove critical distinctions between men and women and pointed to the ways that women would gain educational, housing, and employment benefits through military service.[10] And, most importantly, proponents argued, equal rights required equal obligations. Massachusetts representative Louise Day Hicks stated on the House floor in October 1971, "there is no reason why women should not carry equally the burdens as well as the rights of full citizenship."[11] The Senate Judiciary Committee explained the connection more directly in its report to the full chamber: "equality of rights is incomplete without equality of responsibilities."[12]

Opponents insisted that women and men did not bear equal responsibilities when it came to the military. Senator Sam Ervin (D-NC) represented this viewpoint most vocally and most dramatically. Although Ervin was a Harvard-educated attorney, he famously characterized himself as a country bumpkin and, as he often did on other occasions, laced his arguments against the ERA with biblical references and melodrama. When he took the floor of the Senate chamber in March 1972, he proposed two amendments that he hoped would, if not defeat the ERA, weaken its effect. The first proposed to exclude women from military conscription, the second to exclude women from combat roles. In arguing for both exclusions, Ervin insisted that gender and biology were irrevocably linked and that any attempt to equalize men's and women's military obligations was a misguided attempt to "crucify American womanhood upon the cross of dubious equality and specious uniformity."[13]

Invoking his World War I experiences, Senator Ervin painted a vivid tale of how the ERA would result in women being "drafted and sent into combat, where they will be slaughtered or maimed by the bayonets, the bombs, the bullets, the grenades, the mines, the napalm, the poison gas, or the shells of the enemy." He repeated this phrase, nearly verbatim, four times.[14] It was not actually clear that the ERA would force the military to remove all restrictions on women in combat, nor that there was any direct connection between conscription and combat. What did seem likely was that the amendment would require the armed forces to develop specific qualifications for combat roles instead of excluding women wholesale. The Senate Judiciary Committee determined that military commanders would retain their ability to assign all individuals based on "their qualifications and the service's needs."[15] Even the ERA's staunchest advocates suggested that conscripting women would not overhaul the military's last remaining gender divisions. Representative Griffiths suggested that once drafted, women would continue to serve as stenographers and telephone operators.[16] Other supporters noted the relatively small percentage of conscripted men who served in combat units in Vietnam and suggested that women would bear no greater risk, perhaps less.[17] Senator Ervin acknowledged none of the nuances but insisted that the ERA would require women and men to be drafted and sent to combat "under exactly the same conditions."[18]

When Senator Ervin's proposal to exempt women from conscription failed, he proposed another to exempt women from combat. Here, he shifted his focus more explicitly to conventional gender roles in the family. When "God made physiological and functional differences between men and women," Ervin insisted, he intended them for separate roles. Men were destined to "beget" children, women to "bear" and nurture them. Men were to provide "a habitation and livelihood," women to "make the habitations homes."[19] The ERA's proponents went to great lengths to explain that mothers would not be dragged away from their babies. Senator Birch Bayh of Indiana characterized Ervin's insistence that the ERA would result in every mother being "dragged, kicking and screaming from the cradle of her child" as "a bit farfetched, to be kind."[20] The Senate Judiciary Committee argued that such fears were "totally and completely unfounded."[21] Others took great care in explaining that fathers had often been exempted or deferred from the draft and that the ERA would merely require that mothers and fathers be treated equally.[22]

Such assurances did little to appease Senator Ervin or the ERA's other opponents. Nonetheless, in the fall of 1971 and spring of 1972, both houses of Congress rejected all attempts to limit the ERA's reach, including Ervin's proposals to limit its effect on women's military service. When Congress sent the ERA to the states for ratification, it intended equal rights to incur equal obligations, including in the military. Lawmakers acknowledged the likelihood that the amendment's passage would result in women's conscription and the service of qualified women in combat.[23]

The armed services swiftly responded. Military officials expected that the states would quickly ratify the amendment to become part of the U.S. Constitution, and they anticipated that its ratification would require many changes to personnel policies and practices. Two weeks after the Senate sent the ERA to the states, the DOD instructed each of the services to "eliminate all unnecessary distinction in regulations applying to women." Assistant Secretary of Defense (Manpower and Reserve Affairs) Roger Kelley insisted that "women must be given equal opportunity and treatment" and cautioned that "separate organizations and restricted assignments do not provide adequate career opportunity for women."[24] The Central AVF Task Force and the DOD general counsel agreed that any policy that treated men and women differently would likely be challenged in the courts, including assignments to ships, aircraft, and combat.[25] If the AVF had increased opportunities for women in the military, the ERA seemed destined to remove all remaining limitations.

Initial discussions about the ERA's effects on the military focused on different regulations and standards for women and men. Some stirred little controversy. Women had to meet higher mental standards to enlist than did men, for example, but because the armed forces comprised far fewer women than men, recruiters could essentially choose the best applicants regardless of requirements.[26] Military officials faced the most resistance when they proposed changes that threatened to remove gender distinctions. Top women in the services objected to some regulations that differentiated between men and women, including different minimum enlistment ages, the exclusion of young women from JROTC programs, limitations on the number of women who could serve in the Army Judge Advocate General's Corps, and the requirement that women's—but not men's—dependents rely on them for more than half of their subsistence to receive benefits. Yet they did not call for a complete removal of all differences between the sexes. Only the U.S. Air Force's highest-ranking female officer called for women to be admitted to the service academies. None of the military's top women advocated for women to serve in combat. The House Committee on Armed Services' Subcommittee on Utilization of Manpower in the Armed Services decried "a degree of complacency on the part of the women officers" in opening MOSs and noted an overall "satisfaction with the status quo."[27]

It was not that the military's top women did not want advancement and increased opportunities for women, but for those who had entered the armed forces during World War II, the erasure of all sexual distinctions seemed not only risky but also potentially devastating. After the secretary of the army ordered plans in March 1973 to merge women's promotion and assignment lists with the rest of the army and to designate all noncombat jobs as interchangeable, WAC Director Gen. Mildred Bailey protested that without the women's corps, female soldiers would have no advocate on their behalf, no one to "ensure that the Army lived up to its promises and commitments to women."[28] She vehemently resisted any changes to prohibitions against pregnancy and single parenthood and clung to the gender and sexual ideals of an earlier era, ideals that prioritized women's maternal possibilities over anything else.[29]

Despite some resistance, sex-based regulations continued to fall, and women continued to expand their presence in the AVF. By 1976, they could serve in more than 80 percent of all enlisted occupations.[30] Gender seemed to matter less and less in the AVF as men and women trained together and performed the same jobs. Put another way, fewer and fewer positions remained the exclusive purview of men. Combat seemed to be the last remaining masculine domain, but by the mid-1970s, even that seemed under threat.

In the fall of 1976, the first integrated classes of women and men entered the service academies. Women had long been excluded, and every service secretary and the Joint Chiefs of Staff had preferred to keep them out, citing their exclusion from combat. Secretary of the Army Howard "Bo" Callaway had testified before the House Armed Services Committee that admitting women to West Point would lower standards and "irrevocably change the Academy . . . for the worse."[31] Three months after making that statement, he advocated to end the WAC as a gesture of recognizing women "for what they are, full and equal members of the Army in every sense."[32] Very likely, Callaway saw no contradiction in the two positions. There were simply separate roles for women and men to play in the armed forces based on their gender. But after having passed the ERA, Congress was less willing to endorse sexual differences. Ultimately, a government study showing that 12.3 percent of academy graduates on duty in October 1974 had never served in combat convinced many in Congress that combat exclusions should not prevent women from entering the academies.[33]

In some ways, even combat roles seemed up for debate. Two army studies in 1977 and 1978 tested the effectiveness of female soldiers in integrated combat support and combat service support units, and both found that they had no negative influence on unit effectiveness. In fact, a report about women's performance in an annual Cold War training exercise blamed "considerable bias against women" on poor leadership and management.[34] Personnel demands pressed the navy to move quicker on the issue. Because of legal prohibitions against women on ships, the navy was facing the prospect of reaching the maximum number of women it could enlist by 1983. Naval officials did not want to remove all combat restrictions but asked Congress to approve legislation that would permit women on training and research ships. Secretary of Defense Harold Brown thought that the move did not go far enough and called instead for legislation that would remove all "artificial legal restrictions on women serving on ships of the Navy and certain aircraft of the Navy and Air Force."[35]

Increasingly, the civilian leaders of the armed forces seemed at odds with its uniformed leaders. A study conducted for the secretary of Defense and published in 1977 made a case for a serious reexamination of women's roles in the military, including the possibility of their participation in combat. The study criticized both proponents and opponents of women's expanding roles for basing their arguments on "emotionalism[,] . . . unsubstantiated generalities, or isolated examples." It took aim at army leaders who cited national security as justification for resisting women and asked if "recruiting a big, dumb, male high school dropout in preference to a smaller, weaker, but higher quality female [was] erring on the side of national security, in view of the kinds of jobs which must be done in today's military?" And it pointed to the ways that combat itself varied depending on circumstance, the ways that definitions of combat were fluid, and the ways that definitions could mean little in war anyway.[36] According to the then-current definition of "combat," Brown later testified to the Senate, women had served in combat in World War II, Korea, and Vietnam, while nurses had been in combat for over a century, despite all of them having been noncombatants.[37]

But, by 1979, Congress no longer appeared interested in the nuances of women's service, its relationship to combat, or even whether it could be compelled in the right circumstances. The AVF had its opponents, and in early 1979, Senator Harry F. Byrd Jr. of Virginia introduced a bill to reinstate Selective Service registration. Secretary of Defense Brown noted that if this bill became law, women should have to register. In 1972, when Congress passed the ERA, women's registration seemed a foregone conclusion, but in 1979, the subject of registering women derailed Byrd's bill. The Senate Armed Services Committee reported that its membership "feels strongly that it is not in the best interest of our national defense to register women."[38]

A few months later, when the House held hearings on the DOD's proposal to remove combat restrictions on women in the navy and air force, growing congressional resistance to an expanded place for women in the armed forces seemed even more apparent. Similarly, it no longer appeared certain that the ERA would mandate equal opportunities and treatment for servicewomen, even if it was ratified. Although women's rights advocates revived their earlier arguments about equal rights and equal obligations, opponents—including many former military leaders—framed women's expanding footprint in the military as a challenge to conventional gender, sexual, and family norms. Phyllis Schlafly, who founded the Eagle Forum to organize opposition against the ERA, urged the nation to remember that "there are different roles for men and women," while General Westmoreland, who had kissed the first two female generals, testified that "no man with gumption wants a woman to fight his nation's battles."[39] The hearings illuminated the deepening divides over women and gender and presaged an even larger debate that would begin a few months later.

President Jimmy Carter had been a staunch advocate of the volunteer force during his presidency, and so when he announced in his State of the Union address on January 23, 1980, that he intended to revive Selective Service registration, he took many by surprise. His administration had long insisted that registration was not necessary to meet the DOD's projections for mobilization needs in the event of war. But after the Soviet

Union invaded Afghanistan in December 1979, a move that Carter characterized as threatening to most of the world's oil production, he decided that reviving registration would serve as a useful show of force. Although he acknowledged the "men and women of America's Armed Forces [who] are on duty tonight in many parts of the world," he did not announce that evening that he intended to seek legislation granting him authority to register women alongside men.[40]

Carter's advisors knew from the beginning that the prospect of registering women would be divisive, even "volatile," as the chairman of the Democratic National Committee warned.[41] The president could not claim military necessity because the DOD was clear that women would not be immediately required under its mobilization plans. Of the first 100,000 inductees who would be needed, it projected, "virtually *all* would be trained and used in combat occupational specialties." Some medical personnel—including women—could be required in the first 180 days after mobilization, but the DOD expected that it would be able to meet its immediate need for women strictly through volunteers.[42]

Still, most interest groups consulted by administration officials, including young people, students, religious groups, and veterans organizations, supported the registration of women, though they also preferred to keep women out of combat roles. Early polling suggested that the majority of the American public held the same opinion.[43] Yet Carter's advisors warned of congressional defeat and a bloody public fight over the issue. Chief Domestic Policy Advisor Stu Eizenstat characterized the move as "an unnecessary point of controversary" that would lead to "almost certain Congressional defeat."[44] Senator Sam Nunn (D-GA) had fought for several years to revive military conscription and was eager to support its return, but he warned Carter that seeking legislation to register women "would be 'disastrous' politically and would undermine everything that you have done to improve your standing in the polls."[45] Even with "significant support in both Houses," the director of the Office of Management and Budget warned, a bill to register women would likely not make it out of the House Armed Services Committee in an election year.[46]

Perhaps more problematic, those who favored the registration of women were lukewarm advocates. No organization was loudly calling for Selective Service registration as a symbol of women's equal obligation as citizens. No grassroots effort had mobilized women from across the country to beat on their representatives' doors asking to register themselves or their daughters. Most feminist organizations opposed military conscription on principle and interpreted Carter's calls to revive Selective Service registration as the first step on a slippery slope toward another draft. If it occurred, they believed that women should be registered equally, but they were not actively advocating for the cause.[47] It was an "unusual situation," Eizenstat warned Carter, in which excluding women from Selective Service "would not likely bring any political wrath down upon you," but calling to register women could alienate "many of your moderate-to-conservative supporters."[48] Indeed, in the two weeks after the State of the Union address—but before the president had officially announced his intention to seek legislation to register women—the overwhelming majority of calls and letters to the White House opposed such a move.[49]

Despite the risk, Carter, a staunch proponent of the ERA and advocate for women's equality, saw no option but to call for their registration. In his statement to the press on February 8, 1980, the president drew a clear line connecting equal rights and equal obligations. "In every area of our national life," Carter noted, "women are meeting the responsibilities of citizenship." They were already serving in expanded roles in the military, just as they were in many other areas of national life. And, he insisted in a plug both for women's registration and the ratification of the ERA, if they were assuming these "additional responsibilities, it is more urgent than ever that the women in America have full and equal rights under the Constitution. Equal obligations deserve equal rights."[50] Carter maintained that he was willing to take the political risk of proposing women's registration because he believed it was "necessary and right," regardless of "whether it is assured of passage or not."[51] Even then, the president made the political calculation to separate his legislative requests to fund the Selective Service System and to provide him the authority to register women.[52] He was not willing to risk the prospect of registration entirely for the sake of women's equality.

Carter knew that his proposal would raise questions about women's exclusion from combat, and he knew that the connection could be potentially "destructive" to the ERA.[53] Thus, he tried to parse his position very carefully. He had to be careful, in part, because the DOD was continuing to press Congress to "remove the inflexible statutory restrictions presently in effect for the assignment of women in the Navy and Air Force."[54] But Carter insisted that even as women might be assigned "in or near combat zones" in the event of war, he did not seek to change current policies excluding them from units "where engagement in close combat would be part of their duties."[55] An early draft of his statement had clarified that "close combat" would not be part of women's "*primary* duties," perhaps acknowledging that anything could happen in the fog of war, but by the final statement, that qualification had been removed.[56] Still, the president saw no conflict between calling for women's equal obligation and their exclusion from ground combat. Equity, he argued, did not require equal numbers nor equal work. It did require that "both men and women are asked to serve in proportion to the ability of the Armed Forces to use them effectively."[57]

When the House Armed Services Committee took up Carter's proposal in March 1980, opponents successfully dominated the discussion by shifting it from a debate about Selective Service registration to a dogfight over women in combat. They did not contemplate the projections of the DOD's mobilization plans but conflated the differences between Selective Service registration and an actual draft in the event of war. In a gross simplification of a complex issue, opponents claimed that registration would send women straight to combat. When one witness reminded the committee's chair, Representative Richard C. White (D-TX), that the purpose of registration was to provide personnel for both combat and support positions, the congressman replied, "this committee won't consent to that," dismissing outright a fact he did not wish to acknowledge.[58] He and his colleagues failed to reckon with the likelihood that any draftee—male or female—would be assigned to the combat arms and all but ignored the intricacies of legal scholars' evaluations of the ways that the ERA might, or might not, force the military to allow women to apply for positions in the combat arms.[59]

Instead of analyzing the DOD's mobilization plans and dealing with the realities of slots assigned by gender, of who might be needed in a future war of indeterminate size or nature, and of thinking about how registration could be used to solicit different kinds of critical skills, opponents characterized registration as the first step down a steep slope toward dragging mothers away from babies and throwing them straight into the worst kind of combat imaginable. "We don't want our daughters taught to kill," insisted Kathleen Teague of the Coalition against Drafting Women, another of Schlafly's organizations. "Women's mission is to participate in the creation of life, not in destroying it," Teague reasoned. Men had to be "tough enough to defend us against any enemy," but women should wait at home, "to be feminine and human enough to transform our servicemen into good husbands, fathers, and citizens upon their return from battle."[60] Conservative columnist George Will acknowledged that in war, prohibitions against combat were "somewhat artificial," but he insisted that "the distinction is worth trying to preserve." He argued that women were not *excluded* but *exempted* from combat in an effort to prevent "the encroachment of violence upon havens of gentleness." Like Teague, he understood essential gender differences as conferring "upon women a privilege of decency."[61] The vivid language that Senator Ervin had utilized to no avail in 1972 resonated with far more Americans in 1980—and, indeed, with Congress.

That language of loss reflected the broader national political climate. As historians have noted, the gains women made in the 1960s and early 1970s faced increasing challenges by the late 1970s and 1980s. Political conservatives, and more particularly, conservatives calling for a return to a mythic era of nuclear families in which everyone knew their place, were gaining steam, influence, and power. Organized and vocal, they tapped into widespread concerns about changing gender and family structures.[62] For members of groups like the Eagle Forum, the Moral Majority, and the Coalition against Drafting Women, protecting women from combat seemed to many the last chance they had to withstand the dismantling of all gender differences between women and men.

In the early 1980s, that movement secured two key victories. The House Armed Services Committee overwhelmingly defeated Carter's proposal to register women for Selective Service. A little over a year later, the Supreme Court weighed in on registration in *Rostker v. Goldberg*. The case had originated in 1971, when four young men challenged the Vietnam War–era draft on many grounds, but by 1980, when Carter proposed to reinstate Selective Service registration, it focused exclusively on sexual discrimination. Three days before registration was scheduled to begin, a U.S. district court ruled that male-only registration violated the equal protections guaranteed by the Constitution. The decision threatened to derail Selective Service entirely, but the Supreme Court granted a stay, allowing registration to proceed. Then in June 1981, the court ruled in the government's favor. Citing the military's restrictions on women in combat, justices ruled that the government could exclude women from Selective Service registration.[63] Women could volunteer, but they could not be compelled to serve in the nation's military.

In the more than forty years that have followed, women have pushed even further into the military's last remaining male echelon: combat. Their involvement in military incursions into Panama and Grenada high-lighted the ways that combat and combat-support roles were increasingly hard to distinguish. War in the Persian Gulf blurred the lines further, and by the post-9/11 era, many wondered if drawing lines was even worth the effort.[64] Finally, in 2015, Secretary of Defense Ashton Carter announced the removal of all remaining restrictions on women's military service. In part, the policy change simply caught up to the reality that women served in combat regardless of their particular assignment. But more broadly, it reflected a fundamental change in the military's thinking about women, a change that began with the advent of the AVF in 1973. Secretary Car-ter justified the opening of all military roles to women as an effort to make the armed forces better, to improve their effectiveness. Integrating women fully was good for the military, not just for women.[65]

Neither the AVF nor the final removal of all service restrictions erased gender as a consideration in the military. Neither completely severed centuries-old associations between martial duty, particularly combat, and masculinity. Yet the beginning of the AVF began a long process in which those associations have been challenged by hundreds of thousands of women in uniform, including many serving in combat.

In the early 2020s, the only remaining distinction between men's and women's obligations as citizens is registration for Selective Service. Men are required by law to register, while women are forbidden from doing so. This distinction remains, though the legal justification for excluding women from registration—combat—no longer applies. The prospect of including women in Selective Service registration remains a political lightening rod and has united an odd assortment of strange political bedfellows, both in support and in opposition. The DOD; the congressionally created National Commission on Military, National, and Public Service; and organizations as diverse as the American Civil Liberties Union, the National Organization for Women, and the men's rights organization National Coalition for Men have all urged the inclusion of women in Selective Service registration. Indeed, another odd political assortment of parties continues to oppose the expansion of registration to women, ranging from the pacifist, feminist organization Code Pink to several socially conservative representatives and senators. In 2017 and 2021, those conservatives successfully stripped a provision requiring women's registration from the National Defense Authorization Act.[66] The military remains a volunteer force, just as it has always been for women. Time will tell whether women's service will be accepted, or required, on any other terms.

Notes

1. A rich literature on women and the U.S. military analyzes this history. On the Civil War, start with Jane Schultz, *Women at the Front: Hospital Workers in Civil War America* (Chapel Hill: University of North Carolina Press, 2004). For the beginnings of the Army Nurse Corps and the Spanish-American War, see Mary T. Sarnecky, *A History of the U.S. Army Nurse Corps* (Philadelphia: University of Pennsylvania Press, 1990), chaps. 1–2. On the world wars and early Cold War, start with Elizabeth Cobbs, *Hello Girls: America's First Women Soldiers* (Cambridge, MA: Harvard University Press, 2019); Leisa D. Meyer, *Creating GI Jane: Sexuality and Power in the Women's Army Corps during World War II* (New York: Columbia University Press, 1996); and Linda Witt, Judith Bellafaire, Britta Granrud, and Mary Jo Binker, *"A Defense Weapon Known to Be of Value": Servicewomen of the Korean War Era* (Lebanon, NH: University Press of New England, 2005). My work on the Vietnam War details the history described here. See

Kara Dixon Vuic, *Officer, Nurse, Woman: The Army Nurse Corps in the Vietnam War* (Baltimore: Johns Hopkins University Press, 2010), 55 (quote).

2. Beth Bailey, *America's Army: Making the All-Volunteer Force* (Cambridge, MA: Belknap Press of Harvard University Press, 2009), 141–142.

3. GE Tempo, "Innovations for Achieving an AVAF" (December 15, 1971), xii, 25, in *I Want You! The Evolution of the All-Volunteer Force*, by Bernard Rostker (Santa Monica, CA: RAND, 2006), accompanying CD, G0338.pdf (hereafter cited as Rostker CD). GE's Center for Advanced Studies (GE Tempo) produced this report for the Office of the Assistant Secretary of Defense (Manpower and Reserve Affairs).

4. U.S. Army, *Provide: Project Volunteer in Defense of the Nation*, vol. 2, *Supporting Analysis, Directorate of Personnel Studies and Research* (September 15, 1969), 9-5, 9-16, Rostker CD, G0335.pdf.

5. Quoted in Bailey, *America's Army*, 141–142.

6. Army, *Provide*, 9-8 (2d quote), 9-16 (1st quote).

7. "Innovations for Achieving an AVAF," 24, 25n2, 47, Rostker CD, G0338.pdf.

8. Bettie J. Morden, *The Women's Army Corps, 1945–1978*, Army Historical Series (Washington, DC: Center of Military History, 1990), 265.

9. Morden, *Women's Army Corps*, 263–274; Jeanne Holm, *Women in the Military: An Unfinished Revolution*, rev. ed. (Novato, CA: Presidio, 1992), chaps. 18, 19, 22; Bailey, *America's Army*, 154–156.

10. Congressional Record–Senate, 92d Cong., 2d sess., March 21, 1972, 9333, https://www.govinfo.gov/content/pkg/GPO-CRECB-1972-pt7/pdf/GPO-CRECB -1972-pt7-7-2.pdf.

11. Congressional Record–House of Representatives, 92d Cong., 1st sess., October 6, 1971, 35324, https://www.govinfo.gov/content/pkg/GPO-CRECB-1971-pt27/pdf /GPO-CRECB-1971-pt27-2-2.pdf.

12. Senate Committee on the Judiciary, *Equal Rights for Men and Women*, 92d Cong., 2d sess., 1972, S. Rpt. 92-689, 20.

13. Congressional Record–Senate, 92d Cong., 2d sess., March 22, 1972, 9567, https://www.govinfo.gov/content/pkg/GPO-CRECB-1972-pt8/pdf/GPO-CRECB -1972-pt8-1.pdf.

14. Congressional Record–Senate, 92d Cong., 2d sess., March 21, 1972, 9333–51.

15. Senate Committee on the Judiciary, *Equal Rights for Men and Women*, 13.

16. Congressional Record–House, 92d Cong., 1st sess., October 6, 1971, 35323.

17. Congressional Record–House, 92d Cong., 1st sess., October 6, 1971, 35324; Congressional Record–Senate, 92d Cong., 2d sess., March 21, 1972, 9332.

18. Congressional Record–Senate, 92d Cong., 2d sess., March 21, 1972, 9333.

19. Congressional Record–Senate, 92d Cong., 2d sess., March 22, 1972, 9565.

20. Congressional Record–Senate, 92d Cong., 2d sess., March 21, 1972, 9331.

21. Senate Committee on the Judiciary, *Equal Rights for Men and Women*, 13.

22. Congressional Record–House, 92d Cong., 1st sess., October 6, 1971, 35324; Congressional Record–Senate, 92d Cong., 2d sess., March 21, 1972, 9332.

23. The Office of the Secretary of Defense General Counsel concluded in October 1977 that the ERA's "legislative history indicates that . . . , if enacted, would probably require that women be subject to the draft, if any existed. It is also possible,

though not so clear, that women would be permitted to volunteer for any military assignment, including combat, and to serve in such assignment so long as they were qualified." Department of Defense Office of General Counsel Memorandum for Vice Admiral Finneran, June 23, 1977, in House of Representatives, *Women in the Military: Hearings before the Military Personnel Subcommittee of the Committee on Armed Services, . . . November 13, 14, 15, 16, 1979 and February 11, 1980* (Washington, DC: U.S. GPO, 1981), 35 (quote).

24. Central All-Volunteer Force Task Force, Office of the Assistant Secretary of Defense (Manpower and Reserve Affairs), "Utilization of Military Women (A Report of Increased Utilization of Military Women FY 1973–1977)," December 1972, 2, Rostker CD, S0026.pdf.

25. Central All-Volunteer Force Task Force, "Utilization of Military Women," 30–31. See also in this report Carole L. Frings, Office of the General Counsel, OSD, "The Effect of the Equal Rights Amendment on Women in the Military," speech to Defense Advisory Committee on Women in the Services, November 12–16, 1972 (tab G), 134–158.

26. Bailey, *America's Army*, 147–148, 156–157.

27. House of Representatives, *Report by the Special Subcommittee on the Utilization of Manpower in the Military of the Committee on Armed Services*, 92d Cong., 2d sess. (Washington, DC: U.S. GPO, 1972), 14661–14662 (quote, 14661).

28. Morden, *Women's Army Corps*, 310–318 (quote, 314).

29. Morden, *Women's Army Corps*, 303–310; Bailey, *America's Army*, 147–154.

30. Martin Binkin and Shirley J. Bach, *Women and the Military* (Washington, DC: Brookings Institution, 1977), 2.

31. Quoted in Morden, *Women's Army Corps*, 321.

32. Quoted in Morden, *Women's Army Corps*, 315.

33. Morden, *Women's Army Corps*, 318–322; Bailey, *America's Army*, 159–160.

34. Karl E. Cooke, *Department of the Army Historical Summary, Fiscal Year 1978* (Washington, DC: Center of Military History, 1980), 79–80 (quote, 80), available at https://history.army.mil/books/DAHSUM/1978/index.htm (accessed October 16, 2020); Office of the Assistant Secretary of Defense (M, RA, & L [Manpower, Reserve Affairs, and Logistics]), "America's Volunteers: A Report on the All-Volunteer Armed Forces," December 31, 1978, 76, Rostker CD, S0194.pdf.

35. "Hearings before the Committee on Armed Services on S. 2571, U.S. Senate, 95th Cong., 2nd Session, February 7, 1978, Part 1—Authorization Posture Statement, Secretary of Defense Harold Brown and General George S. Brown, Chairman Joint Chiefs of Staff," 330 (quote), Rostker CD, S0451.pdf; R. W. Hunter, "Background Study: Use of Women in the Military," (Washington, DC: Office of the Assistant Secretary of Defense [M, RA, &L], 1977), 39, Rostker CD, G1440.pdf; Assistant Secretary of Defense (M, RA, & L), "America's Volunteers," 77.

36. Hunter, "Background Study."

37. "Hearings before the Committee on Armed Services on S. 2571," 329.

38. Quoted in Holm, *Women in the Military*, 349–350 (quote, 349).

39. Bailey, *America's Army*, 166–170 (quotes, 169); Holm, *Women in the Military*, 344.

40. Jimmy Carter, "State of the Union Address 1980," January 23, 1980, Jimmy Carter Presidential Library and Museum (hereafter JCPL), https://www.jimmycarter library.gov/assets/documents/speeches/su80jec.phtml (accessed December 15, 2020). Bernard Rostker, who had been confirmed as the new director of the Selective Service System in November 1979, provides a detailed history of the Carter administration's plans for registration in *I Want You!*, chap. 12.

41. Rostker, *I Want You!*, 436.

42. James T. McIntyre Jr., "Memorandum for the President, Subject: Registration of Women for Selective Service," February 2, 1980, 3 (quote), Collection: Office of Staff Secretary; Series: Presidential Files; Folder: 2/8/80; Container 150, JCPL, https://www.jimmycarterlibrary.gov/digital_library/sso/148878/150/SSO_148878 _150_04.pdf (accessed October 22, 2020).

43. Anne Wexler, "Memorandum for Jim McIntyre, Subject: Presidential Decisions on Selective Service Reform," February 2, 1980, Collection: Office of Staff Secretary; Series: Presidential Files; Folder: 2/8/80; Container 150, JCPL, https://www .jimmycarterlibrary.gov/digital_library/sso/148878/150/SSO_148878_150_04.pdf (accessed October 22, 2020).

44. Stu Eizenstat, "Memorandum for the President, Subject: Selective Service Reform and Registration," February 2, 1980, 2, Collection: Office of Staff Secretary; Series: Presidential Files; Folder: 2/8/80; Container 150, JCPL, https://www.jimmy carterlibrary.gov/digital_library/sso/148878/150/SSO_148878_150_04.pdf (accessed October 22, 2020).

45. Frank Moore, "Memorandum for the President, Subject: Weekly Legislative Report," January 26, 1980, 3 (quote), Collection: Office of Staff Secretary; Series: Presidential Files; Folder: 1/28/80 [3]; Container 148, JCPL, https://www.jimmyc arterlibrary.gov/digital_library/sso/148878/148/SSO_148878_148_10.pdf (accessed October 23, 2020). See also Moore, "Memorandum for the President," February 6, 1980, Collection: Office of Staff Secretary; Series: Presidential Files; Folder: 2/9/80 [1]; Container 150, JCPL, https://www.jimmycarterlibrary.gov/digital_library/sso/14 8878/150/SSO_148878_150_02.pdf (accessed October 23, 2020); and Anne Wexler, "Memorandum for the President, Subject: Activities Report Week Ending February 1, 1980," February 2, 1980, Collection: Office of Staff Secretary; Series: Presidential Files; Folder: 2/4/80; Container 149, JCPL, https://www.jimmycarterlibrary.gov/di gital_library/sso/148878/149/SSO_148878_149_08.pdf (accessed October 23, 2020). For more on polling information, see John Ryor to Anne Wexler and Mike Channin, "Memorandum RE: Outreach Strategy for President Registration Legislation," undated, Rostker CD, C0004.pdf; and Melina Beck, "Women in the Armed Forces," *Newsweek*, February 18, 1980.

46. McIntyre, "Memorandum for the President," 5–6 (quote, 5); Richard Halloran, "Carter Draft Plan Urges Registration of Men and Women," *New York Times*, February 9, 1980.

47. Sarah Weddington, "Meeting with Presidents of Women's Organizations, Selective Service Registration of Women," February 28, 1980, Collection: Office of Staff Secretary; Series: Presidential Files; Folder: 2/12/80 [2]; Container 150, JCPL, https://www.jimmycarterlibrary.gov/digital_library/sso/148878/150/SSO_148878_150_07

.pdf (accessed October 23, 2020); Sarah Weddington, "Memorandum for the President, Subject: Registration of Women," February 4, 1980, Collection: Office of Staff Secretary; Series: Presidential Files; Folder: 2/8/80, Container 150, JCPL, https://www.jimmycarterlibrary.gov/digital_library/sso/148878/150/SSO_148878_150_04.pdf (accessed October 22, 2020).

48. Eizenstat, "Memorandum for the President," 1.

49. Hugh Carter, "Memorandum for the President, Subject: Draft Registration Mail and Calls," February 6, 1980, Collection: Office of Staff Secretary; Series: Presidential Files; Folder: 2/9/80 [1]; Container 150, JCPL, https://www.jimmycarterlibrary.gov/digital_library/sso/148878/150/SSO_148878_150_02.pdf (accessed October 23, 2020); Steven Shoob, "Memorandum for Hugh Carter, Subject: Comment Office Week-Ending Report," February 8, 1980, Rostker CD, C0007.pdf.

50. "Carter Statement on Draft Registration," *New York Times*, February 9, 1980, 8.

51. Rick Her and Chris Matthews, "Memorandum for the President, Subject: Meeting with students," February 14, 1980, Collection: Office of Staff Secretary; Series: Presidential Files; Folder: 2/15/80 [2]; Container 151, JCPL, https://www.jimmycarterlibrary.gov/digital_library/sso/148878/151/SSO_148878_151_02.pdf (accessed October 23, 2020).

52. Draft A-1, Draft Registration Announcement, February 7, 1980, 3, Collection: Office of Staff Secretary; Series: Presidential Files; Folder: 2/8/80; Container 150, JCPL, https://www.jimmycarterlibrary.gov/digital_library/sso/148878/150/SSO_148878_150_04.pdf (accessed October 22, 2020).

53. Sarah Weddington, "Meeting with Presidents of Women's Organizations," January 30, 1980, Collection: Office of Staff Secretary; Series: Presidential Files; Folder: 1/30/80 [1]; Container 149, JCPL, https://www.jimmycarterlibrary.gov/digital_library/sso/148878/149/SSO_148878_149_02.pdf (accessed October 23, 2020).

54. Her and Matthews, "Memorandum for the President."

55. "Carter Statement on Draft Registration."

56. Draft A-1, Draft Registration Announcement, February 7, 1980 (emphasis mine); Draft P-1 Draft Registration Announcement, both in Collection: Office of Staff Secretary; Series: Presidential Files; Folder: 2/8/80; Container 150, JCPL, https://www.jimmycarterlibrary.gov/digital_library/sso/148878/150/SSO_148878_150_04.pdf (accessed October 22, 2020).

57. "Presidential Recommendations for Selective Service Reform: A Report to Congress Prepared Pursuant to PL 96-107," February 11, 1980, 4, 24–28 (quote, 28), Rostker CD, S0561.pdf.

58. "Hearings on H. R. 6569 Registration of Women, Military Personnel Subcommittee of the Committee on Armed Service, House of Representatives, 96th Congress, 2nd Session, March 5 and 6, 1980," 64 (quote), Rostker CD, G1175.pdf. See also Linda K. Kerber, *No Constitutional Right to be Ladies: Women and the Obligations of Citizenship* (New York: Hill and Wang, 1998), 267–302.

59. Legal scholars came to many conclusions, but they all acknowledged that Congress had historically given the military great latitude, especially in times of war, and that an ERA very likely would simply forbid blanket sexual discrimination, not

overturn the military's ability to set particular qualifications for combat that women may or may not have been able to meet. See Stephen L. Teicher, Department of the Air Force Office of the General Counsel, "Memorandum for Mr. Reichart, Subject: Constitutionality of an All Male Draft," May 9, 1979, Rostker CD, S0602.pdf; Robert L. Gilliat, "Memorandum for the Deputy Assistant Secretary of Defense (M, RA, & L)," January 2, 1980, Subject PRM 47 (Selective Service System Comments, December 12, 1979), Rostker CD, S0608.pdf; John M. Harmon, "Memorandum for Honorable John White, Subject: Constitutionality of All-Male Draft Registration," January 31, 1980, Rostker CD, S0607.pdf; and Jane J. Mansbridge, *Why We Lost the ERA* (Chicago: University of Chicago Press, 1986), 47, 61–66.

60. "Hearings on H. R. 6569 Registration of Women," 103.

61. George F. Will, "Armies Should Win Wars," *Newsweek*, February 18, 1980.

62. Robert O. Self, *All in the Family: The Realignment of American Democracy since the 1960s* (New York: Hill and Wang, 2012); Natasha Zaretsky, *No Direction Home: The American Family and the Fear of National Decline, 1968–1980* (Chapel Hill: University of North Carolina Press, 2007); Donald G. Mathews and Jane Sherron DeHart, *Sex, Gender, and the Politics of the ERA* (New York: Oxford University Press, 1990); Bailey, *America's Army*, 132–134.

63. Kerber, *No Constitutional Right to be Ladies*, chap. 5.

64. Rostker, *I Want You!*, 571–572; William A. Taylor, *Military Service and American Democracy: From World War II to the Iraq and Afghanistan Wars* (Lawrence: University of Kansas Press, 2016), 149.

65. Ash Carter, "Remarks on the Women-in-Service Review," December 3, 2015, U.S. Department of Defense, https://www.defense.gov/Newsroom/Speeches/Speech/Article/632495/remarks-on-the-women-in-service-review/ (accessed December 16, 2020).

66. Office of the Under Secretary of Defense for Personnel and Readiness, *Report on the Purpose and Utility of a Registration System for Military Selective Service*, March 2017, 17–20, https://hasbrouck.org/draft/DOD-report-17MAR2017.pdf (accessed January 22, 2021); "Inspired to Serve: The Final Report of the National Commission on Military, National, and Public Service," Homeland Security Digital Library, March 2020, https://www.hsdl.org/?abstract&did=841630 (accessed October 25, 2022); Connor O'Brien, "Lawmakers Drop Proposal to Add Women to the Draft as Defense Bill Headaches Mount," *Politico*, December 6, 2021, https://www.politico.com/news/2021/12/06/ndaa-women-draft-dropped-523829 (accessed October 25, 2022); Etta Lanum, "Selective Service Reform AWOL in 2022 NDAA (Again): What Happens Now?," *Lawfare*, March 17, 2022, https://www.lawfareblog.com/selective-service-reform-awol-2022-ndaa-again-what-happens-now (accessed October 25, 2022).

6

Military Benefits

Jennifer Mittelstadt

When the United States ended conscription and created the modern all-volunteer force in 1973, military leaders, manpower experts, sociologists, and journalists initiated investigations to learn how the military would fill holes left behind by the exiting conscripts. No longer able to force young people to join, the armed forces would have to convince them. Who would join? What would motivate them to enlist?

Answers from these studies emerged within a few years. In 1975, a typical young man who joined the U.S. military was nineteen and came from a lower-working-class background. He had graduated high school, spent a year or two trying to find good employment, but had little luck during the recession of the early 1970s. While the weak economy pushed some young men toward the armed forces, it was not sufficient to fill the ranks.[1] Advertising also lured new recruits, as the new AVF propagated popular themes of consumer society using the latest advertising technologies of targeted ads in specific media.[2] And traditional appeals to patriotism and a newly professionalized image of the military also helped draw new volunteers. But one of the key discoveries of those 1970s reports was that young people hoped for access to military benefits.

Offering first-term recruits access to a full complement of benefits—both for them and their families—would mark a major shift for the U.S. armed forces. For hundreds of years, active-duty benefits had been limited to basic food, shelter, clothing, or allowances for lower ranks, with more fulsome benefits—family housing, family access to post amenities, health care, and more—offered as perquisites of service for career personnel and officers. The switch to the AVF in the 1970s forced the U.S. military to offer much more. It began expanding traditional benefits and building new social and economic-support programs for all ranks and their families. Millions of Americans who volunteered for active duty after 1973—and millions more family members—found an AVF that offered housing assistance, subsistence payments, child care, medical and dental programs, commissary and post-exchange privileges, tax advantages, education and training, social services ranging from financial counseling to legal aid, and dozens of family welfare programs.[3] With the AVF, spending on benefits skyrocketed. In many years since 1972, manpower costs accounted for the bulk of Defense Department expenditures.[4]

The AVF initiated a historic transformation of traditional active-duty military benefits, with expanded forms, functions, and long-term consequences. The coming of the AVF refashioned them into universally accessible, family focused services, which over time functioned as essential components of military recruitment, retention, and readiness. This benefits expansion occurred in tandem with the growing political popularity of and federal spending on the AVF in the late 1970s and 1980s. But the growth and transformation of military benefits under the AVF brought complicated outcomes. These benefits have furthered the gap between military personnel and civilians by providing a dedicated wraparound welfare state in the armed services not available to most civilians.[5] In addition, the growth of military benefits has subjected programs and personnel to some of the debates and trends associated with civilian social-welfare politics. As central and costly components of the AVF, military benefits have become closely tied to the larger political economy of the AVF, which, while expansive in the 1980s, has faced privatization and outsourcing since the mid-1990s.

Benefits Prior to the AVF

Before the United States created the modern AVF in the early 1970s, military benefits for active-duty personnel were shaped by two primary factors—the contours of rank and hierarchy and the limits placed on military family life. Officers and career noncommissioned officers enjoyed fuller benefits than enlisted personnel. And while enlisted personnel were prohibited from marrying and, even if surreptitiously married, received no benefits for family members, officers and senior career personnel welcomed their families in the web of military support. This unequal and relatively spare system of military benefits operated without great resistance or major difficulty before World War II. But the creation of the massive draft armed forces during that conflict and the persistence of a large standing military during the Cold War began to test these limited benefits. Due to the buildup for World War II, the armed forces rescinded the marriage prohibition but otherwise did not meaningfully extend benefits to the millions of enlisted men's families. The problems exposed during the several decades after the war, and some of the solutions that were initially developed, paved the way for major expansions of benefits after the creation of the AVF.

Rank determined military benefits in the era before the modern AVF. Beginning with the Revolutionary War and continuing into the nineteenth century, the U.S. Army and U.S. Navy offered daily support to its conscripts and volunteers during wartime and peacetime. There were the basics—rations, shelter in either tents or barracks, and uniforms—or, later, allowances for such. Enlisted personnel could also expect to receive medical care as needed and as available, though services varied widely depending on location and whether soldiers were in the field or on an installation. After the Civil War, the PXs offered enlisted personnel a military-run site at which to shop, and in the early twentieth century, clubs and programs for morale, welfare, and recreation—sports, music, arts, and so forth—offered diversions and personal development for the enlisted man.

During these same periods, officers and higher-ranked enlisted career personnel received more fulsome benefits than their enlisted compatriots. Officers and NCOs lived in more private and commodious quarters, apartments, or houses, depending on rank and family status. They had access to military service providers who managed their household cooking and cleaning or an officers' mess. They received allowances for subsistence and clothing. And they accessed health care of the best quality available in the circumstances in which they found themselves. The clubs opened for the career force and officers were more luxuriously outfitted and offered fuller service than enlisted gathering places.[6]

As the military grew and established more permanent posts in locales around the nation—and, after the Spanish-American War, around the world—military leadership undertook installation planning and construction that offered access to additional pastimes and institutions that enlisted personnel and officers, in their separate manners, could enjoy. Take, for example, the churches and chapels that offered not only worship services but also dinners and dances. By the 1920s and 1930s, many posts included bowling alleys, swimming pools, and movie theaters. Post lending libraries made books available. Groups like the Red Cross and the United Service Organizations might offer special events for military personnel on post or even in theater. While not technically military benefits, these outlets for recreation and morale allowed both enlisted personnel and officers fuller participation in standard American middle-class activities.

The generosity of military benefits and the wraparound feel of life on post was most encompassing for officers and career NCOs, the only people whose families were welcomed into military life. Thus, the second major factor shaping military benefits prior to the advent of the AVF was the acceptance or rejection of families.

In the period from the American Revolution through the first half of the nineteenth century, single men filled military ranks.[7] The army and navy lured soldiers and sailors with monetary rewards and promises of land, which they might use as the basis for supporting a family, but regulations did not mention family members, nor did it officially provide anything for them. Then, in 1847, Congress prohibited married men from enlisting in military service, and once in the ranks, policies discouraged marriage for nearly a century.[8]

Discouragement did not stamp out wives and children, however. Some enlisted men defied regulations and married, entered common-law relationships with women, or had children. If discovered, a serviceman was either immediately discharged or prevented from reenlisting when his current term ended. Either in the shadows or when awaiting discharge, enlisted men with family members struggled to survive without military support for wives or children. They stayed in barracks and eked out extra money with second-shift jobs, or they relied on their spouses to work in order to make ends meet for the whole family.[9]

By contrast, officers and senior enlisted personnel were allowed to marry and have children. In addition, as a reward for their rank and career service, they were offered sponsored support for their families. The nature and level of support varied by availability of some services and by local command, but Congress in the early twentieth century made sure such personnel were entitled to official "family support" of housing, some access to dispensaries, and a subsistence allotment. Officers and career enlisted men could expect to receive family quarters, in-kind subsistence, and domestic service or allowances that supported the same. Family members were eligible to the use of military medical facilities when not too taxed, especially as in wartime. When officers or senior enlisted personnel were reassigned to new posts, the military sponsored the moves from end to end.[10] Larger posts offered schools. And officers' families partook of the rich environment of clubs, tennis and golf, and other amenities that many installations offered. As one army wife recalled: "It was like a small elite club. We had a rich man's life on a small income."[11]

This regime of rank-based limited benefits continued even as the massive manpower demands of World War II placed new pressures on the systems. To meet an overwhelming demand for personnel—nearly 15.5 million men and 500,000 women would serve—the U.S. government in 1942 had to rescind the family ban for enlisted personnel and allow husbands and fathers into the ranks. Marriage inclusion continued after the war, as the United States reinstituted the draft in 1948 and maintained a large peacetime Cold War military, which still needed married men to meet personnel goals. By the end of the 1950s, the marriage-inclusion policy had produced a revolution in military life in which family members on base often outnumbered military personnel.[12]

Even though the early postwar military had more than 3.7 million family members in its midst, it nevertheless continued to exclude from benefits those of lower-ranked enlisted personnel—the bulk of the armed forces. This refusal spawned a series of crises. In 1949, *Life* magazine reported that decrepit housing and severe shortages plagued the military. Enlisted men were spending their small paychecks on dented, drafty metal trailers; windblown, jerry-rigged shacks; and even "huts" and "chicken coops," all clumped together haphazardly near a post.[13] In 1956, stories of military wives and children being unable to access care, or provided inappropriate care, prompted Congress to pass the Civilian Health and Medical Program of the Uniformed Services (CHAMPUS), which provided regular health coverage to military families. But economic and social problems persisted, especially among lower-level enlisted personnel. In 1955, the National Committee on Social Work in Defense Mobilization warned the military brass, "of all the social welfare problems confronting military community [*sic*] none are more difficult than those falling in the general area of child and family welfare." If the armed forces did not catch up, both military families and military performance would be affected.[14] A slew of community-service, volunteer-operated "lending closets" and other social groups that emerged in the services in the 1960s could hardly make a dent in the problems.[15] Even as the system generated embarrassment and frustration, the DOD stood by its rank-based system of economic and institutional supports and to its limitations on family support. Leadership and many career members and officers clung to these limitations of military benefits as a perquisite of the perceived commitments they made to the military. All in all, the military's disregard for enlisted personnel and their family members' needs reflected the classic joke, "If the army had wanted you to have a family, it would have issued you one."

The AVF and the Transformation of Military Benefits into Readiness and Recruitment Tools

The decision by President Richard M. Nixon and bipartisan allies in Congress to end conscription forced the military to alter its benefits structures and rules by extending benefits to all ranks and incorporating all family members into the benefits system. Leaders of the new AVF understood the necessity for what might be thought of as an "officerization" of the force, in which all personnel were treated as valuable members of a potential career cadre of trained, professional servicemembers, and they argued that full benefits for all symbolized this transformation.[16] They also actively undertook a "familialization" of the armed forces, welcoming families of all ranks and incorporating them into the concept of military readiness. Both decisions resulted not only in significant expansion of existing benefits but also the creation of totally new forms of military benefits that served both the universal ethos of officerization and the commitment to families. Popular with both Republicans and Democrats, these grew with remarkable speed and without significant political opposition, partaking of the growing political legitimacy of the AVF and the militarization of American life in the 1980s.

The massive growth and transformation of military benefits under the AVF was not predestined, however. President Nixon's prime architects for the new volunteer force were economists, not military personnel, and they opposed the extension of traditional military benefits to all members of the armed forces. Indeed, they opposed even those existing for officers and career personnel, preferring instead a purely cash-based system of military compensation. Milton Friedman and the free-market economists who staffed the President's Commission on an All-Volunteer Armed Force opposed most government programs and disliked military-provided housing, health care, recreation, and more. They preferred that personnel and their families receive a salary just high enough to allow them to purchase the "benefits" they needed or wanted in the private sector ("on the economy").

Military leadership rejected the economists' cash-based model as incompatible with the more professionalized, career-focused armed forces they hoped to foster with the AVF. Secretary of the Army Stanley Resor worried that reliance on income incentives alone would "attract the man on the economic margin," someone not fully committed or able to perform military duties.[17] The powerful senator John Stennis (D-MS) echoed these doubts, arguing in hearings about the AVF, "we are abandoning the essential spirit of the modern services when we say we are going out to do whatever is necessary to induce a man solely based on the money."[18]

But more than undermining service values, military leadership felt that economists' proposals for cash incentives could not meet the goals of the new AVF—a permanent, highly trained force entirely reliant on volunteers and large numbers of career personnel. They believed the military would need to recast itself with an ethos professionalism that amounted to an officerization of the armed forces—the assumption of leadership and mission extending to every member at every rank. As they studied the possibilities of the new AVF, officials determined that benefits would provide incentives needed to maintain the force and also help produce the kind of professionally minded, career-oriented soldiers required.

For one, benefits for all ranks helped generate the loyalty and cohesion necessary for the high-skilled volunteer era. Army leaders argued that such benefits and programs demonstrated institutional support and commitment that soldiers wanted in order to commit to being career servicemembers. The army's "cohesiveness," Gen. Harold Moore insisted in his 1976 annual report to *Army Magazine*, "is based on our ability to provide benefits and services that offset the conditions, unexpected demands and hazards of service."[19] The extension of benefits to all ranks would nurture necessary institutional loyalty, cohesion, and efficiency. Secretary of the Army Martin Hoffman testified to Congress, "The old Army leadership adage 'Take care of your people and they will take care of you' was never more true" than in the modern volunteer era.[20]

Military research confirmed the importance of benefits to enlisted personnel and the necessity of incorporating them in the professional vision of the AVF. In the early 1970, army surveys of soldiers confirmed that they consistently named benefits and supports such as housing, health care, and the PX as among the most important factors in their decisions about recruitment and, even more important, about retention. If military life was difficult, what could the armed forces offer to compensate? Soldiers wanted security, protection, health care, an environment in which to raise a family, and job training for the future.[21] They also wanted opportunities for education and training, together a source of long-term earnings and potential upward socioeconomic mobility.[22]

Military leaders worked with sympathetic members of Congress to expand benefits and supports to all junior enlisted personnel and to all of their family members. By 1977, six of ten servicemembers were married—about 50 percent of enlisted personnel, 78 percent of career enlisted personnel, and over 80 percent of the officer corps.[23] Through the changes to its benefits, the AVF thus underwent a simultaneous officerization and a closely related familialization of the force.

Many of the very same worries regarding recruitment, retention, and professionalization driving the armed forces to "officerize" the modern AVF also pushed them and their congressional allies to advocate opening benefits to all military families. Congress reported, "adequate family housing . . . was one of the primary factors influencing the retention of qualified married military personnel in the services." If the military was to keep its married junior enlisted personnel, then it needed more family housing. It would also need to allow servicemembers to bring their families on "accompanied tours of duty" like those of higher rank were entitled to do. Commanders in Europe reported instances of junior en-

listed soldiers who refused to leave their families behind in the States and
brought them to Germany "on their own dime."[24] Forced to live off post,
sometimes without a kitchen, heat, or appliances, they became isolated
and disillusioned. "This type of situation," a member of the House Armed
Services Committee pointed out, "is hardly conducive to force morale and
retention and we are losing some very good people as a result."[25] Failure to
extend benefits to families of all ranks could, as one staff sergeant put it,
"single-handedly bring down the Army's volunteer concept."[26] "If we are
to maintain a volunteer military," wrote a spouse to *Army Times*, the entire army community "should be campaigning for the right of all military
men to the same family care."[27] Ongoing military research supported the
wisdom of personnel, military leaders, and Congress in extending benefits to all ranks and all families.[28] Of enlisted soldiers' wives, 55–65 percent
reported that the army would be "much or a little better" by expanding
programs like family housing, health care, and educational opportunities.
If these benefits were upgraded, these wives indicated, they would be
more inclined to have their husbands reenlist.[29]

The military thus embraced benefits expansion to all ranks and all families as a solution to recruitment and retention in the AVF era. "Chances
are," an advertisement for reenlistment explained, "a man's not going to
stay in the Army if his wife doesn't want him to." But by the end of the
1970s, the army expressed confidence that a spouse would want a soldier
to "re-up" given the "housing, child care, medical care, and all the other
things she doesn't have to spend his paycheck on."[30]

As the AVF progressed, the officials envisioned family benefits as central not only in recruitment and retention but also in military readiness
and effectiveness—the ability of a servicemember to perform his or her
function effectively. Immediately upon allowing accompanied tours for
lower ranks, commanders noted that the thousands of new young families
quelled all manner of poor conduct and infractions. "At three dozen major U.S. military bases in West Germany," the presence of these "dependent families" served as "a moderating influence" on soldiers. "Married
men," *Time* magazine quoted an army general as saying, "tend to be more
stable and much less subject to the dangers of alcohol, drug abuse and
sexual adventures with the locals, provided family are with them at these
overseas posts."[31]

The equation between family benefits and readiness was confirmed by
more than just anecdotes. Military branches developed research programs
that explored the relationship between families and military readiness
beginning in the 1980s.[32] In the army, new military family researchers
analyzed how "polices, programs, and practices" with respect to families also affected readiness.[33] Their findings demonstrated that "family

problems detract from a soldier's . . . ability to perform."[34] Soldiers were rated as having higher personal readiness when they felt that their supervisors showed "support for families."[35] Units were rated as having better readiness when servicemembers' spouses perceived that they supported families.[36] Family benefits and supports thus became central to improving military readiness.

Such research helped press the armed forces not only to expand benefits to all military families but also to create entirely new ones oriented toward improving military family life. With the support and prodding of Congress and the administration of President Ronald Reagan, the services invested hundreds of millions of dollars into new facilities. First came an explosion of childcare programs; each year from 1984 through 1989, the army added between one and two dozen new childcare programs to posts around the world.[37] Then the armed forces developed specialized services like family counseling, youth and adolescent programs, premarital guidance, crisis prevention and intervention, and a rich collection of family recreation activities. By 1985, the army counted eighteen distinct "family programs" constituting a web of nearly comprehensive social-welfare services for soldiers and their dependents.[38]

Military benefits reached their height in the 1980s and were generally viewed as an uncontroversial good for the services and society. The general popularity of the armed forces and the AVF in the 1980s lent political legitimacy to programs that served military personnel. By the end of the Reagan presidency in the late 1980s, military benefits had grown so much and become so comprehensive that more than one observer noted it had become its own welfare state. It was, as one longtime defense reporter quipped, a "Great Society in Camouflage."[39] The switch to the AVF transformed military benefits into a universal, comprehensive social-welfare program unprecedented in the U.S. armed forces or in American life.

Long-Term Consequences of the Expansion and Transformation of Military Benefits in the AVF

The creation of vast, comprehensive, and expensive active-duty benefits within the AVF changed the ways that millions of military personnel and family members lived their everyday lives. Servicemembers, spouses, and children enjoyed suburban-like communities on installations boasting clean, safe amenities. And major medical, childcare, and housing supports offered them unprecedented social and economic security. Yet the massive expansion of military benefits also produced consequences beyond individual well-being. AVF benefits have heightened distinctions between military personnel and civilians by providing targeted, comprehensive, and specialized programs not available to most Americans. At the same time, the growth of social-welfare benefits in the armed forces have subjected military programs and personnel to some of the debates and trends associated with civilian social-welfare politics. And, as expensive elements of the AVF, military benefits have been swept up in the privatization and outsourcing of military services since the 1990s.

Benefit expansion under the AVF played a role in enlarging what many scholars call the military-civilian gap—the geographic, social, and political divide between military personnel and their civilian counterparts that has been growing since the end of conscription. The gap is partly quantitative: without the draft, and without the large peacetime Cold War military, fewer Americans experience military service. But the distance is also fostered by different lived experiences among armed forces personnel and civilians. As scholars have noted, the AVF has developed a more insular military culture, physically separated from civilian society on ever-more-strictly guarded posts. The AVF offers substantially unique, challenging, and immersive work-life experiences that diverge from most of the civilian world.[40] And the professionalized, career nature of the AVF fosters high rates of reenlistment and family legacy service as compared to the era of conscription.[41]

Military benefits have played a role in sharpening these differences. As early as 1970, the nation's most eminent military sociologist, Charles Moskos, pointed out how the expansion of benefits would set servicemembers apart from their civilian peers. "The establishment of family-service agencies within the armed forces can . . . be interpreted as another indication of the emerging differentiation of the military and civilian spheres. That is, to the degree that family needs are increasingly served by the formal organization of the military, to that extent will military families be removed from ties with civilian associations and institutions."[42] The decision by policymakers to expand traditional military benefits contributed to isolating AVF participants from the civilian world while also providing personnel social and economic benefits that differ from it.

These benefits were not only different from but also, on average, significantly fuller and higher quality than those available in civilian life. Beginning in the 1970s, a bipartisan movement spearheaded by conservatives began attacking the civilian welfare state, particularly means-tested programs and those targeting poor people. At the same time, new proposals for social-welfare programs like universal health care, a guaranteed minimum income, the provision of child care, and the opening of Social Security to include more types of workers all failed.[43] Though some Americans found excellent benefits in private-sector employment, the decline of unionization and the outsourcing of traditional manufacturing jobs to plants overseas meant that even these benefits declined as those in the armed forces grew and stabilized.[44] As a result, military personnel and their families during the AVF era not only have received different benefits from civilians but also have enjoyed a larger number of them that were both comprehensive and higher quality.

The AVF's benefits created additional consequences beyond widening the military-civilian gap. Some observers have drawn connections between military social programs and the less popular civilian social-welfare programs. As the AVF expanded its benefits in the 1970s and early 1980s, a vocal group of retired military officers and active-duty midcareer officers opposed benefits expansion on the grounds that the military was subverting its warfighting purpose by devoting resources to social programs. The influential Beard Report of 1978, written by Rep. Robin Beard (R-TN), a member of the Marine Corps Reserves, typified this view, predicting a disastrous transformation of the army "into a social welfare institution." Joined later by retired naval officer James Webb—later secretary of the navy and U.S. senator (D-VA)—Beard cited interviews with officers and NCOs who feared the army was becoming a haven for low-income, less educated, and nonwhite soldiers and their families, people who mirrored stereotypical images of civilian welfare clients. As more women and low-income Americans indeed have joined the AVF, other observers have predicted that universal access to social-welfare benefits would drain the army's power, with commanders forced to "teach kindergarten" to the uneducated rather than train soldiers for battle. They also forecast the transformation of the army into a "babysitter," with the new family and child care programs.[45]

These critics were always a minority, however, and never successfully halted the growth of military benefits. But worries about the armed forces' conversion into a "welfare state" persisted into the 1990s and eventually reshaped the stated goals of some benefits for families. In the early 1990s, civilian "welfare reform" policies turned welfare into "workfare," and just as civilian policymakers pressed low-income civilians into "independence" through mandatory employment, so did the armed forces begin to worry about the "dependency" of its own programs. In the wake of the massive deployments of the Persian Gulf War in 1991, after-action reports voiced new concerns about families who were "overly dependent" on army programs and had "relied too much" on its social supports during the deployment.[46] Cued by family sociologists and psychologists who also studied civilian welfare clients, the army, for one, called its benefits and supports into question.

Fearful of having its support program labeled as "welfare" or "encouraging dependency," officials "redefine[d] how the Army supports and assists families" along the lines of civilian welfare reform.[47] The army announced plans to "make soldiers" rather than the army "responsible for family readiness."[48] Morale, welfare, and recreation leaders discussed media strategies that communicated how the army's "programs are not social services to 'help people when they are down' . . . [but instead] encourage self-support."[49] Over the next several years, the army created initiatives like "Army Family Team Building" that taught families "how to serve the army." It changed the name of "Family Support Groups" to "Family Readiness Groups."[50] And instead of the motto "The Army Takes Care of Its Own," it now pledged to produce independence: "The Army Takes Care of Its Own So That They Can Learn to Take Care of Themselves."[51] Army leadership pulled back on their commitment to social and economic support at the same time, and in much the same way, as "reformers" of the civilian welfare state.

If servicemembers and families have had to become more self-reliant, they have also had to deal with private corporations and contractors rather than with the armed forces personnel in the provision of their benefits. Since the mid-1990s, as part of the larger push of DOD's political economy toward outsourcing major elements of the AVF's functions—logistics, technology and communications, payroll and administration, and strategic analysis—military benefits have been contracted to the private sector.

In the late 1980s and 1990s, amid the post–Cold War drawdown, the combination of smaller defense budgets and President Bill Clinton's National Performance Review (NPR), popularly called "Reinventing Government," created intense political pressures to outsource benefits. The NPR imported corporate practices of outsourcing and privatization in all government agencies, including the armed forces, to meet budgetary requirements.[52] Clinton named a Wall Street privatization expert for a newly created post at the Pentagon that would privatize and outsource as much as possible.[53]

Meanwhile, when the post–Cold War defense drawdown forced commanders to slash spending and seek savings, they and their staff turned to corporate budget and management strategies. The army joined leading corporations on the Conference Board, created a Captains of Industry Conference, consulted with business schools, and hired scores of consulting firms. In the hopes of reducing budget lines, they sent major elements of soldier- and family-support programs, from housing to health care to counseling to recreation, into the private sector.[54] In the process they transformed the government-provided social-welfare system the AVF had just built into a delegated provision of services handled in large part by private companies.[55] In less than a decade, political leaders, economists, corporate advisors, and military leaders dramatically altered the military's benefits programs from mostly public to mostly private. Servicemembers and their families thus received many benefits from private contractors: doctors contracted by national health-care corporations, managers for multinational real-estate corporation, or contracted social workers staffing family support programs.

Conclusions

Traditional military benefits for active-duty personnel were transformed by the rise of the modern AVF from perquisites of service for limited numbers of career personnel into essential components of military effectiveness, playing vital roles in recruiting, retaining, and maintaining readiness among the volunteer servicemembers. The results generally have been to further distinguish military personnel from civilians through a dedicated wraparound welfare state. But also, the growth of military social-welfare programs has subjected these benefits to some of the politics and trends associated with civilian social welfare. Finally, as central and costly components of the AVF, military benefits have been closely tied to fate of all armed services, which, since the 1990s, have faced a historically unprecedented privatization and outsourcing of their functions to the private sector.

Notes

1. See the following studies: Sar Levitan and Karen Cleary Aldeman, *Warriors at Work: The Volunteer Armed Force* (Beverly Hills, CA: Sage, 1977); Charles Moskos, *The American Enlisted Man* (New York: Russell Sage Foundation, 1970); David R. Segal, "Military Organization and Personnel Accession: What Changed with the AVF . . . and What Didn't," in *Conscripts and Volunteers: Military Requirements, Social Justice, and the All-Volunteer Force*, ed. Robert K. Fullinwider (Totowa, NJ: Rowman and Allanheld, 1983).

2. Beth Bailey, "The Army in the Marketplace: Recruiting an All-Volunteer Force," *Journal of American History* 94, no. 1 (June 2007): 47–74.

3. Department of Defense, Office of the Under Secretary of Defense for Personnel and Readiness, "Population Representation in the Military Services," Fiscal Year 2006, http://www.defenselink.mil/prhome/PopRep_FY06/ (item removed).

4. Levitan and Aldeman, *Warriors at Work*, 95.

5. Unlike European countries that provided nearly universal social welfare to all citizens, the United States had only a patchwork social-welfare system, consisting of various public and private safety nets. So, military benefits and their growth occupied a unique space in the American polity.

6. Andrew Byers, *The Sexual Economy of War: Discipline and Desire in the US Army* (Ithaca, NY: Cornell University Press, 2019), 31.

7. Sondra Albano, "Military Recognition of Family Concerns: Revolutionary War to 1993," *Armed Forces and Society* 20, no. 2 (Winter 1994): 284.

8. Albano, "Military Recognition of Family Concerns," 284–285, 286.

9. Byers, *Sexual Economy of War*, 31.

10. Albano, "Military Recognition of Family Concerns," 286–288.

11. Quoted in Edward Coffman, *The Regulars: The American Army, 1898–1941* (Cambridge, MA: Belknap Press of Harvard University Press, 2004), 259.

12. Albano, "Military Recognition of Family Concerns," 289.

13. *Life*, March 7, 1949, 34–35.

14. Elizabeth Wickenden, *The Military Program and Social Welfare* (New York: National Committee on Social Work in Defense Mobilization, 1955), 23, 23–25.

15. Wickenden, *Military Program and Social Welfare*, 23–25. For the full history of these social-welfare programs, see Jennifer Mittelstadt, *The Rise of the Military Welfare State* (Cambridge, MA: Harvard University Press, 2015).

16. Thanks to Michael Allen for suggesting the useful term "officerization."

17. Robert K. Griffith, *The U.S. Army's Transition to the All-Volunteer Force, 1968–1974* (Washington, DC: Center of Military History, 1996), 37.

18. U.S. Senate, Committee on Armed Services, *Hearings on Selective Service and Military Compensation, Ninety-Second Congress, First Session, February 2, 4, 8, 9, 10, 19, and 22, 1971* (Washington, DC: GPO, 1971), 50.

19. Harold G. Moore, "A Busy Year of the 'Hard Look' at People Policies," *Army Magazine* 25, October 1975, 10, 45.

20. Memorandum, William B. Fulton, Director of the Army Staff, to Assistant Secretary of the Army for Manpower and Reserve Affairs, January 23, 1976, folder 11, box 13, ser. II, All Volunteer Army Collection, U.S. Army Heritage and Education Center, Carlisle, PA, 2. The motto "The Army Takes Care of Its Own" originated during World War II through the Army Emergency Relief Program, a volunteer organization that helped army families in emergencies.

21. Griffith, *U.S. Army's Transition*, 39.

22. Memorandum, Carl S. Wallace, Assistant Secretary of the Army, to Principal Deputy, Assistant Secretary for Defense, October 19, 1973, folder 6, box 7, ser. II, All Volunteer Army Collection, 1–2.

23. Laurie Weinstein and Christie White, *Wives and Warriors: Women and the Military in the United States and Canada* (Westport, CT: Bergin and Garvey, 1997), 27, 28; Levitan and Aldeman, *Warriors at Work*, 16, 56.

24. U.S. Senate, Committee on Armed Services, *Hearings on Selective Service and Military Compensation*, 41, 46.

25. Rep. Bob Wilson (R-CA) quoted in "Jr. EM Travel Pay Pushed," *Army Times*, May 29, 1978, 22.

26. SSGT (E-5) Larent P. Fronts, USAF, letter to the editor, *Times Magazine*, August 7, 1978, 35.

27. Joan Hodges, letter to the editor, *Times Magazine*, August 7, 1978, 42.

28. Memorandum, Robert G. Nivens to Lieutenant Colonel Doctor, June 7, 1972, Final Evaluation Report, Modern Volunteer Army Experiment, Fort Benning, GA, July 1972, folder 2, box 8, ser. II, All Volunteer Army Collection, Tab B-155.

29. Memorandum, Nivens to Lieutenant Colonel Doctor, inclusion 26.

30. Advertisement, "Want Your Soldier to Re-Enlist?," *Army Times*, September 19, 1975, 17.

31. "G. I. Dependents: Aid and Comfort," *Time*, April 14, 1980, 67.

32. Mady Weschler Segal and Jesse J. Harris, *What We Know about Army Families* (Alexandria, VA: U.S. Army Research Institute for the Behavioral and Social Sciences, 1993), 26, 27, 29.

33. Segal and Harris, *What We Know about Army Families*, 27.

34. U.S. Army, Office of the Deputy Chief of Staff for Personnel, *The Army Family Action Plan III* (Washington, DC: U.S. Army Chief of Staff, 1986), 42, 43.

35. Segal and Harris, *What We Know about Army Families*, 26.

36. Segal and Harris, *What We Know about Army Families*, 30.

37. Comptroller of the Army, *The Army Budget: Fiscal Year 1988–89* (Washington, DC: U.S. Department of the Army, 1987), 73.

38. List from Zahava D. Doering and Bette S. Mahoney, "Briefing Notes: A Discussion of Military Dependents' Issues," March 18, 1986, Defense Manpower Data Center, Arlington, VA, Center for Military History Collection, 29; Comptroller of the Army, *The Army Budget: Fiscal Year 1986* (Washington, DC: U.S. Department of the Army, 1985), 94; Comptroller, *Army Budget: Fiscal Year 1988–89*, 73; John Wickham, "Leadership Is Key in Coping with Wide Threat Spectrum: Annual Army Green Book Report of the Chief of Staff, 1985–86," October 1985, in *Collected Works of the Thirtieth Chief of Staff, U.S. Army: John A. Wickham Jr., General, United States Army, Chief of Staff, June 1983–June 1987* (Washington, DC: U.S. Army Center of Military History, 1987), 126; and John Wickham, "Opening Statement before the Armed Services Committee, U.S. Senate, Washington, DC, February 5, 1987," ibid., 212.

39. Quote from Tom Ricks, "The Great Society in Camouflage," *The Atlantic*, December 1996, 24.

40. Mady Wechsler Segal, "The Military and the Family as Greedy Institutions," *Armed Forces and Society*, January 1986.

41. "The Military-Civilian Gap: Fewer Family Connections," Pew Research Center: Social and Demographic Trends, November 23, 2011, https://www.pewsocialtrends.org/2011/11/23/the-military-civilian-gap-fewer-family-connections/ (accessed September 10, 2020); Segal and Harris, "What We Know about Army Families," 55.

42. Moskos, *American Enlisted Man*, 70.

43. Alan Derickson, *Health Care for All: Dreams of Universal Health Care in America* (Baltimore: Johns Hopkins University Press, 2005); Sonya Michel, *Children's Interests, Mothers Rights: The Shaping of American Child Care Policy* (New Haven, CT: Yale University Press, 1999); Brian Steensland, *The Failed Welfare Revolution: America's Struggle over Guaranteed Income Policy* (Princeton, NJ: Princeton University Press, 2008).

44. G. A. "Sandy" Mackenzie, *The Decline of the Traditional Pension: A Comparative Study of Threats to Retirement Security* (Cambridge: Cambridge University Press, 2010).

45. Jerry Reed, "An Analysis and Evaluation of the U.S. Army: The Beard Study," appendix to U.S. Senate, Committee on Armed Services, *Status of the All-Volunteer Armed Force: Hearing before the Subcommittee on Manpower and Personnel, Ninety-Fifth Congress, Second Session, June 20, 1978* (Washington, DC: GPO, 1978), 141, 257.

46. "Family Support: Desert Storm AAR," May 29, 1991, folder 407, box 24, U.S. Army Heritage and Education Center, Carlisle, PA, 1; D. Bruce Bell et al., "Helping U.S. Army Families Cope with Stresses of Troop Deployment to Bosnia-Herzegovina," paper presented at the 1997 Inter-University Seminar on Armed Forces and Society Biennial International Conference, Baltimore, MD, October 24–26, 1997, Military Families Collection, Center of Military History, Washington, DC.

47. "Family Support: Desert Storm AAR," 1.

48. "Family Support: Desert Storm AAR," 1.

49. "Memorandum from Rice to Evan Gaddis (BG) et al., Subject: Knight Ridder Interview," n.d., folder Media Queries, 1997, box 26, Harriet Rice Papers, U.S. Army Heritage and Education Center, Carlisle, PA.

50. Chris Murray, "Basic Training for Army Families," *Army Times*, November 22, 1993, 12, 13; "Information Paper, Subject: Family Readiness Groups, CFSC-SF-A," February 8, 2000, folder Papers from the Commanders Conference—Carlisle—24 FEB 2000, Military Families Collection, Center of Military History, Washington, DC.

51. "Briefing Slides," folder Community and Family Support Center Briefing Slides, box 15, Harriet Rice Papers.

52. Inspiration for Reinventing Government came from David Osborne and Ted Gaebler, *Reinventing Government: How the Entrepreneurial Spirit Is Transforming the Public Sector* (New York: Penguin, 1993), cover, 31, 45. On the importance of outsourcing in the NPR, see, for example, Alice M. Rivlin, OMB, "NPR Phase II: Remarks," December 1994, National Performance Review Papers, University of North Texas, http://govinfo.library.unt.edu/npr/library/speeches/234a.html.

53. Transcript, Joshua Gotbaum radio interview, *The Business of Government Hour*, October 2, 2000, IBM Center for the Business of Government, https://www.businessofgovernment.org/sites/default/files/JG.txt; U.S. Senate, Committee on Armed Services, *Statement of Joshua Gotbaum, Assistant Secretary of Defense (Economic Security), before the Subcommittees on Personnel and Readiness*, 104th Cong., 1st sess., May 15, 1995.

54. CMH, *DAHSUM: FY 2000* (Washington, DC: GPO, 2011), 103–104; Assistant Secretary of the Army for Installations and Environment, "RCI Plan: Where We Are Now," 2010, www.rci.army.mil/programinformation/rcioverview.html (item removed). The privatized health-care program, TRICARE, began in 1993.

55. See Kimberly Morgan and Andrea Louise Campbell, *The Delegated Welfare State: Medicare, Markets, and the Governance of Social Policy* (Oxford: Oxford University Press, 2011).

7

Socioeconomics

Titus Firmin

Conventional wisdom holds that the U.S. all-volunteer force was, and is, a poor man's army because only Americans without other opportunities would be willing to fight and die for a paycheck. After 1973, many observers noted the overrepresentation of poor and working-class Americans in the AVF, particularly in the U.S. Army. That impression persists, despite that recruits are more likely to have graduated high school than their peers and more come from the middle to upper socioeconomic quintile than from the bottom.[1] It is true that during the first twenty-five years of the volunteer army, many recruits came from poor and working-class backgrounds as a result of the draft. Still, in the last twenty-five years, the AVF pivoted to provide a solid middle-class army.

The idea that the U.S. Army is currently made up of the poor is as politically problematic as it is inaccurate. The common belief that most recruits who join the military are from poor and working-class backgrounds was fed by reality and myth through popular culture and movies about the Vietnam War.[2] Indeed, the draft and such initiatives as Project 100,000 channeled many poor and working-class men into the army during the Vietnam War. Yet research suggests that a person's belief of why they think recruits join reveals more about their own political affiliations and leanings. Political conservatives generally believe recruits enlist for patriotic reasons, while liberals contend soldiers join for primarily financial reasons.[3] The belief that the army is composed of America's poor and working class is a vestige of Vietnam and the subsequent culture wars. Misconceptions about who serves when not all serve may exacerbate societal divisions based on politics and class when, at this time, many Americans already believe gross economic inequality and political polarization is a danger to our nation.

Servicemembers frequently hear expressions of appreciation—"thank you for your service"—and receive free meals while in uniform. Over the course of the last twenty years, many servicemembers have deployed at least once, still, even deserving soldiers may feel uncomfortable to be showered with such praise and generosity. They may find themselves asking, "why do they think I need money?" While the AVF may be physically integrated within American society, a significant disconnect exists between the perception and reality of who serves when not all serve.

The U.S. Army's pursuit of high-tech equipment and quality soldiers reshaped it from a poor and working-class into a middle-class force in the decades after the Vietnam War. Over the past fifty years, in response to changes in policy and doctrine, army leaders reorganized units and rethought how they prepared for war. First, after Vietnam, the army grappled with how to fight outnumbered against modern Soviet forces. Second, victory in the Cold War and the Persian Gulf War created the expectation that the army, whatever its size, would succeed throughout the spectrum of conflict from peacekeeping to large-scale combat operations. Finally, the shock of the terrorist attacks of 9/11 and the subsequent Global War on Terrorism saw the army shift from conventional warfare to counterinsurgency. These reorganizations gradually moved the army toward a high-tech American Expeditionary Force. Each restructuring demanded higher-quality recruits from increasingly advantaged backgrounds and shifted the class composition of new enlistees from America's poor to the American middle class.

This chapter is synthetic and relies on the scholarship of eminent historians as well as official accounts and doctrine from the U.S. Army and the Center for Military History. Its penultimate argument—that the class-composition of the AVF is predominantly middle class—relies on social-science research. But ascertaining class composition has proved difficult because the Department of Defense in 1982 stopped reporting and collecting information about the socioeconomic background of recruits. Therefore, census tract data informs the conclusion that the U.S. Army is a thoroughly middle-class institution.

In addition, force structure refers to the combat capabilities of a military organization that constitutes how personnel, their weapons, and materiel are organized to accomplish their mission and tasks based on service doctrine or actual circumstances in the field. While the purview of this book covers the AVF, this chapter specifically focuses on the U.S. Army to explain how force structure has changed the army since 1973 and challenges the notion of the "poor man's army."

Historiography

Few scholars give much thought to how the U.S. Army organizes to fight the nation's wars during the AVF era. Those who do examine the structure of the institution usually focus on recruitment, personnel policies and benefits, and family support programs. In the 1970s and 1980s, army recruitment campaigns promoted generous pay and benefits to dismiss the idea that many soldiers joined from poor and working-class backgrounds. Recruitment and retention were crucial to meet the army's strength goals and indirectly supported the national military strategy and the army's accompanying operational posture between 1973 and 2023. Still, service and support elements exist to sustain combat operations.

Some of the first scholars to focus on the class demographics of the AVF, specifically race, were sociologists Charles Moskos and Jon Sibley Butler. In their 1996 work *All That We Can Be*, they argued that the army achieved successful, albeit imperfect, racial integration largely due to the middle-class origins and values of the majority of soldiers.[4] Moskos and Butler praised the army as a model for racial integration and equal opportunity for Americans to truly be all that they can be. But they did not consider how the army filled its ranks with middle-class soldiers to successfully obtain relative racial equanimity.

Beth Bailey, in *America's Army*, recognized that recruiting efforts and goals were shaped by changes to the army's mission, emerging technology, and doctrinal shifts since Vietnam.

> America's army—even its enlisted ranks—is fairly solidly middle class. . . . Young people from America's poorest families, by and large, don't meet current army standards. They are more likely to have dropped out of high school. Poor schools leave them ill-prepared for written qualification tests. They are more likely than their peers to have criminal convictions or significant health problems. In times of peace, for those who see the army as a site of intervention and producer of social good, such standards seem to discriminate against the poor. In times of war, they could be seen as a protection from exploitation. So while most upper- and upper middle-class youth make other choices, and the poor find themselves with one fewer option, the army draws primarily from those in between.[5]

Bailey demonstrates that the army eventually obtained its recruitment focus on higher-quality recruits over time, in part, because the level of sophistication required of soldiers increased and the end strength of the army declined dramatically in the years following the war in Vietnam.

In *The Rise of the Military Welfare State*, Jennifer Mittelstadt focuses on how financial incentives and support programs offered by the army enticed poor and working-class Americans to enlist after the switch to the AVF. She originally approached the topic from the field of welfare history. While some historians reject her use of the term "welfare" for what are essentially job benefits, Mittelstadt emphasizes that many of the benefits offered fall into the category of social welfare: free medical and dental coverage; allowances for food, clothing, and housing; and subsidized childcare.[6] She suggests that these benefits, coupled with the scarcity of enlistees with college degrees, noticeably attracted poor and working-class Americans. While she details substantial changes to the army's family and soldier support programs during the 1970s and 1980s, Mittelstadt does not examine changes to the army's doctrine and force structure.

Several other works are significant here. William A. Taylor, in his broader study *Military Service and American Democracy*, shows that shifts in personnel policies made military service more inclusive for African Americans, women, gays, and lesbians and also served to redefine citizenship. Taylor suggests that, at various times, changes in organization, personnel policy, and military service leveled inequalities related to race, class, gender, and sexuality. A model for this essay is Brian Linn's *Elvis's Army*. Linn focuses on the period preceding the AVF and analyzes the relationship between Pentomic reorganization and the social demographics of the Cold War army.[7] He contends that the army's only tangible revolutionary claim in the 1950s was that it was one of the first and only egalitarian institutions in American society regardless of class or race. Linn and Taylor both provide a useful blueprint for understanding the relationship between the military's organizational structure and socioeconomic demographics.

Class matters because, in the early years of the AVF, the army thought it mattered. Army officers defined high-quality recruits as those with at least a high school diploma and who scored in the top-two quantiles on the Armed Services Vocational Aptitude Battery (ASVAB). Typically, recruits with a high school or some college education scored better on entrance exams, which also generally transferred to better-than-average performance in service. This definition of quality enlistees established assumptions about class. A recruit who dropped out of high school or had a General Educational Diploma (GED) came from a poor or working-poor background, a high school graduate came from a solidly working-class or lower middle-class background, while a recruit with some college education or a degree was a product of a middle-class background. While a sturdy indicator, these assumptions are problematic given that other gauges of quality and class exist and that many recruits join between the ages of seventeen and twenty-four years old with little work experience and education that does not factor in their middle-class backgrounds. Educational obtainment as an indicator of quality recruits and as a proxy of their class or socioeconomic status continues to inform the army and much of society.

Income and education are common metrics for determining class in the United States because of accessible source material. Class is historically difficult to define because of inflation, class indicators, and the quality of life associated to specific groups continue to change over time. In addition, self-reporting is faulty because the majority of Americans self-identify themselves as middle class regardless if their annual family income is less than $40,000 or more than $200,000.[8] For the purpose of definition, this chapter relies on sociologist Dennis Gilbert's stratification of class in the United States into six distinct groups (see the illustration following).[9] In the absence of data on income or wealth, scholars also examine educational obtainment as a stand-in. Still, education as a metric for class is less than ideal because, historically, many Americans acquire middle-class income with simply a high school diploma.[10] Wealth or financial assets are a better determination of class or socioeconomic status, yet that information is far more difficult to obtain. Homeownership used to be an indicator of middle-class status, but the subprime mortgage crisis and the Great Recession revealed that homes may not be a reliable asset for those aspiring toward the middle class. In addition, the average price of a home sold in the United States increased from $257,000 in 2009 to roughly $543,000 in 2022.[11] This data suggests regular Americans cannot afford the average home and that homeownership is an indicator of upper-class status. Far from perfect, educational obtainment and income are good indicators of class in the United States, but they are not the only ones.

Acknowledgment of socioeconomic demographics is made more difficult due to a lack of data. Army recruitment data on enlistees has not been collected since 1982, when the Military Manpower Task Force announced, "the social origins of those who freely choose to accept the burdens and benefits of military service should not be a recruiting criterion" and that no effort should be made to "attempt to identify recruits by social origin."[12] Faced with a lack of information, scholars since have relied on outdated and anecdotal evidence to maintain that the army is a refuge for the poor. Military service has often had a compressing effect on social, racial, and class divisions. Still, when the army has served as a vehicle for socioeconomic uplift or reflected a more diverse American society, it has been within the confines of its mission to close with and destroy the enemy in ground combat. The volunteer army is organized around deploying, fighting, and winning America's land wars as part of a joint force across the global spectrum of conflict. Thus, its structure is organized around its ability to defend the nation or to wage war. Given

Class	Education	Income	Population (%)
Poor	Some High School	$17,238.92	1
Working Poor	Some High School or GED	$29,306.17	15
Working	High School or GED	$60,336.23	34
Lower Middle	High School or College	$103,433.53	30
Upper Middle	College and Postgraduate	$215,487.53	16
Elites	Prestigious College	$1,723,892.22	1

Educational Obtainment and Income
The six distinct socioeconomic classes in the United States are here illustrated by their education, income, and percent of the total U.S. population.

the immense scale of such a task, some scholars may miss the army's primary and institutional purpose—war.

Over the last three decades, various scholars have explored the class composition of the volunteer army. Some of their studies concentrate on the changes in force structure. A few have combined examinations of force structure and class composition in depth. Still, most scholars treat force structure and the class composition of the AVF as separate topics.

Previous historians have emphasized the racial and gendered aspects and changes while acknowledging the army's middle-class aspirations and status. Still, scholars of the AVF generally focus on whether the racial and gender demographics within the army change over time and how they have shaped its relationship with civilian society. The primary argument of this chapter relies on these assessments and offers a causal explanation of the relationship between the all-volunteer army and class.

Background

In the United States, the president establishes national-security policy, then military leaders shape their strategy to fulfil the president's charted policy or doctrine. In the process, they determine the size, organization, and type of military forces, resources, and necessary training required to accomplish the desired objectives. Because Congress retains the power of the purse and the authority to declare war, military leaders propose budgets that will allow them to fulfill their commander's intent. Generally, if lawmakers approve the military's requested budget, then Congress tacitly approves the president's national-security policy.

Prior to World War II, military planners prepared the United States to simultaneously fight a global conflict in two separate major theaters and a third minor theater to extinguish a small war or insurgency. During the Korean War, the U.S. armed forces were still structured to fight "2½ wars," after which President Dwight D. Eisenhower's policy of Massive Retaliation and New Look with nuclear weapons seemingly negated the need to fight a traditional conflict in two separate ground theaters. The administrations of John F. Kennedy and Lyndon B. Johnson developed the policy of Flexible Response, and the Reorganization Objective Army Division (ROAD) instructed the military, especially the army, to fight limited and small wars short of nuclear conflict. In 1969, President Richard M. Nixon's so-called Guam Doctrine, however, instructed army leaders to prepare for a "1½ war" contingency—one major and one minor theater of conflict.

Simultaneously, Nixon instructed military leaders to be prepared to fight a 1½ war and transition to the AVF. In the two decades after the Vietnam War, army leaders concentrated the volunteer force's training, equipment, organization, and doctrine on fighting the Soviet Union in Europe in a short war of maneuver with heavy tanks and mechanized infantry. This focused investment in a numerically smaller army was significant. Between 1969 and 1989, the size of the active-duty U.S. Army shrunk by 49 percent, resulting in 742,428 fewer soldiers.[13] As the army reorganized and invested in technology to overcome its numeric disadvantage, the need for qualitatively superior soldiers increased throughout the late Cold War and beyond.

Such plans for a quality, high-tech force reshaped the social composition of the army. Military leaders realized that without the draft, the Soviet Union overwhelmingly outnumbered the United States and its allies. As a result, the army acquired better equipment and more skilled and educated soldiers to even the odds. That decision was validated by its performance in the Persian Gulf War, as the quality of its personnel and organization mattered much more than sheer numbers. Preference for technology and quality recruits continued throughout the 1990s, as U.S. political leaders compelled the army to restructure the force again. The post–Cold War peace dividend allowed the army to select higher-quality recruits from more advantaged backgrounds as its numbers continued to shrink. The shock of the terrorist attacks of 9/11 and the surge of soldiers needed in Afghanistan and Iraq spurred one of the latest organizational restructurings, which required soldiers with even greater levels of education, skills, and training to meet a host of complex global challenges. As a result, since the 1990s, middle-class Americans are overrepresented in the ranks of the U.S. Army.

Active Defense to AirLand Battle

In the first two decades of the AVF, army leaders restructured training, doctrine, and equipment to focus on limited conflict, short of nuclear war, in Western Europe. They rewrote doctrine and reorganized units in anticipation of massive clashes similar to the Battle of Kursk, fought between the Nazis and Soviets during World War II. In preparation, the army invested in soldier education and training to prepare them for World War III. Soviet forces outnumbered the U.S. Army and its European allies; still, army leaders developed and acquired high-tech weapons systems to ensure they would not be outmatched on the battlefield.

As the commander of the U.S. Army's Training and Doctrine Command (TRADOC), General William E. DePuy later believed he oversaw a "historic turning point in the evolution of the army" and, through doctrine, reshaped the army's officer corps. The 1973 Arab-Israeli War convinced DePuy that the Warsaw Pact planned to fight a quick ground war before the United States and its NATO allies could mobilize. By the time American reinforcements arrived, Soviet armies would already be at the English Channel and in possession of Western European cities, making nuclear retaliation untenable. The brainchild of DePuy, *FM 100-5, Operations* (1976), which formed the basis of the Active Defense doctrine, declared, "battle in Central Europe against forces of the Warsaw Pact is the most demanding mission the US Army could be assigned."[14] Active Defense prescribed formulaic force ratios and mass firepower for defending units. DePuy calculated how army divisions might defend against Soviet forces with current and future weapons.

DePuy recommended an increased number of technicians and combat-support troops to sustain significantly fewer, more specialized combat soldiers and units in the field.[15] Even individual combat soldiers became increasingly specialized. Recruits who enlisted in the infantry were assigned a military occupancy specialty of 11X until they were designated as an 11B light infantry, 11C mortarman, 11M mechanized Bradley, 11H antiarmor, or stayed 11X until they completed special-forces training and were then classified as 18 series MOS. Units remained unchanged at the company level, however authority to request fire support was removed from the company commander and required authorization from the battalion commander.[16] DePuy's TRADOC successor, General Donald Starry, worried such processes hindered speed and stifled junior leaders from exercising battlefield initiative and so created the Division 86 study to improve on Active Defense.

General Starry's Division 86 reexamined Active Defense's doctrinal organization and recommended new weapons and equipment to enable army leaders and soldiers to outwit and outfight their adversary. The study group proposed delegation of authority and span of control down to junior leaders at the company level as well as reorganized heavy armored divisions with six tank battalions and four mechanized-infantry battalions. Known as Army 86, this study proposed various changes to unit organization so that infantry divisions, corps, and larger could be lighter to transport and deploy rapidly. The argument of some army officers that light infantry divisions were, to quote one critique's title, "Not Light Enough to Get There, Not Heavy Enough to Win," led to an inconclusive search for high-tech experiments with the motorized Ninth Infantry Division at Fort Lewis, Washington.[17] Still, the army adopted the findings of Division 86 prior to the approval and publication of AirLand Battle, or *FM 100-5, Operations*, in 1982.

Starry's AirLand Battle officially replaced DePuy's Active Defense as the army's operational doctrine, yet both focused on modern land warfare in Europe against a numerically superior adversary. The most noticeable differences between the two were at the tactical and operational levels as well as questioning what type of fighting disposition and spirit army units should possess for victory. AirLand Battle valued maneuver over the defense to "use the advantages of surprise, psychological shock, position, and momentum which enable smaller forces to defeat larger ones." *FM 100-5* (1982) also promoted the concept of deep battle to disrupt second-wave Soviet forces with air assets. The dispersion of forces over a large area required reliable technology to communicate and coordinate fire support on the battlefield. Deep battle also made it necessary for soldiers to exercise decentralized leadership initiative and synchronize movement, fires, and communications at the tactical and operational levels.[18] Both Active Defense and AirLand Battle recommended sophisticated heavy armor and mechanized weapons systems for the army to succeed on the battlefield.[19]

The Big Five

The army's smaller, reorganized units needed increased speed, survivability, lines of communication, and lethality to defeat a larger enemy. Both Active Defense and AirLand Battle called for armor and mechanized forces to "fight outnumbered and win," and they resulted in the development of five main weapons systems: the M1 Abrams main battle tank, UH-60 Blackhawk utility helicopter, AH-64 Apache attack helicopter, M2/3 Bradley Infantry Fighting Vehicle, and a new family of mechanized air-defense vehicles and precision-guided artillery and rocket systems and munitions.[20] Leaders calculated that with high-tech weapons systems, the army could defeat a Soviet army three times its size.[21]

The M1 Abrams balanced speed, protection, communications, and firepower. Its low-profile hull composed of layers of ceramic and metal balanced mobility and armor. A high-tech fire-control system stabilized the 105/120-mm cannon to fire accurately even while moving. The laser rangefinder, thermal night sights, and digital gunnery system only required a four-person crew.

Designers planned for the M2/3 Bradley IFV to accompany the M1 Abrams, but it also needed to carry enough infantrymen. The Bradley functioned as a mobile firebase, with its 25-mm cannon, 7.62-mm machine gun, and antiarmor TOW missiles. Its personnel capacity, however, fell short of an infantry rifle squad and thus required changes in tactical doctrine.[22]

The third weapons system developed by the army was the AH-64 Apache attack helicopter. Equipped with night-vision and high-tech targeting-device systems, the Apache was heavily armed with a 30-mm chain gun, high-precision Hellfire missiles, and rockets. Less striking yet just as important, the UH-60 Blackhawk utility helicopter provided quick troop transport for an infantry squad or could transport artillery.

Finally, the Patriot missile system, equipped with computer-guided missiles and radar apparatus, made it versatile against enemy aircraft and ballistic missiles. In addition to these five weapons systems, the army also developed the Multiple-Launch Rocket System (MLRS), the high-mobility multipurpose wheeled vehicle (HMMWV), and a host of other modern communications, intelligence, and information systems.[23]

Army leaders secured sophisticated, high-tech military hardware and weapons systems to survive and thrive in a hypothetical war with Soviet armies. Outnumbered badly, the U.S. Army augmented its smaller forces with sophisticated weapons and support systems to increase firepower, communications, speed, and protection on the battlefield. Weapons modernization provided the ability to win against an enemy three times more numerous. Still, these high-tech systems required trained officers and planners, as well as skilled technicians and combat-support troops, to sustain them and the army.

"Train as You Fight"

Armed with such new military hardware, army leaders recognized that they also needed the soldiers necessary to operate, troubleshoot, and coordinate these high-tech systems at the tactical and operational level.

Throughout the 1970s and 1980s, they heavily invested in education, training, and assessment of the volunteer army at the unit and individual levels. Hi-tech systems required new MOSs and skilled training as well as soldiers who could pass the training. The army designed various realistic exercises that tested soldiers' knowledge, training, and leadership skills.

Officials viewed training and education as vital to ensure troops were prepared for the rigors of battle. For officers, at each key career point, training schools furthered their grasp of the concepts and language of AirLand Battle from second lieutenant to lieutenant colonel.[24] In 1983, the Advanced Military Studies Program taught at the School of Advanced Military Studies (SAMS) was established by the U.S. Army Command and General Staff College (CGSC) at Fort Leavenworth, Kansas. SAMS functioned as an additional one-year honors course for captains and majors as planning officers at the CGSC.[25] Professional military education was also required for noncommissioned officers starting at their local NCO academies and concluding with the Sergeants Major Academy at Fort Bliss, Texas. An officer could expect to spend one out of every four years in some sort of school, either as a student or as an instructor.[26]

After soldiers acquired the requisite knowledge and skills through professional military education, the army tested them. At the most basic, units conducted regular evaluations through the Army Training and Evaluation Program (ARTEP). Followed by periodical stints at the army's recently established training centers, soldiers conducted realistic joint- and field-training exercises. They scrimmaged against other troops posing as oppositional forces in mock battles armed with blank ammunition, simulated munitions, lasers, and advanced sensors to realistically replicate combat.[27] Heavy tank and mechanized infantry units within the United States attended the National Training Center at Fort Irwin, California, while those in Europe conducted exercises at the Combat Maneuver Training Center (CMTC) at Hohenfels, Germany. Light infantry units attended field exercises at the Joint Readiness Training Center (JRTC) at Fort Polk, Louisiana.[28] In addition, soldiers conducted regular coalition exercises, including REFORGER (Return of Force to Germany), Team Spirit in Korea, and Bright Star with Egypt.[29] Continual evaluations and intense field exercises certified whether soldiers could coordinate and apply schoolhouse doctrine, operations, and tactics with their high-tech equipment in a combat environment.

Starting in the late 1970s and throughout the 1980s, army leaders invested significant time and resources to ensure soldiers had high-tech equipment and realistic training. Greater emphasis on professional military education trained officers and NCOs to plan, coordinate, and lead units with complex and sophisticated equipment. The army increasingly relied on technology to enhance training to test its high-quality soldiers through numerous scenarios and exercises for certification.

Transformation and Terrorism

Interventions in Lebanon, Grenada, and Panama revealed that U.S. Army units needed to be more flexible and rapidly deployable. The victory of the Persian Gulf War, however, validated the Cold War concentration on high-tech, heavy armor, and mechanized infantry. In addition, between 1987 and 1997, congressional budget cuts and base realignment and closure (BRAC) reduced the army by 289,108 soldiers, or 62.9 percent.[30] Still, President William J. Clinton's national-security strategy sought to advance U.S. interests through broadened engagements and interventions overseas but with a substantially smaller force.[31]

Throughout the 1990s, army leaders were tasked with even more complex missions beyond traditional battlefield operations. Rapid deployments for raids and humanitarian operations demonstrated the value of special-forces units as well as the army's reliance on technology, such as digital network-centric warfare, GPS, night-vision devices, unmanned aerial vehicles (UAVs), and precision-guided missiles. Effective command and control relied on advanced communications equipment to coordinate over vast geographic areas and conduct joint operations with various governmental organizations and nongovernment organizations as well as host nation and allied military partners. After President Clinton appointed him army chief of staff in 1999, General Eric K. Shinseki revealed new doctrine in *FM 3-0, Operations* (2001) for full-spectrum operations intended to enhance the army's expeditionary capabilities. Shinseki also initiated the development of the Stryker—a wheeled, light-armor infantry vehicle that could operate more easily in urban environments and be transported on the U.S. Air Force's C-130 and C-17 cargo aircraft. In order to rapidly deploy the U.S. Army anywhere on the globe, Shinseki's reforms of the 1990s continued its reliance on high-tech equipment and skilled soldiers.

The terrorist attacks on September 11, 2001, disrupted the army's planned transformation and drastically increased its missions despite its small size. Army leaders struggled to simultaneously conduct counterinsurgency operations in Afghanistan and Iraq while also developing new doctrine. Still, a joint effort by Lieutenant General David H. Petraeus of the army and Lieutenant General James F. Amos of the marine corps produced *FM 3-24, Counterinsurgency* (2006). Army leaders configured the modular brigade combat teams for counterinsurgency operations.

Cavalry, field artillery, and armor soldiers found themselves tasked with low-tech convoy missions and grunt roles, such as dismounted patrols in villages and along dusty roads. Still, between 2003 and 2011, Afghan and Iraqi insurgents relied on low-tech improvised explosive devices (IEDs) with deadly results. A small army conducting counterinsurgency operations and facing the invisible threat of IEDs necessitated armored vehicles; individual body armor for soldiers; mine-resistant, ambush-protected vehicles (MRAPs); vehicle cage armor; and various other anti-insurgency accoutrements. In addition, the size of the active-duty army grew from 480,000 in 2001 to a peak of 565,000 in 2011—roughly 85,000 soldiers in the span of ten years.[32] Military leaders in the 1990s had prepared a small U.S. Army for the full spectrum of operations, yet the impetus of the Global War on Terrorism inhibited such a development and abruptly focused the force on countering two different insurgencies.

Political considerations also shaped the size and force structure of the army. In 2008, presidential candidate Barack Obama campaigned on ending the war in Iraq. Still, after his inauguration as president, the number of soldiers on active duty increased in 2009–2010 by about 23,000 as the war in Iraq wound down and fighting in Afghanistan surged.[33] In 2011, President Obama withdrew U.S. forces from Iraq after negotiations over the Status of Forces Agreement with that country's government broke down. But the rise of the Islamic State in Syria and the Levant (ISIL) in 2013 resulted in the redeployment of the U.S. military to Iraq and then into Syria. Between 2011 and 2015, however, the size of the army shrunk by over 75,000 soldiers.[34] By 2019 the active-duty strength of the army was 479,000, roughly 1,000 fewer soldiers than in 2001, as U.S. forces shifted focus toward China in the Indo-Pacific region. Between 2001 and 2020, the size of the army fluctuated significantly in response to various military threats and policy decisions.

Army leaders continue to work toward preparing the force despite shifting political considerations, military challenges, and resource constraints. The U.S. Army Futures Command has sought to modernize, develop, and acquire new weapons systems for great-power competition and prepare for the entire spectrum of conflict. With fewer soldiers and resources, army leaders have worked toward multidomain operations/battle or joint all-domain operations to enhance the interoperability between the army, navy, marine corps, air force, and the nascent space force. Doctrine, force structure, equipment, and soldier training continue to be vital, especially given technological developments in cyber, space, and artificial intelligence. Still, the quality and quantity of U.S. soldiers also matters, whether the task is related to cyber, counterinsurgency, or urban operations. In 2018, the U.S. Army had 122,000 fewer active-duty sol-

The active-duty strength of the U.S. Army was smaller in 2018 than before the outbreak of the Korean War in 1950. Data for 1951 and 1952 are unavailable. (Courtesy Defense Manpower Data Center)

diers than in 1950 before the outbreak of the Korean War. Technological advancements, military budgets, political considerations, and multiplying problems remain common topics in American military history; thus, the size of the army continues historically on a downward trajectory.

The end of the draft and the advent of the AVF in 1973 forced the army to reorganize combat units based on the reality that, in a future conflict, they would have to compete against numerically superior adversaries. Leadership envisioned that a potential World War III would involve massive tank battles and quick strikes from combined-arms maneuver units. In support of this vision, they developed new military equipment and weapons systems during the 1970s and 1980s. Advancements in strategy and doctrine guided army officers as they reorganized, reequipped, and retrained soldiers for the challenge of the Cold War. Investments in high-tech weapons systems provided a distinct edge and emphasized the need for greater soldier education and training. Army leaders invested in soldier skills, education, and training to increase the quality and lethality of U.S. forces against a numerically larger foe.

Despite the celebratory end of the Cold War and victory in the Persian Gulf War, the U.S. Army has been uniquely challenged since the early 1990s. The disintegration of the Soviet Union enabled the expansion of the U.S. military globally for various missions and operations other than war. Simultaneously, the army coped with substantial reductions in personnel and funding. Army leaders positioned for a force-structure transformation similar to the post–Vietnam War era, but the primacy of the Global War on Terrorism stifled their efforts. Since 2001, officials and officers have adapted to varied conditions and constraints imposed by this new type of war but are now positioning the force for renewed great-power competition.

Over the past fifty years, the missions assigned to the U.S. Army have increased in number as well as complexity. Simultaneously, the overall size of the force has decreased as the requirement for high-tech equipment and the complexity of operations necessitated highly educated, skilled, and trained soldiers.

Class Composition of the Volunteer Army

While many who enlist do so for financial incentive, that in and of itself does not define recruits as poor or working class in origin—their family income and wealth does. Historically, class is difficult to define. Still, what do the claims about poor and working-class recruits reveal about those who make them?[35] How do their assumptions about income diverge from how much middle-class American families actually earn? How much do they presume poor and working-class Americans make?[36] How little or how much money do they believe these poor, working-class soldiers make when basic pay, allowances, and allotments are considered? The disconnect between Americans may be amusing when someone like Bill Gates cannot guess the price of grocery staples, but it may be disastrous if Americans are uninformed about who actually serves in the armed forces when not all do. The high-tech force structure has increasingly attracted middle-class recruits who qualify to enlist in the army since the 1990s.

Today, the volunteer U.S. Army primarily comprises middle-class recruits. That, however, was not always the case. Uneven draft policies during the Vietnam era produced an army of primarily poor and working-class soldiers who the AVF then built upon. In the late 1950s to the early 1960s, American officials expressed concern that stringent enlistment criteria excluded poor and working-class men from providing service to the nation. As a result, defense officials and policymakers pushed for increased military participation from these groups while the United States deployed large numbers of troops to Vietnam.[37] Casualties then suggested that Vietnam was a working-class war, which elicited a backlash of demands from the American public that included withdrawal from Indochina and the end of the draft.

After 1973, the AVF continued to attract poor and working-class recruits similar to those drafted during Vietnam. Organizational reform within the army during the late 1970s and 1980s, however, gradually re-quired more middle-class recruits and slowly raised enlistment criteria as military pay and benefits increased. By the 1990s, U.S. politicians re-duced the number of active-duty soldiers in the army by nearly half, yet the number and complexity of overseas deployments increased. Still, sig-nificant reductions in force allowed the army to cut less-skilled soldiers, who tended to be poorer recruits, and gradually enlist new members who met relatively more rigorous criteria, many from middle-class families. After the 9/11 terrorist attacks, more eligible recruits from middle- and upper-middle-class families enlisted to prosecute the wars in Afghanistan and Iraq. Despite concerns about lowered standards and the quality of soldiers, middle-class recruits joined in greater proportions than both poor and wealthy Americans. In addition, middle-class recruits primarily enlisted in combat arms and made up a disproportionate number of casu-alties in the Global War on Terrorism.

In the early years of the Cold War, army leaders dreamed of a futur-istic high-tech Pentomic reorganization and modernization to transform the service into a flexible and mobile force. In a 1957 lecture at the Army War College, Major General Donald Booth argued: "The ground warfare of the future will be won by the Army that has the greatest innovations in mobility, firepower, and dispersion. Success cannot be won by units clut-tered with sub-caliber personnel."[38] Still, the U.S. Army did not possess the necessary personnel for such a desired force structure. Army lead-ers spent considerable resources and time providing education to poor and working-class draftees. These modernization efforts did not succeed. Still, they succeeded at creating a force that was comparatively egalitarian and representative of society in terms of class. During the 1950s, the U.S. Army was the most egalitarian institution in American society, where men of all races and social backgrounds came together.

Army budget cuts during the 1950s, combined with the draft, allowed the army to more selectively induct recruits. President Eisenhower's New Look reduced the ranks by 560,577 soldiers, or nearly 58 percent. This smaller size encouraged local draft boards to offer more deferments and increased recruitment criteria. In 1962, the Selective Service System disqualified one-third of the selectees, many for mental ability or physical fitness.[39] Alarmed, President Kennedy maintained: "A young man who does not have what it takes to perform military service is not likely to have what it takes to make a living. Today's military rejects include to-morrow's hardcore unemployed."[40] In 1963, Daniel P. Moynihan, assis-tant secretary of labor, reported that poor men from families with annual incomes of less than $4,000 were primarily rejected from service. He recommended lower requirements to military service and special training for those previously rejected.[41] In response to repeated concerns, Secretary of Defense Robert McNamara announced Project 100,000 in August 1966. McNamara planned to utilize this initiative to support President Johnson's Great Society program by salvaging poor men for "productive military careers and later for productive roles in society."[42] While the U.S. Army increased the quality of soldiers inducted into its ranks, public leaders worried that the draft discriminated against poor and working-class men who might profit from military training and service.

Policymakers intended for Project 100,000 to reduce socioeconomic inequality, though it also allowed the army to meet its wartime personnel requirements. Project 100,000 directed over 350,000 "New Standards" men from poor and working-class backgrounds into the military. It placed roughly 40 percent of these recruits into combat arms and deployed around 125,000 of them to Vietnam. While the New Standards men did not make up the majority of the U.S. armed forces in Indochina, many came from poor and working-class families. Of the 2.5 million servicemen who participated there, roughly 80 percent came from poor and working-class backgrounds.[43] By 1968, American casualties mounted to over 1,000 per week in Vietnam.[44] The total number of servicemembers killed there increased from 9,378 in 1967 to 14,592 in 1968, many of them poor and working-class draftees, leading to the perception that Vietnam was a working-class war.[45] The mounting toll suggested a "casualty gap" existed based on class divisions, and many Americans clamored for changes to draft-exemption policies.

Politicians quickly acted to address these new socioeconomic inequities of military service. Weeks before the 1968 presidential election, Republican candidate Nixon called for an end to the draft; once elected, he moved to reform Selective Service. Wealthy and middle-class young men with the resources and connections had avoided conscription through broad deferments and exemptions based on medical issues, education, vocation, and conscientious objection.[46] The Nixon administration implemented a random lottery system and phased out educational deferments, producing a relatively fair class composition. Historian Jennifer Mittelstadt noted that, by 1970, Nixon's draft reforms "produced a military with 28.2 percent of the total force . . . having attended college, a good marker of middle-class status."[47] The administration moved with haste to increase the number of middle-class recruits and inductees between 1969 and 1972.

Nixon worked to make the draft more equitable until the conclusion of conscription in 1973. Still, many poor and working-class Americans continued to fill the ranks. In 1975, nearly 10 percent of army recruits came from families with incomes of less than $2,900 a year, and 53 percent of enlistees' families earned under $10,999 a year. The following year, the number of recruits from families earning less than $5,000 a year rose from 16 percent to 30 percent. By 1978, fewer than 6 percent of army recruits enlisted with any college experience.[48] According to Mittelstadt, the army operated as "more of a welfare state than civilian society" through on-post family housing; tax-free post exchange and commissary privileges; travel expenses for all soldiers, not just career officers; child care; counseling; and finance and legal aid.[49] The volunteer army attracted poor and working-class recruits with increased funding for pay, benefits, and social services. Nevertheless, it moved to address new military threats and political considerations after 1973.

Army leaders initiated changes to the structure of the force, informed by the strategic guidance of the Nixon administration. The commander of the newly created Training and Doctrine Command in 1973, General DePuy, took this as a historic opportunity to reshape the army's officer corps. Still, his formulaic assessments and combat ratios perceived soldiers and leaders as mindless cogs. Historian Brian Linn has noted that DePuy's Active Defense doctrinal transformation "treated combat commanders as midlevel executives whose primary tasks were to master their organization's materiel and methods, plan military operations, and train and supervise an unintelligent and unmotivated labor force."[50] DePuy envisioned a transformational army under the assumption that it would be manned by a cadre of skilled volunteers and expanded with an army of inexperienced draftees.

Army officers shared DePuy's overarching vision. They believed, however, that the new force structure necessitated qualitative changes in personnel and soldier training. General Starry, DePuy's successor as TRADOC commander from 1977 to 1982, insisted the AirLand Battle doctrine required individual soldier skills, initiative, leadership, and technical synchronization with tactical and operational units.[51] Infantrymen previously only required discipline, stamina, and courage, not "a particularly high order of intelligence nor sophisticated training." In contrast, the "modern infantryman, [was] expected to master a wide range of skills and think for himself on an extended battlefield, [and] faced a far more daunting challenge."[52] As a result, army leaders sought recruits from middle-class backgrounds who would likely have the requisite critical thinking skills, education, or, at the very least, aspirational motivation.

Military and civilian officials aimed to rebrand the image of soldiers as coming from poor backgrounds to as primarily middle class in their origins. Major General Maxwell Thurman, commander of U.S. Army Recruiting Command, spearheaded the "Be All You Can Be" campaign and imposed standardization on recruitment practices and quality control. Advertisements communicated that the army sought enlistees who wanted to reinvent themselves, to be better, stronger, disciplined, and more mature. In addition, it offered educational support with the Army College Fund in 1982 and then the Montgomery G.I. Bill of 1986.[53] Money for college contributed to its rebranding away from an army of the poor and working class and toward an image of a smart, ambitious middle-class military. In addition to marketing, the army took tangible steps to improve the quality of enlistees through more stringent recruitment criteria. While in 1980 only 54 percent of new soldiers had graduated from high school, by 1987, over 90 percent enlisted having earned a high school diploma.[54] New recruitment campaigns with increased criteria found success in not just rebranding the army but also in reshaping it into a middle-class institution.

New political and military considerations at the conclusion of the Cold War occasioned significant reductions to the size of the U.S. Army, yet these assisted it in becoming a middle-class force. After victory in the Persian Gulf War, officials perceived opportunities to transform and modernize the army into an even more high-tech and professional force. Chief of Staff General Shinseki envisioned a transformation of the army into an expeditionary force that leveraged technological advancements in communications, surveillance, and intelligence to coordinate forces over large spans in space and time. This rapidly deployable force required soldiers to be highly versatile and critical thinkers in order to operate throughout the range of missions, from humanitarian crises to total war. Shinseki asked commanders, "how have you prepared your youngsters both intellectually, from a point of being trained and prepared, and with equipment, to be able to very quickly prevail in that more intense higher mission requirement?"[55] By 1999, army leaders required 90 percent of new recruits to have at least a high school diploma, not a GED.[56] Higher recruitment standards during the 1990s increased the quality of recruits in the peacetime army while also barring those without the requisite education, men and women who were more likely to come from poor and working-class families.

After 2001, leadership continued to restructure and modernize the army into a high-tech and skilled force while also meeting the challenges of insurgencies in Iraq and Afghanistan during the Global War on Terrorism. Between 2001 and 2018, they increased the size of Special Operations Command from 33,000 to 70,000 soldiers and created seven expeditionary Stryker brigades.[57] Still, to meet the challenge of the wartime surges, the army began accepting more recruits without high school diplomas and issued more waivers for those with moral or criminal offenses. Continuous and prolonged army deployments were accompanied by a spike of reported soldier suicides, which actually exceeded the number of combat casualties, and a significant increase in reports of sexual harassment and assault.[58] Nearly two decades of active campaigning and incessant deployments to the Middle East strained the volunteer army and its soldiers.

The 2003 invasion of Iraq and the U.S. Army's subsequent growth elicited concerns about diminished quality of the force. After the terrorist attacks of 9/11, Americans from all walks of life enlisted in the armed services, though the 2003 invasion of Iraq divided them as the subsequent situation there devolved into insurgency and civil war. Popular support remained divided, but unlike the Vietnam War era, antiwar proponents did not directly accost individual soldiers or officers. Rather, they criticized the perceived class composition of the army.[59]

Public commentators and politicians contended that the army recruited too many troubled soldiers from poor and working-class families. In 2008, Representative Charles Rangel referred to the Iraq War as a "death tax . . . on the poor," while the New York Review of Books argued, "the military has set its sights on an especially vulnerable population." Even the esteemed historian Andrew Bacevich claimed that "rural Americans, people of color, recent immigrants and members of the working class fill the ranks of the armed forces in disproportionate numbers."[60] Kathy Roth-Douquet and Frank Schaeffer's 2007 book, AWOL: The Unexcused Absence of America's Upper Classes from Military Service—and How It Hurts Our Country, presupposed that the army's three hundred general officers were not drawn from America's elite families. National Public Radio reported on the army's lowered recruiting standards for years. NPR host Madeline Brand asked: "Got a criminal record, got a drug or alcohol problem? Well there may be a place for you in the United States Army."[61] Antiwar advocates implied that the rise in soldier suicides and sexual assaults was related to the class composition and quality of wartime volunteers, rather than acknowledge that the army was stretched too thin and placed in an untenable situation.

Despite concerns about the quality and class composition, between 2001 and 2020, the army enlisted primarily middle-class recruits to fight the Global War on Terrorism. Relatively stringent recruitment standards filtered out many poor and working-class candidates who lacked the requisite education and skills. Despite wartime surges and waivers, interested men and women from poor and working-class neighborhoods were less likely to meet the army's enlistment requirements. From 2001 to 2014, men and women from families with annual incomes between $69,000 and $107,000 were most likely to enlist.

Recruits who enlisted during the Global War on Terrorism also came from families with middle distributions of wealth, with net worth and capital assets between $29,000 and $219,000 per family.[62] Another study of 695,000 U.S. Army recruits between 2000 and 2010 suggested that most who became enlistees came from middle-class families. Most strikingly, it reported white families with above-average incomes tended to provide the bulk of soldiers in combat arms, those more likely to deploy and experience higher rates of battle injury and death.[63] Unlike Vietnam-era soldiers, most volunteers during the Global War on Terrorism, and many of its casualties, came from predominantly middle-class families.

Shifts in the socioeconomic composition of the U.S. Army have been accompanied by changes in force structure. Army leaders unsuccessfully attempted to build a skilled and futuristic atomic army with draftees after the Korean War. Still, increased standards and draft deferments filtered out predominantly poor and working-class men during the 1950s and 1960s. Americans concerned about economic inequality facilitated the creation of Project 100,000, which inadvertently channeled hundreds of thousands of poor and working-class men to battlefields in Vietnam and prompted the creation of the AVF. In the 1970s and 1980s, the AVF drastically altered its force structure and attempted to shake its Vietnam-era image as a poor man's army. The reductions during the 1990s then forced the army to cut its personnel drastically and established more stringent recruitment criteria. Despite concerns about the quality of the army during the Global War on Terrorism, the volunteer soldiers primarily represented the American middle class. While the public worries about the decline of the political and economic standing of the middle class, there is little evidence that Americans worry about its overrepresentation in the army.

Conclusions

Various changes in mission and force structure over the last fifty years have transformed the class composition of the AVF from a poor man's army into one that is solidly middle class. In the AVF's early years, poor and working-class volunteers enlisted in large numbers, while middle-class recruits did not. Still, the class composition of the army did not direct its force structure—politics, strategy, and the economy also mattered— rather the army's push toward a progressively high-tech and professional force stiffened enlistment criteria that moved its class composition toward middle-class origins. As the army organized around sophisticated technology and complex operations, enlistment criteria became even more stringent, especially as its overall numerical strength declined. Over the last twenty-five years, America's army has shifted decidedly toward middle-class recruits. Still, the misconception remains that the AVF is a poor man's army. The U.S. military does not track the class composition of recruits, with the unintended consequence that it is more difficult for the AVF to prove that it is representative of society.

After fifty years, twenty of them fighting the Global War on Terrorism, the AVF has reached a "mid-life crisis."[64] It is customary for opponents of U.S. foreign policy and the AVF to advocate reinstating the draft. Some Americans earnestly believe that some form of compulsory service may narrow political polarization, economic inequality, the perceived civil-military divide, and deter aggressive foreign policies. Indeed, the U.S. Army's recent focus and restructuring to conduct large-scale combat operations means the force will struggle to fill division- and corps-sized infantry units without a compelling incentive or systematic channeling. Still, reinstating the draft could not occur independent of major revisions to U.S. domestic politics, foreign policy, and the national defense strategy.

What are the implications of America's middle-class army? Most leaders prefer a professional volunteer force. Still, they should consider the implications of expanding one of the nation's oldest vehicles for social and economic mobility during war and peace. The National Commission on Military, National, and Public Service's 2020 report and the response to the COVID-19 pandemic attest to the desire and propensity of many Americans to serve their country and community. Yet military service is one of the few clearly defined paths toward national service.[65] Perhaps what we should ask is whether the army should be one of the only pathways to provide for the common defense.

Notes

1. Shanea Watkins and James Sherk, "Who Serves in the U.S. Military? The Demographics of Enlisted Troops and Officers," Center for Data Analysis Report 08-05, Heritage Foundation, www.heritage.org; "Demographics of the U.S. Military," Council on Foreign Relations, https://www.cfr.org/backgrounder/demographics-us-military. Enlisted recruits are consistently drawn from middle-class neighborhoods. Recruits from families who earn between $53,549 and $87,850 are overrepresented, while those above and below that range are underrepresented.

2. Christian G. Appy, *Working-Class War: American Combat Soldiers and Vietnam* (Chapel Hill: University of North Carolina Press, 1993); Appy, *American Reckoning: The Vietnam War and Our National Identity* (New York: Viking, 2015).

3. Ronald R. Krebs and Robert Ralston, "Patriotism or Paychecks: Who Believes What about Why Soldiers Serve," *Armed Forces and Society* 20, no. 10 (2020): 1–24, https://doi.org/10.1177/0095327X20917166.

4. Charles Moskos and Jon Sibley Butler, *All That We Can Be: Black Leadership and Racial Integration the Army Way* (New York: Basic Books, 1996), 11–12.

5. Beth Bailey, *America's Army: Making the All-Volunteer Force* (Cambridge, MA: Harvard University Press, 2009), 258.

6. Jennifer Mittelstadt, *The Rise of the Military Welfare State* (Cambridge, MA: Harvard University Press, 2015), 43.

7. Aaron O'Connell, *Underdogs: The Making of the Modern Marine Corps* (Cambridge, MA: Harvard University Press, 2012) also served as a model to demonstrate the ways in which an institution's culture shapes its operational structure and strategic posture.

8. For the purpose of definition, this chapter relies on sociologist Dennis Gilbert's stratification of class in the United States into six distinct groups: underclass, working-poor, working, lower-middle, upper-middle, and upper or capitalist class. Gilbert, *The American Class Structure in an Age of Growing Inequality*, 11th ed. (Los Angeles: SAGE, 2021).

9. Gilbert, *American Class Structure*.

10. In addition, an American with a high school diploma may have less annual income than a college graduate, though they may have invested their income in assets other than student-loan debt.

11. U.S. Census Bureau and U.S. Department of Housing and Urban Development, "Average Sales Price of Houses Sold for the United States [ASPUS]," Federal Reserve Economic Data (St. Louis Federal Reserve Bank), 2022, https://fred.stlouisfed.org/series/ASPUS, accessed October 30, 2022.

12. Quoted in Jennifer Mittelstadt, "Military Demographics," in *At War: The Military and American Culture in the Twentieth Century and Beyond*, ed. David Kieran and Edwin A. Martini (New Brunswick, NJ: Rutgers University Press, 2018), 97.

13. "DoD Personnel, Workforce Reports & Publications," Defense Manpower Data Center, https://dwp.dmdc.osd.mil/dwp/app/dod-data-reports/workforce-reports.

14. Quoted in Brian McAllister Linn, *The Echo of Battle: The Army's Way of War* (Cambridge, MA: Harvard University Press, 2007), 203.

15. Richard W. Stewart, ed., *American Military History*, vol. 2, *The United States Army in a Global Era, 1917–2008*, 2d ed. (Washington, DC: Center of Military History, 2010), 392.

16. *Field Manual 100-5, Operations* (1976), http://cgsc.contentdm.oclc.org/cdm/compoundobject/collection/p4013coll9/id/42/rec/9.

17. William B. Caldwell IV, "Not Light Enough to Get There, Not Heavy Enough to Win: The Case of US Light Infantry," report, School of Advanced Military Studies, Army Command and General Staff College, 1987, https://apps.dtic.mil/sti/citations/ADA191406; Stewart, *American Military History*, 392.

18. Linn, *Echo of Battle*, 210.

19. Stewart, *American Military History*, 383.

20. Linn, *Echo of Battle*, 201.

21. Stewart, *American Military History*, 384.

22. Stewart, *American Military History*, 387.

23. Stewart, *American Military History*, 388.

24. Stewart, *American Military History*, 394.

25. Linn, *Echo of Battle*, 212.

26. Stewart, *American Military History*, 395.

27. Linn, *Echo of Battle*, 215.

28. Anne W. Chapman, *The National Training Center Matures: 1985–1993* (Fort Monroe, VA: Military History Office, U.S. Army Training and Doctrine Command, 1997); Chapman, "The Origins and Development of the National Training Center 1976–1984" (Fort Belvoir, VA: Defense Technical Information Center, 1992), https://apps.dtic.mil/sti/pdfs/ADA252825.pdf.

29. Stewart, *American Military History*, 395.

30. "DoD Personnel, Workforce Reports & Publications."

31. White House, *A National Security Strategy of Engagement and Enlargement* (Washington, DC: Historical Office, Office of the Secretary of Defense, 1994), https://history.defense.gov/Portals/70/Documents/nss/nss1994.pdf?ver=2014-06-25-121219-500.

32. "DoD Personnel, Workforce Reports & Publications."

33. "DoD Personnel, Workforce Reports & Publications."

34. "DoD Personnel, Workforce Reports & Publications."

35. Krebs and Ralston, "Patriotism or Paychecks."

36. John Lynch, "Billionaire Bill Gates Failed Miserably at Guessing Grocery Prices in a Quiz Game on 'Ellen,'" *Business Insider*, February 22, 2018, https://www.businessinsider.com/bill-gates-failed-guessing-grocery-prices-in-ellen-quiz-game-2018-2.

37. William A. Taylor, *Military Service and American Democracy: From World War II to the Iraq and Afghanistan Wars* (Lawrence: University Press of Kansas, 2016), 89–132.

38. Quoted in Brian McAllister Linn, *Elvis's Army: Cold War GIs and the Atomic Battlefield* (Cambridge, MA: Harvard University Press, 2016), 133.

39. Bailey, *America's Army*, 94.

40. Quoted in Bailey, *America's Army*, 95.

41. Appy, *Working-Class War*, 30.

42. Quoted in Bailey, *America's Army*, 94.

43. Appy, *Working Class War*, 18.

44. Allan R. Millett, Peter Maslowski, and William B. Feis, *For the Common Defense: A Military History of the United States from 1607 to 2012*, 3d ed. (New York: Free Press, 2012), 560.

45. Appy, *Working Class War*, 29.

46. Mittelstadt, "Military Demographics," 93.

47. Mittelstadt, "Military Demographics," 93–94; Bailey, *America's Army*, 2.

48. In 1975, $2,900 and $10,999 would be roughly $14,350 and $54,424 as of June 2020. In 1976, $5,000 would equal $23,183 in 2020.

49. Mittelstadt, "Military Demographics," 95.

50. Linn, *Echo of Battle*, 205.

51. Linn, *Echo of Battle*, 210.

52. Stewart, *American Military History*, 393–394.

53. Bailey, *America's Army*, 195.

54. Bailey, *America's Army*, 197.

55. Quoted in Bailey, *America's Army*, 232.

56. Bailey, *America's Army*, 233.

57. Todd South, "Special Operations Command Asks for More Troops, Biggest Budget Yet," *Military Times*, February 24, 2018, https://www.militarytimes.com/news /your-army/2018/02/23/special-operations-command-asks-for-more-troops-biggest -budget-yet/; Congressional Research Service, "U.S. Special Operations Forces (SOF): Background and Issues for Congress" (Washington, DC: Congressional Research Service, 2020), https://fas.org/sgp/crs/natsec/RS21048.pdf; W. J. Hennigan, "The New American Way of War," *Time*, November 30, 2017, https://time.com/5042 700/inside-new-american-way-of-war/; Todd South, "The Army Is Converting Two BCTs as It Beefs Up Its Fighting Force for the Next Big War," *Army Times*, September 20, 2018, https://www.armytimes.com/news/your-army/2018/09/20/the-army-is -converting-two-bcts-as-it-beefs-up-its-fighting-force-for-the-next-big-war/.

58. "U.S. Military Suicides Exceed Combat Deaths," CBS News, January 14, 2013, https://www.cbsnews.com/news/us-military-suicides-exceed-combat-deaths/.

59. David Kieran first made this argument about the antiwar critiques following the 2003 invasion of Iraq in *Signature Wounds: The Untold Story of the Military's Mental Health Crisis* (New York: NYU Press, 2019).

60. Quoted in Andrea Asoni, Andrea Gilli, Mauro Gilli, and Tino Sanandaji, "A Mercenary Army of the Poor?: Technological Change and the Demographic Composition of the Post-9/11 U.S. Military," *Journal of Strategic Studies* 45, no. 4 (January 2020): 574, https://doi.org/10.1080/01402390.2019.1692660.

61. Libby Lewis, "'Redefining' Quality among Army Recruits," *Weekend Edition Saturday*, National Public Radio, July 15, 2006, https://www.npr.org/templates/story /story.php?storyId=5559563; Steve Almasy, "Former Soldier at Center of Murder of Iraqi Family Dies after Suicide Attempt," CNN, February 18, 2014, https://www.cnn .com/2014/02/18/us/soldier-steven-green-suicide/index.html; Madeleine Brand and Alex Chadwick, "U.S. Army Recruits Offered Waivers for Past Crimes," *Day to Day*, National Public Radio, February 14, 2006, https://www.npr.org/templates/story/sto ry.php?storyId=5205754. Lewis's story for *Weekend Edition Saturday* chronicled soldiers such as Steven Green, who enlisted with a moral waiver then raped an Iraqi girl and murdered her family. A federal court convicted Green, who in 2014 committed suicide in prison.

62. Asoni et al., "Mercenary Army of the Poor?," 568–614.

63. Susan Payne Carter, Alexander A. Smith, and Carl Wojtaszek, "Who Will Fight? The All-Volunteer Army after 9/11," *American Economic Review: Papers & Proceedings* 107, no. 5 (2017): 415–419, https://doi.org/10.1257/aer.p20171082.

64. Hugh Liebert and James Golby, "Midlife Crisis?: The All-Volunteer Force at 40," *Armed Forces and Society* 43, no. 1 (2017): 115–138, https://doi.org/10.1177/0095327 X16641430.

65. The National Commission on Military, National, and Public Service, *Inspired to Serve: Final Report* (Washington, DC: National Commission on Military, National, and Public Service, 2020), www.inspire2serve.gov.

III

Challenges

8

Viability

Major General Dennis Laich

Forty-seven years ago in 1973, two decisions were made in our nation's capital that affected the social fabric of our republic. One of those decisions has been litigated, debated, and challenged regularly. The other one has never been rigorously examined or challenged. The first decision came from the Supreme Court in *Roe v. Wade*, legalizing abortion. The other decision came from Congress to move to the all-volunteer force model of manning our armed forces and thereby to abandon conscription. As a result of the AVF decision, 330 million Americans lay claim to rights, liberties, and freedoms that not a single one of them is obligated to protect and defend. The task of defending the nation falls to a small segment of the populace that is not racially, geographically, or socio-economically representative of the broader population. This represents a threat not only to our national security but also to the social fabric of our democracy.

The issue of how to man a nation's military is not new. Writers, politicians, and pundits often invoke the wisdom of our founding fathers. General George Washington, perhaps the most respected of those men, said in 1783, "It may be laid down as a primary position, and the basis of our system, that every citizen who enjoys the protection of a free government, owes not only a portion of his property, but even of his personal services to the defense of it."[1] The AVF model is clearly at odds with General Washington's counsel.

In this chapter, I will question whether the AVF is working and will work in the future based on fairness, efficiency, and sustainability. I will also suggest that it contributes to the civil-military gap and the militarization of U.S. foreign policy. This is a framework for a fact-based national dialogue that is preferable to asking the question, "What if we had a war and no one showed up on our side?" As Americans engage this difficult and important dialogue, the counsel of President John Kennedy may be helpful:

We must move on from the reassuring repetition of stale phrases to a new, difficult, but essential confrontation with reality. For the great enemy of truth is very often not the lie—deliberate, contrived, and dishonest—but the myth—persistent, persuasive, and unrealistic. Too often we hold fast to the clichés of our forebears. We subject all facts to a prefabricated set of interpretations. We enjoy the comfort of opinions without the discomfort of thought.[2]

History

A brief review of how the United States came to embrace the AVF model may be helpful. Richard Nixon's 1968 presidential campaign focused on a commitment to end both the Vietnam War and conscription. Whether the commitment to end the draft was enlightened social policy or political opportunism by a soon-to-be-disgraced president remains an open question. The American people were receptive to sacrificing conscription to atone for the sins of the most unpopular, and arguably unfair, draft coupled with the most unpopular war in their history. After winning the election, Nixon set about implementing his promise to create an all-volunteer military and a presidential commission to "study" the issue and make "recommendations."

Nixon chose former secretary of defense Thomas Gates to chair the commission, which became known as the Gates Commission. All its members were well respected and, although some had reservations about an all-voluntary military, many of the most outspoken among them and most of the research staff were primarily economists who favored abandoning conscription. It was reasonable to predict the commission's "recommendation," given the president's campaign promise, the composition of its membership and research staff, and, perhaps most importantly, Nixon's charge "to develop a comprehensive plan for eliminating conscription and moving toward an all volunteer armed force." In December 1968, after six months' work, the commission unanimously recommended moving to an AVF. The final report, however, identified nine "objections" that the commissioners anticipated would be raised and responded to each of them. Most of the "objections" proved to be legitimate and prescient.[3] They included the following:

- The AVF would be so expensive that the nation could not afford it. Commission members responded by citing economic costs rather than Pentagon budget costs of $2 billion per year based on the difference in the current pay rate for draftees and what they would receive in the private sector, a cost that would be eliminated by their higher pay as part of the AVF, and ignored the budget costs. They considered this low pay a form of taxation on those who served. In 2012, Secretary of Defense Leon Panetta said that "the escalating growth of personnel costs must be confronted. This is an area of the budget that has grown by nearly ninety percent since 2001."[4]

- The AVF would lack the flexibility to expand rapidly in times of crisis. The commission argued that the National Guard and reserves would serve as a credible backup when necessary and that "preparedness depends on forces in being, not on the ability to draft untrained men." Since 1973, the ability of the Guard and reserves to serve as a credible backup has been mixed. In every major war prior to 1973, the nation relied on "an ability to draft untrained men," who won every conflict except Vietnam. Americans did not seriously consider conscription when the AVF faced its first real test in 2003 following the terrorist attacks of 9/11.
- The AVF would undermine patriotism by weakening the traditional belief that every citizen has a moral obligation to serve the country. In response, the commission held that "a voluntary decision to serve is the best answer morally and practically." The broad-based concern in the media, social sciences, and political discourse with the current civil-military gap indicates that there is merit to this objection.
- Finally, those joining the AVF would be from the lower socioeconomic classes and would be motivated to join by financial rewards rather than patriotism; the force would be manned by "mercenaries." The commission suggested that the AVF would not differ from the existing force of conscripts and volunteers with respect to socioeconomic class. In fact, the move to the AVF legitimized this inequality by granting a mass exemption from military service to all Americans, particularly the first socioeconomic quintile, while offering unprecedented enlistment bonuses that are disproportionately attractive to the lower socioeconomic quintiles.

Fairness

Fairness suggests that something is marked by impartiality and honesty and is free from self-interest, prejudice, and favoritism. Do all citizens participate, contribute, and sacrifice in manning the force, and should they? Is the force representative of the nation in terms of race, gender, class, and region, and should it be? Fairness regarding military service is usually defined in terms of either serving or not serving. It could also be defined as all qualified citizens between the ages of eighteen and twenty-four being subject to enlistment based on a transparent and random selection process. The fairness question has been historically framed by the philosophical tension between libertarianism and egalitarianism. Libertarianism holds that an individual citizen has no responsibility to society or the state other than to respect the liberty and property of others; the individual, according to this philosophy, has absolute, unrestricted, liberty of thought and action. Egalitarianism, on the other hand, is a belief in human equality with respect to social, political, and economic rights, privileges, and responsibilities and advocates for the removal of inequalities among people. Elliot Cohen writes, "we may sum this up crudely by saying that liberals hope to minimize coercion and egalitarians to spread it evenly."[5]

The perception of fairness regarding the manning of a nation's military is influenced not only by the philosophical tensions described above but also by the methods used. This is particularly relevant regarding conscription. In the United States, this perception is mixed from the Civil War to the current day. Article I of the Constitution gives Congress the power to "raise and support Armies." The Mobilization Act of 1862 gave President Abraham Lincoln the authority to draft men into the Union army. The threat of conscription initially provided a sufficient number of volunteers until casualties became so great that a broad-based draft became necessary. On March 3, 1863, Congress passed the Enrollment Act, which included a provision for substitution and commutation, allowing a draftee to purchase exemption by paying someone $300 to serve in his place. The public response was cries of "a rich man's war and a poor man's fight" and led to the New York City Draft Riots, in which 2,000 people died and 8,000 were injured. As a policy and method, conscription had a bad start in America.

The lessons of the Civil War draft informed subsequent wartime conscription methods. During World War I, almost 24 million men registered for the draft, and 3 million were inducted. Exemptions were rare, and noncompliance was dealt with harshly. The constitutionality of the 1917 draft law was challenged in court, with the Supreme Court unanimously ruling in *Arver v. United States* (also known as the *Selective Draft Law Cases*) that it was legitimate. That 1918 ruling stands to this day, and its opinion states that "it may not be doubted that the very conception of a just government and its duty to the citizens includes the reciprocal obligation of the citizen to render military service in case of need, and the right to compel it." On September 16, 1940, America's first peacetime draft became law in anticipation of World War II, during which the United States eventually had 8.3 million men in uniform, two-thirds of whom were draftees. The draft methods in both world wars were generally considered fair and supported by the public.

Conscription continued after World War II due to significant shortfalls in army recruiting and the threat of the Soviet Union to U.S. interests globally as Congress passed the Selective Service Act of 1948. As a result, the army's ranks were filled with conscripts and "draft induced volunteers." The beginning of the Korean War in June 1950 validated the need for the Selective Service. The draft remained in place through the 1950s and 1960s despite some periodic objections and was viewed as a symbol of American resolve against Soviet aggression.

The Vietnam War and the draft that supported it have a profound influence almost fifty years later on the American public's perception of conscription. Mass educational deferments, racial inequality, and inconsistencies among local draft boards led to campus riots, sit-ins, mass demonstrations, and civil disobedience that tested the social fabric of our republic. Remedies to the draft injustices in the war's later years were not enough to offset the consequences of the earlier errors.

Setting aside the libertarian position and focusing on the egalitarian, what might constitute a fair military draft? Perhaps a lottery-based draft of men and women, with no deferments and no exemptions, with three options available to the relatively few selected from among the 4 million Americans who turn eighteen each year might work. Their three service options might be two years of active service, six years of National Guard or reserve service, or, if they choose to attend college, a requirement to enroll in ROTC (discussed later). This structure ensures that all socioeconomic classes have some "skin in the game" and, arguably, is therefore fair. If the benefits of national defense are shared equally among the citizens, then it stands to reason that the cost of defending it—risk of life and limb and surrender of personal liberties—should be shared equally among the citizens.

In 1840, Alexis de Tocqueville, in his classic book *Democracy in America*, warned that the U.S. government must appeal "to the whole community at once; it is the unequal distribution of the weight, not the weight itself, which commonly occasions resistance." Currently, the weight of national security on U.S. citizens is unequally and unfairly distributed socioeconomically, racially, and geographically. The AVF structure contributes to this. Eventually, resistance may manifest itself in the failure of "volunteerism," the weakening of national defense, or a threat to the social fabric of our democracy.

Efficiency

Efficiency suggests that the method of manning a nation's armed forces produces the desired effect without waste or redundancy at a reasonable cost. Does the military efficiently "provide for the common defense" in fighting and winning the nation's wars? If so, at what cost and to whom? Personnel costs have risen dramatically over the past twenty years, and some national-security experts have expressed concerns that, if the overall defense budget remains flat with inflation, they will crowd out such other areas as training, operations, maintenance, and procurement. Personnel costs of the U.S. AVF consume a large portion (25–33 percent) of a defense budget that is larger than that of the next ten nations in the world combined. Even with such heightened spending, the win/loss record of the AVF is poor compared to that of conscripted forces in American history.[6]

Going back to the Civil War, the United States has never been able to achieve an efficient mass mobilization to fight a large or sustained war without conscription. So, when the first major war of the AVF era came in response to the terrorist attacks of 9/11, the Pentagon faced several choices once realizing they had too much war and not enough warriors: recommend conscription, restrict the scope of the war based on available personnel, or change policies and practices to maximize the use of existing forces. Each alternative had political, social, and strategic consequences. The path of least resistance to the decision makers was to change policies and practices that they controlled, with the effects being borne by servicemembers and their families and largely ignored or invisible to the general public. Although perhaps more efficient, they never seriously considered the conscription option.

Opting to change policies and practices, officials sought to get the most from the existing AVF model and those serving. One of the first to be changed was the longstanding "dwell time" policy of two years recovery time for each year in combat, allowing soldiers the opportunity to recover from the physical and emotional stress of war. The emotional stress is particularly acute in asymmetric wars like Iraq and Afghanistan. Dwell time went from a two-to-one ratio to a one-to-one ratio or even less. The Pentagon also changed its policy about prescribing psychotropic drugs to treat servicemembers suffering from depression, anxiety, depression, PTSD, and other psychiatric or emotional conditions. Dispensing powerful drugs such as Seroquel and Risperdal as well as other anticonvulsant and antipsychotic medications was rationalized by decision makers "to conserve the fighting strength" of the military. In March 2010, Senator James Webb said that the increase in prescribing these drugs was "on its face, pretty astonishing and troubling." It was particularly distressing because the servicemembers prescribed these drugs were deemed emotionally and psychologically fit prior to enlistment. The drug and dwell-time policy changes enabled the repeated deployment of soldiers to the war zones. By 2010, it was not uncommon for an active-duty soldier to have three or four combat tours or for a reservist or National Guardsman to have two or three combat tours—no horse was so dead that it could not be beaten one more time.

Changes in administrative practices also were implemented to compensate for personnel shortages. Stop-Loss was a controversial example. According to Section 12305 of Title 10 of the U.S. Code, the president, after declaring a national emergency or presidential call-up, may "suspend any provision of law relating to promotion, retirement, or separation applicable to any member of the armed forces determined to be essential to the national security of the United States, and determine, for the purpose of said section, that members of the armed forces are essential to the security of the United States." Stop-Loss restricted servicemembers from voluntarily separating from the military at the end of their commitment if the unit to which they were assigned was scheduled to deploy to the combat zone in the next ninety days; if already deployed, their active service was extended until ninety days after their unit redeployed. More than 120,000 servicemembers had their enlistments extended by this "back door draft" made necessary by an inefficient AVF model. The Pentagon was also forced to use civilian contractors at an unprecedented level to accomplish traditional uniformed-military tasks because the AVF model could not generate a sufficient number of troops.

Although some in the Pentagon expressed concern that these practices and policies, along with the personal stresses they generated, would "break the force." While the force did not break, thousands of individual servicemembers and their families did. PTSD, increased drug and alcohol abuse, divorce, homelessness, domestic abuse, and suicides became the signature consequences of stressing a too-small force of volunteers and providing an inefficient VA system to deal with them.

The efficiency of the organizational structure supporting the AVF is an additional factor to consider. The U.S. Army Recruiting Command has 10,900 recruiters and 1,400 recruiting stations. Most of these people are highly qualified noncommissioned officers who would otherwise be training and leading soldiers; none of them enlisted to be a recruiter. In Fiscal Year 2019, the army enlisted 91,488 soldiers, or 8.4 enlistees per recruiter.[7] Put another way, the average recruiter succeeds in enlisting a new soldier every forty-three days. In order to achieve even this level of efficiency in manning the AVF, waivers from "standards" were granted for between 10 percent and 12 percent of enlistees and for an additional 1.9 percent (more than 1,700 men and women) who were classified Category IV (CAT IV), scoring between the tenth and thirtieth percentile on the Armed Services Vocational Aptitude Battery. A RAND study found that a CAT IV enlistee will perform from 15 percent to 30 percent less effectively than a higher-scoring peer.[8] The Pentagon caps CAT IV enlistees at 4 percent. In order to achieve even this level of efficiency, the army paid more than $424 million in enlistment bonuses. If military service in a democracy is a measure of patriotism, enlistment bonuses place a price on patriotism and foster a "poverty draft." A concerned taxpayer might ask, "if it's an all-volunteer force, why do we pay someone to volunteer?" These facts suggest that the nation pays a high price to attract minimum quantities of marginally qualified recruits to serve in its army. Many argue that this is necessary because a small percentage of U.S. youth can meet enlistment standards (that is, are able to join), and an even smaller percentage have a propensity to serve (that is, are willing to join). A brief review of AVF arithmetic informs this argument.

Accommodating these compromises and inefficiencies are unique to the AVF and surrender the Pentagon's greatest source of competitive advantage in the competition for human talent—conscription. Consider the arithmetic of the AVF. Approximately 4 million Americans turn eighteen each year. About 30 percent of them (approximately 1.2 million) meet the minimum standards for enlistment and thus are able to serve. Around 15 percent of American youth exhibit a propensity to enter the armed forces and thus are willing to serve. This results in 180,000 young men and women who are both *willing* and *able* to serve. The armed forces normally needs to recruit about 150,000 new members per year, leaving little room for error between supply and demand under the AVF model. Combat casualties and forces beyond the control of the military, such as low unemployment or widespread health issues, can compound this challenge.

If, however, volunteerism were to be complemented by conscription from a pool of 1.2 million Americans able to serve, using the lottery-based model mentioned earlier, standards could actually be raised, waivers and CAT IVs eliminated, the U.S. Army Recruiting Command downsized, high-quality NCOs returned to troop duty, enlistment bonuses eliminated, and a measure of equality of sacrifice restored. Additionally, in this larger pool would be numerous high school valedictorians who would make solid cyber warriors and all-conference linebackers who would make great infantrymen who, with the AVF model, are granted mass deferments. Finally, the United States would not be subject again to the dilemma of too much war and not enough warriors and the resulting consequences to those who do serve.

Richard Nixon spoke to the issues of fairness and efficiency in his 1980 book, *The Real War*

I considered the end of the draft in 1973 to be one of the major achievements of my administration. Now seven years later, I have reluctantly concluded that we should reintroduce the draft. The need for the United States to project a strong military posture is now urgent, and the volunteer army has failed to provide enough personnel of the caliber we need for our highly sophisticated armaments. Its burden should be shared equally by all strata of society, with random selection and as few deferments as possible.[9]

Sustainability

Sustainability denotes the capacity of a system to maintain current or future expected results over a period of time appropriate to the mission and at acceptable costs. In this regard, is the volunteer system capable of providing the required quality and quantity of personnel for military service today and in the future at an acceptable cost? Five issues inform the response to this question: propensity to serve (willingness), fitness to serve (ability), costs of the AVF, full mobilization, and expanded and complex military missions.

Propensity to serve is a function of a person's familiarity with and knowledge of the military, their attitude toward the military, their association between the military and a set of valued outcomes, and their perception of how supportive various people would be of them joining the military. The Department of Defense uses surveys such as the University of Michigan's Monitoring the Future and its own Youth Poll Survey.[10] The Youth Poll Survey for 2017–2018 provides data from 2001 forward, identifying a propensity to serve highest at 16 percent in 2003 and lowest at 9 percent in 2007, with the most recent reading at 14 percent. From 2014 to 2017, the propensity averaged 13.4 percent (recall the conservative 15 percent used when describing AVF arithmetic earlier). Of the top-ten reasons expressed in the survey to join the military, "To pay for future education" was first, "pay and money" was third, and "it is my duty/obligation to my country" ranked eighth.

Among the top-ten reasons for not joining the military, "possibility of physical injury/death" and "possibility of PTSD and other psychological issues" ranked first and second, respectively. The armed forces cannot eliminate the risks that concern potential recruits and may not be able to continue to offer the benefits that attract them; wars and civilian unemployment rates and educational benefits are beyond the Pentagon's control. Since 2005, propensity has reached the 15-percent threshold in only three of the twenty-eight reported periods. There is little reason to believe that it will rise above the 13.4-percent level, and each decline of 1 percent removes 12,000 potential enlistees from the pool of those able to serve.

Many Americans are surprised that only 30 percent of the nation's youth can meet the minimum standards for enlistment in the armed forces. But when considering the physical, mental, and emotional elements necessary in an active, global force striving to integrate technological advances into its day-to-day operations, it is not so surprising. Physical shortcomings rooted in adolescent obesity and high school dropouts are leading factors in disqualification. About 30 percent of U.S. youth are obese, and from 20 percent to 25 percent fail to graduate from high school. Neither statistic is likely to improve in the foreseeable future. Other issues, such as criminal records, illegal drug use, asthma, and emotional issues such as anxiety and depression, also contribute to the shrinking pool of those able to serve. The Pentagon cannot control any of these factors, but it can lower "standards" and grant waivers, thereby compromising the quality of the force. In 2006, a few years after the first real test of the AVF began, General William Wallace, commander of the Army Training and Doctrine Command, stated:

> I have serious thoughts about the future and it's got less to do about the recruits than . . . with the education and fitness of American youth, because all of the trends are going in the wrong direction. Only three out of ten young men and women ages 17–24, are fully qualified to be soldiers. One kid drops out of high school in the United States every 29 seconds—over a million kids dropping out of school. And we have fitness and obesity problems within our youth population, so in an organization like the Army, which values intellect, fitness, and morals, and all the trends are going in the wrong direction—that does, indeed, cause me some concern, unless we do something about it.

To date, "something" has not been done about "it"—sustaining the AVF. The percentage of American youth who are fully qualified to serve in the military is stable at best and may be declining.

Fifty years ago, the Gates Commission acknowledged the possibility that the AVF would be expensive, so much so that the nation could not afford it. Today, the federal government is 26 trillion dollars in debt and running annual deficits of a trillion dollars. Responsible taxpayers and legislators may begin to look at places to reduce these burdens. A

Congressional Budget Office (CBO) report titled *Approaches to Changing Military Compensation* states, "To attract and retain high quality military personnel, assign them to needed occupations, and motivate them to perform their best, the Department of Defense (DoD) must offer compensation packages that adequately reward service members for the rigors of military life."[11] It goes on to state: "To determine the competitiveness of its pay, DoD sets a benchmark goal: Regular Military Compensation for service members should be approximately equal to the 70th percentile of wages and salaries for comparable civilians. In CBO estimates, cash compensation, including nontaxable housing and food allowances, exceeds DoD's benchmark in almost all cases (often by large margins) for civilian workers of comparable age and education levels." DOD is therefore paying a large premium to market for personnel to support the AVF in addition to bonuses ($427 million for the army in FY 2019) to induce enlistments (draftees are not paid such bonuses). The study identifies that the median enlisted servicemember's total annual compensation is $112,800. This means that the total compensation of the 10,900 recruiters assigned to the U.S. Army Recruiting Command is more than $1.2 billion per year. This money, $1.2 billion, would pay the starting annual salary of 33,000 public-school teachers in Ohio, applying the construct of President Eisenhower's "military-industrial complex" speech. Informed taxpayers in a debt- and deficit-plagued republic might question this level of spending to support the AVF.

Two generations of Americans who were able but unwilling to volunteer to serve in the U.S. armed forces have not had to be concerned with defending the nation militarily. But the world continues to be a dangerous place, as the most recent national-security strategy identifies China, Russia, Iran, and North Korea as threats to U.S. security. To think that the United States could prosecute wars against China, Russia, or Iran with a volunteer force, given the current propensity to serve, is wishful thinking at best and dangerous at worst. The nation has never fought a war against a peer competitor without implementing conscription. Nonetheless, some lawmakers have advocated defunding the Selective Service System, and Congress has created the National Commission on Military, National, and Public Service to address the question. Fortunately, the panel has recommended that not only men but also women register with Selective Service. At some point, Congress and the American people may be forced, amid a security crisis, to address the issue of conscription. How will two generations of absence affect the decision process?

A final challenge to the sustainability of the AVF is captured in the title of Rosa Brooks's 2016 book, *How Everything Became War and the Military Became Everything.* Successive administrations and Congresses, with the prodding of a vocal "defense" lobby, have richly funded the Pentagon while starving the State Department and the U.S. Agency for International Development (USAID) with the American people's acquiescence. This trend has operationalized the phrase, "If your only tool is a hammer, everything looks like a nail" and leads to an "all options are on the table" mindset in international approach: In effect, do as we say or face the military response. Notwithstanding its fundamental purpose, to fight and win the nation's wars (with a lackluster record since World War II), the Pentagon has been tasked, for example, with fighting Ebola in Liberia, establishing economic-development projects in Africa, training Afghan judges, developing television soap operas for Iraqi audiences, conducting antipiracy patrols in Somalia, protecting the U.S. southern border from "caravans" of asylum seekers, and forcefully ejecting U.S. citizens peacefully protesting from Lafayette Square in their nation's capital.

In the view of Michael T. Klare, author of *All Hell Breaking Loose*, the demands on the U.S. military will only increase due to climate change, as natural disasters will be more frequent and powerful and the Pentagon will receive the 911 emergency call to rescue, remove, restore, feed, and assist domestically. Future demands are foreshadowed by the simultaneous missions to respond to hurricanes in Puerto Rico and Texas along with raging wildfires in California. Climate change will create failed states in other parts of the world due to droughts, famine, mass migration, and social unrest, and the U.S. military is likely to receive that 911 call as well. Can we expect an exhausted, overextended volunteer force to sustain this heavy burden?

The Civil-Military Gap

The civil-military gap identifies the disconnect between the American public and the servicemembers and veterans who defend and protect their rights, liberties, and security. Academics, politicians, national-security experts, and the armed forces attribute the gap to the concentration of military bases in the South and Far West, a smaller force as a result of the "peace dividend" of the early 1990s, or a self-centered, consumer-focused culture. Few acknowledge the contribution of the AVF to this gap. Today, most Americans view the military in general and the way we recruit the armed forces, in particular, through a lens of fear, apathy, ignorance, and guilt. This often leads to identifying servicemembers and veterans as either heroes or victims, which in turn begs the question, if all who serve are heroes, what does that make those who do not—laggards at best, cowards at worst? It is a rare veteran who sees himself or herself as a hero. The victim label is equally problematic because most of those serving see themselves as responsible citizens doing important work. At the same time, many in the military do not hold the society they serve in high regard.

Civilian contact with the armed forces is often limited to watching the Blue Angels perform at an air show or shouting "USA, USA" as an Iraq or Afghanistan veteran and his or her family is recognized and applauded at halftime of an NFL game—pageantry patriotism. Other forms of faux patriotism include allowing servicemembers to board airplanes before other passengers, hosting job fairs exclusively for veterans, and veteran discounts at restaurants and national-chain stores. U.S. brewers even participate in "supporting the troops": Budweiser with its "Salute from the Stands" campaign, and Miller countering with its "Give a Veteran a Piece of the High Life" initiative. Few Americans know the size of the defense budget, the number of servicemembers killed in Iraq and Afghanistan, or how many of their fellow citizens even serve. They view national defense as a job for someone else—if they think about it at all. Patronizing acts of gratitude may cause some to feel briefly connected to the military, but few attend a military funeral or visit a wounded patient at their local VA hospital.

On the other side of the civil-military gap, the servicemembers feel taken for granted, patronized, misunderstood, and ignored, notwithstanding repeated expressions of "thank you for your service" with a handshake. When so greeted, I often ask the other party if they served, and if not, why not. A recent *Military Times* survey identified that more than 75 percent of active-duty and reserve personnel agreed with the statement, "The military community has little in common with the rest of the country and most civilians do not understand the military." It also reported that majorities of both military and civilian respondents agreed that "military culture and way of life . . . is very different from the culture and way of life of those who are not in the military" and that "the military has different values than the rest of the country."

A feckless succession of Congresses since World War II has legitimized the civil-military gap by declining to discharge its constitutional obligation to declare war when U.S. troops are committed to harm's way. Other democracies have acted more responsibly. In Athens in the fifth century B.C., for example, the Greek historian Thucydides described how the Athenians decided to go to war. The city-state's assembly met to hear both sides of the issue. "Every argument was made, heard, and discussed before the full assembly." The same men who would be required to fight in any war that might result from the decision debated the issues and determined the course to take by their own votes. The Athenians had "skin in the game"; by contrast, Americans have "support the troops" bumper stickers. This difference is inherent in the AVF and leads to a militarized U.S. foreign policy.

Militarization of U.S. Foreign Policy

The link between the militarization of U.S. foreign policy and the AVF was acknowledged years before the AVF became reality. Among the "objections" the Gates Commission identified in its final report was that the AVF would encourage military operations and interventions, leading to an irresponsible national-security policy and reduce civilian concerns about militarism. Without "skin in the game," the average citizen would not be concerned with military actions. The commission dismissed this by arguing having the entire armed forces composed of volunteers would have no effect on the national command authority's decision to go to war or initiate military actions. They noted that domestic politics, financial costs, and the nature of threats to national security drives such decisions, thereby discounting the effects of a feckless Congress and deficit spending.

The wisdom of dismissing this objection is informed by the reality of pre- and post-AVF overseas military deployments since World War II. In the twenty-seven-year draft period (1946–1973), 19 such deployments occurred, while in the forty-seven years of the AVF, 144 such deployments have taken place. This comparison represents a deployment rate more than five times higher per year for the AVF period than that of its immediate predecessor.[12] Although some may argue that a such an increase is not decisive proof of increased U.S. militarism due to the AVF, it is certainly suggestive and should not be dismissed out of hand.

When I and others speak publicly, we have asked audiences how long the United States would have continued to deploy large numbers of troops in Iraq after invading and occupying the country in 2003 if we had a conscripted armed forces. Rarely does anyone suggest that we would have remained beyond 2005 or 2006. We did withdraw most of our volunteer force in 2011, but some still remain. Many suggested that if we had a conscripted force in 2003, we would not have invaded Iraq in the first place. Considering the cost of the resulting war in blood and treasure, this is a sobering suggestion. These speaking opportunities have delivered an unexpected exchange with pacifists and peace activists who seem to be attracted to such events. I have asked them if U.S. militarism overseas would be reduced, thus advancing their agenda, if the United States returned to conscription. They reluctantly agree that it would while reminding me that they would not support any war, whatever the composition of U.S. forces.

Conclusions

Given the various political, financial, and social issues we face as a nation, it is not surprising that the issue of how personnel procurement for our armed forces is not urgent. But it is important. Individually, Americans are faced with the day-to-day challenges of employment, health care, and saving for retirement and children's education, among other things. The issue of who defends the rights, liberties, and security of 360 million Americans is fundamental and important to a just, vibrant, and prosperous democracy. Throughout human history, other democracies have failed, among them Athens, of which Demosthenes said: "There is one source, O Athenians, of all your defeats. It is that your citizens have ceased to be soldiers."[13] All Americans cannot be soldiers. But a fact-based national dialogue to engage the question of whether the AVF is working and will work in the future will strengthen not only our national security but also the social fabric of our democratic society by everyone putting a bit more skin in the game.

Notes

1. George Washington to Alexander Hamilton, May 2, 1783, https://www.mount vernon.org/library/digitalhistory/quotes/article/it-may-be-laid-down-as-a-prima ry-position-and-the-basis-of-our-system-that-every-citizen-who-enjoys-the-protec tion-of-a-free-government-owes-not-only-a-proportion-of-his-property-but-even -his-personal-services-to-the-defence-of-it-and-consequently-that-th/.

2. John F. Kennedy, "Commencement Address at Yale University," June 11, 1962, Public Papers of the President.

3. The President's Commission on the All-Volunteer Force, chap. 12, "Objections to the All-Volunteer Force," 129.

4. Leon E. Panetta, "Secretary of Defense Statement on Fiscal 2013 Budget," January 26, 2012, 5, https://www.hsdl.org/?view&did=707164.

5. Eliot A. Cohen, *Citizens and Soldiers: The Dilemma of Military Service* (Ithaca, NY: Cornell University Press, 1985), 151.

6. Defense Business Board (2018), Fully Burdened and Lifecycle Cost of the Workforce, DBB FY 18-01, Washington, DC.

7. U.S. Army Recruiting Command Public Affairs, U.S. Army Recruiting.

8. The RAND Corporation, "Determinants of Productivity for Military Personnel" (2005), 27.

9. Richard M. Nixon, *The Real War* (New York: Simon & Schuster, 1980), 201.

10. Department of Defense Youth Polls, Joint Advertising Research Studies.

11. Congressional Budget Office, "Approaches to Changing Military Compensation," Congressional Budget Office Report, January 14, 2020.

12. Karl W. Eikenberry, "Reassessing the All-Volunteer Force," in *The Modern American Military*, ed. David M. Kennedy (Oxford: Oxford University Press, 2013), 217.

13. Demosthenes, Athenian general and orator.

Efficiency

Lawrence B. Wilkerson

According to the *Oxford English Dictionary*, "efficiency" means: "Fitness or power to accomplish, or success in accomplishing, the purpose intended. Adequate power; effectiveness." Employing this definition as a starting point, one can make certain assertions with regard to the method by which the United States has populated its military since the Gates Commission recommended the all-volunteer force in 1970.[1] That method provides for armed forces composed of mainly bought-and-paid-for volunteers—"contracted individuals," to use the army's jargon—who largely come from the third and fourth quartiles of the U.S. population and constitute less than 1 percent of that population. A central question must be asked: does this method produce an efficient force for the American empire?[2]

In the post–World War II era, and perhaps even more so in the post–Cold War period, metrics for the success of the use of military force are subject to debate regardless of the protests of those old warriors and others who, siding with General of the Army Douglas MacArthur, still cling to the ringing words "there is no substitute for victory" and believe they know very well how to define it.[3] For instance, is it fair even to use "victory" in a more traditional sense as a metric, and if so, what precisely is modern victory? Answering this query is made all the more difficult and complex in reference to the world's sole superpower, for which "winning" might be argued to have a number of more complex and sophisticated implications than it would for, say, Colombia, Norway, or even a country as large and facing major security challenges as India. Ancient Rome's leaders likely felt they had won even when they had lost—if referring to the catastrophic loss at Cannae when set against the eventual Roman routing of Carthage some seventy years later, they might have a point. But the twenty-first century A.D. is decidedly not the third century B.C. Certain words about war, however, will likely resonate forever, such as these from Book 8 of Carl von Clausewitz's *Vom Kriege* (On War): "every age [has] its own kind of war, its own limiting conditions, and its own peculiar preconceptions."[4]

In a more modern sense, then, not losing outright, or maintaining "the shadow of power"—as Dean Acheson defined "prestige"—might rank almost as high for a U.S. president and his national-security team as an outright traditional win would for a less powerful country.[5] Similar reasoning might even make claims to a losing stalemate, as in the U.S. struggle in Afghanistan, some twenty years in duration being a positive outcome of sorts—one composed of the electrifying initial and swift defeat of major al-Qaeda and Taliban elements in that country immediately after the terrorists attacks of September 11, 2001, as well as the bitter and indecisive struggle afterward—because it maintains U.S. military force in a critical region vis-à-vis China and the potentially unstable nuclear stockpile in neighboring Pakistan, regardless of the immediate on-the-ground and much-debated situation in Afghanistan presently.[6] One might even argue, as does one well-informed author, that Afghanistan from the beginning has been all about oil and gas pipelines, and thus, a troop presence there is essential for as long as oil and gas remain vital security interests.[7]

Similarly, containing an enemy state or states might be acceptable, even though on the surface more standard metrics could reveal a certain defeat, and perceived to be, even more so, all that could have been accomplished without an unprecedented resort to maximum power, including nuclear weapons, an option out of the question for an empire trying to uphold at least a modicum of imperial decency. The recent fight in Iraq and Syria against the Islamic State could be characterized in such a way. To claim that ISIS is defeated in the face of its spread from Syria and Iraq to Libya, Afghanistan, Nigeria, and elsewhere would be too much. But to claim it was dealt a severe blow perhaps not so, and its claim to holding extensive territory has largely vanished.

For this short analysis, the metric used will be the preservation and advancement of real U.S. national-security interests with an admixture of informed speculation about the costs, both in blood and treasure, of such preservation.[8] Moreover, these also will be examined in the light of the opposite conclusion, that is, when U.S. real interests were not preserved and advanced but, on the contrary, quite badly damaged and the costs—blood, treasure, and such intangibles as reputation and stature—seem commensurately extravagant.[9] This is to say nothing of the opportunity costs—education, infrastructure, healthcare, and general investment in the welfare of the greater U.S. population, for example—of such heavy and ultimately questionable expenditures.[10]

Moreover and critically, this analysis examines *war*, not its euphemisms such as "conflict" or "hostilities."[11] That is to say, for examples of the latter, U.S. actions on Grenada (October 1983); the air raid on Libya (April 1986); Operation Praying Mantis against Iran (October 1987); the "largest no-knock drug bust in history," called Operation Just Cause and conducted against Panama (December1989–January1990); the massive aerial bombing in the Balkans (1999); and other such imperial policing actions will not be tallied. The Persian Gulf War (1990–1991), Afghanistan (2001–2021), the Iraq War (2003–2011), and a look at potential wars with Russia and China will all be examined.

Using such modernized metrics as these, we could easily claim that, since the inception of the AVF in 1973, the United States has won outright only one war, that being the Persian Gulf War, known in U.S. military terminology as Operation Desert Shield / Desert Storm. There, the U.S. military and its several allies fulfilled the U.N. mandate and expelled Saddam Hussein's army from Kuwait, restoring that country's territorial integrity.[12] The efficiency of the AVF was therefore at its peak, for not since that war has it done well by the more traditional metrics or even by the modernized ones that are more pertinent.

Yet even in this "successful war," there were problems, one of them quite dramatic. Would any critic argue, for instance, that had the U.S. armed forces continued to pursue that campaign to Baghdad, as some pundits, both at that time and well afterward, claimed it should have, it would have ultimately faired any better than the AVF that did precisely that in the Iraq War?[13] Probably not, as most if not all forces allied with the United States (the total force with allies numbered over 600,000 troops) would have abandoned the effort—as happened largely in 2003, with the sole meaningful exception of the British—and the same problems would most likely have developed in 1991 as they developed in 2004.[14] And herein lies one of the fatal flaws of the AVF in terms of efficiency: it is far too small for an empire of the size that the United States has forged since World War II.[15] So, the AVF's "fitness or power to accomplish the purpose intended," as we might say on an efficiency scale, has ranged from somewhat deficient to woefully lacking.

Second, as to "adequate power, adequate effectiveness," one can readily assert or perhaps even demonstrate that the AVF could not stand up to and win, possibly even could not survive, a full-blown war with a major power—referred to in the current Pentagon jargon as a "peer power war"—such as Russia or even more significantly, China. Moreover, referring back to the Gates Commission, which presented its report to President Richard Nixon on February 21, 1970, we find that its members never really concluded that the AVF should be so tested. Here it is helpful to look back a moment at that commission, created by Nixon in the closing years of the Vietnam War to terminate conscription—a force-manning tool that in 1953 had been judged by general-turned-president Dwight D. Eisenhower to be an absolute necessity for waging the Cold War and for being maximally ready in case it turned into a hot war, which at any moment might have occurred.[16]

This commission included its chair and namesake, Thomas Gates, a former secretary of defense; economists Milton Friedman and Alan Greenspan; Father Theodore Hesburgh, Notre Dame's president and, importantly for the commission's mission, chair of the U.S. Commission on Civil Rights; and Generals Lauris Norstad of the U.S. Air Force and Alfred Gruenther of the U.S. Army, who was also head of the American Red Cross. Other noted Americans served as well. In short, the Gates Commission comprised members who one would think knew what they were considering, even though as with most such panels, there was more than a patina of politics associated with it. President Nixon felt strongly that public opposition to the war in Vietnam had been whipped up and fed by young citizens vulnerable to the draft. Thus, he was predisposed to the commission's "discovery" that conscription was not the best way to secure the nation. The draft, Nixon felt strongly, had inhibited his ability to wage successfully operations in Vietnam so that he could, as he had promised the American people, "end the war with honor."[17]

But, even with these associated and powerful politics, commission members actually included the following in their final report:

- "We unanimously believe that the nation's interests will be better served by an all-volunteer force, *supported by an effective stand-by draft*, than by a mixed force of volunteers and conscripts [emphasis added]."
- "We have satisfied ourselves that a volunteer force will not jeopardize national security, and we believe it will have a beneficial effect on the military as well as the rest of our society."

Despite these conclusions, or perhaps because of them, the members went on to conclude: "Conscription should be used only when the size of the forces required for the security of the nation cannot be supplied by the existing system [that is, the AVF]." Going further and interestingly, after debating whether Congress or the president should have the authority to invoke this "national emergency" conscription, the commission declared:

A standby system which authorizes the president to invoke the draft at his discretion would capture the worst of two worlds. On the one hand, it would make it possible for the President to become involved in military actions with a minimum of public debate and popular support. On the other hand, once the nation was involved, especially in a prolonged limited conflict, the inequities of the draft would provide a convenient point for opposition to the policy being pursued.[18]

With this, the commission let the proverbial cat out of the bag.

Its conclusions and recommendations acknowledged the fundamental political reason that presidents objected to the draft and pointed out equally well how their claim to the warpower might be made far easier to assert and execute by not having a draft.[19] Such defense experts as Gordon Adams have elucidated this very point since, how the AVF has not only facilitated the president's use of the warpower with almost no check from Congress—the branch of government empowered in Article I of the Constitution with the warpower—but also militarized U.S. foreign policy to a murderous extent and to the almost total negation of nonlethal tools of national power such as diplomacy.[20]

More than one expert in the field has noted such developments. Sarah Chayes, calling on her recent experiences in Afghanistan, writes eloquently in her book *Thieves of State*:

> If Western countries wish to reduce the likelihood of extremists or revolutionary violence abroad, if they want to curtail their use of military force when emergencies erupt—with the staggering financial and human costs and uneven chances of success such use of force entails— they must be willing to take political risks ahead of time. They must work to create redress for legitimate grievances. They must show as much courage in deploying leverage as they have, to date, in deploying soldiers.[21]

In fact, "deploying soldiers" does not cut the mustard more often than not these days. But this has become almost facile because, as another critic of the AVF has demonstrated, Americans have no "skin in the game" with the AVF.[22] Here it seems the Gates Commission was eerily prophetic but chose to ignore its own vision.

In terms of national security and perhaps most critically of all, as has been pointed out elsewhere, the AVF will likely prove an abject failure when confronted with the most serious test of efficiency possible, a major war. In such a war, the AVF would be consumed and destroyed so swiftly as to call into question whether any further action—full national mobilization, for instance, as the Gates Commission seemed to recommend—could be accomplished or would even be effective if it could. In short, it would call into play the potential surrender of the nation, an eventuality surely contemplated in those early years from 1776 to 1820 not only with some trepidation but also with a recognition of reality, as three formidable global empires—Spain, France, and Britain—vied with one another on an almost daily basis and had their own significant claims in "the New World." But such a possibility of utter defeat, with the exception perhaps of a nuclear holocaust during the Cold War, has seemed remote ever since that age, and most certainly since 1992, thus making it almost impossible to believe possible today. Such a well-established but clearly unsubstantiated belief (in terms of the history of empire) might be part of the challenge confronting anyone today wishing to change America's force-manning system.

But such might be the results were either, one, a major war on the plains of Europe against Russia's sizeable land army, great strategic depth, and ample nuclear weapons or, two, a largely air and naval battle, at least initially, with China in the South China Sea, either over more belligerent and outrageous Chinese territorial claims or, as far more likely, over China's use of military force to reclaim Taiwan.[23]

In the European scenario, the United States and its NATO allies—NATO allies President Donald Trump seemed bound and determined to alienate and dispense with—just might be able to hold long enough to achieve a stalemate, but with China, not even that would be likely. The almost 24 million citizens of Taiwan would be subject to the rule of Beijing posthaste. In fact, it is difficult even to believe that the United States would today contest an outright takeover of the island by Beijing. Washington would protest vociferously, to be sure, but to commit the AVF to oppose such a takeover would likely be out of the question. An eventual and wholesale retreat from Asia would be the far more probable ultimate outcome. There simply are not sufficient U.S. military forces to oppose such huge numbers as China could field. What would surely be a fait accompli would not be contested militarily; to do so would be foolhardy in the extreme.

In an excellent and succinct article appearing in the prestigious magazine *Proceedings* (the article was awarded first prize by the Chief of Naval Operations in the "Rising Historian" category), Lieutenant Commander Jeff Vandenengel, U.S. Navy, looks closely at the 1982 Falklands War.[24] Though it occurred more than a generation ago, like the American Civil War forecast dramatically the carnage of the First World War, the Falklands War forecasts the carnage—particularly naval—of any modern war between the United States and China. "Fighting along a Knife Edge," the title Vandenengel gives to his article, provides the most succinct yet tellingly descriptive preview of what a war with China would probably be like. One citation from the article demonstrates this: "A single submarine

The USS *Dwight D. Eisenhower* (CVN 69), a nuclear-powered *Nimitz*-class aircraft carrier, transits the Mediterranean Sea. (Courtesy Department of Defense)

launched a single salvo that sank a single ship—and defeated an entire navy with a devastating deterrent impact."[25]

Perhaps no more vulnerable capital ship exists in the world today than a $14 billion-plus U.S. aircraft carrier, with its extremely expensive air wing and its approximately 5,000 sailors. That a Chinese submarine could easily sink such an asset is common knowledge among sailors and others expert in the ways of the U.S. war machine.[26] After describing how a single Argentine submarine almost immobilized the British fleet in the Falklands, Vandenengel writes: "Confronted by dozens of Chinese submarines in the western Pacific, the U.S. Navy will be faced with a significantly more challenging problem."[27]

With 5,000 Americans dead, wounded, in the water, or otherwise incapacitated—notably, there are not even sufficient spaces on a carrier's normal escort ships to take these people on board should it be sunk and many of its crew be in the water—what will Washington do?[28] And how is this particular scenario, one far more likely than any U.S. defense expert will admit in public, relevant to the inefficiency of the AVF? One must wonder indeed what American officials would do. Multiple exercises in which the author has participated demonstrate a quick turn to nuclear-weapons use, or at least recommendations for such deployment from military participants. Civilian participants roleplaying the national-security council members are not normally so inclined—not immediately, in any event.

The relevance to the AVF is twofold. First, the U.S. Navy is almost as vulnerable to the inefficiency of the AVF as is the U.S. Army. For example, if the navy were suddenly to find the money and the congressional support to raise its total ship numbers to 350-plus, as President Trump indicated was his wish, it is highly doubtful it could recruit sufficient men and women to crew those vessels. The AVF concept is incapable of providing them unless the nation is willing to provide such monetary bonuses and inducements that military budgets would have funding for little else. Second, the shock of the reality that the United States had just lost a significant number of the 5,000 men and women on board an aircraft carrier, not to mention one of the most expensive ships in the U.S. Navy's fleet, with in a single shot, so to speak, would produce one of two outcomes: rage or deep despair—possibly both across the national spectrum, that is, from elites to the general population. It is not beyond the possible, either, that the loss might be not just one carrier but two or three and almost simultaneously. If the outcome is national rage, where is the military force—other than nuclear weapons—to respond to that rage? If the outcome is national despair, China has won—in the more complete sense of the traditional meaning, more or less, of that term. A nation that cannot mobilize for the longer and more sweeping war thus required in such circumstances is a defeated nation, most certainly a defeated empire.

Sadly, the far more likely outcome would be a resort to nuclear weapons, first in small and low-yield numbers, then, as more than a half century of nuclear-escalation doctrine indicates, to a general strategic exchange. At the moment, because China has far fewer such weapons, the United States might "win," but the resulting Pyrrhic victory might be of very little comfort. Logically enough, too, Beijing is rumored to be considering a change in its nuclear-weapons philosophy—constant since Mao Tse-tung devised it—so as to build more of them and more sophisticated models. Clearly, China's leaders see the handwriting on the wall.[29]

Moreover and as seriously, we court today a negative answer to the very real question that former assistant secretary of defense Lawrence Korb has raised: "What if we had a war and no one showed up on our side?"[30] Some, particularly in the progressive political camp, might immediately exclaim, "Excellent!" Given the last nineteen or so years of utterly catastrophic national-security decision making in Washington, many realists might just join them in their ecstasy. But then a certain knowledge of the way power works in the world would intervene and inform them that such a feeling, while euphoric and feel-good, is also utopian and thus ultimately very dangerous.

More realistically and even more dangerous, perhaps, is what one U.S. senator remarked as we were debating these issues in his congressional offices recently. Exasperated with arguments regarding the need for conscription and utterly convinced that the resurrection of the draft was a political dead end, he exclaimed, "If the enemy were on the beaches, by God, the American people would rouse themselves!" I reminded the senator of a little history. I asked if he knew what had happened in 1863 when President Lincoln initiated a draft. "Yes," he said, "The northern states answered him." "True," I responded. "They answered with so much opposition that Lincoln had to dispatch a sizeable troop formation to New York, where the riots were quite out of hand and where people were being killed. These were troops the Union could ill afford to divert from the war. Only then did the situation settle a bit and could the Union army get on with its central business." I continued, "And remember, all one needed to escape that grossly unfair draft of 1863 was 300 U.S. dollars or someone whom you could direct to fill your place, like a slave—oh, yes, there were still slaves in such positions that they could be directed to serve, even in the North."

Despite this, it appeared to me that the senator was unmoved, just like all the other members of Congress with whom I have discussed this issue.[31] But adding to this dire scenario, polls today show that those Americans under twenty-five years old—the so-called postmillennials—have as little propensity or desire to serve in the military as any young people in our history. Moreover, polls show that the heretofore most powerful indicator of vulnerability to recruitment into the AVF—that the young man or woman comes from a military family—is not so active anymore. In fact, these polls demonstrate that such potential recruits are now being advised by members of that very military family—moms, dads, granddads, and others—not to enlist.[32]

In short, if a sudden call for conscripts were made today, would the response be any different than in 1863? Very likely the situation would be worse, perhaps much worse. Add to this the prospect that, were a draft called, women by necessity would have to be included in Selective Service, and one begins to visualize the utterly catastrophic circumstances that could be generated, perhaps vastly exceeding the 1863 riots in their ultimate consequence.[33] Having traveled the country in the past ten years, one of the most volatile issues I have uncovered in the heartland is the issue of drafting women: grandmothers, grandfathers, mothers, and fathers, even the young women themselves, have registered full-throated, powerful dissent. Go outside the beltway in Washington, D.C., and such dissent is extraordinary. Government's elitist views mask this fundamental grassroots antipathy to "the absolute equality of women." And such antipathy to conscription, particularly if they are under forty years old, is palpable. One can mount the argument that in the United States it has always been so for men, so why should it be any different for women; that is a powerful point. In the past, however, there has been time to demonstrate the danger of such views: after the sinking of the *Lusitania* in 1916, after the attack on Pearl Harbor in 1941, and even after the headlong route of the South Korean army and their few U.S. allies on the Korean Peninsula in 1950. And in Vietnam, the draft sort of sneaked up on men, slowly over several troop escalations. Post 9/11, there was a patriotic surge of enlistment, but it dissipated rather rapidly.[34]

Finally, there is a quite powerful, persuasive argument that future wars will be far less consuming of manpower (and womanpower) than those of the past; that cyberoperations, network attacks, and other digital-age methods will constitute the order of battle. Two counters seem logical, however. First, these methods are already available and being employed today. But it remains to be seen if, one, they are truly effective—some contend they will be devastatingly so—and, two, when and if states will begin to employ them on a "replacement basis," that is, spending time, energy, and money on these methods at the expense of the more traditional bombs, bullets, and bayonets. Should that eventually happen, fielding military forces of any type might be highly dubious. An entourage of highly trained hackers might be far more appropriate.

Second and more importantly, the need for large numbers of pliable, trained, and ready young men and women will not disappear as the century progresses; quite the contrary, the need will grow and perhaps exponentially so. By midcentury—slightly less than a generation away—the climate crisis will be upon the planet, perhaps with a vengeance.[35] Already, sea rise and hurricanes alone have demonstrated to military leaders that large numbers of responders will be necessary—numbers eventually well beyond the capacity of state militias (National Guard) and in time even the AVF, particularly if its primary mission remains the security of empire from its 750–800 overseas bases. Combine this domestic need with the five- to tenfold increase in humanitarian- and disaster-relief requirements internationally, and one can readily imagine the need for 2–3 million men and women in some degree of readiness—not unlike, perhaps, the Civilian Conservation Corps (CCC) of the 1930s.

In every serious respect of efficiency, the AVF comes up dramatically short. It represents trillions of dollars spent on an instrument of security that will fail at the most important moment of need because it is so inefficient. Trillions of dollars spent on a force that enables and even invites wars that are long, brutal, bloody, and unwinnable. Trillions of dollars spent on a force that, in other words, aids and abets wars that cannot be won while being unready for wars that must be won. And the AVF is unready, indeed, for the coming crisis of climate change.

Notes

1. For more on the President's Commission on an All-Volunteer Armed Force and Selective Service Reform (1969–1970), also known as the Gates Commission, see Bernard Rostker, *I Want You!: The Evolution of the All-Volunteer Force* (Santa Monica, CA: RAND, 2006), 61–108. Its final report was entitled *The Report of the President's Commission on an All-Volunteer Armed Force* and was presented to President Nixon on February 21, 1970.

2. Douglas L. Kriner and Francis X. Shen, *The Casualty Gap: The Causes and Consequences of American Wartime Inequalities* (Oxford: Oxford University Press, 2010). There is a new analysis that seems to refute much of what Kriner and Shen have conveyed. See Andrea Asoni, Andrea Gilli, Mauro Gilli, and Tino Sanandaji, "A Mercenary Army of the Poor?: Technological Change and the Demographic Composition of the Post-9/11 U.S. Military," *Journal of Strategic Studies* 45, no 4 (January 2020): 568–614, https://doi.org/10.1080/01402390.2019.1692660. Its abstract reads as follows:

Is the American military a mercenary army of the poor, as some critics of U.S. foreign policy suggest? In this article, we analyze individual-level data of two national representative samples covering the period 1979–2008. We find that, in contrast to the accepted wisdom, the U.S. military no longer primarily recruits individuals from the most disadvantaged socioeconomic backgrounds. Technological, tactical, operational, and doctrinal changes have led to a change in the demand for personnel. As a result, on different metrics such as family income and family wealth as well as cognitive abilities, military personnel performs [*sic*], on average, like or slightly better than the civilian population.

There are significant problems with this analysis, not the least of which is that, if it is accurate, the authors are contending that the U.S. "middle class" borders on infinitesimal, that the military targets for recruitment almost exclusively that middle class—gaining almost all of that segment's high school graduates, for example—and that such success constitutes a win for the military and an even bigger win for the society it is pledged to secure. Furthermore, the authors contend that the very high-tech demands of the military probably could not be met in any other way since only these "middle class" men and women have the capacity to perform in such a largely technical environment, a change that has positively altered recruiting success, as if by some mysterious magic. Aside from these conclusions and analytical problems, the study takes no account of increased induction of Mental Category IVs by, particularly, the U.S. Army in order to meet end-strength demands or the increased use of waivers of such misconduct as illicit drug use, convictions for misdemeanors and even felonies, and other less than stellar activities. More significantly, the study makes no attempt to address the indisputable reality that the top tier in the United States has almost zero representation in the military—it is, in fact, AWOL—and the second tier is largely absent as well, so that the very small middle class, squeezed in as it were between the top half and the bottom half (even less, as one-third of the youth population are too obese for military service and another third intellectually incapable of it) is what mainly composes the U.S. military. It is at best a very strained point of view and at worst a complete misrepresentation of the recruiting challenges faced by all the armed services, particularly the army. Perhaps indicative of these challenges are two points: in 2019, the army alone spent $427 million on recruitment bonuses and more than $1 billion on almost 10,000 recruiters, who are some of the very best NCOs in the army and, when recruiting, not doing the jobs for which they were intended. These recruiter numbers constitute more than an entire combat brigade of soldiers.

3. "In war there is no substitute for victory." Douglas MacArthur, "Farewell Address to Congress," April 19, 1951, https://www.americanrhetoric.com/speeches/douglasmacarthurfarewelladdress.htm. MacArthur also expressed this sentiment in a letter to Congressman Joseph W. Martin Jr., March 20, 1951, sent from Tokyo. "Message from Douglas MacArthur to Joseph Martin," World War II Database, https://m.ww2db.com/doc.php?q=408.

4. Carl von Clausewitz, *Vom Kriege*, ed. and trans. Michael Howard and Peter Paret (Princeton, NJ: Princeton University Press, 1976).

5. Robert L. Beisner, *Dean Acheson: A Life in the Cold War* (Oxford: Oxford University Press, 2006), 335.

6. Lawrence B. Wilkerson, "A Strategic Reappraisal of Afghanistan," March 2020, unpublished paper submitted to the U.S. Joint Chiefs of Staff, copy in author's possession.

7. Charlotte Dennett, *The Crash of Flight 3804: A Lost Spy, a Daughter's Quest, and the Deadly Politics of the Great Game for Oil* (White River Junction, VT: Chelsea Green, 2020).

8. "Real" as opposed to "vital"—a much overused term—simply denotes, for example, what a statutorily composed National Security Council populated by the best possible men and women in deliberation would determine worthy of a fateful decision—that is, a decision that would send young men and women to die and to kill others for state purposes. In my thirty-five years serving in the military or the U.S. government, I have encountered such a group of people only once, but I have encountered real interests several times. The only such interest I have ever considered *vital* is the one implied by that word—national survival, in whatever guise. Examples of this are the 1961 crisis over Berlin and the standoff with the Soviets, which led to the building of the Berlin Wall, and the almost-contemporaneous Cuban Missile Crisis of October 1962. Nonvital interests can be important, even supremely so, but they are not existential.

9. Dwight D. Eisenhower was the last president to demand a formal budget annex to national-security decision documents—that is, an analysis that, for better or worse, demonstrated to the best abilities of his director of the Bureau of the Budget

and staff just how much a national-security decision might cost the nation in dollars. To demonstrate how irresponsible presidents have become in adhering to any sort of fiscal restraint vis-à-vis such decisions, in 2002, when President George W. Bush was considering military action in Iraq and asked his National Security Council for a cost estimate, Vice President Richard Cheney responded: "[President] Reagan proved deficits don't matter." Deputy Secretary of Defense Paul Wolfowitz later told the Senate Armed Services Committee that the coming war would not cost the United States any money at all, that Iraq would pay for it, presumably with its abundant oil resources. In fact, the official and unofficial estimates for the war's costs were wildly off the mark. Senator Robert Byrd was the only member of the U.S. government who came close when, in a speech on the floor of the Senate, he exclaimed, "Why this war could cost billions, even trillions!" According to the Costs of War Project at Brown University, the war's total cost exceeded $5 trillion. See note 10.

10. The Costs of War Project is a joint effort between Brown University's Watson Institute for International and Public Affairs and Boston University's Frederick S. Pardee Center for the Study of the Longer-Range Future. Together, these two groups of experts have published analytical studies of the dollar costs of the so-called Global War on Terrorism. Several findings were made, but the conclusion that received widespread coverage was the $6.4 trillion price tag, which, of course, included the massive war in Iraq begun in 2003. See specifically Nita C. Crawford, "United States Budgetary Costs and Obligations of Post-9/11 Wars, through FY 2020: $6.4 Trillion," in 20 Years of War, Watson Institute, November 13, 2019, https://watson.br own.edu/costsofwar/files/cow/imce/papers/2019/US Budgetary Costs of Wars November 2019.pdf.

11. Here we mean to rule out such uses of military force as cited in the narrative. The U.S. Marine Corps sometimes refers to certain of these as "small wars," but they are more accurately labeled by the appropriate military terminology as "raids," "surgical and limited strikes," "peacekeeping or peace-enforcement operations," and so on.

12. See U.N. Security Council Resolution 678, adopted November 29, 1990, http://unscr.com/en/resolutions/doc/678.

13. See Michael Gordon and General Bernard Trainor, *The Generals' War* (Boston: Little, Brown, 1995). Most famously in this regard, the secretary of defense during the Persian Gulf War, Richard B. Cheney, directly afterward explained several times that Baghdad was not worth the life of a single soldier or marine; later as George W. Bush's vice president, Cheney was one of the strongest advocates for "going to Baghdad" in 2003.

14. In addition to the United States, coalition members consisted of thirty-four other nations, including Saudi Arabia, Syria, Egypt, Bangladesh, France, the United Kingdom, Belgium, and South Korea.

15. See David Vine, *Base Nation: How U.S. Military Bases Abroad Harm America and the World* (New York: Henry Holt, 2015). The "empire" now has somewhere between 750 and 800 military bases and installations scattered across the globe.

16. Generals Eisenhower and George C. Marshall had voiced their views of such personnel issues on several occasions, including before, during, and after World War II. Marshall, of course, and President Harry S. Truman had strongly advocated not simple

conscription but universal military training (UMT). Under UMT, every able-bodied and capable young American male would receive some military training and then, were a crisis to demand it, join one of the armed services. Marshall, in particular, saw this as essential to making the "militia" (the National Guard) a robust strategic reserve for the United States. As laudable as this concept might seem, at least to some of us, it is today probably unaffordable in terms of dollar costs. We are simply too populous a nation to submit all our able-bodied men and women to, say, six months of military training. See, in particular, General Marshall's testimony before the Senate Armed Services Committee on March 17, 1948, "Hearings before the Committee on Armed Services, United States Senate, Eightieth Congress, Second Session, on UNIVERSAL MILITARY TRAINING."

17. Robert Dallek, *Nixon and Kissinger: Partners in Power* (New York: HarperCollins, 2007), 127ff.

18. The Gates Commission, or the President's Commission on an All-Volunteer Armed Force, 1970, https://www.nixonlibrary.gov. The first two bullets are from page iii of the report and are part of the transmittal letter from Thomas Gates to President Nixon, the letter which forwarded the report to the president and thus became an official part of the report. The remainder of the citation is from the body of the report, specifically pages 120–121.

19. All one need do is examine the struggle between Congress, the DOD, and President Donald Trump over the war in Yemen, where U.S. military intelligence and logistical support is essential to the coalition prosecuting the conflict, led by the Kingdom of Saudi Arabia. More than once, a majority of Congress has voted to withdraw funding from the DOD in order to halt U.S. participation in this brutal war. The president has vetoed the legislation each time and, because his party controlled the Senate by a slight margin, the veto was not overridden. One could argue that, according to the War Powers Act, which bestows the power on Congress to check the president's power to continue participation in such conflict situations, a simple majority should be all that is required. Apparently not, given the nation's current acquiescence to this state of affairs. Having an overwhelming 99 percent of Americans with "no skin in the game" clearly contributes to this attitude.

20. Gordon Adams and Shoon Murray, eds., *Mission Creep: The Militarization of US Foreign Policy?* (Washington, DC: Georgetown University Press, 2014). Also see Karl W. Eikenberry, "The Militarization of U.S. Foreign Policy," *Journal of the National Committee on American Foreign Policy* 35, no. 1 (2013): 1–8; and Robert M. Gates, "The Overmilitarization of American Foreign Policy," *Foreign Affairs* 99, no. 4 (July/August 2020). Gates served as secretary of defense under Presidents George W. Bush and Barak Obama.

21. Sarah Chayes, *Thieves of State: Why Corruption Threatens Global Security* (New York: W. W. Norton, 2015), 204.

22. Dennis Laich, *Skin in the Game: Poor Kids and Patriots* (Bloomington, IN: iUniverse, 2013).

23. The author participated in numerous wargames during his thirty-one-year army career, particularly when on the faculty of the U.S. Naval War College and, later, at the U.S. Marine Corps War College, where he crafted many of the games.

Taiwan was often the game scenario's focus when the exercises occurred in the Pacific theater. At the Marine Corps War College, students characterized the Taiwan-focused games as "The Shark and the Elephant." China, the elephant, could not get at the U.S. Navy seriously, while the United States, the shark, could not invade China. Use of nuclear weapons was almost always contemplated to break this stalemate after nonnuclear fighting had attrited both countries' conventional forces quite dramatically. Cooler heads prevailed, however, and the games usually terminated there.

24. When the author was on the faculty of the Naval War College, U.K. admiral Sandy Woodward, commander of the British forces in the Falklands War, told a special seminar of faculty and students in 1987 that if had he lost another ship in that brief but quite destructive war, he would have recommended to Prime Minister Margaret Thatcher that U.K. forces withdraw. It was, he said, "like Napoleon declared after Waterloo, a very close-run thing."

25. Jeff Vandenengel, "Fighting along a Knife Edge in the Falklands," *Proceedings* 145, no. 12 (December 2019): 62.

26. In exercises such as Pacific Rim, it is common for a U.S. attack submarine to surface inside the antisubmarine-warfare screen of a participating U.S. aircraft carrier, break radio silence, and transmit simply "Bang, you're dead" to the skipper of the carrier, much to the latter's frustration and chagrin. Such is a well-kept secret in navy circles, as the reader can well imagine. Submarines are still relatively invulnerable if their skippers and crews are well trained, smart, and on top of their game. And their weapons—such as 65-cm wake-homing torpedoes—do not even have to strike the carrier directly but rather just explode underneath it, thereby breaking its back (that is, keel) and sinking it extremely swiftly.

27. Vandenengel, "Fighting along a Knife Edge in the Falklands," 65.

28. For a thorough examination of the aircraft carrier, the extremely costly central ship of the U.S. Navy, see Henry J. Hendrix, "At What Cost a Carrier?," Center for a New American Security, Disruptive Defense Papers, March 2013, https://www.cnas .org/publications/reports/at-what-cost-a-carrier.

29. Many Asia scholars—in the region and outside of it—have written on the possibilities of China's nuclear policy undergoing significant change. Since Mao Tse-tung devised this policy, based simply on his belief that the country did not need any more nuclear weapons than the small number that constituted deterrence, China has more or less adhered to that basic common-sense approach. Of late, scholars have written about forthcoming changes, largely based on China's growing sense that deterrence could fail and it might need to ride out a first strike and retaliate. One of the most recent treatments of this situation is Michael Mazza and Henry Sokolski, "China's Nuclear Arms Are a Riddle Wrapped in a Mystery," *Foreign Policy*, March 13, 2020, https://npolicy.org/chinas-nuclear-arms-are-a-riddle-wrapped-in-a-myst ery-foreign-policy/.

30. Lawrence J. Korb, foreword to Laich, *Skin in the Game*, xii.

31. I cannot reveal the name of the senator thus quoted because of a confidentiality agreement.

32. Numerous sources, including the U.S. Army's Recruiting Command, the *Military Times* newspaper, strictly civilian newspapers such as the *New York Times*, and

magazines such as *Fortune* have published stories on both the failures and the successes of military recruiting over the past decade and particularly in the last three years, largely due to the increasing controversy over what is actually causing the current AVF to have enormous problems filling its ranks. For a recent example, see William Arkin, "Fewer Americans Want to Serve in the Military: Cue Pentagon Panic," *Guardian*, April 10, 2019. The military is wont to concede difficulties but claim overall success; critics seek to claim disaster or something just short of it. The reality seems to be a bit of both, depending on one's point of view. For instance, when the U.S. Army does well, it usually omits the facts that it took in a higher number of Mental Category IVs or issued a higher number of waivers for illicit drug use, for failure to meet weight standards, or even for felony convictions. Likewise, it is less than forthcoming about the millions of dollars in "bribes" it has paid to get the numbers it did acquire. Just as the analysis in the article by Asoni et al. is highly questionable in terms of its overall implications—some counterarguments being repeated here—so are some of the official revelations somewhat suspect. See note 2 above. At the day's end, it is fair to conclude that serious challenges exist today and are likely to grow in seriousness in the future. It is also fair to say that, despite shifts in recruiting tactics and procedures, increased sums of money—almost half the annual budget for defense is already dedicated to personnel—is the only real answer, and it might become questionable that even that solution will work at some future date. In FY 2022, for example, the U.S. Army failed to meet its target for annual recruiting by 25 percent, or 15,000 recruits; the U.S. Navy raised its maximum enlistment age to forty-one years; and the U.S. Air Force remained dramatically short of fighter pilots—1,650 in 2021, with the future outlook little better.

33. The National Commission on Military, National, and Public Service published its final report on March 25, 2020. It recommended that, so long as the Selective Service System continues to exist, women as well as men should be subject to call-up. See National Commission on Military, National, and Public Service, "Inspired to Serve: The Final Report of the National Commission on Military, National, and Public Service," March 2020, https://www.volckeralliance.org/sites/default/files/attachments//Final Report - National Commission.pdf.

34. See James Dao, "They Signed Up to Fight," *New York Times*, September 6, 2011; and N. Branker, "Post 9/11 Military: What Has Changed since That Terrible Day?," *Purple Heart Foundation* (blog), September 8, 2017, https://purpleheartfoundation.wordpress.com/2017/09/08/post-911-military-what-has-changed-since-that-terrible-day/.

35. See Michael T. Klare, *All Hell Breaking Loose: The Pentagon's Perspective on Climate Change* (New York: Henry Holt, 2019).

10

Reserve Components

Major General Jeffrey E. Phillips

The reserve components of the U.S. armed forces comprise two major elements: the federally controlled reserves and the National Guard. Each service's federal reserve is led by a commissioned flag officer—a general or admiral—responsible for the readiness of the command's resources for use worldwide. This officer's chain of command runs through the respective service chief, such as the chief of staff of the air force, to the national command authority. The reserve components are governed by the same federal law that governs the armed forces.[1]

The federal reserves have army, marine corps, navy, and air force elements as well as the U.S. Coast Guard Reserve, which is considered one of the uniformed services but operates under the control of the Department of Homeland Security. (The coast guard and its reserve may be transferred to control of the Department of Defense by presidential decree or act of Congress). As of this writing, the newly formed space force does not have a "reserve" element.

The National Guard has the Army National Guard and Air National Guard. National Guard elements, although largely funded with federal dollars, are directed under normal circumstances by their respective state's governor. When so operating, the Guard is governed by Title 32, United States Code. Typical of their employment in this relationship is domestic service during crises. The directors of the Army National Guard and Air National Guard function much as the chiefs of the federal reserve components, ensuring the readiness of their components through their respective unit chains of command. Each state's units are commanded by an adjutant general appointed by the governor, normally of two-star rank. The chief of the National Guard Bureau, a four-star general responsible for ensuring the readiness of all Guard assets nationwide, is a presidentially appointed, Senate-confirmed member of the Joint Chiefs of Staff and is the chief military adviser to the president, secretary of defense, and National Security Council, serving also as the Pentagon's principal communications channel to state governors and their adjutants general. The National Guard can be "federalized" by the president, at which time it comes under the president's direction and may then operate under Title 10 authority. When Army and Air National Guard units deployed during Operations Enduring Freedom and Iraqi Freedom, they operated within this relationship. An important distinction between operation under Title 32 and Title 10 is that, when governed by the former, Guard units may perform law-enforcement roles, such as security of government property. Thus, they may be brought into federal service but remain under state control to perform such missions prohibited by Title 10. Within the reserve components, the National Guard is designated "Component 2," and the federal reserves—such as the Air Force Reserve—are "Component 3."

The reserve components augment the "active component," commonly known as the "active duty" or the "regular" military. Designated as "Component 1," the active component is that element of the national security forces on duty full time under the direction of the president. Normally, these elements are the nation's first responders to crises involving U.S. military force. By law, reserve components are authorized a varying number of training days each year, depending on the category of readiness. The "selected reserve," those members expected to need minimal preparation for mobilization, get forty-eight paid four-hour "unit training assemblies." Normally, a weekend expends four of these periods; thus, the normal number of "drill" weekends per year is twelve, or one per month. The selected reserve also gets two weeks of "annual training." It is this training schedule that has earned reservists the uncharitable moniker "weekend warrior." That has changed dramatically, however. In today's all-volunteer force, the U.S. military cannot successfully operate without its reserve components. According to the Reserve Forces Policy Board's 2017 transition briefing for the incoming administration, these components provide:

Surge capacity: supplementing the active component, the Reserve and National Guard provide the resources to enable an expeditious enlargement of forces available to the nation.

Active component / reserve component integration: Gone are the days of a wholly "strategic reserve" intended for use only in a major conflagration. The current and improving integration of the components is a source of military readiness and capability.

Bargain capability: While in "dwell"—home-station presence, not deployed—the reserve components cost the nation far less than active component units also in dwell. Constituting some 38 percent of the total force, the reserve components account for about 16 percent of the total defense budget. The fully burdened, per-capita cost of the reserve component is about one-third the cost of the active component, as it needs less infrastructure and overhead.

Continuum of service: The reserve components provide a variety of service options, from inactive service to full-time duty virtually indistinguishable from that of the active component. The services are making transition between the components more feasible; that helps retain service members who for any number of reasons need to change from one intensity of service to another, such as full-time to part-time.

Roughly beginning with the advent of the AVF, the transformation of the nation's reserve force was heralded by then–army chief of staff General Creighton Abrams, ruing the disaster of Vietnam: "Never again will I send or be part of sending America's Army into conflict without Main Street USA." Four decades later, incoming army chief of staff General Mark Milley echoed what had become a theme. "We cannot conduct sustained land warfare without the Guard and the Reserve," he said. "It is impossible for the United States of America to go to war today without bringing Main Street—without bringing Tennessee and Massachusetts and Colorado and California. We just can't do it."[2] This is the story of those decades of immense change.

History of the Reserves

The original "citizen-soldier" was the militiaman. In the American colonies, the militia secured villages and settlements. The English crown, consumed with protection of its vast dominion as well as internal conflict, regarded as a low priority the protection of its North American colonies and granted them authority to provide their own defenses. In 1623, the Virginia General Assembly directed "that men go not to work in the ground without their arms; That no man go or send abroad without a sufficient partie well armed." The Massachusetts Bay Colony in 1636 organized what is recognized as the first colonial militia, the direct forebear of today's National Guard.[3] Britain did furnish regulars, such as those who arrived in 1677 during the Bacon Rebellion. Boston welcomed such forces in 1689, yet British strength never exceeded 900 troops during this period.[4]

The militia system provided military strength derived from the populace and later served the colonies throughout the War of Independence. At the war's outset, one-third of the 20,000 men in General George

Washington's army were from state militias.[5] Militias did not train as frequently on a large scale as did regular forces; their role was to "drop plow and hammer" to defend their community against indigenous attackers, not a "modern" professional opponent. These earliest of America's citizen-soldiers had to be good, but only good enough for that task. Militia combat readiness, especially at the outset of hostilities, thus tended to be inferior to regulars. "If I was called upon to declare upon Oath, whether the Militia have been most Serviceable or hurtful upon the whole I should subscribe to the latter," Washington told Congress in late 1776.[6] Yet, once Washington learned to use his militia forces in concert with regular Continental troops, the militia's performance improved.[7] The 1777 American victory at Bennington during the Saratoga Campaign was achieved by militia commanded by a Continental officer. At Kings Mountain, North Carolina, militia led by its own colonel defeated loyalist militia, forcing Lieutenant General Charles Cornwallis to change his campaign plans for subduing the South.

The U.S. Constitution's "militia clauses" in Article I, Section 8, give Congress the power to "provide for calling forth the Militia to execute the Laws of the Union, suppress Insurrections and repel Invasions." The section further provides for "organizing, arming, and disciplining the Militia, and for governing such Part of them as may be employed in the Service of the United States, reserving to the States respectively, the Appointment of the Officers, and the Authority of training the Militia according to the discipline prescribed by Congress." Once "called forth" by Congress, the Constitution, in Article II, Section 2, grants the president powers as commander in chief, thus neatly separating military authority among the federal government's legislative and executive branches. Following the War of Independence, reflecting American resistance to large standing armies, as well as with its treasury depleted, the new nation further codified its reliance on state militias. The First and Second Militia Acts of 1792 provided, respectively, authority for the president to "call forth" members of state militias. The second act mandated that every able-bodied white male between the ages of eighteen and forty-five be enrolled in the militia of his locale and be suitably furnished with arms, ammunition, and other basic equipment. It also established rules of discipline and the authority for organizing companies, battalions, regiments, brigades, and divisions, with officer and noncommissioned billets of corresponding rank. Then as now, noncommissioned officers were relied on to take care of the men. Commanding officers, usually captains of companies, were directed to notify local citizens eligible for militia service "by the proper non-commissioned Officer of the company." In reality, the states did not take these acts seriously.[8]

Under President Thomas Jefferson, standing federal forces were reduced with the exception of a standing navy, reflecting the geographic isolation of the continent, yet its vulnerability to Great Britain's seagoing might. Jefferson instead relied, with the consent of Congress, on the state militias. During this period, from about 1800 to 1860, state volunteer militias became popular, filling an important security role within their states' borders.[9]

The breakout of war in 1861 compelled President Abraham Lincoln to call up 75,000 militiamen on a three-month term to augment the 16,000 regular troops then in the U.S. Army. That number increased to 500,000 volunteers, who were federalized. Ultimately, more than 2.5 million men would serve in the Union army.[10] After the Civil War, the militia faded as did the standing force; congressional concern over the use of the military in the South and on the western frontier prompted the 1878 Posse Comitatus Act, prohibiting the performance of law enforcement by the federal military. The law did not apply to state militias, now increasingly being referred to as the National Guard. Simultaneously, momentum built for a navy reserve, with the naval militias of Massachusetts and New York providing a precedent of sorts.

Outbreak of war in 1898 again mobilized volunteers and state militias. U.S. victory in the Spanish-American War notwithstanding, weaknesses in militia performance prompted Secretary of War Elihu Root's advocacy of a federal reserve to augment the militia. The states countered with proposals to strengthen the militias as this federal reserve. Their efforts produced the 1903 Dick Act, which funded militia training and officially designated them the National Guard. The Militia Act of 1908 required the callup of National Guard forces before any use of volunteers. This was a formative period for the reserves, with the Medical Reserve Corps also created by Congress in 1908. In close succession, lawmakers subordinated state naval militias under the U.S. Navy, established the Naval Reserve and the Marine Corps Reserve, and in the 1916 National Defense Act authorized National Guard units to serve in the regular army if called upon by federal authority. Of the nearly 3 million men serving in General John Pershing's American Expeditionary Forces in Europe, some 40 percent were in National Guard units. The Medical Reserve Corps, forebear of today's Army Reserve, also contributed to the victory of 1918. The National Defense Act of 1920 further solidified the role of the reserves, designating the National Guard as a reserve force of the U.S. Army and establishing a federal "Organized Reserve." After Pearl Harbor, the vast increase in U.S. military forces, ultimately totaling 16 million men and women, came mostly from conscripts. By the end of World War II, some three-quarters of the navy on active duty were reservists as was approximately 70 percent of the marine corps, including nearly 20,000 women and a like number of African Americans in its reserve.[11] Reservists made up some 90 percent of the Coast Guard's strength.[12]

Once again, cessation of hostilities drove deep cuts and also brought reform. With the National Security Act of 1947, the Departments of War and the Navy were joined into the Department of Defense. The U.S. Air Force was created, as was the National Guard Bureau, with the Army and Air National Guard subordinated within their respective service head-quarters. In 1948, military retirement was authorized for members of the reserve components, a result of intense lobbying by the congressionally chartered Reserve Officers Association of the United States (ROA).[13] Fighting in Korea reignited a need for reservists, many of them World War II veterans, to augment "green" and poorly trained regular forces that were being mauled in the communist onslaught. The Marine Corps Reserve, as an example, activated some 130,000 marines.[14]

With the lessons of unreadiness learned afresh, Congress passed re-forms that enhanced the ability of the reserves. The 1952 Armed Forces Reserve Act established seven reserve components within the military and organized membership into three categories: the Ready Reserve, the Standby Reserve, and the Retired Reserve. Three years later, Congress increased the size of the Ready Reserve to 2.9 million troops, from among whom the president could unilaterally mobilize 1 million. The National Guard Bureau in 1958 was designated a joint bureau of the army and air force. The Korean War was not followed with the reduction in land forces so characteristic of the American experience after the conclusion of hos-tilities. Indeed, the dawning Cold War drove an elevated troop strength that only waned after the collapse of the Soviet Union.

Notwithstanding President Lyndon Johnson's avoidance of reserve-component mobilization during the Vietnam War, thousands of reserv-ists served voluntarily in Southeast Asia.[15] The Vietnam War otherwise saw no significant use of the reserves. Instead, a titanic battle waged in Washington from late 1964 into 1965 over a proposal by Secretary of Defense Robert McNamara to merge the Army Reserve into the Na-tional Guard, with the former organization disappearing. Such a sug-gestion had been considered and dismissed in 1949 by the nation's first defense secretary, James Forrestal.[16] While McNamara's merger idea was ultimately shelved, as recently as 2015, it was again a short-lived topic that roiled relations within the total force. In the shadow of a historically high post-Vietnam active-component presence focused on readiness for world war, beginning in the mid-1970s, the reserve components assumed the role of strategic reserve and the correspondingly low priority within the defense establishment's "tiered readiness" structure. This would last until Operation Desert Shield in 1990.

The Gates Commission Launches an All-Volunteer Reserve

America's experience in Vietnam was souring fast by 1969. U.S. casualties were piling up without any victory in sight. American youth increasingly resisted compulsory service in a war that many perceived as unjustified, unending, and waged by elders who were out of touch. Within this context, President Richard Nixon in 1969 named a commission to explore the transition from conscripted armed forces to an all-volunteer military. Known as the Gates Commission, it had enormous ramifications for the nation's reserve components. Its 1970 report recommended abolishing conscription in favor of voluntary service, which would "provide (1) active duty forces comparable in strength to those currently projected, 2) reserve forces for quick reinforcement of the active forces and 3) a stand-by draft system as a final measure if large-scale mobilization of untrained men is needed."[17]

At the time of the report, the Ready Reserve comprised those federal reserve forces receiving pay for participation in training and the National Guard. This force numbered about 1 million members. More than 80 percent of the Ready Reserve was in units trained and configured to "fit into" the active-force structure, such as an Army Reserve division that could be attached to an army corps. The rest were individual augmentees who could be assigned where needed. Another 1.3 million reservists were in a "standby" inactive status and would require significant preparation. The president could activate up to 1 million Ready Reserve troops while requiring the consent of Congress to access Standby Reserve forces.[18] Within a total force it estimated must be sized between 2 million and 3 million personnel, the Gates Commission proposed a shrinkage of the existing reserve strength by approximately 113,000 within both the reserves and the National Guard, including officers. That would produce a paid ready reserve strength ranging approximately from 600,000 to 800,000.[19] Then as now, the Army Reserve and Army National Guard composed the largest share of the total reserve force. The commission thus favored a return to the structure used by the nation for much of its history. By and large, only during periods of war had the United States compelled military service. That tradition was voiced on the eve of the nation's lurch into World War II by Senator Arthur Vandenburg, telling the Senate in 1940 that "peacetime military conscription is repugnant to the spirit of democracy and the soul of Republican institutions, and that it leads in dark directions."[20]

Included in the Gates Commission report were "objections" to its recommendations. Objection 2 questioned whether an AVF would be sufficiently flexible to rapidly expand when necessary. Echoing the long-standing rationale for reserves, the commission responded, "Reserve forces provide immediate support to active forces, while the draft provides only inexperienced civilians."[21] Increased pay for enlisted men, another commission recommendation, would increase retention and provide an inducement for those leaving active duty to transfer to the reserves. The commission reasoned that of the 243,000 men leaving the service annually at that time, bolstered reenlistment within and active-duty transfers into the reserves would supply 161,400 men. Relying largely on the effects of increased pay, it predicted with reassuring precision that 90,300 civilians "could be persuaded to enlist" in the reserves, handily filling the remaining requirement for 81,600 new men.[22] On July 1, 1973, the conscription law then in force expired. The recommendations of the Gates Commission would now meet their test.

Post-Vietnam and Cold War

Even as the Gates Commission recommendations became reality with the 1973 dawn of the AVF, the armed services had begun transitioning certain capabilities into the reserve. Army leaders foresaw post-Vietnam force reductions and, to preserve their resources for combat-arms modernization (as some argue), began transferring into the Army Reserve support units such as those in logistics.[23] A result was an enhancement of Army Reserve importance. Active-component reductions amplified the virtues of the relatively cheaper reserves, and the shift of support capabilities dovetailed with new defense policy. In 1969, President Nixon's secretary of defense, Melvin Laird, had issued a total force policy that designated the reserve components as the primary augmentation of the actives in any rapid mobilization, eclipsing the use of conscripts, whose preparation for war was time and resource intensive. The reserves, increasingly seen as a flexible alternative to a large standing force, were beginning a tortuous climb to relevancy.

Vietnam had made service in the reserve components attractive to many men who wished to avoid the war. Three out of four guardsmen responded in a poll that they would not have joined the National Guard if not for Vietnam. With the war winding down and the draft ending, those inflows collapsed. The Army National Guard went from more than

Melvin R. Laird seated near the fireplace in the Oval Office.
September 26, 1974. (Courtesy Gerald R. Ford Library)

100,000 awaiting entry in the late 1960s to only 15,000 in 1971. Barely 3 percent of guardsmen completing their obligation were reenlisting. The Army Guard went from a strength of 410,682 in 1974 to 350,000 four years later. The Air National Guard, regarded as more glamorous, nonetheless declined from a high of 95,000 to 92,000 by 1977.[24]

The services responded with aggressive and even innovative marketing, adding recruiters and loosening unpopular requirements. For example, a guardsman could have long hair if, while on duty, it was kept under a wig. A soldier leaving active duty could "try out" the Guard for a year in a program called "Try One."[25] Congress, loathe during the early AVF period to spend money on manpower, by 1977 could no longer resist. With numbers falling, tens of millions of dollars were appropriated for bonuses that year and in 1978. Through the early 1980s, the reserve components contended with the same societal ills afflicting the country. One retired Marine Corps Reserve general recalls that the "USMC was still struggling with post-Vietnam issues, including drugs, race relations, and low-quality personnel." The corps ultimately benefited from the discharging of some 5,000 "undesirable" marines.[26]

If the legacy of Vietnam was public estrangement from its armed forces, the legacy of World War II and Korea was capability redundancies within the active and reserve components. For example, infantry units existed in all three army components. It would take the reduced defense funding that accompanied the fall of the Soviet Union to force a "rationalizing" of these redundancies. Increased reliance on the reserve components, accentuated within the AVF, revealed the need for a "full-time" presence in reserve units. Part-timers could not, it was argued, maintain sufficient unit readiness to reinforce quickly enough active-component forces presumably by then heavily embattled. Establishing cadres of active-component leaders in reserve units was one concept. What took shape was an outgrowth of a practice begun with the National Defense Act of 1916, which authorized funding in National Guard units for men to care for federally owned horses. With the mechanization of these units, the horse tenders were replaced by maintenance personnel for vehicles and other equipment. By World War II, with the military's growing complexity, clerks and other administrative personal were added to this cadre, extending down to the company level. The navy had its Training and Administration of the Reserves (TAR) program (opened to women in 1980), and the air force had its Air Reserve Technician (ART) program, which served both the reserve and Air National Guard. Reliance on these "technicians" only intensified with the Cold War and the increasing post-Vietnam reliance on the reserves.[27] Since 1960, technicians have had to be "dual status," meeting both civil-service and military qualifications; failure to do the latter prevented a technician's readiness to deploy with the unit. Over time, the percentage of such personnel unable to deploy yet occupying unit billets rose. Unit mobilization strength correspondingly sank. Proposals have been made to reform the programs, including conversion of technicians to uniformed military status. As of this writing, the dual-status dichotomy still causes difficulties in units.[28]

Between Strategic and Operational, during the 1970s and 1980s

If the inflection point marking the change from strategic to operational reserve is largely accepted as the 1990 Desert Shield buildup and the subsequent war, service initiatives from 1970 through the 1980s were already enhancing integration. Defense Secretary Melvin Laird in 1973 stated, "we are placing increased emphasis on the National Guard and Reserve components so that we may obtain maximum defense capabilities from the limited resources available." He termed this initiative "an integral part of the Total Force planning approach." The army took the hint, establishing its Affiliation Program, which would "improve the training and readiness of RC [reserve component] combat battalions and brigades by associating them with AA [active army] units. Under this program AA divisions formed training relationships with ARNG [Army National Guard] and USAR [U.S. Army Reserve] units and worked with these units during both AT [annual training] and IDT [inactive-duty training]."[29]

In 1976, combat support and combat service support units were included. Soon thereafter, the Affiliation Program and other force readiness programs were aggregated into a new Capstone Program, which defined the role of every active- and reserve-component unit in the army for either U.S. Army Europe or continental United States use. Capstone established planning and training associations for every unit in the army and thus was the foundation for mobilization training. In 1983, it was expanded to contingencies in the Pacific and Southwest Asia. In 1994, Wartrace replaced Capstone.[30] The round-out relationships stemmed from the affiliation concept. Guard and reserve units were affiliated with active divisions, bringing to full strength brigades and divisions lacking elements, while providing the reserves with dedicated support, training assistance, and—perhaps as important—the promise of relevance.

Years of experience, however, bred cynicism. Richard Wightman, former acting assistant secretary of defense for reserve affairs and himself a retired Army Reserve major general, recalled, "The feeling was, [Capstone] was a continuation of the lip-service the RC had received from our active component brothers." Wightman noted that "the Air Force Reserve was the exception: very little lip-service, and a great deal of trust and positive action by the active duty Air Force."[31] In 1980, Army National Guard units began deploying to train with affiliated regulars in the annual Return of Forces to Germany exercises. For example, the North Carolina Army National Guard's 2d Battalion, 252d Armor (M1 Abrams), rounded out the 2d Armored Division's 2d Brigade. Later, the division was affiliated with the Louisiana Army National Guard's 256th Infantry Brigade until the end of the round-out program in1996. The program ran aground after National Guard round-out units were excluded from Desert Storm deployments. While some 40,000 army guardsmen deployed, performing functions across the combat, combat support, and combat service support spectrum, none of the three Army National Guard round-out brigades deployed, a decision the army justified by pointing to readiness levels in predeployment training readiness evaluations. Lost in the contention was the army's assertion that round-out brigades were never intended to deploy without significant postmobilization training. Nonetheless, it would take widespread use of the Guard a dozen years later in Iraq and Afghanistan to ease the sting and resentments.

The air force, while not establishing a formal round-out program, did begin affiliating reserve units with active units, which paid off in readiness for the demands of the 1991 war. Retired chief master sergeant Ericka Kelly, former command chief master sergeant of the Air Force Reserve, credits the affiliation program with facilitating her service's active and reserve components:

> The Air Force and Air Force Reserve, and Air National Guard needed to train in and use the same gear as it would in war. We realized that we could improve training and save money if we had this association. Usually the Air Force owns the aircraft, and the Air Force Reserve assigns maintainers and crews. Often on a single airplane, the crew is a mix of active and reserve airmen.[32]

The defense buildup under President Ronald Reagan augmented these initiatives. Budgetary growth spurred by the president and bested by Congress was accompanied by the establishment of a new assistant secretary of defense for reserve affairs solely dedicated to reserve-component issues. It is perhaps revealing that the Pentagon opposed the reserves having such a champion. The Reagan years also saw increased reliance on the reserve components: cheaper than the actives, they were also essential to total-force capabilities.

But the ghost of Vietnam moved among policymakers: never again, they said, would the United States go to war "without the people." Engaging "the Guardsman next door" presumably engaged Main Street more effectively than by merely sending in the boy who used to live next door—that is, until he became a regular in the army infantry. It is ironic, given this determination to engage the public, that since World War II, neither the people, Congress, nor succeeding presidents have employed the constitutional mechanism designed for that very purpose: a formal declaration of war.

This reliance on the reserve components forced a recognition that they were unequal to the task. While recruiting had begun to recover, with growth throughout the services and the selected reserve exceeding 1 million people, the complexity of modern warfare had made gaining and maintaining readiness in a unit of "part-time" reservists simply impossible. The old military-technician programs were seized upon as key to reserve and Guard readiness. Congress created a separate authorization for these programs. The active and reserve programs in the Army Reserve and National Guard grew, as did the other services' programs. The Marine Corps Instructor-Inspector program used active-duty officers and

NCOs in reserve units. This program ultimately paid off, as recalled by Lieutenant General Dennis M. McCarthy:

> My first experience with the Marine Corps Reserve was as an active component officer on Inspector-Instructor duty in 1970. The resources given that unit were pitiful—little money, old and antiquated equipment, not even the faintest motivation that the unit would ever be called to action. In 1984–1986 I was an infantry battalion commander as a Reserve Component officer and believed that my well-equipped unit, if mobilized, could function on par with the active component units I trained with regularly. Four years after I gave up command of that battalion, they were mobilized for DS/DS [Desert Shield / Desert Storm].[33]

The Navy Reserve's shift to an operational stance began before Operation Desert Shield. According to retired rear admiral John Cotton, chief of Navy Reserve and commander Navy Reserve Force from 2003 to 2008:

> The Navy started the change in the late 1980s and early 1990s with less people and more work to do. They simply found [operational] missions that Reservists could do with their available man-days and increased [active duty training and active duty for special work support] funding. The 'peace dividend' drawdown of the 1990s created more Reserve operational support opportunities, as did global operations after 9/11. [The] AC preferred RC units and personnel that could show up ready with manpower and equipment, especially if the RC was paying!

The marines eventually placed some reservists on active duty in unit administrative roles. These programs continue to be essential to reserve-component readiness. Indeed, with the increased tempo experienced in today's operational reserve, such "full-time" support is more important than ever.

Dawn of an Operational Reserve during Operations Desert Shield and Desert Storm

Belief that the Soviet Union's collapse meant an end to big wars collapsed with Saddam Hussein's invasion of Kuwait on August 2, 1990. With its combat support and service support capabilities diminished and now contending with the largest mobilization since Korea, the active component required comprehensive augmentation by the reserve and the National Guard. This was not unexpected. Within DOD's 1973 Total Force concept and its focus on Europe, the reserves were to be maintained in readiness to reinforce active units, while conscription (until the AVF, and thereafter Selective Service implementation by the president and Congress) prepared more forces. Either way, the reserves were, in the words of Lawrence Korb and David Segal, a "bridge to conscription."[34] With a draft again in force, the authors observed, "National Guard and Reserve personnel would not have to be mobilized more than one year out of every six," an irony borne out in "dwell times" experienced during the more limited Iraq and Afghanistan campaigns that reached one to one.

Yet, much as doctrine envisioned reserve-component mobilization, absent general war, it was regarded as highly unlikely. Former acting assistant secretary of defense for reserve affairs Wightman noted:

> In the late 1960s and early '70s as an active duty officer, I saw Reservists and National Guardsmen deploy as individuals but not as a unit, so I believed that as a Reservist or National Guardsman you could volunteer to be mobilized or deployed, but if you didn't volunteer, the chances of being deployed into a combat zone were unlikely, even with the Army's decision to have Reserve units Capstoned and National Guard units as Round Out brigades to active duty divisions.[35]

On the eve of the Persian Gulf War, just over 2 million of the U.S. military's total force were in the active component, with some 1.1 million in the reserves of all the services. Between the Army Reserve's 319,000 and the Army National Guard's 436,000, the two primary land reserve components fielded ten divisions and the equivalent of twelve fighter wings.[36] By this time, the Army Reserve comprised primarily support capabilities, such as logistics, medical, and transportation, while the Army Guard was combat heavy, with infantry, armor (tanks), artillery, and attack helicopter units. By Thanksgiving 1990, nearly all the reserve-component activations authorized on August 22 by President George H. W. Bush had answered the call, the first such callup in more than two decades. Under a Presidential Selected Reserve Callup, the president is permitted to mobilize units but not individuals, such as those in the IRR; that would require a partial or full mobilization, which Bush had decided against. On December 1, the president authorized an overall increase to 188,000 reservists of both components, with the army supplying a similar proportion.[37]

The army provided some 70 percent of deployed reserve-component forces, almost equally divided among the 72,000 soldiers who actually deployed to the theater of operations. From the author's vantage point among the troopers of the 1st Battalion, 7th Cavalry Regiment on the 1st Cavalry Division's forward screen line, the air offensive was effectively executed by active and reserve elements. One fighter wing, two fighter groups, and a reconnaissance group came from the Air Force Reserve and Air National Guard, which together supplied more than 34,000 airmen of all ranks and specialties.[38]

Some 20,000 Naval Reserve sailors were mobilized. From the Marine Corps Forces Reserve came an artillery regiment, four infantry battalions, and two armored battalions. While all the services mobilized individual ready reservists, the marines were notable for their high relative number: nearly 20 percent of 32,863 marine corps' mobilizations came from its IRR, double the percentage represented by the Army Reserve's 13,170 IRR mobilizations.[39]

Of the 569,285 U.S. servicemembers deployed, including those from the U.S. Coast Guard, 18 percent were from the reserve components, which suffered 16 percent of the war's American deaths. "The call to active duty and the performance of the National Guardsmen and reservists who have served in connection with that conflict, have been marked by extraordinary success," Assistant Secretary of Defense for Reserve Affairs Stephen Duncan testified to Congress in April 1991.[40] Given the virtual "cold start" they had experienced before deployment, in contrast to their active-component comrades, the reserve components had proved the viability of the Total Force concept.

Under Chairman of the Joint Chiefs of Staff General Colin Powell, the administration had developed in 1991 the Base Force concept, which presupposed a force sized to fight in Europe if required. With the Soviet Union's dissolution, the emphasis was now on regional conflicts, drug interdiction, and nation building (such as the Fuertes Caminos roadbuilding operations in Honduras). The Base Force envisioned total Reserve Component strength dropping from about 1.12 million to some 920,000 by 1997, within a total force drop of some 25 percent.[41] Among the biggest losers was the army's reserve components, with the Army National Guard losing four of its ten divisions. The Persian Gulf War sidelined the Bush administration's moves to downsize the military. But with that war concluded and the Soviet Union no longer a threat, the administration renewed its push to slim down a military sized to fight a potential World War III. Congress, eyeing lost units, bases, and jobs in home districts and states, pushed back. When the Bush administration left Washington in 1993, the Base Force went with it.

With the arrival of a more domestically focused president in William Jefferson Clinton and the lack of a superpower enemy, military reductions become more feasible. The new administration's 1993 Bottom Up

Review (BUR) directed that the armed forces be sufficient to win two major *regional* conflicts that occur *nearly* simultaneously. The reserve components, mostly the army's, lost structure, although the Guard kept eight of its ten divisions. The Army Reserve went down to 208,000; the Air Force Reserve losing five of its air wings, the Navy Reserve lost strength, and the marine corps, which had used its reserves so heavily in Desert Storm, made it through without loss. Where just two years earlier the Base Force had foundered in a congressional minefield, the BUR sailed through.

The BUR-associated personnel and structure losses, however, do not tell the full story. The military, which could not afford an adequately sized active force, needed an accessible, strong reserve force, and Congress agreed.

As a result of congressional pressure and the army's requirements forecast, according to retired major general Roger W. Sandler, former chief of Army Reserve, leaders from the active army, Army National Guard, and Army Reserve met during 1993 at various locations outside the Pentagon, one being at ROA's headquarters on Capitol Hill. The active army wanted to preserve the greatest feasible number of combat units and achieve reductions in reserve-component strengths to help pay the bill. The Guard wanted to preserve its end strength and retain its balanced structure, especially its aviation and special forces units. The Army Reserve was focused on retention of its combat support and combat service support capabilities. Both Guard and reserve leaders wanted to ensure that the army could not make force-structure changes without their involvement.[42]

"After at times acrimonious discussions, the group arrived at what became known as the Offsite Agreement. The U.S. Army Reserve was to reduce its end strength . . . and the Army National Guard would also reduce to a lower number," recalled Sandler. "Additionally, there was a redefinition of missions for each of the components. The Army National Guard would concentrate on combat units while the Army Reserve would concentrate on combat support and combat service support units. The Guard acquired a couple of Army Reserve combat brigades and in return the Army Reserve received a senior signal command. Additionally, in a very contentious decision, the National Guard received most of the Army Reserve's aviation units."[43] Subsequently, the Army National Guard received much of the active army's artillery units in a move to preserve their existence without having the budget to keep them in the active force. Later, Chairman of the Joint Chiefs of Staff General Colin Powell observed, "When we tried to cut back to sensible levels, we had our heads handed to us by the National Guard and Reserve associations and their congressional supporters."[44]

The force structure forged in 1993 remains substantially unchanged in the 2020s. It largely solved the redundancies among the components in combat, combat support, and combat service support capabilities and created a total army able to sustain—if barely—the increased tempo that began in 2001.

In 1995, legislation expanded the president's callup authority to 270 days and enabled IRRs to be activated without the heretofore necessary partial mobilization.[45] With the rising emphasis on regional conflict, smaller, more manageable brigades gained favor over large divisions (the active army would lose eight of its eighteen divisions). While the Army Guard would lose two divisions, with another two converted to cadre status, the BUR ended the round-out program. Fifteen Guard brigades were designated "enhanced brigades," trained and equipped for rapid deployment.[46] The Army Reserve was the reservoir of combat support and combat service support so essential to ground operations. The tradeoffs forged by the BUR—smaller active forces supported by more ready-reserve forces—preserved a total force able to respond in depth to crisis. Those tradeoffs also exacerbated weaknesses in the AVF that, since 2001, have strained that force at times nearly to breaking, and which to some critics could prove the AVF's undoing.

In its Guard and Reserve Overseas Contingency Operations Activations report for March 31, 2020, the DOD announced a milestone: a million members of the reserve components had been activated since 9/11 (1,002,589 to be precise). Currently activated were 38,393 of them—at a time when many Americans had either forgotten about the war or assumed that it was long over.[47] None of this was intended. Secretary of Defense Donald Rumsfeld, weeks before the U.S. invasion of Iraq in 2003, said in response to a question at an ROA-hosted event, "If we want to have a total force, if we want that system to work, we've got to be respectful of the fact that people in the Reserves and Guard have jobs and they're perfectly willing to be called up, but they only want to be called up when they're needed and for something that's a real job."[48]

The reality became something quite different. As the campaign in Afghanistan seemed to be reaching a successful conclusion, President George W. Bush launched the invasion of Iraq in March 2003. The common expectation was that this operation, like Desert Storm, would be brief and victorious. The nearly two decades of inconclusive war that followed would strain the force, its families, civilian employers, and veterans with pressures that persist and, arguably, are increasing. The demands of war overcame the sort of resistance to deploying Guard units into combat that had kept them out of Desert Storm. Two decades of reserve-component performance have measured up to the best provided by the regulars.

What two decades later totaled an activation of a million began with the activation of one: Operation Enduring Freedom initially made heavy use of individual-mobilization augmentees rather than units. These IMAs filled gaps in other units and provided unique skills, validating the long-held belief that reservists are a reservoir of expertise gained in civilian work experience. Initial reliance on IMAs stemmed in great part from the sheer fog of war. Major General John A. Bradley, assistant for reserve matters to the Joint Chiefs of Staff and later the chief of the Air Force Reserve, recalled that the air force's Air Mobility Command, in charge of all strategic airlift, thought the war would be a short affair. Its use of IMAs was echoed in the navy, marine corps, and the army as well. They could be mobilized relatively quickly to fill individual manning requirements, as their duty tended to be performing very specific job functions, such as an Army Reserve public-affairs officer performing IMA duty on the public-affairs staff of an active-duty unit.

As war spread throughout Iraq and then Afghanistan began seeing reversals, demands on active-component units increased. Entire reserve-component units were increasingly deployed. Within a year of the March 2003 invasion of Iraq, strains had developed, largely in the ground-oriented army and marine corps. By October, over a third of the Army Reserve's soldiers had been called up; by January 2004, nearly 70 percent of its law-enforcement personnel had been mobilized at least once.[49] Exacerbating the issue, a 1952 federal law governing partial mobilization prohibited involuntary activation of Ready Reserve units or members for more than twenty-four consecutive months.[50] It envisioned reserve-component elements mobilized to reinforce regulars being themselves replaced or augmented by draftees. But with the AVF in place, the reserves would have to sustain the effort. Seeking to limit the extent of reserve-component use, Secretary Rumsfeld affirmed an interpretation of the 1952 law that replaced "consecutive" with "cumulative." Pentagon guidance to the services in January 2004 limited involuntary mobilizations to "not more than one year in six."[51]

Nonetheless, the pressures mounted. By the end of 2004, about 50 percent of the army's 200,000 reservists had deployed, 15,000 twice, and 2,000 three or more times.[52] The marine corps added its reserves to its rotational schedule to meet the war's needs while maintaining its fleet and Pacific-based force requirements, with many reservists seeing repeated mobilizations.[53] By 2008, just before deployments to Iraq began declining and those to resurgent combat in Afghanistan quadrupled to over 105,000 personnel, some 121,000 members of the reserve components were on active duty supporting the president's partial mobilization; three-fourths of them were from the Army Reserve and the National Guard.[54]

This two-front war created a burden that, by 2005, threatened to overwhelm the reserve components of the army and air force. Army Reserve chief Lieutenant General James R. Helmly in December 2004 wrote Army Chief of Staff General Peter J. Schoomaker the "broken force" memorandum. He warned that "under current policies, procedures, and practices governing mobilization, training, and reserve component manpower management," his force could not do the job required of it in both theaters of war while also adequately resetting and regenerating forces for "follow-on and future missions."[55] Helmly advised Schoomaker, "the Army Reserve is additionally in grave danger of being unable to meet other operational requirements including those in named OPLANS and CONUS emergencies, and is rapidly degenerating into a 'broken force.'" While likely not his intention, the chief's memorandum apparently described similar issues vexing other Reserve Component leaders.[56] Deep in this memorandum was an observation that has received less attention than his "broken force" warning. Helmly opposed mobilizing only volunteers and avoiding involuntary activations. While undermining a sense of obligation among reservists, it placed "the burden of responsibility for service on the Soldiers' back instead of the Army's back. While the Soldier is still protected by USERRA [Uniformed Services Employment and Reemployment Act], the Soldier is seen as having a clear choice by his family and employer. Faced with this, the most likely 'volunteers' are those who often enjoy lesser responsible positions in civilian life." Helmly foresaw reliance on voluntary mobilizations imperiling the integrity of the reserve force. He argued that the bonuses being offered "to induce 'volunteerism' will cause the expectation of always receiving such financial incentives in future conflicts" and warned that such motivation might "confuse 'volunteer to become an American Soldier' with 'mercenary.'"

During this period, both the army and the marine corps began mobilizing IRRs, troops characteristically finishing their terms of service, and inactives. Resorting to IRRs revealed the straits in which the Pentagon found itself. Indicating the readiness problems presented by mobilizing people who had been disconnected from regular contact with the military was the experience early in the war of the marine corps. It mobilized 8,000 IRRs, only to find a quarter of them actually met all deployment criteria. In time, readiness improved, and by 2013, some 80 percent of marine IRRs had served at least one combat tour.[57]

The 2006 Army Force Generation (ARFORGEN) model, adapted in

part from the Army Reserve's system, provided a framework in which units cyclically advanced through three phases. The ARFORGEN model provided for a two-year reset/training phase for units returning from or planned for a deployment; a two-year ready phase for units in advanced stages of training (such as large-unit "collective" training); and a one-year available phase for units ready to deploy. The ARFORGEN process made deployments more predictable. Repeat deployments ground on, and ground down both units and servicemembers. The author, then deputy chief of army public affairs, attended situation briefs in the Pentagon and recalls the mounting concern as the realization deepened that, as he overheard one general say to another, "We're breaking the Army."

So complete was the assumption among defense leaders that the war would be a short one that little attention had been paid to family issues. Slowly, the military increased services for those living on or near installations—by and large the families of active-duty regulars. But for the reserve components, these improvements meant little. National Guard and reserve families live in their hometowns, often far from military installations. They lacked the services such as government health care, child care, and DOD schools as well as the invaluable support of other unit families enjoyed by those of the active component. To a significant degree, they were on their own. Reflecting a broad DOD-wide "paradigm" shift, the National Guard rephrased its family support programs to "family readiness" programs. This shift reflected their more comprehensive nature as they sought to ensure families had the resources and knowledge necessary to overcome the challenges of lengthy and possibly repeated deployments.[58]

By mid-2004, DOD had brought together the separate support programs of the services into the centralized Military OneSource. A twenty-four-hour portal with a toll-free telephone number was answered by a trained counselor, and there was a website inlet to the vast array of individual and family support, from behavioral health to military and veterans benefits; family programs; tax, finance and legal issues; and suicide prevention and counseling. "They helped me deal with my teenage daughter's anger over her dad being gone," said Angie Ayers, whose National Guard husband was deployed to Iraq from 2004 to 2005.[59]

A tenet underlying the improvements was expressed by Army National Guard director Major General Raymond Carpenter in terms all reserve-service leaders would endorse: "You cannot have a mission-effective soldier without the support of the family. . . . If you don't have the support of the family and the employers in the community, you find that, over time, the soldier gives up and leaves the National Guard."[60] Some evidence suggests that families and employers are indeed wearying. An

Army Reserve colonel who as a civilian was running a major corporation's military- and veterans-support program told retired Army Reserve major general Peter Cooke that he had recently been asked by an anxious boss when he himself might again have to deploy. The message, the colonel told Cooke, was clear.

As casualties mounted in Iraq and Afghanistan, the military's health-care system was caught short. It had been a generation since the U.S. military had been faced with any such influx—Desert Storm had resulted in just under 800 dead and wounded. Each year from 2004 through 2006, more than 700 active-duty troops were killed by hostile action.[61] That number would peak above 800 in 2007. Reserve-component families were also grieving, as by 2007, up to 40 percent of the deployed force was from the reserves and Guard. Overall, more than 1,200 reservists and guardsmen would make the ultimate sacrifice.

February 2007 brought a brutal "wake-up call," as an NPR story aired August 31, 2011, later described it. Breaking on February 18 in an exposé by *Washington Post* reporters Dana Priest and Anne Hull headlined "Soldiers Face Neglect, Frustration at Army's Top Medical Facility," conditions at a Walter Reed Army Medical Center building that quartered recovering wounded were shown to be pest-infested, moldy, and foul. The story hit with earthquake force, costing the jobs of a secretary of the army, and top army medical command officers. The army quickly instituted reforms, including better coordination with the Department of Veterans Affairs and its network of some 150 hospitals and nearly 1,000 outpatient centers. This coordination included four VA polytrauma rehabilitation centers specializing in the acute-care treatment of complex injuries and traumatic brain injury as well as a nationwide network of post-acute-care facilities.

With the establishment in 2006 of an annual periodic health assessment, medical readiness began improving. According to retired U.S. Air Force Reserve lieutenant colonel Susan Lukas, a former member of the legislative staffs of the air force and the Department of Veterans Affairs and the former legislative and military policy director of ROA, "The Servicemembers' Health Insurance Protection Act of 2005 became Public Law 109-233; it ensured Reserve and National Guard members could reinstate their medical insurance after deployment without penalty. This was followed with the establishment of TRICARE Reserve Select in the National Defense Authorization Act of fiscal year 2007."[62]

According to a study from 2012, "At the end of the second quarter of FY 2006, the reserve components reported that only 26 percent of forces were fully medically ready, compared with 42 percent of active component forces. By the end of 2009, 47 percent of reserve component forces were fully medically ready, compared with 72 percent of active component forces."[63] Similar improvements were made in dental care, improving the situation from earlier in the war, when many reservists had been disqualified for service based on dental problems. Often, medical issues were fobbed off on the Department of Veteran Affairs—troops were told they had a dental or some other problem and to go to the VA for it to be corrected. The study found that the DOD did not have complete medical records, necessary for VA service-connected medical care. Thus, newly returned veterans were being turned away from VA medical centers. The army implemented the Army Selected Reserve Dental Readiness System in FY 2009 after facing less than a 50-percent readiness standard.[64] By 2011, dental readiness had risen dramatically.[65]

Legislation pushed by House Armed Services Subcommittee on Military Personnel chair Steve Buyer of Indiana, later chair of the House Committee on Veterans Affairs, expanded reserve and Guard TRICARE military health-care benefits. Improvements to these benefits ultimately provided coverage similar to that provided active-component members for up to 180 days before mobilization through demobilization.[66] By the January 2007 arrival in the Pentagon of former Texas A&M University president Robert M. Gates, the armed forces were in crisis under the strain of repeated use, especially the army and marine corps. Reserve-component contributions to the military, which had been about 12 million "man-days" for the six years before 9/11, hit 68 million mandays in 2005.[67] Some deployments had reached fifteen months, with a subsequent deployment looming after a similar period at home, thus providing only a one-to-one "dwell" ratio, the same as experienced in the active component. The effect on families and civilian employers was predictable. A 2006 Joint Staff analysis revealed that, under Rumsfeld's twenty-four-month "cumulative" policy, no army reserve-component combat brigade nor nearly half of the marine brigades could deploy for some eighteen months.[68] Rumsfeld's interpretation of the 1952 law, made by him to preserve the integrity of reserve service, was inadvertently having the opposite effect.

Heeding advice from uniformed leaders, especially National Guard Bureau chief Lieutenant General Steve Blum, Gates changed Rumsfeld's "cumulative" interpretation of the twenty-four-month mobilization limit back to "consecutive," consistent with the 1952 law. Gates ruled that involuntary and unit mobilizations would not exceed twelve months. Further, mobilized-to-demobilized time—the dwell ratio—would be one to five, or one year in six. It was understood within the Pentagon that achievement of the one-to-five ratio was unlikely to be realized, at least for certain high-demand specialties, for some years.[69]

Succeeding Helmly, Lieutenant General Jack C. Stultz warned that the Army Reserve faced two consuming challenges: the need to transform and the need to do that while continuing the job "we're doing now, because we still have to supply about 30,000 soldiers every year to win the war."[70] Stultz struggled with predictability. Speaking to the ROA in January 2012, he said that soldiers want three things, leading off with predictability, which the chief recognized employers also wanted (as well as families, he would have agreed). They also wanted to use their skills and not waste their time in unproductive drill periods and inefficient mobilization processes.[71] "Predictability," said former acting assistant secretary of defense for reserve affairs Wightman, "enables an operational force." Pressures on the force notwithstanding, the reserve components have performed well. In his 2016 book, *On War and Politics*, retired U.S. Marine Corps major general and chairman of the Reserve Forces Policy Board Arnold L. Punaro writes, "At the peak of operations in Iraq and Afghanistan, 45 percent of our ground forces there were Guard and Reserve."[72]

A 2016 Institute for Defense Analyses report commissioned by DOD's Reserve Forces Policy Board (RFPB) noted: "Strategic and operational leaders were generally pleased with RC contributions and performance in support of OIF [Operation Iraqi Freedom]. . . . RC contributions and performance met the intent of leaders at the strategic and operational level. . . . Without the RC, the nation could not have conducted OIF, met other global commitments, and preserved the All-Volunteer Force." The report recognized that DOD "leaders generally lacked knowledge regarding the use of RC forces," noting that, over time, "resource investments and experience mitigated some of these impacts."[73]

Authors Forrest L. Marion and Jon T. Hoffman present several dilemmas associated with the use of the reserve force, perhaps the most significant one being "that the more the nation does to raise the readiness of the reserve component to perform an operational role, the greater the cost, thus undercutting one of the primary rationales for relying on citizen-soldiers to supplement the regulars."[74] Lieutenant General McCarthy, who retired in 2005 after commanding Marine Forces Reserve and Marine Forces North and was confirmed in 2009 as assistant secretary of defense for reserve affairs, has suggested:

The question we should all be asking is: "If the Operational Reserve demands a 1:6 [dwell ratio] mindset for the RC, what kinds of missions should we expect them to fulfill? [Air Force Reserve Command and Air National Guard] units can fill with volunteers, as can [the Navy Reserve]. [The] Army and Marine Corps, in my opinion, cannot. Most of what ground forces supply are units and cohesive units [that] are not easily formed out of disparate volunteers. My sense is that ground forces will have to be more creative about implementing rotational peace time deployments.[75]

But that question has yet to be answered.

The Challenges Confronting a Contemporary Operational Reserve

Perhaps the most pernicious factor in the consistent underresourcing of the reserve components is a persistent undervaluing of the reserves by leaders in the active force. The RFPB, an official DOD organization, comprises among its twenty members a civilian chairman, a nonvoting military executive and senior enlisted representative, a serving or former member of each of the seven reserve components, and ten U.S. citizens versed in national security and reserve affairs. The RFPB "provides the Secretary of Defense with independent advice and recommendations designed to strengthen the Reserve Components."[76] For years, it has advocated an official acknowledgment of the fully burdened and life-cycle costs for all components. The RFPB, which in 2019 made its own analysis using DOD budget requests, contends that "the RC per capita cost ranges from 28% to 32% of their AC [active component] counterparts' per capita costs." In the analysis, the RFPB notes widespread recognition within the Pentagon, Congress, and the national-security community that trends for the fully burdened and lifecycle costs (FBLCC) of the AVF are growing "on an unsustainable basis." It cites a 2012 Center for Strategic and Budgetary Assessment report that found the per-person cost of the active component had risen 46 percent in the previous decade, observing that "if personnel costs continue growing at that rate and the overall defense budget remains flat with inflation, military personnel costs will consume the entire defense budget by 2039." Yet notwithstanding the compelling economies possible through an informed use of the reserve components, the Pentagon in major military manpower decisions "does not know, use, or track" these costs.

The RFPB observes that this "refusal to account for the real estate, facilities, utilities, infrastructure, training and other costs" undermines the myth "held by some that the Guard and Reserve are more expensive that the Active Component."[77] The RFPB has repeatedly cautioned that the operational use of the reserve component is hampered by Cold War policies focused on strategic—and thus infrequent—use, which in turn hampers access to its capabilities in "global contingency operations, especially with current fiscal trends."[78] Since the report's issuance, these fiscal trends have only intensified. The RFPB has recommended adoption of an official definition of operational reserve: "An Operational reserve provides ready capabilities and capacity that are accessible, routinely utilized, and fully integrated for military missions that are planned, programmed, and budgeted in coordination with the Active Component."[79] The proposed definition has not been adopted as of this writing. Defined or not, the reserve's operational tempo is likely to increase. Domestic crises pile on to the demand, as seen with natural disasters, the COVID-19 pandemic, and the events of January 6, 2021, at the U.S. Capitol.

With the Afghanistan War's end, the army's ARFORGEN model is no longer in use. Yet the need for reserve-force readiness has compelled a rotational model of sorts. Units are readied, but instead of being deployed and that readiness "used," they are often merely held in readiness, wearing them out.

One major consequence of this policy mishmash is what retired U.S. Army major general Joseph Whitlock calls "the Army's mobilization problem" in a 2017 Army War College article. Noting the army's "increasing reliance on its Reserve Component as an operational force," Whitlock warns, "The United States is running a high risk that it may lose in a major theater war because it cannot mobilize and deploy the Army quickly enough." He describes how dependence on the reserve components—53 percent of the Army and some 40 percent of the entire U.S. military—has spawned this problem: "The smallest regular [active component] Army in many decades is weighted toward combat-arms forces, but our future war plans demand significant early-entry, 'set-the-theater for war' capabilities provided by Reserve Component combat support and service support units," whose members would need to leave their civilian life for deployment in days rather than months. Paradoxically, the deliberate ARFORGEN model that had brought some order and predictability to the manning crisis from 2004 to 2007 had also mooted the need to tackle such fast mobilizations.[80]

While U.S. military involvement in southwest and southcentral Asia has declined, federal law now permits expanded deployments of reserve and Guard troops to all manner of missions. An active component too small to do everything the nation's military strategy requires must excessively rely on its reserves.

Active-duty generals insist that they regard the reserves as equals, an assertion regarded dubiously by many in the reserve and Guard. Among active-component leaders, service with reserves is limited to brief periods, usually as superior officers. In their advanced military schooling, they see few reserve and Guard colleagues; reservists by and large attend the correspondence (now called "distance education") version of the course that includes relatively brief "residence" sessions—subtle messages. In their younger, formative years, future flag officers live on or near active-duty installations, where reservists and their families are virtually nowhere to be seen. From assignment to assignment, their cohort comprises active-duty peers; their bonds deepen. Active-duty military families do not have backyard cookouts, parties, ballgames, or socials with the families of reservists. Their children attend base schools run by the military, while the children of reservists go to school in their civilian communities.

In an article that appeared with the Iraq War completing its second year, General McCarthy notes that it was "still common to hear senior officers and leaders acknowledge that they know little about the Reserve. Worse, there is little desire to learn."[81] Yet the Iraq War was proof that the U.S. military could no longer go to war without its citizen-soldiers: at no time since the Korean War, with its 858,000 involuntary activations, has the United States used its reserve components more comprehensively than from 2003 to 2023—to date, more than 1 million reservists and guardsmen have been activated.[82]

Voluntarily deployed as an Army Reserve colonel to Baghdad in 2004, the author became the public-affairs officer for Multi-National Force–Iraq's commander, General George W. Casey Jr. One day while walking with *Washington Post* reporter Bradley Graham to an awaiting Blackhawk helicopter, Graham asked, "Jeff, are reservists respected?" Allowing a moment's passage to relish the response, the author, over the thuttering of the Blackhawk's four whirling blades, responded, "Bradley, the commanding general's public affairs officer *is* a reservist!"

The rise of technology is proving the value of reservists who bring civilian skills that are either difficult or impossible to develop in today's military educational systems, including cyber. In most Marine Corps Reserve units by the end of the 1990s, for example, retired major general James M. Lariviere recalls that more than 50 percent of the junior enlisted marines were college students.

> [This] made for a more mature and intelligent enlisted force and is often a shock when RC units mobilize and integrate with AC units, where most junior enlisted are high school graduates. From personal experience I had a master sergeant on my staff with 10,000 hours flying for USAir. A gunnery sergeant platoon commander in 3/25 [3d Battalion, 25th Regiment] was a partner in a Boston law firm. One of my radio operators was studying for his PhD at Harvard. One of my recon team leaders at 3rd Force quit the unit because the internet startup he founded and ran was taking too much time. Of course, not all Marines were of this quality, but generally the RC Marines were of high quality and brought their significant civilian skills to the USMCR.[83]

The reserves are a natural receptacle for such talent, argues Stanford University's Jacquelyn Schneider:

> The citizen portion of a reservist's identity is a unique asset, sometimes more valuable than a member's military qualifications. . . . [T]he reserves should reinvigorate its individual ready reserve, reallocate work by projects instead of billets, and build a database of strategic talent. If done with the right technology and cultural adaptation, the country can have a true strategic reserve—all without competing with the operationally ready reserve.[84]

The kind of future Schneider envisions is increasingly plausible, especially with the advent of the U.S. Space Force. Necessity has "mothered the invention": conscription's end, the shift of capabilities into the reserve components to conserve them in the face of a shrinking active force, and the demands of a long war have undercut old biases.

Yet if "sharing the foxhole" has improved reserve-component readiness and integration, the U.S. exit from Iraq and Afghanistan will reduce opportunities to serve together with the active component. Among those troubled about what may happen is RFPB chairman Punaro, a veteran of the Vietnam and Persian Gulf Wars and a former Senate Armed Services Committee staff director. "I worry that after this is over, and once the budget knives come out, we'll go back to where we were. We can't let that happen."[85]

The near-death experience of the Coast Guard Reserve is illustrative. The reserve, which made up over 92 percent of the coast guard's manning in World War II and has continued to play a key role in wartime missions such as port security, nearly succumbed to budget cuts proposed by the Nixon administration, which would have eliminated its personnel funding. Fierce advocacy in Congress by ROA and other supporters won back that funding in 1971.[86]

Punaro's concern is echoed by a fellow retired marine general, Dennis McCarthy: "The RC will respond to what the AC asks. But to many in the AC, the RC remains 'the force of last resort' so the 'ask' will be reluctant and later than it should be."[87] General Casey, with his unique perspective as having commanded Multi-National Force–Iraq and then as being the U.S. Army's senior officer, offered his perspective. "What hurt us in those early days after September 11, was that we were adapting a very good 20th Century army for the very different security challenges of the 21st Century, and we had to do it while we were at war. It was very hard, because institutionally we were still trying to be a garrison-based force that lived to train for conventional war." Referring to ARFORGEN and the succeeding Sustainable Readiness model (SRM), General Casey explained, "The rotational model is especially important to the reserve components—we owe them a 'contract'; the reserves are our ability to adapt and increase the Army." The SRM, which replaced ARFORGEN in FY 2017, nonetheless retained the latter's five-year train-up and one-year deployment structure.[88]

Succeeding SRM, the Regionally Aligned Readiness and Modernization model (ReARMM), announced by the Army in 2020 and now in implementation, adapted a rotational model with a focus of both active and reserve forces on specific regions, or theaters, in support of combatant commanders. ReARMM includes dedicated time for equipment modernization. That enhancement corrected a significant flaw in the old ARFORGEN model, which accommodated modernization, according to one general, "when we can find a window to fit it in."[89]

Rotational policies create some predictability. But rotation does not reduce operational tempo, it merely regularizes it. This does not help a young captain or staff sergeant whose regular and predictable deployments annoy her employer, especially if these deployments are not to war but to a training exercise in eastern Europe or the Baltics. As of this writing, U.S. employers have sustained their support for their citizen-soldier employees, but signs are emerging that such support may be fraying. General McCarthy has noted:

> Shifting to an operational reserve should trigger a review of USERRA and the demands placed on employers. As far as I know, USERRA is the only Federal Labor statute that places equal demands on all employers regardless of size. Asking a mom and pop operation with five employees to bear the same burden as Walmart doesn't make sense if you plan to use the RC routinely. RC members who chose to make a career in the operational reserve should realize that not all jobs are equally compatible with that career choice. RC leaders should help with that realization.[90]

Beginning with the 2001 U.S. invasion of Afghanistan, the operational use of the reserve components, which accelerated from 1990, assumed proportions that have no end in sight. Indeed, reserve-component senior leaders value the enhanced relevance that has attended heavy and sustained use of their forces; they embrace the "operational reserve." That is understandable; all were young officers who, along with General Punaro, experienced "as late as the 1990s [that] little had changed from 1949. The active-duty leadership viewed them as the second string."[91]

Reserve-component leaders will point to recruitment and retention numbers largely adequate to maintain their ranks, although in FY 2022, most services in the three components missed their recruiting goals; persistent shortages also existed in some ranks. The army, not alone among services in the challenge to compete for active-duty recruits in a strong economy and amid falling interest in military service among young Americans, has looked to its reserve to fill the gap. "The Army will shift about $1 billion to recruiting programs and will rely more heavily on reserve units as its ranks dwindle and the service struggles to attract new soldiers," a July 2022 *Washington Times* article reported.

"Some people say the Reserve was not meant to be operational," observed Susan Lukas. "But the optempo is not going down. Law and policy have not kept up with the use of the reserve components as an operational reserve." Sustainability may be found in a hybrid form of reserve service not unlike tiered readiness, with some portion of the force in the operational role, receiving appropriate educational and health-care benefits, and some in the more "traditional" strategic role.[92] As General McCarthy has observed, "each of the reserve components is comprised of both units and individuals in the strategic and operational elements."[93] Those who want to go repeatedly to the sound of the guns could move to units sent more frequently within earshot. For those who prefer a less "active" reserve experience—perhaps for reasons of family or civilian career—duty in a lower-readiness-tier unit may fit.

As of this writing, the air force is developing a unique and even revolutionary concept in connection with its staffing of the new space force. The concept would essentially eradicate "active" and "reserve" entities. In their place would be a unitary force whose members could seamlessly transition back and forth between "full time" and "part time" service in response to circumstances, either those of the service or of its personnel, the newly named "guardians."

With the (otherwise fortuitous) decline of combat and the operations that alloyed members of the reserve and active components into steel and eroded old biases, there is concern that declining appropriations will spur "tribal" budget knives to carve away at the progress of decades. Any "hollowing out" will have deleterious effects on recruitment, retention, and ultimately readiness. Concern with the viability of overtaxed reserve components is an argument that has been used since the Cold War to preserve funding primarily focused on the active component.

Yet the reserve components have risen to every challenge. "Our Reserve Marines continue to demonstrate their *irrational call to service* as they adroitly balance the requirements of their civilian careers and familial responsibilities," said Marine Forces Reserve commander Lieutenant General David C. Bellon in admiration of his marines.[94] The betting in the Pentagon is that this "irrational call to service" will survive the coming years, perhaps decades, of high operations tempo.

If the future requires an operational capability in the reserve components such as we have seen develop over the past two or three decades, that operational force should no longer be resource differentiated from its active component. Funding and resourcing the reserve should not be seen to weaken the former and prevent the adequate sizing of the latter. Inarguably, since the advent of the AVF, the end of conscription, and the nation's reliance on the reserve components, the men and women who used to be called "weekend warriors" have earned the respect associated with being now known as America's "citizen-warriors."

Notes

1. Title 10, United States Code.

2. James G. Greenhill, "General Milley: 'There Is Only One Army,'" U.S. Army, September 22, 2015.

3. Michael D. Doubler, *Civilian in Peace, Soldier in War* (Lawrence: University Press of Kansas, 2003), 16.

4. Harry Schenawolf, "History of Early Colonial Militias in America," *Revolutionary War Journal*, January 9, 2015, https://www.revolutionarywarjournal.com/militias -in-colonial-america/.

5. H. W. Crocker III, *Don't Tread on Me: A 400-Year History of America at War, from Indian Fighting to Terrorist Hunting* (New York: Crown Forum, 2006), 51.

6. George Washington to John Hancock, September 25, 1776, Founders Online, National Archives, https://founders.archives.gov/documents/Washington/03-06-02 -0305.

7. Thomas Fleming, "Militia and Continentals," *Journal of the American Revolution*, December 30, 2013, https://allthingsliberty.com/2013/12/militia-continentals/.

8. Forest L. Marion, interview with author, 2022.

9. Marion interview, 2022.

10. John K. Mahon, *History of the Militia and the National Guard* (New York: Macmillan, 1983), 97–106.

11. U.S. Marine Corps, "History of the USMCR," 2016, https://www.marforres .marines.mil/USMCR100/History/.

12. U.S. Coast Guard Reserve, "Coast Guard Reserve History," n.d., https://www .reserve.uscg.mil/about/history/.

13. John T. Carlton and John F. Slinkman, *The ROA Story: A History of the Reserve Officers Association of the United States* (Washington, DC: Reserve Officers Association of the United States, 1982), 401–402.

14. U.S. Marine Corps, "History of the USMCR."

15. Marion interview, 2022.

16. Carlton and Slinkman, *ROA Story*, 480–496.

17. President's Commission on an All-Volunteer Armed Force, *The Report of the President's Commission on an All-Volunteer Armed Force* (Washington, DC: GPO, 1970), 154–155 (hereafter cited as Gates Commission, *Report*).

18. Gates Commission, *Report*, 98.

19. Gates Commission, *Report*, 100.

20. Gates Commission, *Report*, 130.

21. Gates Commission, *Report*, 13.

22. Gates Commission, *Report*, 117.

23. James T. Currie, *Twice the Citizen: A History of the U.S. Army Reserve, 1908–1995* (Washington, DC: Office of the Chief, Army Reserve for Chief of Staff, U.S. Army, 1997), 214.

24. John K. Mahon, *History of the Militia and the National Guard* (New York: Macmillan, 1983), 249–250.

25. Mahon, *History of the Militia and the National Guard*, 250. I recall a fraternity brother in 1977 going to his drill weekends wearing a wig.

26. Maj. Gen. James M. Lariviere, USMC (Ret.), interview with author, n.d. Lariviere is former director of reserve affairs division, Headquarters Marine Corps; former commanding general, 4th Marine Division; former staff director, House Committee on Veterans' Affairs; and former professional staff member, Subcommittee on Military Personnel, House Committee on Armed Services.

27. Currie, *Twice the Citizen*, 217.

28. Currie, *Twice the Citizen*, 218–219.

29. U.S. Army, *Regulation 11-30*, *Army WARTRACE Program* (Washington, DC: Headquarters Department of the Army, July 28, 1995), 3.

30. U.S. Army, *Regulation 11-30*.

31. Maj. Gen. Richard O. Wightman, USA (Ret.), interview with author, 2021. Wightman is a former acting assistant secretary of defense for reserve affairs; former commanding general, 143d Transportation Command (U.S. Army Reserve); and former military executive to the RFPB.

32. Command Master Chief Ericka E. Kelly, USAF (Ret.), interview with author, July 2020. Kelly is a former command chief master sergeant of the Air Force Reserve.

33. Dennis M. McCarthy, interview with author, December 2020. McCarthy is a former assistant secretary of defense for reserve affairs and former commander, Marine Forces North and Marine Forces Reserve.

34. Lawrence J. Korb and David R. Segal, "Manning & Financing the Twenty-First-Century All-Volunteer Force," *Daedalus* (American Academy of Arts and Sciences), 2011.

35. Wightman interview, 2021.

36. Bart Brasher, *Implosion: Downsizing the U.S. Military, 1987–2015* (Westport, CT: Greenwood, 2000), 56.

37. Brasher, *Implosion*, 56–57.

38. Brasher, *Implosion*, 79.

39. Brasher, *Implosion*, 79.

40. Stephen M. Duncan, "Gulf War Was a Test of Reserve Components and They Passed: Testimony to the Subcommittee on Manpower and Personnel of the Senate

Armed Services Committee," April 24, 1991, https://www.globalsecurity.org/military/library/report/1995/p162.pdf.

41. Brasher, *Implosion*, 56, 71, 82.

42. Doubler, *Civilian in Peace, Soldier in War*.

43. Roger W. Sandler, interview with author, 2020.

44. Doubler, *Civilian in Peace, Soldier in War*.

45. Forrest L. Marion and Jon T. Hoffman, *Forging a Total Force: The Evolution of the Guard and Reserve* (Washington, DC: Office of the Secretary of Defense, Historical Office, 2018), 94.

46. Ronald E. Sortor, "Army Active/Reserve Mix: Force Planning for Major Regional Contingencies," RAND, 1995, https://www.rand.org/content/dam/rand/pubs/monograph_reports/2005/MR545.pdf.

47. ROA *Reserve Voice Online*, April 15, 2018, March 15, 2019, March 2020.

48. *CNN*, January 20, 2003.

49. Marion and Hoffman, *Forging a Total Force*, 126, 128.

50. Title 10, United States Code § 12302—Ready Reserve.

51. Marion and Hoffman, *Forging a Total Force*, 127.

52. Marion and Hoffman, *Forging a Total Force*, 134.

53. Marion and Hoffman, *Forging a Total Force*, 129.

54. Marion and Hoffman, *Forging a Total Force*, 166.

55. James R. Helmly, "Memorandum through Commander, United States Forces Command for Chief of Staff, United States Army," December 20, 2004, https://www.globalsecurity.org/military/library/report/2005/usar_memo-20dec2004.pdf.

56. Marion and Hoffman, *Forging a Total Force*, 135.

57. Marion and Hoffman, *Forging a Total Force*, 144–145.

58. Marion and Hoffman, *Forging a Total Force*, 115.

59. Gregg Zoroya, "Hotline Helps War-Weary Troops, Families," *USA Today*, February 27, 2008, http://veteransforcommonsense.org/2008/02/27/hotline-helps-war-weary-troops-families/.

60. Marion and Hoffman, *Forging a Total Force*, 148.

61. Defense Casualty Analysis System, n.d., https://dcas.dmdc.osd.mil/dcas/app/home.

62. Susan Lukas, interview with author, October 2020.

63. Marygail K. Brauner, Timothy Jackson, and Elizabeth Gayton, "Improving Medical and Dental Readiness in the Reserve Components," RAND Corporation, 2012, https://www.rand.org/pubs/research_briefs/RB9670.html.

64. James R. Honey, "The Army Selected Reserve Dental Readiness System: Overview, Assessment, and Recommendations," *Military Medicine* 178, no. 6 (June 2013): 607–618, https://academic.oup.com/milmed/article/178/6/607/4320202.

65. Lukas interview, October 2020.

66. Lukas interview, October 2020.

67. RFPB, 2006 *Annual Report* (Washington, DC: U.S. Department of Defense, February 2007).

68. Marion and Hoffman, *Forging a Total Force*, 157.

69. Marion interview, 2022.

70. Marion and Hoffman, *Forging a Total Force*, 142.

71. C. Todd Lopez, "Reserve Soldiers 'More Relevant' than Ever," U.S. Army, February 1, 2012, https://www.army.mil/article/72873/reserve_soldiers_more_releva nt_than_ever.

72. Arnold L. Punaro, *On War and Politics* (Annapolis, MD: Naval Institute Press, 2016), 203.

73. RFPB, *2016 Annual Report* (Washington, DC: U.S. Department of Defense, 2017), 49.

74. Marion and Hoffman, *Forging a Total Force*, 196.

75. McCarthy interview, December 2020.

76. RFPB, *2016 Annual Report*.

77. RFPB, "Requiring the Use of Fully Burdened and Life Cycle Personnel Costs for All Components in Total Force Analysis and for Budgetary Purposes," September 10, 2019, https://rfpb.defense.gov/Portals/67/Final 2019 Fully Burdened Life Cycle Cost Methodology Report Update 10 SEP 2019_1.pdf.

78. RFPB, *2016 Annual Report*, 75.

79. RFPB, *2016 Annual Report*, 20.

80. Joseph E. Whitlock, *The Army's Mobilization Problem*, U.S. Army College War Room, October 13, 2017, https://warroom.armywarcollege.edu/articles/armys-mobili zation-problem/.

81. Dennis M. McCarthy, "The Continuum of Reserve Service," *Joint Force Quarterly* 36 (December 2004): 34–35, https://ndupress.ndu.edu/portals/68/Documents/jfq /jfq-36.pdf.

82. U.S. Department of Defense, Defense Manpower Data Center, November 2020, https://www.dmdc.osd.mil/appj/dwp/news.jsp.

83. Lariviere interview, n.d.

84. Jacquelyn Schneider, "Moving Beyond Total Force: Building a True Strategic Reserve," *War on the Rocks*, November 2, 2020, https://warontherocks.com/2020/11 /moving-beyond-total-force-building-a-true-strategic-reserve/.

85. Arnold L. Punaro, conversation with author, 2019.

86. U.S. Coast Guard, "Coast Guard Reserve History," n.d.

87. McCarthy interview, December 2020.

88. Congressional Research Service, September 22, 2022.

89. Congressional Research Service, September 22, 2022.

90. McCarthy interview, December 2020.

91. RFPB, *2016 Annual Report*, 203.

92. Lukas interview, October 2020.

93. McCarthy interview, December 2020.

94. David C. Bellon, "Designing the Reserve Component of 2030," *Reserve Voice Magazine* (Washington, DC: ROA, 2021).

IV
Implications

11

Military Culture

Adrian R. Lewis

Citizens willing and able to defend their nation, political system, and way of life are the foundation, the very bedrock of Western civilization. Without their willing, continuous, and loyal participation and support; without their willingness to sacrifice, possibly life itself, for the good of the political and cultural body; and without their physical ability to perform the arduous tasks and duties of soldiers, the nation-state cannot long survive. Peter Risenberg has noted:

> Between the early centuries of the [Roman] Republic's expansion, when the grant of citizenship was used again as a means to hold the state together, citizenship essentially was a status, which conveyed certain legal powers or benefits. It was also a moral demand in that, out of historical and contemporary ethical belief and practice, it placed before a man *a schedule of his responsibilities toward the patria.* . . .
>
> Historically, citizenship had called for a payment of taxes; now Rome was so rich those taxes were no longer required. Moreover, that same wealth did away with the military service every Roman owed his patria. Citizen mercenaries, recruited from the lower classes, now filled the ranks and gave their allegiance to Marius, Sulla, or some other general or politician who promised them good pay and retirement benefits.[1]

In the United States, the schedule of responsibilities toward the patria no longer exists. Today, the American people have no responsibilities toward their patria, no duty to serve their nation or state, even in times of war, while the consumption/obesity epidemic has robbed the majority of them of the physical ability to perform the duties of soldiers.[2] Now, the United States could not fight World War II. Clausewitz's trinity of war—the concert of the people, the government, and the armed forces —a requirement to fight total war, is no longer operative.[3] The United States is a political, administrative, and geographical entity, a state, with professional armed forces that are culturally distinct and primarily serves that state. It is a *state* made up of many *nations*, distinct and unwilling to sacrifice for one another. In 2000, Michael Weiss observed:

> Today, the country's new motto should be "E pluribus Pluriba": "Out of many, many." Evidence of the nation's accelerated fragmentation is more than anecdotal. . . . American society today is composed of sixty-two distinct lifestyle types. . . . The lifestyles represent America's modern tribes, sixty-two distinct population groups each with its own set of values, culture, and means of coping with today's problems.[4]

In 2016, Nancy Isenberg further documented the cultural, economic, and class divisions in the United States:

> "Make America Great Again" is another way of saying that hard work is no longer automatically rewarded as a virtue. It tapped the anxieties of all who resented government for handing over the country to supposedly less deserving classes: new immigrants, protesting African Americans, lazy welfare freeloaders, and Obamacare recipients asking for handouts. Angry Trump voters were convinced that these classes (the takers) were not playing by the rules. . . . This was how many came to feel "disinherited."[5]

The election of Donald Trump in 2016 said more about America than it did about Donald Trump. The sustained support for Trump of 45 percent of the population—even though most Americans believe he is a racist, even though his public anti-immigrant rages have been widely condemned—sheds light on the acute political, social, racial, class, cultural, and regional divisions in the United States. There is a lot of hate and anger in America.[6] This hate destroys the sense of community, causes fractures that make unified action impossible to achieve, and creates opportunities for foreign governments to exploit these cracks with the goal to harm and diminish the United States. At the height of the Vietnam War, in 1968 during the Tet Offensive, another war—a political, cultural, racist, regional war—was going on in the United States, making a unified effort in Vietnam impossible.[7] This hate is not new. It rises and falls with political, social, and economic conditions and circumstances, and how it is managed matters. But a state divided into multiple nations/tribes, where primacy is placed on differences, where tribalism is more important than patriotism or the cause for which we fight, is incapable of fighting total war, of effectively fighting limited war, of unified actions even during periods of crisis, and of conscripting a national army.

The divorce between the American *nations* and the *state* took place during the Korean and Vietnam Wars and was completed in 1973, when conscription came to an end. The divorce was confirmed on 9/11, when in the wake of the terrorist attacks that bought down the World Trade Center in New York, the George W. Bush administration told the American people to go shopping and directed the armed forces and private military firms to fight the Global War on Terrorism.[8] This divorce was again confirmed from 2008 to 2009, during Operation Iraqi Freedom (the Iraq War), when the U.S. Army and U.S. Marine Corps were too small to accomplish the missions established by the president and no effort was made to call upon the American people to serve.[9] Instead, the Bush administration relied on private contractors (the new mercenaries) and placed the burden of two long wars on the shoulders of the all-volunteer force. The administration was more willing to accept defeat in Iraq and/ or Afghanistan than to call upon the American people to serve.

Further confirmation of the inability of the United States and the American people to act in a cohesive, unified manner came in both 2016 and 2020. Vladimir Putin's Russia, employing social media and other means, exploited fractures in American society and culture, influencing the outcome of the 2016 national elections without consequences.[10] In 2020, during the COVID-19 pandemic, Americans again demonstrated who they are. States competed against one another to acquire protective equipment to fight the virus, individual states entered into agreements with foreign governments to acquire needed supplies and equipment, and regional alliances of states were formed to organize partially coherent responses.[11] There was no national strategic plan, no mobilization of the vast intellectual and productive resources of the country, no common sense of shared sacrifice, and no unified actions. As a consequence, by June 2020, more Americans were dead—more than 100,000 in six months—than were killed in both the Korean and Vietnam Wars combined, and *every other state on earth* outperformed the United States in managing the pandemic.[12] The modern American nation-state, the cohesive, cultural entity that fought World War II and the subsequent Cold War, no longer exists. The evidence at this point is overwhelming. The fact is, the only armed force the United States is capable of employing is an AVF. It is incapable of manning a conscripted, national army. The American people will not support it. Why does this matter?

The Global Responsibilities of the Armed Forces of the United States

The AVF is incapable of meeting the security needs of the United States and its allies. It is incapable of maintaining the U.S. led and created post–

World War II order, which is under attack from both China and Russia.[13] And, the AVF is destroying, arguably has destroyed, the tradition and cultural norm of citizenship as it has evolved in Western civilization since the days of Ancient Greece and Rome. One observer writing during the Bush administration's "elected" war in Iraq concluded:

> The United States now has a mercenary army. To be sure, our soldiers are hired from within the citizenry, unlike the hated Hessians whom George III recruited to fight against the American Revolutionaries. But like those Hessians, today's volunteers sign up for some mighty dangerous work, largely for wages and benefits—a compensation package that may not always be commensurate with the dangers in store, as current recruiting problems testify. . . . Since the time of the ancient Greeks through the American Revolutionary War well into the 20th century, the obligation to bear arms and the privileges of citizenship have been intimately linked. . . . That tradition has now been all but abandoned.[14]

The American-initiated war in Iraq in 2003 was unnecessary. Saddam Hussein did not have weapons of mass destruction, and even if he did, there was nothing in Iraq that could not have been destroyed from the air. Nevertheless, the war was *not* a national effort. The American people had no part to play. They were bystanders, and unlike the Vietnam War, there was little protest from either them or Congress. And even when it became evident that the administration had misled the American people, no substantive protest arose. The American people are no longer vested in the wars of the United States. They are pacified, overweight, and consumers, physically and culturally incapable of fighting war. They are ignorant of the threats to their security, to the post–World War II security order/structure put in place by the United States, and of the duties and responsibilities their armed forces perform in maintaining stability on earth. How do you support something you have no knowledge of or do not understand? The 2018 edition of *The American Culture of War* states: "It is hard to imagine how the United States can remain a superpower with the majority of its people suffering from the debilitating effects of obesity, drugs, and debt. The American people are deteriorating."[15] I stand by those words, yet I would now add "ignorance" to the maladies. Most Americans have no idea what their armed forces do, no knowledge or understanding of basic global geography, and no desire to learn either one. Since 2018, the rate of deterioration has increased. The majority of Americans, 70–75 percent, cannot qualify to serve in the U.S. armed forces. The status of the United States in 2020 is dangerous not just for the many American "nations" but also for the nations of Europe and Asia.

Let us be clear about what the armed forces of the United States do. They are not just responsible for the security of the lives of the people from San Francisco to New York. They are responsible for the lives of the people in Seoul, Taipei, and Tokyo; for the lives of the citizens of Berlin, London, and Paris; and for the lives of the people in Riyadh, Kuwait, and Tel Aviv. They are responsible for the security of the world economy and the expansion and maintenance of the global capitalist system. And they are responsible for the survival and maintenance of democratic political systems in all parts of the world. Nothing proceeds without security. Stability is a function of security, as are sustained forms of learning, enterprise, art, development, and growth. Political systems, economic systems, promises, commitments, agreements, alliances, or strategic plans not backed by *force in existence* are but empty words, ideas with no force behind them. Since World War II, the United States has maintained a global military presence, keeping stability on earth by ensuring security. The Japanese, Korean, and Taiwanese economic miracles were made possible by the security provided by the U.S. armed forces. The German and French economic and political recoveries were made possible by stability created by the presence of the U.S. armed forces. The flow of Middle East oil was and is made possible by security provided by the U.S. Navy. The armed forces of the United States are responsible for maintaining the post–World War II order established by Presidents Roosevelt, Truman, and Eisenhower.

The American-made global security structure and system have *not* maintained peace but have prevented total wars, tactical nuclear wars, and, most importantly, thermonuclear war; have prevented clashes between the major powers on earth; and have prevented regional wars from escalating into a global war—as a consequence, they have saved many millions of lives and made possible great prosperity in some nations. The global structures and systems put in place were far from perfect. The United States made some horrendous mistakes, and, as a consequence, humanity experienced and witnessed cruel disasters, such as the Vietnam War and the Iraq War. But consider what did *not* happen. In 1961, the Joint Chiefs of Staff estimated that a first strike against the Soviet Union, its Warsaw Pact satellites, and China would result in "roughly six hundred million dead [70 million people were killed in World War II]."[16] In 1970, the nuclear arsenal of the United States included 26,008 devices, while the Soviet Union possessed 11,643 devices.[17] Both sides had sufficient numbers of nuclear weapons and delivery systems to destroy all the major cities in both states. The miracle was what did not happen.[18]

The American-made security structure and system did not eliminate threats—it effectively managed them. Force in existence, backed by the willing commitment of a people and the productive and intellectual resources of the nation-state, created security and stability. Briefly, what did Roosevelt, Truman, and Eisenhower create?

- The Massive Retaliation strategic doctrine, the threat of thermonuclear war using nuclear weapons (the destructive power of each "bomb" measured in megatons of TNT) deployed by bombers and missiles, which was the main element of U.S. strategic-deterrent policy. In the second term of the Eisenhower administration, tactical nuclear weapons entered the U.S. arsenals, and the theory of waging a limited, tactical nuclear war was born. It was not until the later 1950s and early 1960s that the United States and Soviet Union actually possessed sufficient bombs and delivery systems to conduct thermonuclear war.
- Forward deployment of the armed forces of the United States in chains of naval and military bases stretching across the planet, from Central Europe to the Korean Peninsula, supported the first line formed by allied nation-states in execution of the Containment policy.
- Strategic reserves, active-duty forces trained, equipped, and deployable, stationed in the United States, and strategic transportation resources (air and sea) capable of rapidly moving major units to reinforce forward-deployed and allied forces formed the second layer of defense. National Guard and reserve divisions and units that could be mobilized for war formed the third layer of defense.
- Global command and control structure, known as the combatant commands, which are unified and specified commands that exercise regional responsibilities to maintain security in accordance with international law and contingency plans to manage crises. During World War II, the earth was divided into major theaters of operations. In the early days of the Cold War, this system evolved into the current structure, for example, U.S. Indo-Pacific Command (USINDOPACOM), U.S. Central Command (USCENTCOM), and U.S. European Command (USEUCOM).
- Mutual-security agreements, such as NATO and the Southeast Asia Treaty Organization (SEATO), which call on all members to provide military forces for regional security, were signed. The United States also concluded separate security agreements with individual nation-states. These nation-states formed the perimeter between the two blocs.
- The Eisenhower Doctrine (an extension of the Truman Doctrine)

continued and expanded programs designed to provide military and economic assistance, including weapons, training, and education, to states fighting communist insurgencies in the "gray areas." This included extending U.S. security promises to regions and states considered vital to the West, such as the oil-rich Middle East states.

- Foreign military sales, major weapons and equipment sold to allies, including ships, aircraft, missiles, ammunition, and other military hardware and systems, became a significant part of the national-security program. Nations such as Japan, South Korea, Britain, Israel, Saudi Arabia, Iran, Iraq, and numerous others purchased billions of dollars of American-made military equipment annually. The United States became the biggest arms producer on earth.

- Intelligence agencies, the employment of the Central Intelligence Agency, National Security Agency, National Reconnaissance Office, Defense Intelligence Agency, and others to conduct worldwide surveillance and espionage wars to undermine the Soviet Union, People's Republic of China, and the international communist system; collect intelligence on Soviet and Chinese capabilities, strategies, and plans; carry out a disinformation campaign to degrade Soviet and Chinese capabilities; and overthrow and/or undermine unfriendly governments, became a major part of the Eisenhower national-security strategy.[19]

- Science and technology influenced the outcome of World War II. During the Cold War, the research-and-development race intensified as both sides sought the most advanced weapons and military technology. The arms race became a major tenet of the American culture of war under the Eisenhower administration. This received enormous attention, resources, and emphasis after the Soviets launched Sputnik, the first artificial satellite, in 1957. This event caused the creation of the Defense Advanced Research Projects Agency, National Aeronautics and Space Administration, and other agencies and greatly expanded the relationships between U.S. universities and the DOD.

- The Defense industrial base, maintaining the industrial capacity and the know-how to mass produce the weapons, ships, tanks, airplanes, and other materials of war, grew in significance as war technologies became more sophisticated and difficult to produce. New facilities had to be built, and senators and representatives became greatly involved in this process, in part, to secure resources and jobs for their states and districts.

- "Peace and Prosperity," fiscal conservatism, balanced budgets, and increased domestic spending and consumption such as, for example, the construction of the interstate highway system and the national airport system, were part of Eisenhower's defense policy. Quality of life mattered to people everywhere. The demonstrative superiority of the American system to produce the greatest good for the greatest number of people was the element of Eisenhower's strategy that had the greatest importance in winning the Cold War. Communism as an economic system did not work. The great American grocery store, with all its abundance, helped win the Cold War.

• Ultimately, Americans believe the rest of the world has to look like them, which is achieved through the exportation of culture. During the Eisenhower years, the United States started the mass exportation of culture, democracy, capitalism, free trade, and, ultimately, music, MacDonald's, blue jeans, and other staples of the American way of life. The presence of hundreds of thousands of American military personnel stationed overseas, the enormous U.S. military and economic assistance program, the export of weapons through arms sales, and the globalization of business all facilitated this exportation of culture.

By the end of the Eisenhower administration, the United States had developed and deployed a global security structure and system that grew to encompass every American and most of the world. This imperfect system prevented major wars between the great powers and created the stability required for the greatest expansion of economic activity in history. The quality of life enjoyed—and taken for granted—by many people in Europe, Asia, and the Middle East was acquired through security and stability attained and maintained primarily by the armed forces of the United States. Citizenship formed the bedrock of this system, a cohesive people willing and able to sacrifice for something greater than themselves. The foundation of this system was conscripted armed forces and the knowledge that, in the event of war, the government could call upon the American people to show up and fight.[20]

The end of the Cold War with the collapse of the Soviet Union did not signal the end of this American-made security structure. The revolution from 1989 to 1991 was incomplete. It did not achieve the two most important elements of the victory: the elimination of nuclear weapons and great-power competition and the will and desire to change the status quo by leaders in the People's Republic of China or Russia. At present, China and Russia are again threatening the world order put in place at the end of World War II.

In the wake of that war, the American people accepted the responsibilities of world leadership. They projected military power across the planet, not for conquest, but for security. They maintained an imperfect system that benefited humanity. The big question facing them has been: will current and future generations of Americans continue to accept these responsibilities, including the sacrifices they require, to preclude total war? Will they accept the responsibilities handed down to them by the World War II and Cold War generations? The answer seems to be a re-sounding "no." As a result, humanity must now determine what nation, what system, will fill the vacuum created by the retreat of the United States from world leadership. The AVF is not just an American issue: It is an international issue. It is an issue for our allies. It is an issue for NATO. It is an issue for Koreans, Japanese, Israelis, and other nations. We are witnessing a fundamental shift in the global power structure, and the American people have demonstrated they are unwilling and unable to perform the required duties of soldiers to sustain the post–World War II order.

What Went Wrong

The unpopular Vietnam War and the draft that supported it dealt the final blow to the world-wars system of manpower procurement. But the process of its destruction, the erosion of the system, started at the end of World War II with the revolution in warfare caused by the development of nuclear weapons. It started when the United States became a superpower with worldwide responsibilities for the security of people who were culturally, racially, or ethnically different from most Americans. It started when the United States created a global network of military bases and manned them with conscripted forces. It started when senior military leaders theorized that future wars would be dominated by airpower and advanced technologies, including missiles and satellites. The responsibilities of the United States and its armed forces expanded enormously after 1945 at the same time a revolution in the conduct of war was taking place. That change was not what theorists predicted or Americans expected, however, and the American people only gave limited approval, limited acceptance, to their new role in world affairs. In other words, the responsibilities accepted by the *state* were acknowledged by the *nation*, but, at that time, no price tag was attached.

THERMONUCLEAR WEAPONS AND AIRPOWER

Nuclear weapons promised a new era of warfare, a fundamental change in the conduct of human conflict. The development of airpower and missile technologies greatly amplified this understanding that the conduct of war was forever changed. Many came to believe that armies and navies were obsolete, that the great struggles between legions of soldiers and fleets of ships that had characterized all history had come to an end. In his 1948 book *Crusade in Europe*, General Eisenhower, supreme commander of Allied forces in Europe during World War II, writes about the advent of atomic weapons:

> In an instant many of the old concepts of war were swept away. Henceforth, it would seem, the purpose of an aggressor nation would be to stock atom bombs in quantity and to employ them by surprise against the industrial fabric and population centers of its intended victim. Offensive methods would largely concern themselves with certainty, the volume, and the accuracy of delivery, while the defense would strive to prevent such delivery and in turn launch its store of atom bombs against the attacker's homeland. Even the bombed ruins of Germany suddenly seemed to provide but faint warning of what future war could mean to people of the earth.[21]

Then, in the mid-1950s and as president of the United States, Eisenhower stated after the development of the hydrogen bomb:

> You cannot possibly say that the kind of unit and organization that I took to war or took over across the Channel in 1944 would have any usefulness today whatsoever. For example, you will recall we landed on June 6; we got out of that narrow little beachhead on about July 25. All right; behind that we built up two artificial harbors and we were landing over the beaches. What would two atomic bombs have done to the whole thing?[22]

Between 1945 and 1953, a revolution in warfare took place. The United States and the Soviet Union invented thermonuclear war. In 1949, the Soviet Union acquired nuclear weapons. In 1952, the United States detonated the first hydrogen bomb, with an explosive power that measured fifteen megatons, enough to destroy a city the size of New York with one bomb. By comparison, the bomb dropped on Hiroshima generated only fifteen kilotons of explosive power. In 1953, the Soviet Union followed suit and detonated its first hydrogen bomb; thus was born thermonuclear war. Over the decades that followed, both states constructed weapons each with the explosive power of more than fifty megatons and developed missile technologies capable of striking every location on earth. In 1953, Robert Oppenheimer, the man most responsible for the production of the atomic bomb, concluded: "We may anticipate a state of affairs in which the two Great Powers will each be in a position to put an end to the civilization and life of the other, though not without risking its own. We may be likened to two scorpions in a bottle, each capable of killing the other, but only at the risk of his own life."[23] Thermonuclear war is extermination warfare.

Before the first atomic bomb was tested, the argument was made that airpower was the decisive instrument for the conduct of war. During World War II, U.K. Royal Air Force and U.S. Army Air Force leaders again and again advanced the thesis that wars could be won exclusively from the air. General Henry "Hap" Arnold, commander of Army Air Forces in World War II, observed:

> War has become vertical. We are demonstrating daily that it is possible to descend from the skies into any part of the interior of an enemy nation and destroy its power to continue the conflict. War industries, communications, power installations and supply lines are being blasted by attacks from the air. Fighting forces have been isolated, their defenses shattered and sufficient pressure brought by air power alone to force their surrender. Constant pounding from the air is breaking the will of the Axis to carry on. . . . Strategic air power is a war-winning weapon in its own right, and is capable of striking decisive blows far behind the battle line, thereby destroying the enemy's capacity to wage war.[24]

Such other technologies as the V-2 rocket, the world's first guided missile, and jet aircraft supported the airpower thesis, which seemed to usher in a new age of warfare. The late 1940s and 1950s were rich in technological developments. Mankind envisioned traveling in space, flying saucers, and push-button warfare. Science fiction, with the help of the military, sold a new futuristic vision of war to Americans. It was a vision based primarily on airpower and nuclear weapons. In 1947, the U.S. Air Force was born, finally separating itself from the army. The air force claimed primacy among the armed forces. It was the future of warfare, and Americans, wrongly, came to believe that airpower would maintain security.

There was pushback to this vision of war. Gen. Mark Clark, who commanded Allied forces in Italy during World War II and the United Nations Command in the Far East during the last year of the Korean War, challenged the thinking of the Eisenhower administration and the airpower theorists, writing in 1954:

There is much talk these days about push-button warfare and the fact that the technical experts have developed such weapons of mass destruction that the role of the infantryman is now secondary. . . . However, in my opinion, and without in any way disparaging the vital roles of the Air Force and the Navy, the infantryman remains an indispensable element in any future war. Certainly he must be supported by the Air and the Navy and every kind of technical weapon, but he never will be relegated to an unimportant role. He is the fellow with the stout heart and a bellyful of guts, who, with his rifle and bayonet, is willing to advance another foot, fire another shot and die if need be in defense of his country.[25]

The weight and force of the airpower argument, however, was overwhelming. When the United States entered the Korean War and then later the Vietnam War, airpower was supposed to be the decisive instrument for the conduct of each. The U.S. Army and U.S. Marine Corps fought the entire Vietnam War on the strategic defense. The only offensive element to American strategy was airpower—Operation Rolling Thunder.

THE COLD WAR AND NEW GLOBAL RESPONSIBILITIES

At the end of World War II, the political objectives that had directed U.S. national and military strategies and the energies and intellect of the American people for two hundred years radically changed; as a consequence, the American paradigm for war changed. Two superpowers emerged from the unparalleled carnage of World War II. Secretary of State Dean Acheson noted:

Since the defeat and surrender of Germany and Japan, the disappearance of the great empires of Europe, and the eclipse of China, the United States and the Soviet Union had emerged unrivaled—saved each by the other—among the powers of earth. Each had been molded by its position, its experience, and its conception of its interests to view the other with distrust amounting to hostility. Unfortunately, but inevitably, this attitude has affected the replacement of the old world-order of the nineteenth century. . . . Even now, after a quarter of a century, agreement has been impossible. Only an uneasy *modus vivendi*, based upon a balance of terror between the superpowers, has led them to place some restraint upon their client-states.[26]

The Soviet Union emerged from World War II a wounded superpower. During the war, it and the United States were allies. The Americans provided tens of billions of dollars in Lend-Lease Aid to the Soviets. Still, the United States and United Kingdom failed to open the "second front" in Europe, requested by Stalin in 1942, until June 1944. This meant that the people of the Soviet Union bore the heaviest burden of the war, suffering from 25 million to 30 million casualties. World War II was a source of friction afterward. Even without that, they were not natural allies. The Soviet Union, a communist state, possessed political and economic systems that were incompatible with the American way of life, and Stalin was considered a brutal dictator. Between 1945 and 1950, the Cold War emerged as a worldwide struggle, kept cold by the threat of nuclear war.

In that aftermath of World War II, American power and influence, both economic and military, stretched around the earth. More so than any other factor, the war advanced the process of globalization.[27] As technologies and trade connected the world in new ways; as old Europe collapsed under the weight of two world wars; as wars of national liberation erupted in Asia, Africa, and the Middle East; and as the Cold War intensified, the United States necessarily assumed new responsibilities and new roles in world affairs. By 1950, the United States was, in fact, both a European power and an Asian power, responsible for the security of over 200 million people in Asia, Europe, and other parts of the world. In 1945, it also assumed occupation duties and became directly responsible for the security of Japanese, Koreans, Filipinos, Germans, and Italians and indirectly responsible for the security of Western democracies. Americans were responsible for defending people who were racially and ethnically different, people for whom they had little or no cultural affinity.

The new political objectives of the United States were to stop the spread of communism, deter nuclear war, implant American capitalism and practices of trade, support democracies, and transplant American culture—in other words, remake the rest of the world to look like America. Permanent readiness for war and defensive national strategy and doctrine were the results of these new political objectives. The American people accepted ever larger defense budgets and embraced a new form of militarism.[28] Defense industries and foreign military sales created new opportunities, new wealth. The United States became the world's largest arms producer and dealer. Yet this new mission and strategy were not in accord with the traditional American practice of war and not in accord with American thinking about the nature and conduct of war.

ARTIFICIAL LIMITED WAR
In June 1950, on the Korean peninsula another new form of war was born, artificial limited war (ALW). The Korean War was not another world war, but it was not a nuclear war. It was something new. In Korea, the costs of America's new responsibilities came clear. ALW was a direct

function of the development of thermonuclear war and the American acceptance of new, worldwide responsibilities. It created artificial rules of engagement, wars in which willing limitations were imposed on political objectives, weapons employed, geographic boundaries of the battlefield, nationalities engaged, commitment of resources, the investment of the passions and intellect of the people/citizens, and the actions and words of military leaders. During the Korean War, both sides, without formal agreement, continuously exercised restraints, placing limitations on their conduct of the war, while seeking total military and political objectives. It never escalated to a potential World War III or, officially, a clash between the superpowers. Both sides, both alliances, engaged in subterfuge and accepted lies; the other side knew what was a lie, but still accepted it. Fear of nuclear weapons kept the Cold War cold.

But while the *state* could fight ALW, the *nation* could not. In Korea, the American nation ultimately rejected ALW for the obvious reason: there is nothing limited about dying. There is no difference between limited war and total war at the edge of the battlefield where the killing takes place. There, a nation ultimately pays the price in blood. From the Korean War to the end of the Vietnam War, a contradiction manifested in the American culture and practice of war. That contradiction ended in the final year of the Vietnam War when the *state* and the *nation* agreed to end the draft, relieving Americans of the responsibility to serve the state during times of war.

The Korean peninsula was divided at the thirty-eighth parallel at the end of World War II. The United States took the surrender of the Japanese south of that latitude, and the Soviet Union north of it. Korea's division was supposed to be a temporary expedient; yet as the Cold War emerged and friction between the United States and the Soviet Union intensified, the thirty-eighth parallel became a border between two separate states, the Republic of Korea (ROK), formed in the south on August 15, 1948, and the Communist Democratic People's Republic of Korea (DPRK), which emerged in the north on September 9, 1948. Both sides sought to reunite the country under their respective governments but were held in check by their respective superpower patron. In 1950, Kim-Il Sung, the leader of the DPRK, requested permission from Stalin and Mao Zedong, to invade the ROK to reunify the peninsula. Stalin and Mao Tse-tung approved, believing that the United States would not intervene. They were wrong. President Truman committed the armed forces of the United States to the defense of the ROK, setting the stage for a great-power conflict, for a potential World War III, and for a possible nuclear war.

By September 1950, following the Inchon amphibious landings, the

United States had achieved its primary political objective of saving the ROK; in October, however, ROK and U.S. forces crossed the thirty-eighth parallel to complete the destruction of the Korean People's Army and re-unify the peninsula. At this point, the United States sought a total political objective and total victory on the Korean peninsula but was unwilling to fight a total war. Now the United States miscalculated. In November, the People's Republic of China (PRC) entered the Korean War to save the DPRK, a major escalation that brought a clash between the armed forces of the United States and People's Liberation Army (PLA) of the PRC, which called itself a *volunteer force*. This was subterfuge, but it was an important lie, having the intent of precluding war between the two nation-states.[29] It worked. There were no formal declarations of war.

The attack caught the U.S. Eighth Army by surprise, forcing a costly, long, and bloody retreat.[30] At that moment, from November to December 1950, the United States possessed the nuclear weapons and delivery systems to destroy the PLA and isolate the battlefield. Had Truman employed nuclear weapons, he would have had the support of his generals, his soldiers and marines, and the American people. Truman, the only person to date ever to approve the use of nuclear weapons, decided *not* to employ the weapon, decided to let his army continue to fight and suffer on battlefields most Americans could not find on a map. In Korea in November 1950, ALW became the new American way of war.

Explain Truman's decision to the American people and at the same time ask for their continued support, for their sons and daughters to fight the war. Explain to the American people why the United States was not employing the weapons it so richly possessed and committed vast resources to develop. Explain why they should continue to support a bloody ground war for the security of foreigners, when their government had no intention of completing the destruction of the enemy. Explain why the army and marine corps were fighting a defensive war of attrition when they had the capacity to conduct offensive operations to destroy the enemy. Neither Truman nor later Presidents Johnson or Nixon could do so. It was in Korea that the divorce between the *nation* and the *state* was initiated. From the Korean War until the end of the Vietnam War, Americans tried to adapt traditional cultural tenets and traditional ways of thinking and acting in war to the new national missions, the Cold War environment, and the new paradigm of ALW. Ultimately, this adaptation process in relation to Korea failed; in Vietnam, it collapsed. What emerged was a new American practice of war—one that virtually eliminated the American people from the conduct of war. As a result, today the United States is more *state*, a political/military entity, than *nation*, a culturally cohesive entity.

The Cold War and nuclear weapons changed the American equation for war. While ALW was necessary in the age of nuclear weapons, it was and remains nonsense to most of humanity because there is nothing limited about dying and killing. Limited war is limited at the strategic and operational levels, and then only limited for the superpowers and major Western nations. At the tactical level, where the killing, dying, and suffering take place, there is nothing limited about limited war. Weapons produce the same effect in "limited war" as they do in "total war." They destroy life. To ask Americans to commit their most valued sons and daughters, to war and then hold back resources that would hasten its end and perhaps save their children was inexplicable. The restraints in limited war were artificially imposed, and because everyone understood this, there was an internal illogic to war and an internal contradiction. Political and military leaders accepted and fought limited wars, but the American people and many of the soldiers who were drafted to fight them never accepted the ALW doctrine or strategy. Defensive, protracted wars of attrition—a function of the limitations imposed—were un-American and could not be reconciled with long-held traditions and cultural norms. In the 1950s and 1960s, when Americans said "war," the Civil War and World War II immediately came to mind—offensive war aimed at the destruction of the enemy's armed forces, means of production, and ultimately political system. ALW expanded the fissure between the American people and their understanding of war and the U.S. government and its practice of war.

"Revolutionary technologies" held the promise of sealing the fissure but instead only expanded it. These never achieved what the government and airpower theorists claimed. The Korean and Vietnam Wars were not "push-button" wars, nor was airpower the decisive instrument. The army and marine corps fought another dirty, bloody ground war to save South Korea. And, that effort was more primitive than World War II had been. Later, it took combat ground forces to stabilize South Vietnam, more bloody battles that required American lives. The most advanced airpower in history could not stop the flow of weapons, men, and supplies down the Ho Chi Minh Trail. And the Vietnam War was more primitive than the Korean War. The promises made to the American people were not kept. There was an irreconcilable contradiction between the realities of war and the imagined, futuristic, technological vision of war sold to the American people by the U.S. government and the armed forces. The promises of military technology were never fulfilled, and while the promises were being made, the government was demanding more sons and daughters to fight ALWs in lands most Americans had never heard of.

The Vietnam War marked an important transformation in the American practice of war. The citizen-soldier army was eliminated, effectively removing the American people from the wars of the United States. By the time of the Persian Gulf and Iraq Wars, the American people had no legal, positive duties. The terrorist attacks on 9/11 and George W. Bush's Global War on Terrorism did not change this. When the army and marine corps were fully engaged in fighting two long wars in Iraq and Afghanistan while grossly understrength, no effort was made to call upon the American people to serve. Amid the Global War on Terrorism, the president of the United States promised the American people they would not be called upon to fight or to sacrifice. Rather than compel the American people to serve through conscription—an act that both Bush and 2004 Democratic presidential candidate John Kerry considered political suicide—the Bush administration chose to increase the burden on active-duty, reserve, and National Guard personnel and to employ private military firms. The administration extended tours of duty, put in "stop-loss policies" to preclude people from leaving the services, and rotated soldiers and marines back to Iraq after a relatively brief dwell time at home. This was a first for the United States, confirming the separation between *state* and *nation*.

American Citizenship and the Future of Warfare

The elements and dynamic process for the decline of the United States and the disintegration of the post–World War II order are already in play and well advanced. The ability of the United States to produce combat soldiers has diminished continuously since 1945; as a consequence, the ability of the United States to maintain the postwar security structure and system has deteriorated.

War demands that individuals perform the two most difficult tasks that can be asked and required of a human being: first, to risk one's life, to enter the battlefield; and second, to take another's life, to kill. To get individuals to perform these tasks, to get them to recognize and accept that they belong to something greater than themselves, requires significant attachments. Citizenship requires cultural cohesion, significant attachments to a formal and informal union of people, a political-cultural body. It requires a shared identity, a common set and systems of values, ethics, and beliefs. It requires recognition of the importance and legitimacy of the political-cultural body to the security and welfare of its members. And it requires acceptance not only of the privileges granted and guaranteed to citizens but also of the obligations and responsibilities required of them. Citizens are both sovereign and subject. "Sovereign" is defined as "the supreme repository of power in a political state," "a political unit possessing or held to possess sovereignty," or "possessed of controlling power, ruling, predominant." In theory and, to some degree, in practice, citizens are the sovereign; it is the great power of citizenship. They elect their leaders, whose actions then are supposed to reflect the will of the people, the sovereign. If elected leaders fail to act in ways that reflect the will of the people, they can vote them out of office. The power of this is that the will of the people determines the duties required of citizens. If an elected political leader determines war is necessary, that decision reflects the will of the sovereign people.

The three pillars of citizenship are all in an advance state of decay in the United States. First, the individual's connections to the state are tenuous, superficial, and mostly for ostentatious displays.[31] Second, the individual's connections to other members of the political and cultural body, to other citizens, has fragmented into tribal and clustered communities that are disconnected from the larger American community and incapable of supporting one another.[32] Third, because of overconsumption, which has resulted in an epidemic of obesity and near obesity, the vast majority of Americans are physically unfit and incapable of serving as soldiers. Thus, there is no other alternative to the AVF, supported by private military firms. The majority of Americans are politically, socially, culturally, and physically incapable of serving in the armed forces. One of the essential elements of the modern nation-state, the citizen-soldier, a dual role of sovereign and subject, no longer exists in the United States of America.

During President Bush's Global War on Terrorism, as the need for forces increases, the demands on the AVF grew, and the role of private military firms increased. This is what happened in Afghanistan and Iraq during Operations Enduring Freedom and Operation Iraqi Freedom. The AVF was too small to do all that was required, and private military firms, at great expense, stepped in to perform needed functions, including employing weapons and providing security. Today, the armed forces of the United States cannot get themselves to the battlefield or sustain themselves on it without private contractors. In other words, defense contractors have assumed a large part of the responsibilities for the security of the United States and the maintenance of the post–World War II order that citizen-soldiers used to perform. This is the future of warfare— mercenary armies, in some cases populated by foreigners. The most significant transformation in the American conduct of war since World War II and the invention of the atomic bomb was not technological or doctrinal, but cultural, social, and political: *the elimination of the American people from the conduct of the wars of the United States.* As a consequence, the occupant of the White House has enormous, king-like powers to go to war and to fight as he sees fit. The responsibility of the president to limit the use of the armed forces to actions acceptable to the American people has greatly diminished. The White House and Pentagon have greater freedom to go to and fight wars as they see fit. And the American people have greater freedom to pursue the "American Dream," to accumulate wealth and debt and to consume. They are uninvolved. Out of 300 million Americans, fewer than 1 percent carried the burden of the Global War on Terrorism. This is the new American practice: war without the people. It is not sustainable.

In many ways, the United States has returned to the political-military system prevalent in Europe during the seventeenth and eighteenth centuries, the period of the absolute monarch, when an elite ruling class, the aristocracy, gave small, professional armies military objectives and fought limited wars for political and economic gains. The other clusters, the majority, had nothing to do with war. Robert R. Palmer, in his description of Europe during the "Old Regime," the period prior to the French Revolution and the granting of citizenship to all the people of the state, observes: "A good people was one that obeyed the law, paid its taxes, and was loyal to the reigning house; it need have no sense of its own identity as a people, or unity as a nation, or responsibility for public affairs, or obligation to put forth a supreme effort in war."[33] Palmer further notes: "The tie between the sovereign and subject was bureaucratic, administrative, and fiscal, an external mechanical connection of ruler and ruled, strongly in contrast to the principle brought in by the Revolution, which, in its doctrine of responsible citizenship and sovereign people, effected an almost religious fusion of the government with the governed." The people, according to Palmer, "felt that they participated in the state, that they derived great advantage from their government, and therefore should fight for it loyally and with passion." "Religious fusion" and "passion" do not describe the American people today. The United States in the early twenty-first century is a *state*, an entity made up of many nations that are incapable of fighting major wars. The AVF is not sustainable. Against near-peer adversaries such as the People's Republic of China, it will fail.

Notes

1. Peter Riesenberg, *Citizenship in the Western Tradition: Plato to Rousseau* (Chapel Hill: University of North Carolina Press, 1992), 73, 80.

2. The thesis and analysis advanced in this chapter are based in part on Adrian R. Lewis, *The American Culture of War: The History of U.S. Military Force from World War II to Operation Enduring Freedom*, 3d ed. (New York: Routledge, 2018).

3. Carl von Clausewitz, *On War*, ed. and trans. Michael Howard and Peter Paret (Princeton, NJ: Princeton University Press, 1976), 89.

4. Michael J. Weiss, *The Clustered World: How We Live, What We Buy, and What It All Means about Who We Are* (New York: Little, Brown, 2000), 10, 11.

5. Nancy Isenberg, *White Trash: The 400-Year Untold History of Class in America* (New York: Penguin, 2016), xxii. Also see Charles Murray, *Coming Apart: The State of White America, 1960–2010* (New York: Crown Forum, 2012).

6. Minority groups, particularly African Americans, can see, feel, and experience the hate in America with greater clarity than the majority white populations. Still, the hate is evident on social media, on the southern borders of the United States, in police brutality against minorities, in the courts and hospitals, in Congress, and in every segment of American society.

7. In 1968, Robert Kennedy, a candidate for president, and Martin Luther King Jr. were assassinated, causing riots and discord across the country.

8. For discussions on the rise of private military firms, see P. W. Singer, *Corporate Warriors: The Rise of the Privatized Military Industry* (Ithaca, NY: Cornell University Press, 2003); Allison Stanger, *One Nation under Contract: The Outsourcing of American Power and the Future of Foreign Policy* (New Haven, CT: Yale University Press, 2009); Dina Rasor and Robert Bauman, *Betraying Our Troops: The Destructive Results of Privatizing War* (New York: Palgrave Macmillan, 2007); and Paul R. Verkuil, *Outsourcing Sovereignty* (Cambridge: Cambridge University Press, 2007). Also see Sarah E. Kreps, *Taxing Wars: The American Way of War Finance and the Decline of Democracy* (New York: Oxford University Press, 2018), 141–178.

9. Adrian R. Lewis, "Conscription, the Republic, and America's Future," *Military Review* 89, no. 6 (November/December 2009): 15–24.

10. U.S. Department of Justice, *The Mueller Report*, Washington Post ed. (New York: Scribner, 2019), 59.

11. The governor of Maryland entered into agreements with the government of South Korea to secure personal protective equipment and other needed supplies. He then employed Maryland National Guard units to protect the equipment from confiscation by the federal government. The governor of New York formed a regional alliance with contiguous states to battle the pandemic.

12. The United States, with 4.25 percent of the world's population in May 2020, had 32.3 percent of COVID-19 infections and had suffered 27.9 percent of global deaths, far worse than any other country. National-security-forum@googlegroups .com.

13. Michael Pillsbury, *The Hundred-Year Marathon: China's Secret Strategy to Replace America as the Global Superpower* (New York: St. Martin's Griffin, 2015), 1–16; Angela Stent, *Putin's World: Russia against the West and with the Rest* (New York: Twelve, 2019), 3.

14. David M. Kennedy, "Sons, Brothers, Soldiers," *Dallas Morning News*, Sunday, July 31, 2005.

15. Lewis, *American Culture of War*, 37. This statement was in the first edition of my book, and each year the situation has gotten worse. In 2025, the Center for Disease Control estimates that half of the population of the United States will have

diabetes or be prediabetic. These people have eliminated themselves from the wars of the United States.

16. Daniel Ellsberg, *The Doomsday Machine: Confessions of a Nuclear War Planner* (New York: Bloomsbury, 2017), 3.

17. Colin S. Gray, *War, Peace, and International Relations: An Introduction to Strategic History* (New York: Routledge, 2007), 238. By 1989, the Soviet Union's nuclear inventory counted 39,000 devices, while the United States held 22,217 devices.

18. This thesis is not accepted by all. For an alternative perspective, see John Mueller, *Retreat from Doomsday: The Obsolescence of Major War* (New York: Basic, 1989).

19. Some of the agencies, such as the National Reconnaissance Office, did not come into full existence until after the Eisenhower administration, but they were conceived and initiated during this period. Spy-satellite and aircraft technologies were conceived and developed during the Eisenhower years.

20. Dennis Laich, *Skin in the Game: Poor Kids and Patriots* (Bloomington, IN: iUniverse, 2013), 9. Laich writes: "Ninety-nine percent live in the land of the free and the home of brave because 1 percent who have skin in the game chose to be brave and call that land home. The 99 percent succumb to fear, apathy, ignorance, and guilt to become limited-liability patriots with 'Support the Troops' bumper stickers on their cars. They lack the commitment in their minds and hearts that would be required to enlist."

21. Dwight D. Eisenhower, *Crusade in Europe* (New York: Doubleday, 1948), 456.

22. Dwight D. Eisenhower, "The President's News Conference on March 17, 1954," *US National Security Policy and Strategy: Documents and Policy Proposals* (New York: Greenwood, 1988), 55–58.

23. J. Robert Oppenheimer, "Atomic Weapons and American Policy," *Foreign Affairs* 31, no. 4 (July 1953): 529, quoted in *The Evolution of Nuclear Strategy*, by Lawrence Freedman (New York: St. Martin's, 1983), 94.

24. Gen. Henry H. Arnold, "Air Strategy for Victory," *Flying* 33, no. 4 (October 1943): 50.

25. Mark W. Clark, *From the Danube to the Yalu* (Summit, PA: TAB Books, 1954), 196.

26. Dean Acheson, *The Korean War* (New York: W. W. Norton, 1971), 3, 4.

27. Globalization is frequently described as an economic process, "the emergence and operation of a single, worldwide economy"; yet global communications systems, social media, air travel, energy resources, war, terrorism, and even diseases are connecting the peoples of earth as never before.

28. See Alfred Vagts, *A History of Militarism: Civilian and Military*, rev. ed. (New York: Free Press, 1937), 17; Andrew J. Bacevich, *The New American Militarism: How Americans Are Seduced by War* (New York: Oxford University Press, 2005), 2.

29. Shen Zhihua, *Mao, Stalin, and the Korean War: Trilateral Communist Relations in the 1950s* (New York: Routledge, 2012), 151–153; Chen Jian, *China's Road to the Korean War: The Making of the Sino-American Confrontation* (New York: Columbia University Press, 1994), 175, 176.

30. David Halberstam, *The Coldest Winter: America and the Korean War* (New York: Hyperion, 2007), 393.

31. Michael Walzer, *Obligations: Essays on Disobedience, War, and Citizenship* (Cambridge, MA: Harvard University Press, 1970), 99. Walzer addresses the first pillar:

The extraordinary transformation in social scale which has occurred in the past century and a half created a radically different kind of political community—one in which relations between individual and state are so attenuated (at least their moral quality is so attenuated) as to call into question all the classical and early democratic theories of obligation and war. The individual has become a private man, seizing pleasure when he can, lone, or in the narrow confines of his family. The state has become a distant power, captured by officials, sometimes benevolent, sometimes not, never again firmly within the grasp of its citizens.

Walzer envisions a new status of citizenship, "resident aliens at home," in which the people have no obligation to fight the wars of the nation-state. He concludes: "He [the resident alien at home] has incurred limited, essentially negative duties to the state that regulates and protects his social life. He is bound to respect the regulations and to join at critical moments in the protection. But that is all he is bound to do."

32. Weiss, *Clustered World*, 10–15. Weiss notes:

Cultural dissonance has developed, to some degree, in communities all around the country. On the eve of the twenty-first century, America has become a splintered society, with multi-ethnic towns . . . reflecting a nation more diverse than ever. [T]he term cluster . . . refers to population segments where, thanks to technological advancements, no physical contact is required for cluster membership. . . . [T]he clusters simply underscore realities already apparent, such as the widening gap between the richest and poorest Americans. . . . Sociologists say global competition and the cyber-revolution have widened the gap that divides the haves from the have-nots."

No longer are Americans rising and falling together, as if in one large national boat, former labor secretary Robert Reich has observed. "We are, increasingly, in different, smaller boats. And not all are assured of life rafts."

33. Robert R. Palmer, "Frederick the Great, Guibert, Bulow: From Dynastic to National War," in *Makers of Modern Strategy from Machiavelli to the Nuclear Age*, ed. Peter Paret (Princeton, NJ: Princeton University Press, 1986), 92, 119.

12

Force Structure

Mark F. Cancian

As the United States considered moving from a draft to an all-volunteer force in the early 1970s, concerns arose that the higher personnel costs required to attract volunteers might make the active-duty force smaller. That has, in fact, happened. Unexpectedly, the higher cost and smaller numbers of active-duty personnel drove a restructuring of the armed forces. The United States now relies more heavily on reserves, government civilians, capital assets, and contractors. This shift has allowed it to sustain a global national-security strategy with a much smaller active-duty force but, in doing so, has changed the way the United States fights its wars.

The Rising Cost and Declining Numbers of Military Personnel

A key driver of the force changes has been the rising cost of military personnel, especially those on active duty. Under the AVF, the military must pay a competitive wage in the national labor market to recruit and retain quality personnel. The Gates Commission, in recommending an AVF, saw this as a good thing, with conscription no longer acting as a hidden tax on those who served.[1] A one-time bump up in compensation at the beginning was not enough, however. Military labor has continued to get more expensive over time. Since the establishment of the AVF in 1973, inflation in the economy as a whole (measured by the GDP index) has been 370 percent, but labor inflation, as measured in the military personnel account, has been 581 percent.[2]

The increase in costs for military compensation has been particularly steep since 2000. From 2000 to 2019, pay and benefits for the average servicemember have risen 64 percent in constant dollars, driven especially by large increases in health benefits.[3] As a result, servicemembers now earn more than nearly all their civilian counterparts with comparable education and experience.[4]

Cost is not the only factor acting to shrink the active-duty force. As described elsewhere in this volume, recruiting is becoming more difficult, even with competitive compensation. The propensity to enlist has declined over time from 23 percent in the 1980s to 13 percent today.[5] This has occurred for many reasons, but one of the clearest is the increasing numbers of young people who attend college. In 1973, when the AVF was established, there were 10 million students in college. By 2020, the number had doubled to 20 million. This constitutes about half of eighteen- to twenty-one-year-olds, thus narrowing the military's primary recruiting pool for enlisted personnel.[6] Further, as federal financial aid for higher education has increased, the value of military college benefits like the G.I. Bill has decreased. Finally, of the young people in the seventeen- to twenty-four-year-old cohort, the prime target group for enlistment, 71 percent are not qualified because of drug use, criminal history, low academic achievement, or, increasingly, obesity.[7]

The result has been a long-term decrease in the size of the active-duty force. This decline exhibits a ratchet effect; that is, the force decreases in major steps, not gradually, and once it reaches a lower level, it does not return to the higher level, even if budgets increase. Thus, the armed forces declined during the post-Vietnam drawdown and as the AVF was established in the early 1970s. During the defense buildup of the 1980s, force size stayed relatively constant. Personnel funding increases during this period went to compensation to recapture competitiveness in the labor market. At the end of the Cold War, the AVF took another large reduction and has stayed at that level ever since. The Trump administration's defense budget increases produced little personnel expansion, and the Biden administration will likely cut personnel, though long-term plans are not yet publicly available.[8] The reserve force has similarly declined in numbers, though less steeply (as described later).

This decrease was not entirely unexpected. On the one hand, the Gates Commission forecast a "stable force," arguing: "Since World War II, our peacetime armed forces have been consistently supported at high levels. The public has supported large forces because it has felt them essential to national security. The change from a mixed force of volunteers and conscripts to an all-volunteer force cannot significantly change that feeling."

On the other hand, the commission did foresee some force changes: more personnel in units, arising from longer enlistments, and an opportunity to reduce overall numbers as a result; a shift of duties from military personnel to civilians; mechanization to reduce labor requirements; and a general "economizing" of personnel as the full costs became apparent.

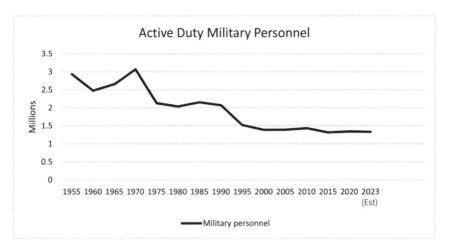

The total number of active-duty military personnel in the U.S. armed forces from 1955 to 2020 (and 2023, estimated) in millions.

This was quite foresighted, as all these changes occurred. Yet the commission saw the decline in active-duty personnel numbers as a one-time "period of transition," not a long-term challenge. It further missed the increasing importance of the reserves, expecting that they would decline as their feature as a draft haven disappeared.[9]

The Military's Response

The military has responded rationally to these challenges. Indeed, it has reacted much as American business has when faced with the rising costs of a core, often unionized, workforce. Thus, business has reduced the number of expensive core personnel, increased its use of part-time employees, substituted capital for labor, used less expensive personnel where possible, and outsourced. For the military, this means increasing reliance on the reserves, fielding more sophisticated weapon systems, expanding the number of government civilians, and using contractors. Let us look at each of these in turn.

INTEGRATING GUARD AND RESERVE FORCES
Just as Amazon hires thousands of part-timers during the Christmas shopping rush, so too do the military services use their National Guard and reserve forces for surge capacity in times of high demand. Guard and reserve forces, when not mobilized, cost much less than active-duty forces.

The Reserve Forces Policy Board calculated that the average reservist costs 28 percent of an active-duty servicemember. RAND Corporation, using a different methodology, calculated that the cost varied depending on the type of unit. Thus, a reserve unit with little equipment costs about 25 percent of an equivalent active-duty unit, while an aviation unit with expensive equipment and requiring extensive training costs much more, 70 percent of an active-duty unit for some (F-16s, for example) but over 100 percent for others (KC-135s). RAND found that the average across all units was about one-third of active-duty costs. Regardless of the methodology, however, reservists are demonstrably much cheaper.[10]

Historical data on the active/reserve mix of the armed forces illustrate these cost dynamics. During the draft era, when active-duty personnel were plentiful, the proportion of Guard and reserve forces in the total force stayed in the 26–28 percent range. With the introduction of the AVF in the early 1970s, the proportion surged to 32 percent. Another surge occurred during the post–Cold War era of the 1990s, when reserve forces declined less than active-duty forces. The proportion dipped a bit during the wars in Iraq and Afghanistan, when the active-duty force grew to meet wartime demand, but seems to have stabilized at about 38 percent during the postwar period.

Numbers do not convey the full extent of this policy shift. As one study notes:

> During the first half of the Cold War, from 1948 to 1970, the reserve forces constituted a second line of defense, significantly less ready than active forces and requiring a long lead time to be effective after being mobilized. The reserve forces were designed to be a source of augmentation for a large, lengthy war and were to be mobilized, equipped, and trained after the start of the war. During this period, the reserve forces (except for the air reserve components) were too unready to immediately augment active forces.[11]

That began to change in 1970, when Secretary of Defense Melvin Laird announced the Total Force concept, which became fully established in 1973, when Defense Secretary James Schlesinger proclaimed it as policy. Total Force policy required, "Guard and Reserve units and individuals of the Selected Reserves will be prepared to be the initial and primary source of augmentation of the active forces in any future emergency requiring a rapid and substantial expansion of the active forces."[12] Driving the new policy was a recognition, as the AVF was being established, that the United States could not maintain sufficient forces on active duty to

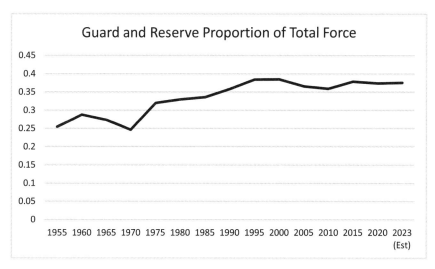

The number of personnel in the reserves and National Guard as a proportion of the total armed forces from 1955 to 2020 (and 2023, estimated).

meet the demands of possible conflict with the Soviet Union, communist China, and other potential adversaries. The reserve component would have to fill the gap.

This policy shift was seen most dramatically in the U.S. Army. Fifty percent of its total force came to reside in its reserve components, a much larger proportion than in the other services (air force, 35 percent; navy, 15 percent; marine corps, 18 percent).[13] A 1974 deal between Secretary Schlesinger and General Creighton Abrams, then army chief of staff, incorporated the army's dependence on reserve components into both its active-duty and reserve force structures. Schlesinger and Abrams were anxious to strengthen deterrence in Europe but recognized that the number of active-duty soldiers was not going to get any larger. Thus, they decided to increase the number of active-duty divisions by three, from thirteen to sixteen, and found the additional personnel by deactivating regular supporting units and transferring their troops. The reserve component thereafter would supply the support in time of war.

This meant that the army could not go to war without calling up large numbers of reservists. The conventional wisdom is that Abrams did this deliberately. He is rumored to have said that he wanted to make sure that no future president did to the army what happened during Vietnam—that is, rely on short-term and unwilling draftees to avoid the political cost of mobilizing reserves. Whether the general said this explicitly, that was the effect.[14] In future wars, those additional forces would come from the reserve components, with all the political costs and national signals that went with a large mobilization.

There were other strategic reasons for increasing reliance on the reserves. For example, strategic mobility is always limited, so overseas deployments in a crisis take a lot of time. It made little sense to have expensive active-duty personnel waiting around for their turn to deploy when they could have been in the reserves and used the wait time to train up and get ready. Reserve components also captured expertise in personnel coming off active duty, so that those skills were not lost to the military. In an AVF with increasingly complex equipment, this expertise comes at a high cost and is worth retaining.

Strategy and cost were not the only drivers of this force-structure shift. The reserve components, particularly the National Guard, have great political power because of their local roots and ties to state congressional delegations. These organizations are not afraid to use this power when they believe that their interests are threatened. For example, in 2001, after the army tried to reduce the size of its reserve component, Congress made the commander of each reserve component a three-star billet to protect the organizations' equities in intraservice decision making.

This new policy had its first major test during Operation Desert Shield / Desert Storm (the Persian Gulf War). In August 1990, during the decision making for the initial deployment, General Colin Powell, then chairman of the Joint Chiefs, told President George H. W. Bush that any deployment would require calling up large numbers of reservists. In the event, the president did not hesitate to order the mobilization. It was not the difficult political step that some had feared. It also meant that the entire nation went to war, however, not just the military enclaves of Fayetteville, North Carolina (82d Airborne Division); Oceanside, California (1st Marine Division); Norfolk, Virginia (Navy Atlantic Fleet); Ogden, Utah (U.S. Air Force fighters), and the like. Yellow ribbons appeared everywhere.

The Department of Defense judged the effort to have been a success, though some questions arose about the length of time needed to train up large combat units like National Guard brigades. As the official history of the Persian Gulf War concludes: "What the Department of Defense accomplished in resolving the Persian Gulf crisis simply could not have been done without the full integration of the capabilities of thousands of reservists and National Guard personnel. . . . The mobilization and use of reserve forces validated the key concepts of the nation's Total Force Policy."[15]

Reliance on the reserve components received another boost in 2008 with the announcement that they would no longer be considered a "strategic reserve" that participated only in the most extreme situations. Instead, they would be an "operational reserve," defined as "R.C.s [reserve components] participat[ing] in a full range of missions according to their Services' force generation plans."[16] This change recognized what was happening in the field, as virtually the entire reserve component was mobilized bit by bit to conduct the long wars in Iraq and Afghanistan. Indeed, the army called 2005 "the year of the reserves" in Iraq because the active-duty force had been used up during the first two rotations, and the third rotation consisted mostly of National Guard brigades.

Yet there are limits to reliance upon reserve components, and the military services are probably at that limit now, at least for the current strategy. The primary reason is the obvious one: Guard and reserve units are just not as ready as active-duty forces. They train thirty-eight days a year, and there is only so much that they can accomplish in that time. In a mobilization, these forces must be alerted, administratively brought on active duty, trained, and then deployed. This process takes time. For individuals and small units of specialists, the delay may only be a few weeks. For large units, particularly combat units, the delay will be many months.[17] This limits the ability of the reserve component to meet the timelines required in operational plans.

Even with adequate training time, concerns continue about how effective reserve-component units can be. This is particularly true for combat units because they require skills to coordinate complex operations involving many different kinds of capabilities—fires, aviation, maneuver, engineers, logistics, and others. Although recent studies have shown that, with enough train of time, Guard and reserve units were as effective as active-duty units in Iraq, this concern persists.[18] Reserve-component forces also face the same recruiting challenges faced by active-duty counterparts and have struggled to meet their personnel targets, particularly in the army. Expansion is not possible under the current conditions.

Finally, there are structural constraints in each of the services. The army, which supplies much of the theater support for all the armed forces, relies heavily on its reserve components for these capabilities, but those units have limits in what they can provide. The Army National Guard seeks to maintain a balanced force that includes a full set of combat capabilities. Thus, it is unwilling to become too lopsided toward support functions and is reluctant to deploy anything smaller than full units. The Army Reserve, which consists mostly of support troops, struggles to maintain its current end strength. The other services are also hitting structural limits, although their reserve components are proportionately smaller than the army's. In the air force, for example, equipment is costly, and the savings, when moved to the reserve component, are therefore not as large. The navy and marine corps have extensive day-to-day commitments for forward deployment of forces. These frequent deployments must be done primarily by active-duty units.

As a result, the reserve component has stabilized at about 38 percent of the total force. A different strategy—for example, one that reduces global commitments—might open opportunities for a change in the active/reserve mix. That, however, requires a major shift away from the strategy that the United States has pursued since the end of the Cold War and, arguably, since the end of World War II.

EXPANDED USE OF GOVERNMENT CIVILIANS

The United States is unusual in that it has always had a large number of government civilians working in its military establishment in roles where other countries use military personnel. These civilians are often viewed as "overhead" who staff various Washington headquarters. In fact, most civilians (96 percent) are employed outside Washington. Only about 4 percent (31,000) work in management headquarters, and only 27,000 of these work in Washington.[19] DOD's civilians perform a wide variety of support functions in intelligence, equipment maintenance, medical care, family support, base-operating services, and force management.

Use of government civilians has increased since the beginning of the AVF. The chart below shows the proportion of civilians to total full-time personnel (civilian and military) in the DOD. Three trends are apparent: a big jump between 1970 and 1975 reflecting the beginning of the AVF; a decline during periods of conflict, when the military grows faster than the civilian workforce; and a long-term increase, which continues to the present.[20]

This shift to government civilians has occurred for several reasons.

- DOD argues that civilians "are key to warfighter readiness, essential enablers to DoD's mission capabilities and operational readiness, and critical to supporting our All-Volunteer Force and their families."[21]
- Civilians can act with the full authority of the government, just as military personnel can. This is important because some functions, deemed "inherently governmental," can only be performed by federal personnel.[22]
- Civilians cost less. Although government civilians are expensive, they still cost from 25 percent to 40 percent less (depending on the skills and years of service) than equivalent military personnel,

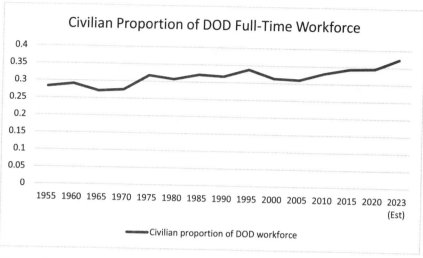

The total number of civilians as a proportion of the DOD full-time workforce from 1955 to 2020 (and 2023, estimated).

whose benefits, as described earlier, make them extremely expensive.[23]
- Civilians have a more flexible personnel system. The civilian personnel system, for all of its limitations, is more flexible than the military system in that civilians do not need to meet the strict standards for health, fitness, combat skills, career progression, and worldwide assignment that servicemembers do.
- Civilians provide long-term expertise, staying on the job an average of 7.5 years, whereas military personnel rotate every 2–3 years.[24]

As a result of this shift, many functions that military personnel performed in the past are now done entirely or primarily by government civilians. For example, commissaries, post exchanges, and maintenance depots now have few military personnel working in them. In theory, civilians could perform more military functions, given that 60 percent of active-duty military personnel are currently in overhead or infrastructure positions.[25] There are, however, limits on transfers of functions from military to civilian personnel.

- Perceptions of civilians being "overhead" limits the number that Congress is willing to authorize.
- Deployment limitations prevent civilians from participating extensively in overseas operations. Secretaries of defense, from Donald

Rumsfeld to James Mattis, have wanted to make DOD civilians more expeditionary to reduce dependence on contractors and ease the stress on military personnel. DOD did take steps to give deployed civilians comparable benefits to servicemembers in areas such as family separation, disability, medical care, and tax benefits. It also established an "Expeditionary Civilians" program manager and recently updated its directive on implementation.[26]

- Yet this effort remains small. Only about 1,000 government civilians were in Afghanistan in October 2019, compared with 15,000 military and 27,000 contractor personnel. There is no mechanism for involuntary deployments; civilians deploy individually, thus leaving vacancies in their parent organizations; and such assignments are not considered "career enhancing" in the same way they are for the military.[27]
- Finally, there is the longstanding weakness of the federal personnel system in ensuring employee performance. Civil-service protections against political interference are so strong that they also protect poor performers. The federal government terminates only 0.2 percent of career employees for poor performance in a given year, a rate far below that of the private sector.[28] Thus, there is the perception, and likely the reality, that military personnel and contractors perform better on average because of stronger performance-enforcement mechanisms.

These shortfalls limit the number of government civilians in DOD. Recent history indicates that this number may drift up, but large increases are unlikely.

SUBSTITUTING CAPITAL FOR LABOR

Just as the broader economy substitutes capital for labor as labor becomes more expensive, so too do the armed forces. In a military context, this means buying weapons with the most advanced, and therefore costly, technology so that each servicemember has more battlefield effectiveness. Thus, technological quality offsets reduced personnel quantity. This approach has the additional advantage that combat losses are in matériel rather than people, a major consideration for a wealthy democracy that must justify its actions to voters. The chart below illustrates how this approach has played out in the postwar era. It shows acquisition dollars (procurement plus research and development in constant FY 2020 dollars) divided by the number of active-duty personnel at five-year intervals. This ratio gives a sense of the capital intensity of the force.

The level is constant through 1975. Then, as the AVF took hold and

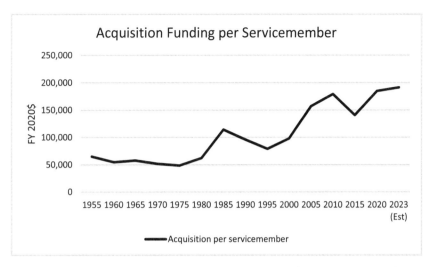

Acquisition Funding per Servicemember

The funding required in FY 2020 dollars to acquire each U.S. servicemember from 1955 to 2020 (and 2023, estimated).

the defense budget emerged from its post-Vietnam decline, the amount increased. It dipped in the late 1990s during the post–Cold War procurement holiday, surged after 9/11 during the defense buildup, and dipped in the post–Iraq/Afghanistan drawdown, but it is rising again. Overall, acquisition funding per servicemember has tripled since the institution of the AVF, rising from $56,600 in 1972 to $184,600 in 2020 (all in FY 2020 constant dollars).

This increase over time signals a change in warfighting approaches. During World War II, the United States pursued a strategy of mass and firepower. This required large-scale production of standard-quality weapons—competitive on the battlefield but not world class.[29]

Tanks provide a good illustration of this. The standard U.S. tank during the latter part of the war was the M-4 Sherman, typically mounting a low-velocity 75-mm cannon. The Sherman was dependable and maneuverable, but was outclassed by German tanks like the Panzer Mark IV and the Panther, with their high-velocity 75-mm guns, and the Tiger, with its 88-mm gun.[30] Victory came from producing more Shermans than the Germans could kill and using their numbers to overwhelm the fewer but better German tanks. As David Johnson, a military historian at RAND, has noted: "The U.S. Army had applied an overwhelming armored bludgeon of inferior machines, complemented by enormous air and artillery resources, against a qualitatively superior German panzer technology."[31]

After World War II, in the face of a rising Soviet challenge and the massive forces that the Soviets could field, the United States changed its approach. Instead of mass-producing standard-quality weapons, which would match the Soviets weapon for weapon, it sought to develop and produce superior-quality weapons so that each could offset several Soviet counterparts. Thus, the United States sought to field the highest-quality tanks, ships, and aircraft. Advanced technology became a central pillar of U.S. military strategy.[32] The results of this approach were most evident in exchange ratios for aerial combat. In the Korean War, the United States shot down 10 adversary aircraft for each American warplane lost, then 5.5 to 1 in the more difficult air-defense environment of the Vietnam War.[33]

This effort to build superior weaponry accelerated after the introduction of the AVF, in part to compensate for declining numbers of personnel, in part to take advantage of the emerging technical revolution in computing and information networks. This revolution produced precision-guided munitions and the sensor-command-shooter networks that enabled their battlefield application. In 1991, the United States crushed the Iraqi army, the fourth largest in the world at the time, in 100 hours of ground fighting with few friendly casualties. It repeated these lopsided victories in Afghanistan in 2001 and in Iraq again in 2003.

To be sure, many other factors came into play in producing these lopsided victories, particularly training. The U.S. military put great emphasis on training personnel so they could get the most out of their equipment. Leaders were taught and encouraged to make decisions for themselves, whereas other militaries, particularly those based on a Soviet model, relied on central direction. Nevertheless, the value of high-technology equipment was an important part of the success. The capital-intensive force has the additional benefit of losses being principally in matériel rather than in human life. At the height of the wars in Iraq and Afghanistan in 2007, the fiscal cost was 66 percent higher than the war in Vietnam at its height in 1968—$204 billion compared to $123 billion (FY 2020 constant dollars), but the human cost to the United States was much lower. In 2007, the United States lost 1,200 killed in action. In 1968, the United States lost 16,899 killed in action, fifteen times as many. To be sure, the nature of the wars was different, but the order of magnitude difference in casualties reflects the effect of a different warfighting approach enabled by technology.[34]

Despite the great successes of U.S. weapons, there are limits to what a capital-intensive strategy can accomplish. A major constraint is cost and the inevitable tradeoff with quantity. As weapons became more capable and more complex, their cost inevitably rises. Each generation of weapon systems cost more in real terms than the previous one. This phenomenon is called "intergenerational cost growth" and runs about 3 percent per year in constant dollars.[35] This is a different phenomenon from cost growth within a single weapon system, where actual costs turn out to be higher than estimated costs. Intergenerational cost growth occurs even if estimates for individual systems are accurate.

Inevitably, numbers decline as costs increase. The experience of the U.S. Air Force illustrates the tradeoff. It bought 2,900 third-generation F-4 Phantom fighters at $24 million each at a time when it flew half a dozen types of tactical aircraft. The air force later bought about 2,000 fourth-generation F-16 fighters at $28 million each to replace about half its tactical aircraft fleet. It now seeks to buy 1,763 fifth-generation F-35 fighters at $105 million each to replace all of its tactical aircraft (all costs in FY 2020 constant dollars).[36] At some point, systems become too expensive and scarce to risk in combat, whatever their individual capabilities might be, or, if risked, are too few to sustain combat attrition for long.[37]

Thus, technology improvements may be at the knee of the curve for legacy systems like aircraft and tanks; that is, revolutionary improvements are unlikely, and evolutionary improvements become increasingly expensive. Future opportunities probably lie in the technologies of long-range precision strike and unmanned systems. A full exploration lies outside the scope of this chapter, but the implication is that opportunities yet exist for capital substitution in the AVF.

Outsourcing through the Increased Use of Contractors

The limited numbers of military personnel, active and reserve, and the difficulty in hiring and deploying large numbers of government civilians have driven defense planners to rely on private military contractors to provide support services that military personnel previously handled. This reliance occurs in two very different environments: domestic and overseas. Although both have increased, there are differences between the two in the composition of their workforces, the reason for contractor use, and their effect on military operations and defense policy.

Contractors have always been a part of the domestic military establishment because, in a market economy, the armed forces will acquire goods and services from the civilian sector. Over time, that reliance has increased. A major boost came in the 1980s when the government issued OMB Circular A-76, declaring that "the Government should not compete with its citizens. The competitive enterprise system, characterized by individual freedom and initiative, is the primary source of national economic strength. In recognition of this principle, it has been and continues to be the general policy of the Government to rely on commercial sources to supply the products and services the Government needs."[38]

This continued in the post–Cold War era with "reinventing government" initiatives in the Clinton administration and government/contractor workforce competitions in the Bush administration.

Because contractors are hired indirectly through a contract vehicle, data for contractor workforce numbers are hazy, unlike for military and government personnel, for which good data exist. The Center for Strategic and International Studies (CSIS) analyzed data on DOD service contracts going back twenty years and found that the amounts increased from $76 billion (in FY 2019 constant dollars) in 2000 to $150 billion in 2018.[39] Although this does not capture personnel numbers or the change since the establishment of the AVF, it does give a sense about the current direction in the Pentagon. DOD reports show that there are approximately 561,000 contractor personnel providing services to the department.[40] What are all these people doing? In general, they perform the same functions that government civilians do—logistics, base operations, and headquarters support. For example, contractors run the dining facilities, daycare centers, and landscaping operations on most military bases.

This shift has had several beneficial effects. First, it has freed military personnel to focus on strictly military tasks. Gone, for the most part, is the soldier's drudgery of mowing the lawn in front of the barracks, cleaning up the trash around the base, and, above all, the notorious kitchen police (KP) duty. Instead, troops can focus on training and maintenance of equipment. Contracting of routine tasks also has the advantage that the government can leverage the expertise and flexible workforce policies of the private sector. Thus, companies specializing in child care can run the daycare centers, companies specializing in meal preparation can run the dining facilities, and landscaping firms can do the landscaping.

Nevertheless, outsourcing has been controversial. The primary controversy concerns relative costs between government and the private sector, with advocates of each arguing that their workforce is cheaper. A Congressional Budget Office analysis showed that government employees were paid 17 percent more on average than the private sector, though the differential decreased with education level.[41] Nevertheless, others, like the Project on Government Oversight, argue that government is cheaper than the private sector.[42] Other criticisms focus on whether the government has enough control to ensure accountability and whether contractors are improperly doing work that is "inherently governmental."

According to the Federal Activities Inventory Report, DOD government personnel perform 175,000 commercial jobs that the private sector could, at least in theory, do instead.[43] Yet congressional action has halted most shifts of functions to the private sector. The use of outsourcing overseas has received more attention because these contractors substitute for servicemembers in an environment—overseas combat operations—that has traditionally been military. While contractors have always supported U.S. forces overseas, the ratio has increased from one contractor to five servicemembers in past conflicts to one contractor to one servicemember today.[44] Further, unlike with the reserve components and civilians, where shifts arose from studies and strategic decisions, this outsourcing of battlefield support to private military contractors has occurred as a result of many small decisions—a contract for security here, a contract for food service there—which, in aggregate, have altered the military force structure.

Despite concerns about "gun-toting mercenaries," 83 percent of battlefield contractors (called "operational support contractors" by DOD) in Syria, Iraq, and Afghanistan performed headquarters and logistics functions. Of the 17 percent who were armed, fewer than half went outside the wire and interacted with civilians. These are the contractors who received much attention during the early twenty-first century, with abuses such as occurred when a Blackwater security detail killed Iraqi civilians at Nisour Square in Baghdad in 2007. Unlike domestic contractors, whose workforce is almost entirely U.S. citizens, the CENTCOM contractor workforce is 43 percent U.S. citizens, 43 percent third-country nationals, and 14 percent locals.[45] Absent such contractors, all of the armed forces, but the U.S. Army especially, would have to convert combat units into support units. Thus, operational-support contractors have allowed the United States to deploy much larger combat forces than it could otherwise.

These contractors have also been effective. Notwithstanding the real abuses that occurred, there were few complaints that they did not do their job, a point acknowledged by the otherwise critical Commission on Wartime Contracting in Iraq and Afghanistan.[46] Concerns that contractors might leave their posts when conditions became dangerous did not materialize, even during the most intense fighting of the Iraq and Afghanistan surges. Finally, the many reforms put into place as a result of the earlier abuses have had a positive effect, with few recent reports about abuses.[47]

The rise of operational-support contractors has not been without criticism. Some commentators have questioned whether governments can fully control these contractors and whether their capabilities will spill out into the private sector and be used in ways that national governments do not condone.[48] Another criticism is that contractor costs are "hidden," but that is not true. These fiscal costs are budgeted and accounted for like any other DOD costs, the department publishes contractor numbers, and the human cost in casualties is publicly available. What is different is that the public does not care as much about contractor sacrifices and casualties as it does about those among servicemembers.[49]

For the U.S. military, the issue has been settled. Contractors continued to support U.S. operations in Iraq, Syria, and Afghanistan in large numbers. The Trump administration made no efforts to reshape military force structure to reduce reliance on contractors. The Biden administration has given no indication, in its national defense strategy or its budgets, that it would do anything different. Instead, the military services have put structures in place to plan for the use of contractors, to deploy them in a crisis, and to manage them in a combat theater. The major uncertainty is whether the system of extensive contractor support would work in a great-power conflict such as the national defense strategy envisions. In these wars, there would be no large sanctuary bases that contractors, and the U.S. military in general, became accustomed to during the wars in the Middle East. There would be contractor casualties on a scale not seen since World War II. Whether contractor support—much of it composed of non-U.S. citizens—would break in such conditions remains an unanswered question.

Looking Ahead: No Change in Sight

Military personnel will continue to be expensive and difficult to recruit. Long term, there is no avoiding the need to pay competitive market compensation. Expanded government entitlements such as "free" college and "free" medical to the general public, whatever their social benefits might be, would undercut major recruiting incentives if enacted and require additional and costly compensation increases to keep the armed forces competitive in the labor market. Social trends, such as a declining propensity to enlist and widespread disqualifications among the target cohort, seem unlikely to reverse. Yet the Trump administration's national defense strategy required large forces to implement. It envisioned extensive global engagement by U.S. forces, a long-term competition against Russia and China, and continued hedges against such regional threats as North Korea and Iran. This approach was broadly consistent with the strategy of the late Obama administration and its focus on five threats: Russia, China, North Korea, Iran, and global terrorism. The Biden administration has continued the broad elements of this strategy. Indeed, the commitment to defend global allies goes back to the end of World War II. Thus, the need for forces in potential future conflicts will continue to be high.

Day-to-day demands for forces to conduct ongoing conflicts, crisis response, peacekeeping, and allied engagement also continue to be high. Even as military forces were withdrawing from the Middle East, additional troops deployed to eastern Europe to reassure allies in enhanced defense in response to Russia's invasion of Ukraine. U.S. administrations have frequently desired to reduce these deployments to ease the stress on forces and perhaps reduce their size—both the Trump and Biden administrations made such reductions a part of their national defense strategy—but the real-world demands on a global superpower always intervene. The navy, for example, year after year, has about 100–110 ships deployed at any particular time, regardless of what strategy documents say about commitments.[50]

Finally, conscription remains unpopular. The military leadership much prefers the AVF because of the well-trained and highly committed personnel it produces. Thus, every strategic review coming out of the DOD discusses the importance of maintaining the AVF. Politicians shy away from conscription because of the political cost it would impose, and the population prefers to let someone else perform military service. Experts can argue whether this is a good or bad thing, but it is a fact and therefore means that the AVF and the force changes it has engendered will continue.

Prospects for the Future

Direct and indirect effects from the establishment of the AVF combined with a longstanding national strategy of global engagement have driven the United States to build a military that is dependent on reserve mobilization, highly capital intensive, employing large numbers of government civilians, and reliant on contractors. That structure is unlikely to change. And it is not a bad thing, as it has produced the most powerful military in the world, crushing other militaries that have tried to meet it conventionally. This has driven adversaries to strategies of the weak—insurgencies and gray-zone competition—which are less threatening. Nevertheless, this structure does shape the way the United States thinks about conflict and fights its wars. The greatest change is a reliance on reserves in order to deploy any force larger than about a division. This reliance means more public involvement and, arguably, requires stronger public support for military operations. Although history shows that reserve mobilization is not a big political hurdle, it is still a hurdle. Further, depending on the reserve component means a slower pace of deployment and, hence, some risk.

The capital-intensive American way of war, employing extremely sophisticated, powerful, and expensive weapons, has been hugely successful in regional wars but has imposed costs and risks of its own. First, it is expensive. A frontline fighter aircraft costs $100 million, and an aircraft carrier costs $12 billion. Sustainment is similarly expensive. Thus, a capital-intensive strategy requires large budgets and highly skilled personnel—military, civilian, and contractor. Second, it allows the United States to fight with a minimum of friendly casualties. The drone strikes against terrorist targets are a principal example. Instead of relying on servicemembers on the ground, even highly skilled Special Operations personnel, the United States uses remotely controlled drones to strike at enemies. If operations go badly, only machines are lost. That is the good news for the United States. The bad news is that this "pushbutton war" makes military operations politically easier and obscures the cost it imposes on non-U.S. societies. Finally, the capital intensity produces some strategic inertia, as the massive investment in legacy systems inhibits innovative operational solutions.

The large number of civilians employed in defense has allowed a bigger national-security establishment than could be sustained with military personnel alone. Given the global strategy that the United States has adopted since World War II, that has been a good thing. There have been no calls to replace government civilians with military personnel. The downside is that, because civilians are much less deployable than military personnel, the United States has had to rely on contractors in overseas conflicts. The widespread use of contractors is the most significant effect of the AVF after the rise of the reserves. Domestically, this increase has not had much effect on warfighting because the domestic jobs done by these contractors are in logistics, base, and headquarters functions where conditions are benign and it matters little who does the function as long as it gets done. Instead, policy discussions have concerned issues of cost, accountability, and unions fighting to retain government jobs.

It is the use of contractors overseas that has raised broader warfighting issues because this use changes the way that the United States fights its wars. As with government civilians, the use of overseas contractors allows the United States to maintain more extensive global commitments than otherwise because, in peacetime, these contractors cost essentially nothing; they are paid only during times of conflict. Such outsourcing also reduces the visibility of conflicts. Although, in theory, the public should perceive no difference between a military casualty and a contractor casualty, in fact, military casualties get much more attention. For deployed military personnel, there are the yellow ribbons commemorating their absence, elaborate rituals for returning casualties, and dozens of charities for "wounded warriors." None of this exists for contractor casualties. Finally, although contractors overseas have proved themselves to be reliable in the kinds of stability operations that the United States has fought in the last three decades, the unresolved question is whether they will be reliable in a high-intensity conflict that would result from a great-power confrontation. This has introduced an element of risk in U.S. warfighting strategy.

Even with all these adaptations, the active and reserve forces available in peacetime are not large enough to handle either a very large or a very long conflict. Government civilians and contractors cannot fill the entire gap. Thus, the number of military personnel must expand during conflicts. That happened to meet the demands of Iraq and Afghanistan, with the marine corps and army increasing by a total of 100,000. The risk is in timing. Force expansion takes time, but political leaders are often reluctant to acknowledge that a conflict will go on long enough or be intense enough to require such expansion. Thus, they may delay, with a penalty on battlefield performance or personnel stress as a result. That happened during the Iraq War. Political leaders did not make a force expansion decision until 2006, two years too late, with the resulting severe stress on personnel from rapid deployments.

Ideally, DOD or the Biden administration would look at all the elements of personnel—active duty, reserve components, government civilians, contractors—together with the weapon systems they operate and make informed decisions about personnel balance and force structure. DOD has done such analyses for active/reserve mix and domestic contractor outsourcing. While that may not have produced what everyone regards as an "ideal" solution, the current structure does have an analytical basis. Applying that discipline across all personnel elements would strengthen the future structure.

Notes

1. Gates Commission, formally known as *The President's Commission on an All-Volunteer Armed Force*, February 1970, 23–35, https://www.nixonfoundation.org/wp-content/uploads/2012/01/The-Report-Of-The-Presidents-Commission-On-An-All-Volunteer-Armed-Force.pdf.

2. Undersecretary of Defense (Comptroller), *National Defense Budget Estimates for FY 2021* (Green Book) (Washington, DC: Department of Defense, 2020), tables 5-1, 5-4, https://comptroller.defense.gov/Portals/45/Documents/defbudget/fy2021/FY21_Green_Book.pdf (hereafter cited as Green Book).

3. Todd Harrison and Seamus Daniels, *Analysis of the FY 2019 Defense Budget, Center for Strategic and International Studies* (Lanham, MD: Rowman & Littlefield, 2018), 12–13,

https://csis-website-prod.s3.amazonaws.com/s3fs-public/publication/180917_Har
rison_DefenseBudget2019.pdf. The authors also published an analysis of the FY 2021
budget, but it does not include data on personnel costs.

4. Compensation relative to civilian peers is 90 percent for enlisted and 83 percent
for officers. *Report of the 11th Quadrennial Review of Military Compensation, Main Report*
(Washington, DC: Department of Defense, June 2012), 31.

5. Bruce R. Orvis, Narayan Sastry, Laurie L. McDonald, *Military Recruiting Outlook: Recent Trends in Enlistment Propensity and Conversion of Potential Enlisted Supply*
(Washington, DC: RAND, 1996), 14; Department of Defense Joint Advertising, Market Research, and Studies, *Spring 2019 Propensity Update* (Washington, DC: Government Printing Office, 2019), 2.

6. Erin Duffin, "U.S. College Enrollment Statistics for Public and Private Colleges
from 1965 to 2020 and Projections up to 2030 (in Millions)," Statista, https://www.st
atista.com/statistics/183995/us-college-enrollment-and-projections-in-public-and-pr
ivate-institutions/ (accessed October 31, 2022).

7. Thomas Spoehr and Bridget Handy, *The Looming National Security Crisis: Young
Americans Unable to Serve in the Military* (Washington, DC: Heritage Foundation,
2018), https://www.heritage.org/sites/default/files/2018-02/BG3282.pdf.

8. For discussion of why the force did not expand during the Trump administration
buildup, see Mark Cancian, "U.S. Military Forces in FY 2020: The Struggle to Align
Forces with Strategy," CSIS Briefs, September 2019, https://www.csis.org/analysis/us
-military-forces-fy-2020-struggle-align-forces-strategy. For a discussion about force
size in the Biden administration, see Mark Cancian, "Force Structure in the National
Defense Strategy: More Capable but Smaller and Less Global," CSIS Commentary,
October 2022, https://www.csis.org/analysis/force-structure-national-defense-strate
gy-highly-capable-smaller-and-less-global.

9. Gates Commission, 19, 29–30, 99–101.

10. Reserve Forces Policy Board, *Requiring the Use of Fully Burdened and Life Cycle
Personnel Costs for All Components in Total Force Analysis and for Budgetary Purposes*,
Report FY19-01 (Washington, DC: Office of the Secretary of Defense, 2019). For
unit costs, see Adele Palmer et al., *Assessing the Structure and Mix of Future Active and
Reserve Forces: Cost Estimation Methodology* (Washington, DC: RAND, 1992). Other
analyses come out in the 20–30 percent range, depending on assumptions about what
to include. See Jacob Klerman, *Rethinking the Reserves* (Washington, DC: RAND Corporation, 2008), 57.

11. Martin Binkin and William Kauffman, *US Army Guard and Reserve: Rhetoric,
Realities, and Risk* (Washington, DC: Brookings Institution, 1989), 58.

12. For the Total Force concept, see cover memorandum to the vice president of
the United States, February 24, 1971, in *Annual Report of the Secretary of Defense on Reserve Forces, Fiscal Year 1971* (Washington, DC: Asst. Secretary of Defense (Manpower
& Reserve Affairs), 1970), 2, https://apps.dtic.mil/dtic/tr/fulltext/u2/a007542.pdf. For
the Total Force policy, see James Schlesinger, "Readiness of the Selected Reserves,"
Secretary of Defense Memorandum, U.S. Department of Defense, August 23, 1973.

13. Office of the Under-Secretary of Defense (Comptroller), *Defense Budget Overview: United States Department of Defense Fiscal Year 2023 Budget Request* (Washington,

DC, April 2022), app. A, tables A-5, A-6, https://comptroller.defense.gov/Portals/45/Documents/defbudget/FY2023/FY2023_Budget_Request_Overview_Book.pdf.

14. There is disagreement about whether General Abrams actually said these words because there is no contemporary written record. His biographer, Lewis Sorley, believes that he did. See Sorley, *Thunderbolt: Gen. Creighton Abrams and the Army of His Times* (New York: Simon & Schuster, 1982), 362–365.

15. Department of Defense, *Conduct of the Persian Gulf War* (Washington, DC: GPO, 1992), 471.

16. Department of Defense Directive 1200.17, "Managing the Reserve Components as an Operational Force," October 29, 2008, https://www.esd.whs.mil/Portals/54/Documents/DD/issuances/dodd/120017p.pdf.

17. Bernard D. Rosker et al., *Assessing the Structure and Mix of Future Active and Reserve Forces: Final Report to the Secretary of Defense* (Washington, DC: RAND Corporation, 1992), 115–153.

18. For an analysis showing that reserve-component units had the same effectiveness as active-duty units when given sufficient training, see Joseph Adams et al., *Sharing the Burden and Risk: An Operational Assessment of the Reserve Components in Operation Iraqi Freedom* (Washington, DC: Institute for Defense Analysis, 2016).

19. Office of the Assistant Secretary of Defense for Manpower and Reserve Affairs, *Defense Manpower Requirements Report, Fiscal Year 2019* (Washington, DC: 2018), tables 1-1, 2-4, https://prhome.defense.gov/Portals/52/Documents/MRA_Docs/TFM/Reports/Final%20FY19%20DMRR%20for%20Posting%20(June%202018).pdf?ver=2018-06-15-103327-750.

20. Green Book, table 7-6.

21. *Defense Budget Overview*, 2–8, 9.

22. Office of Management and Budget, "Circular A-76 Performance of Commercial Activities," Washington, DC, May 29, 2003, https://georgewbush-whitehouse.archives.gov/omb/circulars/a076/a76_incl_tech_correction.html. Appendix A describes functions that are considered "inherently governmental": "An inherently governmental activity is an activity that is so intimately related to the public interest as to mandate performance by government personnel." These functions must be conducted by federal employees. An example is the dispersing of government funds.

23. CBO, "Analysis of Federal Civilian and Military Compensation," January 20, 2011, https://www.cbo.gov/sites/default/files/112th-congress-2011-2012/reports/01-20-compensation.pdf.

24. Data for federal civilian workforce from Bureau of Labor Statistics, "Employee Tenure Summary," table 5, https://www.bls.gov/news.release/pdf/tenure.pdf.

25. Ronald E. Porten, Daniel L. Cuda, and Arthur C. Yengling, *DoD Force & Infrastructure Categories: A FYDP-Based Conceptual Model of Department of Defense Programs and Resources* (Washington, DC: Institute for Defense Analyses, 2002), I-6.

26. DTM 17-004, Department of Defense Expeditionary Civilian Workforce, updated January 25, 2017, https://www.esd.whs.mil/Portals/54/Documents/DD/issuances/dtm/DTM-17-004.pdf?ver=2019-01-02-072423-843.

27. J. P. Lawrence, "Surge of DOD Civilian Employees Is Needed in Afghanistan,

Mattis Says," *Stars and Stripes*, July 11, 2018, https://www.stripes.com/news/surge-of
-dod-civilian-employees-is-needed-in-afghanistan-mattis-says-1.536874.

28. Government Accountability Office, *Federal Workforce: Improved Supervision
and Better Use of Probationary Periods Are Needed to Address Substandard Employee Performance* (Washington, DC: Government Printing Office, 2015), 22; Kathryn Watson,
"Here's Why It's All but Impossible to Fire a Fed," *Daily Caller News Foundation*,
March 3, 2016, https://dailycaller.com/2016/03/03/heres-why-its-all-but-impossible
-to-fire-a-fed/.

29. For a discussion of the U.S. military strategy of employing mass, see Russell
Weigley, *The American Way War: The History of United States Military Strategy and
Policy* (New York: McMillan, 1973), 269–312.

30. Some Sherman tanks were armed with a high-velocity 76-mm gun that made
them equal in firepower to German tanks, but these were relatively few in number.

31. David Johnson, *Fast Tanks and Heavy Bombers: Innovation in the U.S. Army, 1917–
1945* (Ithaca, NY: Cornell University Press, 1998), 201.

32. Thomas Mahnken, *Technology in the American Way of War since 1945* (New York:
Columbia University Press, 2008), 5.

33. William A. Sayers, "The Vietnam Air War's Great Kill-Ratio Debate," *Vietnam Magazine*, June 2018, https://www.historynet.com/great-kill-ratio-debate.htm;
William W. Momyer, *Airpower in Three Wars (World War II, Korea, Vietnam)* (Washington, DC: GPO, 1978), 157–159. There are continuing debates about the ratios. The
Korean ratio may have been overstated because of overly optimistic claims about aerial victories. The Vietnam data have been criticized for being too low because they
include nonfighter losses, with many of the fighter aircraft lost while on bombing
missions. Despite these controversies, there is no question that U.S. forces had large
kill ratios even when fighting in adversaries' home airspace.

34. Iraq Coalition Casualty Count (icasualties), http://icasualties.org/chart/Chart;
"Vietnam War US Military Fatal Casualty Statistics," National Archives, https://
www.archives.gov/research/military/vietnam-war/casualty-statistics; Stephen Dag-
gett, "Costs of Major U.S. Wars," Congressional Research Service, June 29, 2010, 2,
https://fas.org/sgp/crs/natsec/RS22926.pdf; Green Book, tables 2-1, 5-9.

35. CBO, *A Look at Tomorrow's Tactical Air Forces* (Washington, DC: GPO, 1997),
37–38; Norman Augustine, *Augustine's Laws*, 6th ed. (Washington, DC: American
Institute of Aeronautics and Astronautics, 1997), 104–111; N. Davies, A. Eager, M.
Maier, and L. Penfold, "Intergenerational Equipment Cost Escalation," Defence Economics Research Paper, U.K. Ministry of Defense, December 18, 2012, https://assets
.publishing.service.gov.uk/government/uploads/system/uploads/attachment_data/fi
le/280041/18_december_2012.pdf.

36. "F-4 Phantom's Phabulous 40th," Defense, Space, & Security, Boeing (via
WaybackMachine, Internet Archive), https://web.archive.org/web/20110629053417
/http://www.boeing.com/defense-space/military/f4/; "F-16 Fighting Falcon," U.S.
Air Force, https://www.af.mil/About-Us/Fact-Sheets/Display/Article/104505/f-16-fi
ghting-falcon/; "F-35 Lightning II Joint Strike Fighter (JSF) Program (F-35)," Selected Acquisition Report, December 2018, https://www.esd.whs.mil/Portals/54/Do
cuments/FOID/Reading%20Room/Selected_Acquisition_Reports/FY_2018_SARS

/19-F-1098_DOC_33_F-35_SAR_Dec_2018.pdf. Procurement costs adjusted to FY 2020 dollars using Green Book.

37. Many observers argue that aircraft carriers at around $12 billion each have reached the point of being too expensive to risk. For a discussion of how combat attrition would quickly reduce current weapons inventories, see Mark Cancian, "Long Wars and Industrial Mobilization: It Won't Be World War II Again," War on the Rocks, August 8, 2017, https://warontherocks.com/2017/08/long-wars-and-industrial-mobilization-it-wont-be-world-war-ii-again/.

38. Office of Management and Budget, "Circular A-76, Performance of Commercial Activities," August 4, 1983, https://www.whitehouse.gov/wp-content/uploads/legacy_drupal_files/omb/circulars/A76/a076.pdf.

39. Rhys McCormick, Samantha Cohen, Gregory Sanders, and Andrew P. Hunter, "Acquisition Trends, 2018: Defense Contract Spending Bounces Back," CSIS Brief, September 13, 2018, https://www.csis.org/analysis/acquisition-trends-2018-defense-contract-spending-bounces-back-executive-summary.

40. Government Accountability Office, "DOD Inventory of Contracted Services: Timely Decisions and Further Actions Needed to Address Long-Standing Issues," October 2016, 7, https://www.gao.gov/assets/690/680709.pdf. Data from 2015, the last year available. DOD has not issued any more current data than that contained in the 2016 report.

41. CBO, "Comparing the Compensation of Federal and Private Sector Employees, 2011 to 2015," Washington, DC, April 2017.

42. Paul Chassey and Scott Amey, "Bad Business: Billions of Taxpayer Dollars Wasted on Hiring Contractors," Project on Government Oversight, September 13, 2011, https://docs.pogo.org/report/2011/bad-business-report-only-2011.pdf?_ga=2.241455044.710512952.1571838935-1027878366.1571235206.

43. Department of Defense, *Federal Activities Inventory Report* (Washington, DC: GPO, 2015).

44. CBO, "Contractors' Support of US Operations in Iraq," August 2008, 13, https://www.cbo.gov/sites/default/files/110th-congress-2007-2008/reports/08-12-iraqcontractors.pdf.

45. Deputy Assistant Secretary of Defense (Program Support), "Contractor Support of U.S. Operations in the CENTCOM Area of Responsibility," July 2020, https://www.acq.osd.mil/log/LOG_CSD/.CENTCOM_reports.html/FY20_3Q_5A_Jul2020.pdf.

46. Commission on Wartime Contracting in Iraq and Afghanistan, *Transforming Wartime Contracting: Controlling Costs, Reducing Risks* (Washington DC: GPO, 2011), https://cybercemetery.unt.edu/archive/cwc/20110929213820/http://www.wartimecontracting.gov/docs/CWC_FinalReport-lowres.pdf.

47. Whitney Grespin, "Well Behaved Defense Contractors Seldom Make History," War on the Rocks, April 21, 2016, http://warontherocks.com/2016/04/well-behaved-defense-contractors-seldom-make-history.

48. For example, Sean McFate, *The Modern Mercenary: Private Armies and What They Mean for World Order* (New York: Oxford University Press, 2014), esp. chap. 12.

49. For example, such criticism appears in Heidi Peltier, "The Growth of the

'Camo Economy' and the Commercialization of the Post-9/11 Wars," Watson Institute of International and Public Affairs, Brown University, June 30, 2020, https:// watson.brown.edu/costsofwar/files/cow/imce/papers/2020/Peltier 2020 - Growth of Camo Economy - June 30 2020 - FINAL.pdf. U.S. Central Command publishes contractor numbers quarterly, data on individual DOD contracts is available from the Federal Procurement Data System, and the Department of Labor publishes contractor casualty figures.

50. Mark Cancian, "U.S. Military Forces in FY 2022: Navy," Center for Strategic and International Studies, November 2, 2021, https://defense360.csis.org/u-s-military -forces-in-fy-2022-navy/.

13

The Civil-Military Gap

Marybeth P. Ulrich

The civil-military gap refers to a broad array of factors that collectively result in America's armed forces occupying a space in society that increasingly sets them apart from the people they serve. Contributing to the gap are a demographic imbalance in the representation of national regions, socioeconomic groups, racial and ethnic groups, gender, and differences in political attitudes between those who serve and those who do not. Furthermore, there are signs that the increasingly isolated military sphere is spawning a warrior caste among the nation's military families whose children's proclivity to serve far outstrips that of eighteen- to twenty-four-year-olds coming of age in civilian families.

While some gap between civil society and the military institution created to defend it is inherent in the distinct roles and responsibilities of military and civilian actors in any nation, an excessive divide may affect perceptions of one's obligations as a citizen, strain relations between the armed forces and society, weaken constitutional oversight of the use of force and decisions to go to war, and ultimately contribute to the erosion of democratic institutions. This chapter examines the evolution of the civil-military gap through the lens of the all-volunteer force fifty years after its implementation and proposes recommendations to bridge the divide between the nation's armed forces and its citizens.

Origins and Evolution of the Civil-Military Gap

In 1783, George Washington wrote to Alexander Hamilton, "every Citizen who enjoys the protection of a free Government, owes not only a portion of his property, but even of his personal services in defense of it."[1] Military service in colonial times and in the early republic was an obligation of citizenship, and all "free, white, and male" able-bodied men were expected to participate in a common militia to protect their town or city from immediate threats.[2] In the Revolutionary War, General Washington depended on volunteers from these militias to enlist in the Continental Army in order to gain independence from Great Britain. Yet when not enough militiamen were willing to volunteer to campaign against British regulars, the Continental Congress resorted to conscripting them, a practice referred to as a "militia draft."[3] In colonial America, then, militia service was limited to local defense. Historian John Rafuse has described the militiaman and this system of defense: "He did not fight elsewhere. Militia conscription was never meant to provide soldiers for distant wars."[4]

At the nation's birth, the obligation to serve was universal and connected to citizenship. Because familiarity with militia service was widespread, there was no significant civil-military gap. But a focal point of the debate on the new Constitution concerned the establishment of a small standing army of professionals in order to meet the ongoing foreign and domestic threats present in the early republic. Hamilton addressed the dilemma in Federalist No. 8, where he emphasized that the mission of the proposed standing army would be narrow but essential, in that its presence would make "rendering sudden conquests impracticable" while also having the capability to suppress "an occasional mob, or insurrection."[5] Furthermore, he noted that large militias would be an "over-match" for the small professional military and would "stand ready to resist a power" that threatened the community's liberties.[6] Early Americans continued to rely on state militias in the decade following the 1789 establishment of a standing army and navy in the Constitution.

Dealing with the proper mix of professionals, volunteers, and conscripts to address ongoing threats has been a perennial multidimensional challenge for the American people. One aspect is the classic "civil-military problematique," which seeks to balance the quest for security and liberty by ensuring that the arms authorized to preserve the state do not also become the means to vanquish its free government.[7] Another aspect of primary concern is that the armed forces remain connected enough to the society and people whose livelihood and interests they defend. This social value is best achieved by armed forces that are representative of the nation and of its republican ideals—not armed forces set apart from the rest of the nation.

From 1969 to 1970, these questions were completely reconsidered when President Richard Nixon established the President's Commission on an All-Volunteer Armed Force, better known as the Gates Commission, to reexamine U.S. dependence on a national draft that had been in place since 1940 to mobilize for entry into World War II. This conscription was truly universal. A national lottery "determined not who would serve, but rather in what order men would serve."[8] As a result, more than half of the male population between the ages of eighteen and forty-five served in World War II, 8.7 percent of the entire population.[9]

After a brief lapse from 1947 to 1948 a peacetime draft was instituted in June 1948. By 1950, more than one in three men in the United States were veterans, 37 percent of the male population over eighteen years old.[10] In the Korean War era (1950–1953), 6.8 million Americans served on active duty, or 51 percent of the young men between the ages of eighteen and thirty-five registered for Selective Service.[11] In the Vietnam War era (1964–1975), 8.74 million men and women served.[12] Of these, 2.7 million served in Vietnam, representing 9.7 percent of their generation.[13]

The experience of the United States with military service in Vietnam forms the backdrop for the AVF. The Gates Commission concluded that the maladministration of the Vietnam conscription contributed to social unrest and that such a "draft, whether under selective service or a lottery was inequitable."[14] The resulting national decision to implement the AVF has had momentous positive implications for military effectiveness. Yet these gains in the national capacity to apply military power have come at the cost of eroding the societal norm that the burden of military service is shared across all sectors of society.

When the Gates Commission justified its 1970 recommendation to eliminate conscription, it noted the unfair burden that the draft imposed.

> However necessary conscription may have been in World War II, it has revealed many disadvantages in the past generation. It has been a costly, inequitable, and divisive procedure for recruiting men for the armed forces. It has imposed heavy burdens on a small minority of young men while easing slightly the tax burden on the rest of us. It has introduced needless uncertainty into the lives of all our young men. It has burdened draft boards with painful decisions about who shall be compelled to serve and who shall be deferred. It has weakened the political fabric of our society and impaired the delicate web of shared values that alone enables a free society to exist.[15]

Demographic trends and the ramifications of the AVF on the civil-military gap, however, were not the focus of either the Gates Commission's deliberations or President Nixon's decision to adopt the AVF.[16] Still, the commission predicted that the AVF "will be manned largely by the same kind of individuals as today's armed forces," and "the composition of the armed forces will not be fundamentally changed by ending conscription."[17] Yet commissioners did not understand this to mean that either the draft or its successor AVF would be uniformly representative

of society. This was particularly the case with regard to the draft deferments that characterized service in the Vietnam War largely going to
those in the highest socioeconomic classes. As Brandon Archuleta notes
in his essay marking the fiftieth anniversary of the AVF, "The upper class
went to college while the working class went to war."[18]

The AVF at Its Birth

At the advent of the AVF in 1973, African Americans composed 10.6 percent of the armed forces, slightly less than the proportion in the population, and 26.8 percent of army's enlisted.[19] Hispanics made up 3.9 percent
of the armed forces, which was slightly below their numbers in the overall
population.[20] Asian–Pacific Islanders were slightly overrepresented at 2.6
percent.[21] Women were only 1.2 percent of the armed forces, and the
Gates Commission assumed that this would remain the baseline for their
participation in the AVF.[22]

   The underestimation of women's potential contributions to the AVF
was evident in the exploration of the commission's staff of a policy to
replace the few in the military at the time with civilians. This was because women had been relegated to support roles, and "civilianizing"
their positions could reduce the costs associated with using military personnel.[23] Once the AVF was implemented, it was assessed at five- to ten-
year intervals. These studies provide snapshots in time with regard to the
volunteer force's evolving demographic makeup and paint a picture of a
military-civilian gap that grew in various ways despite the Gates Commission's prediction that the AVF would look much like the U.S. military
in the draft era. The downsizing that occurred in the 1990s in the wake of
the collapse of the Soviet Union aggravated the gap in racial, gender, and
socioeconomic characteristics described thus far, contributing to what
some began to call a "growing civil-military divide."[24]

The AVF after Five Years

The renowned military sociologist Charles Moskos noted in 1977, just
five years into the AVF, "In comparison with the peacetime draft, . . . today's Army is much less representative—and becoming increasingly so—
of American youth."[25] He added, "it is incontrovertible that there has
been a sharp rise in black participation—well over double the proportion
in the general population—in the Army's enlisted."[26] Black participation

in 1977 was 16.6 percent of the enlisted forces across the services at a time when African Americans composed 11.6 percent of the population.[27]

Although the Gates Commission did not seriously consider the role women could play in making the AVF a success, their key role was almost immediately evident. In fact, women volunteering at rates from 8 percent to 9 percent of the enlisted force in its early years was "the margin of success in the all-volunteer Army."[28] Furthermore, nearly all the female enlistees had high school diplomas, raising the overall quality of the force.[29] Initially, the military was not interested in appreciably increasing the role of women "unless there is a significant change in public attitudes toward the military services in general and unless military service becomes more attractive to young qualified women as a source of employment."[30]

In light of recruiting shortfalls in the first five years of the AVF, however, by 1977, the military was counting on recruiting enough women to fill 10 percent of the ranks. In addition, the army "authorized [unit commanders] to employ women to accomplish unit missions throughout the battlefield." The Brookings Institution issued a study concluding that women could make up one-quarter of all enlisted personnel without changing the current assignment policies, which still excluded them from combat positions.[31] In addition, at this interval, the pool of seventeen- to twenty-one-year-olds was shrinking, and four of every ten youth of enlistment age were not qualified for military service due to physical or other disabilities.[32] Indeed, by the five-year milestone, the composition of the AVF had significantly changed, and the civil-military gap was developing, with the main trends being the overrepresentation of African Americans in the enlisted ranks and the emergence of women as key contributors to the viability of the force.

The AVF at Ten Years of Service

As the AVF turned ten, it was clear that the composition of the armed forces continued to diverge from that 1970 prediction that its enlisted ranks would not grow to be more than 14.9 percent African American by the early 1980s. In actuality, by 1983, Black servicemembers composed 19.2 percent of the overall armed forces, significantly above the 12-percent rate of Black Americans in the military-age population.[33] Enlisted ranks were 21.4 percent African American, with some wide differences across services. Black servicemembers composed 31.4 percent of enlisted ranks in the army, 20.5 percent in the marine corps, 16.8 percent in the air force, and 12.7 percent in the navy.[34] The attractiveness of military service for African Americans at this time was due to the colorblind nature of military pay scales, given that, in 1979, Black male high school graduates earned 20 percent less than their white counterparts. Black participation was all the more remarkable, considering that this group was two to three times less likely to meet the standards for enlistment. In terms of the civil-military gap, this resulted in 46 percent of qualified Black males enlisting at the ten-year mark of the AVF compared to only 16 percent of qualified white males.[35]

By 1978, women's added value to the quality of the AVF was increasingly appreciated. The Carter administration's secretary of defense, Harold Brown, set a new goal of 11.6 percent for female servicemembers by 1983, doubling the number of women and bringing their numbers up to 200,000. By 1980, the United States had a greater percentage of women in service than any other country.[36] But with Carter's defeat in 1980, the army attempted to roll back the progress, arguing that women lacked the "strength and stamina" needed to sustain readiness.[37] Eventually, the new Reagan administration, which was focused on increasing the end strength of the army by 100,000 troops, realized that women were an essential component of this buildup. Secretary of Defense Casper Weinberger settled the debate that characterized the end of the AVF's first decade: "Women in the military are a very important part of our total force capability. Qualified women are essential to obtaining the numbers of quality people required to maintain the readiness of our forces. . . . This department must aggressively break down those remaining barriers that prevent us from making the fullest use of the capabilities of women in providing for our national defense."[38]

By the end of the AVF's first decade, the lack of representativeness in it was mainly found in the overrepresentation of African Americans and the underrepresentation of women. The Black overrepresentation raised concerns related to the fairness of a sector of society that had "not enjoyed a fair share of the benefits bestowed by the state" bearing a disproportionate burden for the defense of society.[39] Concerns about the female underrepresentation centered around whether women were being arbitrarily held back with both caps on their numbers and restrictions on their service. Women increasingly felt that the military still considered them to be a supplemental resource to "fill in" *man*power gaps.

In addition, it became increasingly evident in the 1970s that political attitudes in the AVF were increasingly diverging from the population as a whole. Ole Holsti's surveys at this time indicated that military officers' identification with the Republican Party far outstripped identification with the Democratic Party. He found a nearly three-to-one ratio of Republicans to Democrats in 1976, with an additional one-third of officers claiming to be independents.[40] This trend was in contrast to the Gates Commission's predications: "Contrary to much dramatic argument, the . . . men who serve will be quite similar in patriotism, political attitudes, effectiveness, and susceptibility to civilian control."[41]

The AVF Turns Twenty

During the 1980s, the percentage of Black enlistees fell into the low twenties. Black enlistments experienced a significant drop in 1991—right after the Persian Gulf War—to the level of 17 percent, which was consistent with the proportion of African Americans in the population.[42] Meanwhile, Hispanic enlistments held steady through the 1980s at about 5 percent and then began a steady uptick that peaked at 14.7 percent in 2008, still slightly below the 17.8 percent of Hispanics in the population of eighteen- to twenty-four-year-olds then.[43]

As the AVF approached the twenty-year mark in 1993, representation in the commissioned-officer ranks was improving markedly for Black officers in the army, reaching 11.4 percent in 1995—up from only 3 percent in 1975. Also by 1990, one-third of senior NCOs were African American. Beth Bailey notes in *America's Army* that these gains were the result of the army leadership's deliberate support for policies promoting affirmative action.[44]

Despite the civilian leadership's general appreciation that women would remain key to the continued success of the AVF, in the 1980s, the services' lack of enthusiasm for both expanded numbers and roles for women stalled their progress. Yet the outstanding performance of the 26,000 women who deployed in the Persian Gulf War shone a national spotlight on their capabilities and paved the way to debate combat-exclusion policies. In 1993, Secretary of Defense Les Aspin ordered the armed forces to allow women to fly combat aircraft. Congress had repealed the ban on women flying combat aircraft in 1991, but the Pentagon had not yet implemented the legislation.[45] By 1993, women made up 15 percent of all accessions.

The downsizing that occurred in the 1990s following the collapse of the Soviet Union aggravated the gap in racial, gender, and socioeconomic characteristics, contributing to a recognizable civil-military divide. In the early 1990s, the active-duty force was reduced by 21.4 percent, and the reserve forces were cut by 6.2 percent to make up the Base Force designed to match the post–Cold War strategic environment.[46] Personnel reductions also included several rounds of base closings, which substantially reduced the presence of the military as an institution throughout the country.

The AVF at Thirty Years of Service

The AVF's thirtieth birthday coincided with the beginning of the Iraq War. The events of September 11, 2001, would set in motion two large and long-term military conflicts that would reenergize the debate over whether the burden of sharing the demands of national defense in wartime were met by an AVF in which all sectors of American society were not uniformly present. The enlisted ranks in 2003 were 17.78 percent African American, 72.94 percent white, 7.22 percent Hispanic, and 1.46 percent Asian. Women made up 20 percent of the enlisted force that year.[47] As for the wider population, Black people composed 12.7 percent of Americans, whites 68.2 percent, Hispanics 13.4 percent, and Asians 4 percent.[48]

In late December 2002, following Congress's Authorization for the Use of Military Force (AUMF) in Iraq that October, Representative Charles Rangel noted in an opinion-editorial in the *New York Times* entitled "Bring Back the Draft" that only one member of Congress "has a child in the enlisted ranks of the military—just a few more have children who are officers." He argued: "If those calling for war knew that their children were likely to be required to serve—and to be placed in harm's way—there would be more caution and a greater willingness to work with the international community in dealing with Iraq. A renewed draft will help bring a greater appreciation of the consequences to go to war."[49]

Rangel was drawing attention to how representativeness in the armed forces had changed markedly since the end of conscription in 1973. This led to concerns that the political class was not sufficiently connected to the portion of the citizenry that it was responsible for sending into harm's way. While the overall demographics had become askew by the thirty-year mark, the proportion of minorities in frontline units did not track the overall trend. In fact, while African Americans were overrepresented in the enlisted ranks, they were underrepresented in ground-combat units. A 2004 analysis of the first 1,000 troops who died in Iraq revealed that 13 percent were black, 12 percent Hispanic, and 70 percent white. Twenty-five were women.[50]

Another aspect becoming increasingly relevant by 2003 was the role of the reserve component, comprising the services' reserve forces and the National Guards of the individual states. The reserve component was no longer the place where well-connected youth sought a safe haven from combat as they had during the draft era. Between 1993 and 2003, the number of active days that reserve forces performed increased eleven fold, from 5.7 million duty days to 63 million duty days in 2003, across the full spectrum of operational missions.[51] The reserve component at this time was 75 percent white (Hispanics included), 16.4 percent black, 2 percent Asian, 0.66 percent Native American/Eskimo, and 6 percent "other."[52] The least diverse component was the Coast Guard Reserve, which was 84.5 percent white, while the most diverse component was the Army Reserve at 65.9 percent white. Women made up 17.3 percent of the overall reserve forces, with the largest share in the Army Reserve at 17.3 percent and the fewest in the Marine Corps Reserve at 4.6 percent.[53]

At this time, demographic and societal trends included the continued shrinking of the pool of fifteen- to nineteen-year-olds, increasing racial diversity of the U.S. population, an increase in youth pursuing higher education in lieu of military service, and an increased focus on Hispanics' role in the AVF as their percentage of the population was projected to grow.[54] Demographers were also noting that the population was becoming increasingly diverse, with 8 percent of people identifying as either "more than 2 races" or "other."[55] In short, by 2003, the youth population that military recruiters targeted had become and was projected to become even more diverse than the population as a whole.[56]

In addition, the military's requirement that recruits be high school graduates and that 60 percent of these score in the top 50 percent of the Armed Forces Qualification Test (AFQT) meant that the services were demanding a high-quality, but unrepresentative, slice of eighteen- to twenty-four-year-olds.[57] Furthermore, survey data indicated that these potential enlistees desired more education during and after military service, prompting recruiters to focus on educational benefits, the armed forces having become by 2003 "one stop on a young adult's increasingly long transition from school to adult career."[58] These educational patterns shaped the nature of the civil-military gap, with Hispanics continuing to be underrepresented due to their lagging grades and test scores. Meanwhile, African Americans continued to be somewhat overrepresented due to the comparatively better employment opportunities in the armed forces than what the civilian world offered.[59]

Finally, by the late 1990s, Holsti's longitudinal study of political attitudes in the officer corps indicated a dramatic change from the 1970s. Officers indicating a Democratic Party affiliation held steady in the low teens, but those who had previously identified as independent almost uniformly changed their party identification to Republican, resulting in a shift over twenty years from one-third of them to two-thirds now declared Republicans.[60]

The AVF Turns Forty

By the time the AVF reached its fortieth anniversary in 2013, the major contours of the civil-military gap that characterize the armed forces today had become evident. Some of the initial concerns about the representativeness of the AVF in wartime had come to the fore. The Gates Commission had recommended that a system for implementing a standby draft be created in the event that "a major increase in forces over an extended period" was required.[61] Some argued that the post-9/11 wars met this criterion, and a draft should have been implemented.

The post-9/11 wars in Afghanistan and Iraq had ground on with the relatively small AVF, and only a small sector of American society has borne the burden of fighting and dying in them. At the peak of the Iraq War in 2010, there were 1.46 million active-duty troops, down from 2 million in 1990. In April 2020, the Department of Defense reported that 1.37 million servicemembers were on active duty.[62] Only 1 percent of Americans over the age of eighteen, 2.4 million, have served in the post-9/11 wars. This figure is 0.5 percent of the total population. As a point of comparison, in World War II, 8.7 percent of the total population was in uniform in a war that was less than half the duration of the post-9/11 wars. In Vietnam, the figure was 1.8 percent at that war's peak in 1968.[63] A smaller AVF also means that there are fewer veterans to serve as adult influencers with military experience to recommend the armed forces to high school students.

Furthermore, the reserves and National Guard were integrated into operations in both conflicts, implementing the "Total Force" concept. These reserve-component forces were rotated into the Iraq and Afghanistan theaters on a regular basis, relieving some pressure from the active-duty force. But the decision to activate the reserve and Guard in this way demanded much more of reservists and guardsmen, who usually balance their civilian jobs with their military service, and limited the availability of true reserve forces to expand the wartime total force. Rather than implement a standby draft, active-duty and reserve-component forces were sent on repeated deployments, raising concerns about the strain on servicemembers and their families and whether it was fair to ask such a small segment of society to bear the burden of what eventually came to be known as the "forever wars."[64]

These concerns were addressed in a Pew Research Center report. "The Military-Civilian Gap: War and Sacrifice in the Post-9/11 Era" opens with this statement: "America's post-9/11 wars in Afghanistan and Iraq are unique. Never before has this nation been engaged in conflicts for so long. And never before has it waged sustained warfare with so small a share of its population carrying the fight."[65] Pew reported that only 26 percent of the public surveyed described the uneven burden borne by military personnel and their families as unfair, while 70 percent considered it "just part of being in the military."[66] Some began to question whether the AVF was sustainable and warned of the expanding civil-military divide, in which "society had become divorced from the service—and vice versa."[67] These trends caught the attention of Secretary of Defense Robert Gates, who remarked in a speech at Duke University, "For a growing number of Americans, service in the military, no matter how laudable, has become something for other people to do."[68]

Focus on the "Gap" as the AVF Reaches Fifty Years of Service

The civil-military gap is not just an issue of small numbers bearing the burden for defending the many. Also significant is the degree to which those who do serve in uniform are representative of society at large. If the 1 percent reflected the participation of all socioeconomic sectors, geographic regions, ethnic groups, and political ideologies—that is, if the 1 percent was a microcosm of the remaining 99 percent—then the concerns associated with such limited participation of the few on the behalf of the many would be substantially mitigated.[69]

But in 2021, the 1 percent is not indicative of the 99 percent. Those who serve are drawn primarily from the middle class, hail predominantly from southern and western states, are politically more conservative, and come increasingly from military families. More and more, the phrase "military" or "warrior caste" appears in the literature on the civil-military gap, implying that the armed forces are not "of society" but rather an "Army Apart."[70] On the eve of his retirement, Secretary of Defense Gates chose to highlight the issue in a speech to the Corps of Cadets at West Point: "There is a risk over time of developing a cadre of military leaders that politically, culturally and geographically have less and less in common with the majority of the people they have sworn to defend."[71]

The gap as the AVF reaches fifty years of service is multifaceted. Contributing to it are a demographic imbalance in the representation of socioeconomic groups, national regions, racial and ethnic groups, gender, and differences in political attitudes between those who serve and those who do not. Furthermore, there are signs that the increasingly isolated military sphere is spawning a warrior caste where children from military families are vastly overrepresented in the armed forces. Finally, the U.S. military's smaller size contributes to the civil-military gap because there are fewer opportunities to serve, and those who do enlist do so for longer periods of time.

THE MIDDLE CLASS IS OVERREPRESENTED, WHILE THE VERY RICH AND VERY POOR DO NOT SERVE

Not only is the burden of military service borne by a few, but these "other people" are not representative of American society. Socioeconomically, societal elites as well as the poor are largely absent from the ranks.[72] According to measures of neighborhood affluence based on their zip codes, enlisted recruits come mostly from the middle three quintiles of households, with incomes between $38,000 and $81,000.[73] Youth from the lowest socioeconomic quintile are underrepresented because they are less likely to earn a high school diploma and are more likely to have an underlying health condition or criminal record, all disqualifying factors for the AVF.[74] Retired U.S. Army major general Dennis Laich, an advocate for returning to the draft, has said, "The all-volunteer force is a mercenary military made up of poor kids and patriots from the third and fourth socioeconomic quintiles of our country. The first socioeconomic quintile is AWOL (Absent Without Leave), but that's where the real decision-makers and policymakers of the country come from."[75]

THE U.S. MILITARY IS NOT GEOGRAPHICALLY REPRESENTATIVE OF AMERICAN SOCIETY

The post–Cold War drawdown also sought savings from reducing defense infrastructure, which, in turn, led to base closings. These developments diminished the frequency of routine interactions between the citizenry and the military. To this point, James Burk has offered the concept of "institutional presence" to refer to the social significance of an institution in society.[76] Burk argues that an institution's material presence, which he defines as the likelihood that members of society would come into contact with a particular institution, has significantly affected the relationship between the armed forces and society.[77] Closing military bases without considering the importance of having a military institutional presence throughout the various regions of the country has resulted in decreased opportunities for contact between servicemembers and the public.

In the Cold War era, the largest military installations were already located primarily in the South and Southwest due to mild climates and the availability of the vast tracts of land needed for training. Several rounds of base closures beginning in the mid-1990s significantly further reduced the military presence in the Northeast and Midwest and consolidated the nation's military presence more firmly in the South and Far West. The army especially concentrated its forces in posts in Texas, Washington, Georgia, Kentucky, and North Carolina, leaving vast portions of the country with little or no military presence.[78] Overall, half of the active-duty forces are stationed in just five states: California, Virginia,

Texas, North Carolina, and Georgia. The list of high recruit-producing counties in the United States tracks well with those that host the largest military installations.[79] In these locations, the public has more frequent and direct contact with servicemembers and military life.

The density of military installations also contributes to higher representation ratios for particular states. Representation ratios compare a state's population of eighteen- to twenty-four-year-olds to its share of recruits. A ratio of one means that a state's share of recruits is equal to its "recruitable" population. In the Northeast, only one state, Maine, had a representation ratio greater than 1, while ten of the fourteen southern states did.[80] Georgia had the highest representation ratio at 1.5, while the District of Columbia had the lowest at 0.29. Recruits from the South and Far West (excluding California) are overrepresented, while volunteers from the Northeast and Midwest contribute less than their proportional share of eighteen- to twenty-four-year-olds.[81] Increasingly, the likelihood of young Americans volunteering for the armed forces depends on the institutional presence of the military in a particular part of the United States.

THE U.S. MILITARY IS INCREASINGLY DIVERSE BUT DEMOGRAPHIC IMBALANCES PERSIST

The United States is becoming more diverse. Census data projects that the country will be majority nonwhite by 2045.[82] In 2017, 40 percent of U.S. active-duty personnel were racial or ethnic minorities, 16 percent were black, 16 percent Hispanic, 4 percent Asian, and an additional 6 percent identified as "other" or unknown.[83] This is up from only 20 percent of active-duty forces coming from racial and ethnic minority groups in 1990. In comparison, 44 percent of Americans eighteen to forty-four years old are racial or ethnic minorities.[84] By 2017, the share of active-duty military who were non-Hispanic white had fallen, while racial and ethnic minorities made up 43 percent of servicemembers. Within that group, African Americans dropped from 51 percent in 2004 to 39 percent in 2017 just as the share of Hispanics rose from 25 percent to 36 percent.

Although the U.S. armed forces have become increasingly more diverse, some differences stand out between their composition and the nation's demographics. Most obviously, women make up only 16 percent of the active-duty force, while the U.S. population is 51 percent female.[85] But the number of women in uniform has risen dramatically since 1970, when only 1 percent of the force was female. By 2017, women composed 18 percent of the officer corps.[86] Female recruits are more diverse that the civilian population and more diverse than male recruits, with 43 percent of enlisted men and 56 percent of enlisted women being Hispanic or another racial minority. Nearly half of all women in the army are African American, and Black men are overrepresented compared to the civilian population in every service except the marine corps.[87] Clearly, women contribute more to the diversity of the enlisted ranks than male recruits do.

The officer ranks are much less diverse. Only 9 percent of the officer corps is black and only 8 percent Hispanic.[88] Furthermore, African Americans and Hispanics compose 8 percent and 2 percent of general and flag officers, respectively.[89] Women make up 18.6 percent of the officer corps across the services but account for only 7.6 percent of the general- and flag-officer positions.[90] This data indicates that some of the patterns with regard to lack of career progression evident in the 1980s and 1990s have persisted into the 2020s, especially in the flag ranks.[91]

THE U.S. MILITARY IS MORE IDEOLOGICALLY CONSERVATIVE THAN THE NATION AS A WHOLE

A consistent trend since the advent of the AVF has been its increased affiliation with the Republican Party.[92] A 2011 Pew survey of post-9/11 veterans found that 36 percent described themselves as Republican compared to 23 percent of the public at large. The poll also found that only 21 percent of veterans from all ranks identified as Democrats compared to 34 percent of the public.[93] Heidi Urben and Jason Dempsey found that Democrats are less likely to join the armed forces than Republicans, and more-liberal Democrats are less likely to stay in the military beyond an initial term of enlistment.[94]

Urben's 2009 survey found that 60 percent of the army officers surveyed identified as Republicans, while only 18 percent identified as Democrats. Furthermore, Dempsey's work parsed out trends across the ranks and revealed that ideological conservatism increases with rank within the officer corps, while the enlisted ranks are more ideologically diverse.[95] This tracks with the greater racial and ethnic diversity found within the enlisted ranks. Black, Hispanic, and female servicemembers lean more Democratic.[96] Exit polling in the 2020 presidential election showed that military members' and veterans' support for Trump declined from 61 percent in 2016 to 52 percent in 2020.[97]

Furthermore, the attack on the U.S. Capitol on January 6, 2021, revealed to the American public the degree to which white supremacists are present in the active and veteran ranks of the U.S. armed forces, which may further discourage enlistment by potential recruits from minority groups.[98] Indeed, the trust the American people have in the military institution dropped markedly following the events of January 6. About 56 percent of those surveyed said they have a "a great deal of trust and con-fidence" in the armed forces, down from 70 percent in 2018.[99]

A WARRIOR CASTE IS DEVELOPING IN THE U.S. MILITARY

A warrior caste is defined as the phenomenon where "the military is in-creasingly composed of those who have an immediate family member who has served."[100] The isolation of military communities from civilian society in many parts of the country has resulted in a generation of chil-dren for whom "military service is an avenue left unexplored and uncon-sidered."[101] In contrast, for the children of servicemembers, the armed forces provide the logical career path. "For such children, the abnormal decision to 'opt out' of military service is akin to the radical choice of the general population to 'opt in.'"[102]

The AVF has resulted in a drastic decline in familiarity with the mil-itary across generations.[103] Polling from 2011 showed that 79 percent of adults ages fifty to sixty-four and 60 percent those aged thirty to forty-nine have an immediate family member who served in the armed forces, while only one-third of eighteen to twenty-nine-year-olds did.[104] DOD statistics from 2015 indicate that approximately one-third of new enlisted recruits had a parent who is a veteran and between 77 percent and 86 percent had a family member who served.[105] Ninety-eight members of the U.S. Air Force Academy Class of 2024 are the children of service-acad-emy graduates, 8.6 percent of the entire class.[106]

Furthermore, the U.S. military's highest ranks are "saturated with legacy families." A 2007 army study found that of the 340 general of-ficers serving in the U.S. Army, 180 had children serving in uniform.[107] These numbers are statistically significant because veterans make up only 7 percent of the U.S. population. The 2019 Senate confirmation hear-ing of General James C. McConville drew media interest when reporters noted that his three children and their spouses in attendance were all army captains.[108] Senator James Inhofe, who chaired the hearing, argued: "Who can vote against a guy, a distinguished general, who has two sons, a daughter—all three captains in the U.S. Army? I say, no one."[109] Close to 100,000 troops are married to another servicemember. The low pro-pensity to serve among youth of military age in the general population has steered recruiters to military bases, where they are more likely to find youth familiar with military service and willing to enlist.

Some observers point to the benefits of the warrior caste and note that, unlike civilians at large, children from military families enter the armed forces with realistic expectations and firsthand knowledge of military life. These well-prepared recruits are service minded, and their successful recruitment indicates that the quality of life in the military must be high for the children of professional servicemembers to seek a career in the armed forces. Others are concerned about the risk that the legacy servicemembers may foster elitism and a sense of superiority.[110] Such a development may make it harder to recruit some sectors of society whose members feel uncomfortable in an institution in which they are underrepresented. Still others point to a "self-replicating cycle of service" among military families, which narrows the pool of people with a propensity to enlist and threatens to make expansion of the force beyond reach without a draft.[111]

Why the Civil-Military Gap Matters

Proponents of the AVF were dismissive of the national value connecting service to the obligations of citizenship. They focused instead on the argument that military service was a tax that restricted the freedoms of the nation's youth. Their solution was to create market forces that would attract sufficient numbers of volunteers to support national-security requirements and to implement a standby draft in the event of sustained military conflicts requiring an expansion of the armed forces beyond what the reserves and National Guard could muster.

Factors they did not sufficiently consider include the opportunity for youth to connect with their national democratic institutions through military service. Fully professional armies also limit the common unifying experience, or "patriotic glue," that widespread military service contributes to the national fabric. In a polarized social and political environment, such opportunities to live, work, and depend on people from all parts of the country for a higher purpose are increasingly rare.[112] Furthermore, declining trust in the armed forces as a result of a perceived overrepresentation of servicemembers and veterans in polarizing political activity, such as the January 6, 2021, attack on the Capitol, seeming to indicate that the military institution contributes to the polarized political environment, further erodes the nation's "patriotic glue." This is significant because, as Republican strategist Karl Rove remarked, "You look at all of our institutions, and [the military] is one where the confidence of the American people cuts across all lines."[113]

The civil-military gap has led to weak governmental oversight of military operations and national-security affairs. This is because use-of-force considerations are far removed from a public without a personal stake in them. A disengaged public does not exert political pressure on representatives to pay attention to wars and troop deployments, giving elected leaders and those vying for elected positions little incentive to pay much attention to the wars either.[114] Furthermore, a 2015 Harvard Institute of Politics poll found that 60 percent of young Americans aged eighteen to twenty-nine were in favor of using military force in Syria to defeat the Islamic State (ISIS), but only 16 percent of this same cohort was willing to serve in such operations.[115] This finding led a Center for New American Security research team to conclude that for the younger generation, "those who serve are seen as either victims or heroes but rarely as relatable people, which may drive down the ability to recruit among the growing majority of the populace who are unfamiliar with military service."[116]

The civil-military gap is also a national-security-expertise gap. Veterans composed slightly less than 17 percent of the 117th Congress elected in 2020, the lowest proportion since World War II.[117] While these numbers surpass the 7 percent of veterans found in the population overall, according to 2010 Census data, it is a precipitous decline from the era when the vast majority of lawmakers had a direct experience with the military institution. The lack of shared risk across society and within the governing class reduces politicians' accountability. Constituents inattentive to national-security affairs make it easier for politicians to deploy troops in their name, with "few consequences for the misuse of force."[118]

These voices argue that without "skin in the game" and the potential of a family member being conscripted, issues of war and peace will remain at the periphery—instead of at the center—of national discourse.[119] This view recommends conscripting a small percentage of eighteen-year-olds so that the youth and their families are more attentive to national affairs, including decisions to deploy the military.[120] Others insist that returning to the draft is simply too impractical. If the overall size of the military remained the same, then those who are enlisted would still compose a very small percentage of the population, which would not appreciably change the military's overall presence in society.[121] Yet the few who are conscripted would improve the military's reach into the areas of the country that are currently underrepresented.

Conclusions

In sum, two generations of the AVF have resulted in the evolution of a civil-military gap where those who choose to enlist are predominantly males from middle-class families in southern and western states. Today's volunteers are healthier, better educated, and are more likely to have come from a military family than their cohort in society at large. African Americans are overrepresented in the enlisted ranks, but 10 percent less so than twenty years ago, while Hispanic representativeness is growing.

The ranks of women in the armed forces continue to grow, and they are just now reaching the highest tiers of military leadership. Servicemembers' ideological conservatism continued to diverge from the nation as a whole, but the military's expanding diversity is mitigating this trend.

As the AVF eclipses fifty years of service, the assumptions of its founders that the demographic makeup of the volunteer force would mirror that of the draft force proved to be wrong. The United States has come to rely on a smaller, unrepresentative force comprised primarily of those with the most exposure to the military. Acknowledging the existence of the civil-military gap and the threat it poses to both military effectiveness and the national value that citizens should be engaged in their own defense is critical. It is the first step toward reversing the inattentiveness of the American people to national-security affairs and to reconnecting them with their government and the measures taken in their name to promote the national interest.

Notes

1. Bernard D. Roster, "The Gates Commission: Right for the Wrong Reasons," in *The All-Volunteer Force: Thirty Years of Service*, ed. Barbara A. Bicksler, Curtis L. Gilroy, and John T. Warner (Washington, DC: Brassey's, 2004), 24.

2. Beth Bailey, *America's Army: Making the All-Volunteer Force* (Cambridge, MA: Belknap Press of Harvard University Press, 2009), 5.

3. John L. Rafuse, "United States' Experience with Volunteer and Conscript Forces," in *Studies Prepared for the President's Commission on an All-Volunteer Armed Force*, vol. 2 (Washington, DC: GPO, 1970), III-1-5.

4. Rafuse, "United States' Experience with Volunteer and Conscript Forces," III-2.

5. Alexander Hamilton, Federalist No. 8, "Militarism, the Inevitable Result of Disunion," in *The New York Packet*, November 20, 1787, reprinted in *The Debate on the Constitution*, vol. 1 (New York: Library of America, 1993), 336.

6. Hamilton, Federalist No. 8.

7. Peter D. Feaver, "The Civil-Military Problematique: Huntington, Janowitz, and the Question of Civilian Control," *Armed Forces and Society* 23, no. 2 (Winter 1996): 150.

8. Rafuse, "United States' Experience with Volunteer and Conscript Forces," III-2.

9. Mark Thompson, "The Other 1%," *Time*, November 11, 2011, 34.

10. Jonathan E. Vespa, "Those Who Served: America's Veterans from World War II to the War on Terror," U.S. Census Bureau, June 2020, https://www.census.gov/content/dam/Census/library/publications/2020/demo/acs-43.pdf.

11. U.S. Census Bureau, *Statistical Abstract of the United States, 1953* (Washington,

DC: GPO, 1953), 230, U.S. Census Bureau, https://www.census.gov/library/pub
lications/1953/compendia/statab/74ed.html.

12. U.S. Department of Veterans Affairs, "Military Health History Pocket Card:
Vietnam," https://www.va.gov/oaa/pocketcard/m-vietnam.asp#:~:text=Approximate
ly%202%2C700%2C000%20American%20men%20and,failed%20to%20meet%20
its%20objectives.

13. Harry Franqui-Rivera, "Vietnam," Center for Puerto Rican Studies, https://
centropr.hunter.cuny.edu/digital-humanities/pr-military/vietnam-war.

14. Frederick B. Dent, Milton Friedman, Stephen E. Herbits, and Theodore M.
Hesburgh, "Reflections from the Gates Commission," in Bicksler, Gilroy, and Warner, *All-Volunteer Force*, 9.

15. *The Report of the President's Commission on an All-Volunteer Armed Force* (Washington, DC: GPO, 1970), 9–10 (hereafter cited as Gates Commission Report).

16. William P. Snyder, "Military Personnel—Procurement Policies: Assumptions—Trends—Context," in *The All-Volunteer Force and American Society*, ed. John B.
Keely (Charlottesville: University Press of Virginia, 1978), 24.

17. Gates Commission Report, 12, 15.

18. Brandon Archuleta, "Fifty Years after the President's Commission on an
All-Volunteer Force," War on the Rocks, February 28, 2020, https://warontherocks
.com/2020/02/fifty-years-after-the-presidents-commission-on-an-all-volunteer-ar
med-force/.

19. Charles C. Moskos, From Institution to Occupation: Trends in Military Organization," *Armed Forces and Society* 4, no. 1 (Fall 1977): 43.

20. Martin Binkin and Mark J. Eitelberg, "Women and Minorities in the All-
Volunteer Force," in *The All-Volunteer Force after a Decade*, ed. William Bowman (Mc-
Lean, VA: Pegamon-Brassey's, 1986), 81.

21. Binkin and Eitelberg, "Women and Minorities in the All-Volunteer Force," 81.

22. Binkin and Eitelberg, "Women and Minorities in the All-Volunteer Force," 82.

23. Binkin and Eitelberg, "Women and Minorities in the All-Volunteer Force," 82.

24. Phillip Carter, Katherine L. Kuzminski, Amy Schafer, and Andrew Swick,
"AVF 4.0: The Future of the All-Volunteer Force," Center for a New American
Security, March 28, 2017, https://www.cnas.org/publications/reports/avf-4-0-the-fu
ture-of-the-all-volunteer-force.

25. Moskos, "From Institution to Occupation," 76.

26. Moskos, "From Institution to Occupation," 72.

27. Snyder, "Military Personnel—Procurement Policies," 27.

28. Moskos, "From Institution to Occupation," 50.

29. Moskos, "From Institution to Occupation," 49.

30. Bernard Rostker, *I Want You! The Evolution of the All-Volunteer Force* (Santa
Monica, CA: RAND, 2006), 560–561.

31. Moskos, "From Institution to Occupation," 50–51.

32. Snyder, "Military Personnel—Procurement Policies," 37.

33. Binkin and Eitelberg, "Women and Minorities in the All-Volunteer Force," 76.

34. Binkin and Eitelberg, "Women and Minorities in the All-Volunteer Force," 75.

35. Binkin and Eitelberg, "Women and Minorities in the All-Volunteer Force," 78.

36. "Women in the Armed Forces," *Newsweek*, February 18, 1980, 34–42.

37. Rostker, *I Want You!*, 565.

38. Rostker, *I Want You!*, 567.

39. Binkin and Eitelberg, "Women and Minorities in the All-Volunteer Force," 86.

40. Ole R. Holsti, "A Widening Gap between Military and Civilians: Some Evidence, 1976–96," *International Security* 23, no. 3 (Winter 1998/1999): 11.

41. Gates Commission Report, 12.

42. Rostker, *I Want You!*, 661.

43. David J. Armor and Curtis L. Gilroy, "Changing Minority Representation in the U.S. Military," *Armed Forces and Society* 36, no. 2 (2010): 230.

44. Armor and Gilroy, "Changing Minority Representation in the U.S. Military," 215.

45. John Lancaster, "Aspin to Open Combat Roles to Women," *Washington Post*, April 28, 1993, https://www.washingtonpost.com/archive/politics/1993/04/28/aspin-to-open-combat-roles-to-women/78a7f11a-6d29-4539-bc10-ac908cff8498/.

46. Eric V. Larson, David T. Orletsky, and Kristin J. Leuschner, *Defense Planning in a Decade of Change: Lessons from the Base Force, Bottom-Up Review, and Quadrennial Defense Review* (Santa Monica, CA: RAND, 2001), 61, https://www.rand.org/pubs/monograph_reports/MR1387.html.

47. U.S. Department of Defense, "Total Force Military Demographics," 54, https://diversity.defense.gov/LinkClick.aspx?fileticket=gxMVqhkaHh8%3D&portalid=51.

48. "Section I: Population," in "Statistical Abstract of the United States," U.S. Census Bureau, 2003, 15, https://www2.census.gov/library/publications/2004/compendia/statab/123ed/tables/pop.pdf.

49. Rostker, *I Want You!*, 690.

50. Ben Werschkul, Matthew Ericson, and Tom Torok, "Interactive Graph: A Look at 1000 Who Died," *New York Times*, September 17, 2004.

51. John D. Winkler, R. Wayne Spruell, Thomas L. Bush, and Gary L. Crone, "A 'Continuum of Service' for the All-Volunteer Force," in Bicksler, Gilroy, and Warner, *All-Volunteer Force*, 297.

52. Defense Manpower Data Center (DMDC), 2003 demographic data, 158, https://dwp.dmdc.osd.mil/dwp/app/dod-data-reports/workforce-reports.

53. DMDC, 2003 demographic data, 158.

54. Rostker, *I Want You!*, 734–737.

55. Martha Farnsworth Riche and Aline Quester, "The Effects of Socioeconomic Change on the All-Volunteer Force: Past, Present, and Future," in Bicksler, Gilroy, and Warner, *All-Volunteer Force*, 120.

56. Riche and Quester, "Effects of Socioeconomic Change on the All-Volunteer Force," 120.

57. Riche and Quester, "Effects of Socioeconomic Change on the All-Volunteer Force," 124. In 2003, recruits with GEDs were limited to only 2–10 percent of total recruits, further increasing the quality of the force but not mirroring the educational profile of all eighteen- to twenty-four-year-olds.

58. Riche and Quester, "Effects of Socioeconomic Change on the All-Volunteer Force," 121.

59. Riche and Quester, "Effects of Socioeconomic Change on the All-Volunteer Force," 132.

60. Holsti, "Widening Gap between Military and Civilians," 11.

61. Gates Commission Report, 9.

62. DMDC, demographic data, 2020.

63. Thompson, "Other 1%," 34.

64. William R. Arkin, "Why America Can't End Its 'Forever Wars,'" *Newsweek*, April 12, 2021, https://www.newsweek.com/why-america-cant-end-its-forever-wars-1582749.

65. Pew Research Center for Social and Demographic Trends, "War and Sacrifice in the Post-9/11 Era," October 5, 2011, http://pewresearch.org/pubs/2111/veterans-post-911-wars-iraq-afghanistan-civilian-military-veterans.

66. Pew Research Center, "War and Sacrifice"

67. Carter, Kuzminski, Schafer, and Swick, "AVF 4.0."

68. Robert M. Gates, "Lecture at Duke University," 2010, https://smallwarsjournal.com/blog/secretary-gates-on-the-all-volunteer-force.

69. Marybeth P. Ulrich, "The US Civil-Military Relations Gap and the Erosion of Historical Democratic Norms," *Oxford Encyclopedia of the Military in Politics*, June 28, 2021, https://doi.org/10.1093/acrefore/9780190228637.013.1932 (subscription required).

70. Thompson, "Other 1%."

71. West Point—The U.S. Military Academy, "2011 Thayer Award Dr. Robert Gates," YouTube, October 7, 2011, https://www.youtube.com/watch?v=z-IoF79U7NQ.

72. Marybeth P. Ulrich, "Mind the Civil-Military Gap: The Republic Depends on All Citizens," *The Hill*, January 29, 2019, https://thehill.com/opinion/national-security/427385-mind-the-civil-military-gap-the-republic-depends-on-all-citizens.

73. "Demographics of the U.S. Military," Council on Foreign Relations, July 13, 2020, https://www.cfr.org/backgrounder/demographics-us-military.

74. Kori Schake and James Mattis, *Warriors and Civilians: American Views of Our Military* (Stanford, CA: Hoover Institution Press, 2016).

75. Schake and Mattis, *Warriors and Civilians*, 28.

76. Peter D. Feaver and Richard H. Kohn, *Soldiers and Civilians: The Civil-Military Gap and American National Security* (Cambridge, MA: MIT Press, 2001), 249.

77. Feaver and Kohn, *Soldiers and Civilians*, 249.

78. Ulrich, "Mind the Civil-Military Gap."

79. National Priorities Project, 2011.

80. "Demographics of the U.S. Military."

81. Ulrich, "Mind the Civil-Military Gap."

82. William H. Frey, "The U.S. Will Become 'Minority White' in 2045, Census Projects," *Brookings*, March 14, 2018, 14, https://www.brookings.edu/blog/the-avenue/2018/03/14/the-us-will-become-minority-white-in-2045-census-projects/.

83. Amanda Barroso, "The Changing Profile of the U.S. Military: Smaller in Size,

More Diverse, More Women in Leadership," Pew Research Center, September 10, 2019, https://www.pewresearch.org/fact-tank/2019/09/10/the-changing-profile-of-the-u-s-military/.

84. Kim Parker, Anthony Cilluffo, and Renee Stepler, "6 Facts about the U.S. Military and Its Changing Demographics," Pew Research Center, April 13, 2017, https://www.pewresearch.org/fact-tank/2017/04/13/6-facts-about-the-u-s-military-and-its-changing-demographics/.

85. U.S. Census, "Quick Facts: United States," 2019, https://www.pewresearch.org/fact-tank/2017/04/13/6-facts-about-the-u-s-military-and-its-changing-demographics/.

86. Erin Duffin, "Distribution of Race and Ethnicity among the U.S. Military in 2018," Statista.com, https://www.statista.com/statistics/214869/share-of-active-duty-enlisted-women-and-men-in-the-us-military/.

87. "Demographics of the U.S. Military."

88. Parker, Cilluffo, and Stepler, "6 Facts about the U.S. Military and Its Changing Demographics."

89. Kristy M. Kamarck, "Diversity, Inclusion, and Equal Opportunity in the Armed Services: Background and Issues for Congress," Congressional Research Service Report, June 5, 2019, R44321, https://crsreports.congress.gov/product/pdf/R/R44321.

90. Kamarck, "Diversity, Inclusion, and Equal Opportunity in the Armed Services."

91. "Demographics of the U.S. Military."

92. Denise-Marie Ordway, "Younger Veterans Are More Likely to Be Republicans Than Democrats," Journalist's Resource, August 23, 2018, https://journalistsresource.org/politics-and-government/veterans-republican-party-affiliation/.

93. Thompson, "Other 1%."

94. James T. Golby, "The Democrat-Military Gap: A Re-examination of Partisanship and the Profession," 2011, paper prepared for the Inter-University Seminar on Armed Forces and Society Biennial Conference, 2, https://themonkeycage.org/wp-content/uploads/2012/02/Golby-IUS.pdf.

Schake and Mattis, *Warriors and Civilians.*

95. Jason K. Dempsey, *Our Army: Soldiers, Politics, and American Civil-Military Relations* (Princeton, NJ: Princeton University Press, 2010).

96. Danielle Lupton and Max Z. Margulies, "Trump's Election Fraud Allegations Suggest Military Voters Uniformly Supported Him. It's Not So," *Washington Post,* November 18, 2020, https://www.washingtonpost.com/politics/2020/11/18/trumps-election-fraud-allegations-suggest-that-military-voters-uniformly-supported-him-its-not-so/.

97. Lupton and Margulies, "Trump's Election Fraud Allegations Suggest Military Voters Uniformly Supported Him."

98. Jaweed Kaleem and Kurtis Lee, "Why Military Veterans and Law Enforcement Joined the Capitol Insurrection," *Los Angeles Times,* January 15, 2021, https://www.latimes.com/world-nation/story/2021-01-15/capitol-riot-police-veterans-extremists.

99. Leo Shane III, "Trust in Military Is Dropping Significantly, New Survey

Suggests," *Military Times*, March 10, 2021, https://www.militarytimes.com/news/penta gon-congress/2021/03/10/trust-in-the-military-is-dropping-significantly-new-sur vey-suggests/.

100. Amy Schafer, "Generations of War: The Rise of the Warrior Caste and the All-Volunteer Force," Center for a New American Security, May 8, 2017, 2, https://www.cnas.org/publications/reports/generations-of-war.

101. Schafer, "Generations of War," 6.

102. Schafer, "Generations of War," 6.

103. Schake and Mattis, *Warriors and Civilians*, 28.

104. Gretchen Livingston, "Profile of U.S. Veterans Is Changing Dramatically as Their Ranks Decline," Pew Research Center, November 11, 2016, https://www.pew research.org/fact-tank/2016/11/11/profile-of-u-s-veterans-is-changing-dramatically -as-their-ranks-decline/.

105. Schafer, "Generations of War," 6.

106. Ray Bowden, "Academy Releases Stats on Class of 2024," U.S. Air Force Academy, July 13, 2020, https://www.usafa.af.mil/News/News-Display/Article/2272 302/academy-releases-stats-on-the-class-of-2024/#:~:text=That%20is%20346%20w omen%2C%2030.2,Hundred%20forty%2Dtwo%20are%20Hispanic.

107. Schafer, "Generations of War," 7.

108. Paul Yingling, "To Fill Civil-Military Gap, Close Base Housing," *Army Magazine*, July 8, 2019, https://www.realcleardefense.com/2019/07/08/to_fill_civil-milita ry_gap_close_base_housing_308876.html.

109. Paul D. Shinkman, "A Photo of a General's Family Highlights Civil-Military Concerns, *U.S. News and World Report*, May 2, 2019, https://www.usnews.com/news /national-news/articles/2019-05-02/a-photo-of-a-generals-family-highlights-civil-mi litary-concerns.

110. Schafer, "Generations of War," 9.

111. Carter, Kuzminski, Schafer, and Swick, "AVF 4.0."

112. Ulrich, "Mind the Civil-Military Gap."

113. Leo Shane III, "Defense Advocates Fear Isolationist Views Endanger Military's Future," *Military Times*, December 7, 2019, https://www.militarytimes.com/ne ws/pentagon-congress/2019/12/07/defense-advocates-fear-isolationist-views-endang er-militarys-future/.

114. Helene Cooper, "In 2010 Campaign, War Is Rarely Mentioned," *New York Times*, October 28, 2010, https://www.nytimes.com/2010/10/29/us/politics/29war.html.

115. Harvard Institute of Politics Fall 2015 Poll, December 10, 2015, https://iop.har vard.edu/survey/details/harvard-iop-fall-2015-poll.

116. Carter, Kuzminski, Schafer, and Swick, "AVF 4.0."

117. Leo Shane III, "Veterans in the 117th Congress, by the Numbers," *Military Times*, December 28, 2020, https://www.militarytimes.com/news/pentagon-congress /2020/12/28/veterans-in-the-117th-congress-by-the-numbers/.

118. Schafer, "Generations of War," 11.

119. Elliot Ackerman, "Why Bringing Back the Draft Could Stop America's Forever Wars," *Time*, October 10, 2019, https://time.com/5696950/bring-back-the -draft/.

120. David Barno, "Civil-Military Relations Amid Domestic Crisis," Johns Hopkins School of Advanced International Studies, June 18, 2020, https://sais.jhu.edu/news-press/event-recap/civil-military-relations-amid-domestic-crisis.

121. Hugh Liebert and James Golby, "Mid-Life Crisis?: The All-Volunteer Force at 40," *Armed Forces and Society* 43, no. 1 (2017): 117.

Conclusion
The AVF's Legacy after Fifty Years of Service

William A. Taylor

After initial recruiting shortfalls caused early yet significant angst among both military leaders and civilian policymakers that the all-volunteer force was failing before it could become well established, the overall situation suddenly and dramatically improved by the fall of 1974. Confident of improved recruiting, Howard H. "Bo" Callaway, secretary of the army, announced on October 9, 1974, that the army would discharge all remaining draftees, roughly 2,500 soldiers, by Thanksgiving of that year instead of having them continue their compulsory military service for a full two years as originally planned.[1]

Among them was the last draftee, Dwight Elliot Stone, who had served almost seventeen months in the army before receiving an honorable discharge on November 14, 1974. His outlook throughout that time was both simple and logical: complete his compulsory military service and get back to his previous civilian life as swiftly as possible. "All I wanted to do was put in my time and get out," Stone remembered. He never harbored any ambivalence regarding whether he would continue to serve in the army after his time as a draftee was over. "My attitude was: I'm in this man's army and the best thing I can do is to get out as quick as I can." After completing his basic training at Fort Polk, Louisiana, Stone served at Fort Monmouth, New Jersey, for the majority of his brief tour in the army. Upon discharge, he returned to Sacramento, California, and assumed his previous job as a pipe fitter for a local oil company, undoubtedly grateful for his much higher salary and newly rediscovered freedoms in civilian life. Reflecting on his brief yet significant stint as the last draftee, which some journalists argued made him "something of a celebrity," Stone demurred: "About the only thing I learned is restraint, patience. What guy wants to carry a rifle and be a hero?"[2]

On November 22, 1974, John M. Crewdson, special correspondent for the *New York Times*, paid tribute to this significant milestone as the transition to the AVF finalized: "By the time the final notes of retreat faded this evening, the last draftee serving in the Army had been discharged." Highlighting that draftees had numbered more than 550,000 at the peak of U.S. involvement in the Vietnam War not long before, Crewdson marveled at the rapid transition to the AVF. He admitted, however, that he did not know what the future would hold for this historic change. One thing was certain, Crewdson remarked: "Tomorrow morning, for the first time since before Pearl Harbor, the United States Army will be an all-volunteer organization." Thus ended an era and launched the true advent of the AVF.[3]

After fifty years of service, the AVF has significantly evolved. It currently totals roughly 1.39 million active-duty personnel, with 1.35 million servicemembers arrayed across the Department of Defense (army, 483,742; navy, 348,064; marine corps, 181,561; air force, 336,459) and an additional 41,500 serving in the U.S. Coast Guard.[4] In addition to these active-duty servicemembers, there are slightly more than 800,000 personnel in the reserves and the National Guard.[5] By comparison, today's AVF is much smaller than when it first began. In June 1973, the active-duty armed services numbered approximately 2.25 million across the DOD (army, 800,973; navy, 564,534; marine corps, 196,098; air force, 691,182).[6]

As the AVF evolved over the past five decades, four important trends emerged regarding its current status. First, it has significantly shrunk over time, both in actual numbers and relative to U.S. society. At the advent of the AVF, roughly 1 percent of Americans served in the armed forces. Today, the percentage is just half that.

Second, the AVF is more expensive, not only in obvious terms of raw costs but also, and more importantly, proportional to its shrinking size. At the same time that it has shrunk, personnel costs have significantly increased related to the smaller size of the armed forces. By one estimate, these have risen 46 percent from what they were in just 2000 when adjusted for inflation.[7] As a result of these two related trends, the AVF is growing relatively more expensive at the same time that it is significantly decreasing in size.

Third, the AVF over time has become more representative of U.S. society writ large. It remains far younger and more male than the broader population. Even so, women's participation in the AVF has risen from less than 2 percent at its inception to 16 percent today. Recruits are largely middle class, with the middle three socioeconomic quintiles slightly over-represented. The top and bottom quintiles, especially the top one, remain notably underrepresented.[8]

Fourth, the AVF has become largely accepted in U.S. society over time. Today, the vast majority of Americans oppose conscription. They also approve current defense-spending levels, some advocating for even more, and maintain either a "great deal" or "quite a lot" of confidence in the armed forces as an institution.[9] Of course, some observers point out that public confidence in the military and public apathy about military matters are not mutually exclusive.

As noted in the introduction, this book consists of four parts: history, results, challenges, and implications. Part one explores the history surrounding the advent of the AVF. In chapter 1, Amy J. Rutenberg surveys the conscription that preceded it. Next, Michael Gibbs and Timothy J. Perri discuss the economics that undergirded the transition to the AVF and the many economists who created, articulated, and promulgated them. William A. Taylor then details the President's Commission on an All-Volunteer Armed Force, which recommended the AVF and made it possible. With chapter 4, Beth Bailey examines the important issue of race within the AVF.

Part two shifts the focus from the advent of the AVF to its major results. In chapter 5, Kara Dixon Vuic explores the influence of the AVF on women in terms of opportunities, norms, and experiences. Jennifer Mittelstadt then details the expansion of benefits within the AVF and relates that critical dynamic to the welfare state. In chapter 7, Titus Firmin investigates the socioeconomics of the AVF, revealing how it has proven to be largely middle class over time.

Part three takes a stark look at some of the many challenges that the AVF has presented. In chapter 8, Major General Dennis Laich argues that the AVF suffers from several troubles related to its viability. Next, Lawrence B. Wilkerson examines the AVF's efficiency, revealing that it has encountered many difficulties related to winning wars, adapting to threats, and converting its vast potential into actual results. In chapter 10, Major General Jeffrey E. Phillips explores the intimate relationship between the AVF and the reserves, two entities inextricably intertwined because of the Total Force policy that accompanied the advent of the AVF in 1973.

The collection closes with part four providing some thought-provoking reflections about the considerable ramifications of the AVF, both today and into the future. In chapter 11, Adrian R. Lewis explains military culture and the many implications that the AVF created for it. Next, Mark F. Cancian provides an exceptional overview of force structure, revealing both past precedents and future directions. Marybeth P. Ulrich then reveals the influence of the AVF on the civil-military gap. Finally, William A. Taylor concludes the volume with some thoughts on the AVF's legacy after fifty years of service.

These cogent chapters speak to the vital issues that remain most relevant today and will likely endure well into the future. For many Americans who have grown up since its advent in 1973, the AVF is the one and only model of military service that they have ever known, even if the vast majority of them have never directly experienced it. The legacy of the draft, however, is certainly not as archaic as it might appear at first glance.

In fact, while Private Stone was the last draftee, Chief Warrant Officer 5 (CWO5) Ralph Rigby was the last continuously serving draftee to retire. After being drafted on April 26, 1972, a little more than one year before Stone, and completing his term of service, Rigby then volunteered to stay in the army, ultimately serving forty-two years, rising to the penultimate chief warrant officer rank of CWO5 before retiring in the fall of 2014.[10]

A brief war scare with Iran following the U.S. drone-strike killing of Iranian major general Qasem Soleimani on January 3, 2020, combined with broad unfamiliarity with the Selective Service System among younger Americans and widespread misinformation on social media about the draft being activated in preparation for a supposed war with Iran— illustrated by the viral social-media tag #WWIII—caused the entire Selective Service System to crash temporarily as scores of young Americans flocked to the agency's website for information. Officials simply and euphemistically characterized the incident as "high traffic volumes."[11]

Economics has always accompanied the AVF. At its inception, a significant group of economists, including Milton Friedman, Alan Greenspan, and W. Allen Wallis, argued that conscription was abhorrent on both economic and libertarian grounds. They convinced key politicians, Nixon chief among them, to enact their recommendations. Economics remains a key issue related to the AVF, although more common today are questions about its "moral hazard" or fiscal sustainability due to skyrocketing personnel costs primarily linked to pay, health care, and retirement, among numerous other military benefits. One estimate revealed that the personnel costs of the AVF had almost doubled from 2001 to 2012, consuming one-third of the entire defense budget. More alarming, it predicted that without either major reforms or enlarged budgets, personnel costs could consume the entire defense budget by 2039.[12]

The Gates Commission has its own recent corollary. Due to heightened interest regarding the AVF and service across all categories, Congress created the National Commission on Military, National, and Public Service through the National Defense Authorization Act for FY 2017.

Over the course of several years, from 2017 to 2020, the group conducted dozens of hearings, consulted with hundreds of organizations, and received thousands of public comments. The commission then issued an interim report in January 2019 and concluded its final report in March 2020. In doing so, it examined many of the same opportunities and challenges that the Gates Commission explored, although the outcome has been far less consequential than its predecessor five decades ago.[13]

Likewise, race continues to be an issue in the AVF. Policymakers have made much progress on improving the diversity of the armed forces over the past five decades. Even so, important challenges remain. While the AVF tends to be racially representative, there is a dearth of African American leaders in senior positions. Recent prominent examples illustrate some progress, including Lloyd Austin, the first Black secretary of defense, and Charles "CQ" Brown, the first African American to serve as chief of staff of the U.S. Air Force (or any of the military services for that matter), although much more work remains to be done.[14]

The AVF fundamentally changed both the representation of and opportunities for women in military service. At its advent, women represented only 2 percent of enlisted servicemembers and 8 percent of officers. The number of women in the AVF has steadily risen since 1973, reaching roughly 16 percent of the enlisted force and 19 percent of officers. The opportunities available for them in the armed forces have also undergone recent transformations. On December 3, 2015, Ashton B. Carter, secretary of defense, announced that the DOD would lift all restrictions on military service for women, beginning in January 2016. While representation and opportunities have both increased, lingering barriers remain. Women still are significantly underrepresented in rates of promotion and retention among officers, especially in the most senior positions.[15]

Socioeconomics remain highly relevant and hotly debated. Several studies highlight that the socioeconomics of the AVF have become relatively balanced over time. Even so, both the lowest- and highest-income families remain underrepresented, the former mostly because they do not meet entrance standards, and the latter largely because they choose other pursuits. As a result, the AVF is primarily drawn from middle-class segments of American society.[16]

Military benefits also remain quite pertinent. With the advent of the AVF, basic pay dramatically increased. In addition, a major expansion in benefits has occurred, which has generated significant, and increasing, costs over time. Efforts to address the rapidly rising costs of benefits have resulted in reforms meant as cost-saving measures in such areas as retirement, compensation, and health care.[17]

The viability of the AVF remains an open question. Several factors contribute to this vital discussion, including both fairness and sustainability. Much of the attention on fairness derives largely from how representative it is. While the AVF is fairly representative regarding race and socioeconomics, it is not so regarding gender and geography. As noted, women have steadily increased their participation in military service but still represent only 16 percent of the AVF compared to 51 percent of the broader U.S. population. Geographically, the South is overrepresented, the West and Midwest are roughly representative, and the Northeast is significantly underrepresented.

Sustainability continues to draw more attention, even concern. Two trends are clear. First, significantly rising personnel costs present a momentous hindrance for the sustainability of the AVF. Second, the Pentagon has begun making changes such as the steeply increasing reliance on the reserves, National Guard, and private contractors. Officials will likely continue reforming the armed forces in order to mitigate the problem, although each avenue opens up important questions all its own.[18]

Efficiency remains an important issue as well. Clearly, the AVF has improved the overall quality of the armed forces. Even so, the hard-fought experience of the United States in the Global War on Terrorism has proven that using the AVF to achieve national interests has been quite difficult indeed. In the cases of Iraq and Afghanistan, lengthy involvement, significant forces, and extreme costs did not produce decisive results in any form or by any metric. The Costs of War Project at Brown University has estimated that the post-9/11 wars have cost the United States more than $6.4 trillion, along with nearly 7,000 troops killed, more than 50,000 wounded, and a staggering 1,000,000 disability claims registered with the Department of Veterans Affairs. In addition, the AVF is generally inefficient, if for no other reason than the vast numbers of individuals it recruits, the tremendous costs of training them, and the large portion of them who then leave military service in short order, thereby necessitating starting the entire process over anew. Emerging threats such as Russia and especially China loom, while technological innovations such as cybersecurity, both offensive and defensive, and artificial intelligence mean that the AVF will have to find new ways to recruit, retain, and promote talent that significantly depart from past procedures.[19]

The AVF clearly affected the reserves and National Guard and continues to do so in numerous and significant ways. Most important, it began to transform the reserve components from a strategic to an operational reserve as the Total Force policy, which accompanied the advent of the AVF, gained momentum during the 1990s, and reached unprecedented heights during the Iraq and Afghanistan Wars. Repeat deployments have stretched units, and personnel, to their limits and raise important questions about ramifications on recruiting and retention moving forward. In the process, these trends have fundamentally transformed the understanding of what it means to serve in the reserve components. As new threats have emerged, some prescient observers have called for a reconsideration of how to rebuild a strategic reserve that can address the challenges of tomorrow. In addition to the Iraq and Afghanistan Wars, the COVID-19 pandemic and civil unrest throughout the nation in 2020 resulted in the most extensive National Guard utilization since World War II.[20]

The AVF has always been inextricably intertwined with U.S. foreign policy. President Nixon created it to end the Vietnam War and the draft that helped sustain that conflict. Since the advent of the AVF, however, concern over the militarization of foreign policy has increased. One worry is that it fosters increased involvement in foreign engagements, by one estimate five times more. Another is that it gives carte blanche to policymakers to embroil the nation in endless wars, largely because so few Americans proportionally have to go fight them. The common moniker given to the Iraq and Afghanistan Wars, "forever wars," reinforces that very point. In response, some policymakers have called for eliminating the oft-used and overly ambiguous 2001 Authorization for the Use of Military Force (AUMF) and its successor from the following year and returning to more stringent congressional war-powers control and formal declarations of war as outlined in the U.S. Constitution.[21]

Military culture remains most pertinent, with many positive aspects. One example is the military's consistent ranking as the "most trusted institution in America," with nearly three-quarters of Americans revering the armed forces compared to less than 10 percent for Congress. Even so, there are warning signs that this constant could be eroding, partly due to pervasive problems with sexual assault and persistent questions regarding extremism in the ranks.[22]

Force structure remains a critical issue to determine the best way to maintain appropriate levels amid declining propensity and diminishing qualifications among American youth. One study revealed that nearly 96 percent of young Americans are either unwilling to serve in the military, unqualified to do so, or both, making recruiting an increasingly difficult, if not impossible, mission without numerous incentives and bonuses that temporarily mask this considerable impediment. Such a recruiting conundrum does not even account for the seismic shifts in the contemporary international security environment and the attendant massive changes that will be necessary for the U.S. armed forces to adapt, including Russia's annexation of Crimea and invasion of Ukraine and China's heightened challenges to Taiwan, along with the nuclear ambitions of

Iran and the nuclear provocations of North Korea. As the U.S. military shifts from two decades of war in the Middle East to renewed great-power competition with Russia and especially China, it will have to rethink force structure to transition from a lengthy emphasis on counterinsurgency to one that builds capacity for large-scale combat operations while innovating new capabilities in cybersecurity, unmanned systems, and artificial intelligence.[23]

Renewed attention on civil-military relations, specifically what many observers critique as a civil-military gap, also demonstrates the continuing challenges of the AVF. Many scholars argue that the gap is only increasing and could become a dangerous chasm before long, with major consequences to the United States. Indeed, even the Pentagon has formally acknowledged it as a problem. Some analysts have made well-reasoned arguments that policymakers should integrate civil-military relations, especially attendant recruiting challenges, into U.S. grand-strategy documents, including the National Defense Strategy.[24]

Overall, the AVF represents one of the most significant shifts in both the U.S. armed forces and the broader American society from the late twentieth century. While its successes and challenges continue to be widely discussed and fervently debated, especially after fifty years of service, one thing is certain: the AVF is an institution that remains critical to both U.S. national security and the fabric of American society. Engaged dialogue about its history, results, challenges, and implications is crucial, to ensure not only that it remains ready to meet and overcome potential threats but also that policymakers address the crucial challenges facing it moving forward. The AVF has garnered both triumphs and shortcomings while continuing to be a vital and essential organization. The insightful, cogent, and at times provocative chapters arrayed in this volume represent a crucial first step toward assessing the AVF fifty years after the end of conscription. It is my sincere hope that these lucid contributions from an august group of leading scholars, military officers, and experienced practitioners—and the overall volume that they form—will spark additional dialogue, inspire further research, spur necessary reforms, and impart to a broad audience an informed understanding of the AVF across the many critical issues that it has faced in the past, continues to grapple with in the present, and will undoubtedly encounter in the future.

Notes

1. "Last Draftees Getting Early Discharges," *Washington Post*, October 10, 1974; "Army to Discharge Its Last Draftees," *Los Angeles Times*, October 9, 1974.

2. "Last Draftee Glad He's Out," *New York Times*, May 31, 1982.

3. John M. Crewdson, "Last Draftees Are Discharged, Making the Army All-Volunteer," *New York Times*, November 23, 1974.

4. Defense Manpower Data Center, "Armed Forces Strength Figures," March 31, 2021, https://dwp.dmdc.osd.mil/dwp/app/dod-data-reports/workforce-reports.

5. Lawrence Kapp, "Defense Primer: Reserve Forces," Congressional Research Service, January 28, 2021, https://fas.org/sgp/crs/natsec/IF10540.pdf; Defense Manpower Data Center, "Department of Defense: Selected Reserves by Rank/Grade," March 31, 2021, https://dwp.dmdc.osd.mil/dwp/app/dod-data-reports/workforce-reports.

6. Defense Manpower Data Center, "Department of Defense: Military Personnel on Active Duty by Grade in Which Serving," June 30, 1973, https://dwp.dmdc.osd.mil/dwp/app/dod-data-reports/workforce-reports.

7. Phillip Carter, Katherine L. Kuzminski, Amy Schafer, and Andrew Swick, "AVF 4.0: The Future of the All-Volunteer Force," March 28, 2017, https://www.cnas.org/publications/reports/avf-4-0-the-future-of-the-all-volunteer-force.

8. Council on Foreign Relations, "Demographics of the U.S. Military," July 13, 2020, https://www.cfr.org/backgrounder/demographics-us-military.

9. Gallup, "Military and National Defense," https://news.gallup.com/poll/1666/military-national-defense.aspx.

10. Michael M. Phillips, "A Reluctant Soldier Completes His Duty," *Wall Street Journal*, November 18, 2014, https://www.wsj.com/articles/a-reluctant-soldier-completes-his-duty-1416337417#:~:text=; Reshema Sherlock, "Last Continuously Serving Draftee Retires after 42 Years of Service," October 29, 2014, https://www.armytimes.com/news/your-army/2014/11/04/last-draftee-retiring-after-42-years-on-active-duty/.

11. Ryan Shepard, "Draft Website Crashes after Soleimani's Death, Selective Service Says 'Business as Usual,'" ABC News, January 4, 2020, https://abcnews.go.com/US/draft-website-crashes-soleimanis-death-selective-service-business/story?id=68068550.

12. Uwe E. Reinhardt, "The Moral Hazard of the All-Volunteer Army," *Economix*, January 31, 2014; Lawrence J. Korb, Alex Rothman, and Max Hoffman, "Reforming Military Compensation: Addressing Runaway Personnel Costs Is a National Imperative," Center for American Progress, May 2012, https://cdn.americanprogress.org/wp-content/uploads/issues/2012/05/pdf/military_compensation.pdf?_ga=2.7750640.316276810.1619792106-193398267.1619792106.

13. National Commission on Military, National, and Public Service, "Inspired to Serve: The Final Report of the National Commission on Military, National, and Public Service," Homeland Security Digital Library, March 2020, https://www.hsdl.org/?view&did=841630; National Commission on Military, National, and Public Service, "Interim Report: A Report to the American People, the Congress, and the President," January 2019, https://inspire2serve.gov/NCOS Interim Report.pdf (site discontinued).

14. Tom Vanden Brook, "Where Are the Black Officers?: US Army Shows Diversity in Its Ranks but Few Promotions to the Top," *USA Today*, September 1, 2020, https://

www.usatoday.com/in-depth/news/politics/2020/09/01/military-diversity-army-sho
ws-few-black-officers-top-leadership/3377371001/; Brakkton Booker, "Lloyd Austin
Confirmed as Defense Secretary, Becomes 1st Black Pentagon Chief," NPR, January
22, 2021, https://www.npr.org/sections/president-biden-takes-office/2021/01/22/95
9581977/lloyd-austin-confirmed-as-secretary-of-defense-becomes-first-black-penta
gon-chie; Stephen Losey, "A New Air Force Era Begins as 'CQ' Brown, the Nation's
First Black Service Chief, Assumes Command," *Air Force Times*, August 6, 2020,
https://www.airforcetimes.com/news/your-air-force/2020/08/06/a-new-air-force
-era-begins-as-cq-brown-the-nations-first-black-service-chief-assumes-command/.

15. "Demographics of the U.S. Military," Council on Foreign Relations, July 13,
2020, https://www.cfr.org/backgrounder/demographics-us-military; Andrew Tilgh-
man, "All Combat Jobs Open to Women in the Military," *Military Times*, December 3,
2015, https://www.militarytimes.com/2015/12/03/all-combat-jobs-open-to-women-in
-the-military/; Emma Moore, "Women in Combat: Five-Year Status Update," Center for a New American Security, March 31, 2020, https://www.cnas.org/publications
/commentary/women-in-combat-five-year-status-update; Beth J. Asch, Trey Miller,
and Alessandro Malchiodi, *A New Look at Gender and Minority Differences in Officer Career Progression in the Military* (Santa Monica, CA: RAND Corporation, 2012),
https://www.rand.org/pubs/technical_reports/TR1159.html.

16. For opposing views, see Dennis Laich, *Skin in the Game: Poor Kids and Patriots* (Bloomington, IN: iUniverse, 2013); Andrea Asoni, Andrea Gilli, Mauro Gilli,
and Tino Sanandaji, "A Mercenary Army of the Poor?: Technological Change and
the Demographic Composition of the Post-9/11 U.S. Military," *Journal of Strategic
Studies* 45, no. 4 (January 2020): 568–614, https://doi.org/10.1080/01402390.2019.16
92660; George M. Reynolds, "How Representative Is the All-Volunteer U.S. Military?" Council on Foreign Relations, April 25, 2018, https://www.cfr.org/article/how
-representative-all-volunteer-us-military; Amy Lutz, "Who Joins the Military?: A
Look at Race, Class, and Immigration Status," *Journal of Political and Military So-
ciology* 36, no. 2 (Winter 2008): 167–188; and Congressional Budget Office, "The All-
Volunteer Military: Issues and Performance," CBO Study, July 2007, 1–49, esp. 27–31,
https://www.cbo.gov/sites/default/files/110th-congress-2007-2008/reports/07-19-mi
litaryvol_0.pdf.

17. Kristy N. Kamarck, "Military Retirement: Background and Recent Develop-
ments," Congressional Research Service, February 16, 2021, https://fas.org/sgp/crs
/misc/RL34751.pdf; Laura J. Junor, Samantha Clark, and Mark Ramsay, "Military
Retirement Reform: A Case Study in Successful Public Sector Change," *Joint Forces
Quarterly* 86 (3d qtr. 2017): 73–80, https://ndupress.ndu.edu/Portals/68/Documents
/jfq/jfq-86/jfq-86_73-80_Junor-Clark-Ramsay.pdf; Beth J. Asch, *Setting Military
Compensation to Support Recruitment, Retention, and Performance* (Santa Monica, CA:
RAND Corporation, 2019), https://www.rand.org/content/dam/rand/pubs/research
_reports/RR3100/RR3197/RAND_RR3197.pdf; Patricia Kime, "Bypassing Pentagon
Please, Lawmakers Say Military Health System Reforms Will 'Stay the Course,'"
Military.com, August 19, 2020, https://www.military.com/daily-news/2020/08/19/by
passing-pentagon-pleas-lawmakers-say-military-health-system-reforms-will-stay-co
urse.html.

18. For contrasting views on fairness, see Dennis Laich, "A Nation of Draft Dodgers," *Military Times*, February 1, 2021; Dana T. Atkins, "In Defense of the All-Volunteer Force," *Military Times*, February 4, 2021; Aline Quester and Robert Shuford, "Population Representation in the Military Services: Fiscal Year 2015 Summary Report," CNA, January 2017, esp. 22–27 on geography, esp. 34–35 on gender, and esp. 35–41 on race, https://www.cna.org/CNA_files/PDF/DRP-2017-U-015567-Final.pdf; and Mark F. Cancian, "The Impact of Rising Compensation Costs on Force Structure," *Joint Forces Quarterly* 79 (4th qtr. 2015): 77–82, https://ndupress.ndu.edu/Media/News/Article/621134/the-impact-of-rising-compensation-costs-on-force-structure/.

19. Bernard D. Rostker, "The Evolution of the All-Volunteer Force," RAND Corporation, 2006, https://www.rand.org/pubs/research_briefs/RB9195.html; Neta C. Crawford, "United States Budgetary Costs and Obligations of Post-9/11 Wars through FY2020: $6.4 Trillion," Watson Institute, November 13, 2019, https://watson.brown.edu/costsofwar/files/cow/imce/papers/2019/US Budgetary Costs of Wars November 2019.pdf; "U.S. & Allied Wounded," Costs of War, Watson Institute, July 2021, https://watson.brown.edu/costsofwar/costs/human/military/wounded; Carter, Kuzminski, Schafer, and Swick, "AVF 4.0," esp. "Waste and Inefficiency"; Tim Kane, *Bleeding Talent: How the US Military Mismanages Great Leaders and Why It's Time for a Revolution* (New York: Palgrave Macmillan, 2012); Samuel Crislip, "Capturing Flags and Recruiting Future Cyber Soldiers," War on the Rocks, August 28, 2020, https://warontherocks.com/2020/08/capturing-flags-and-recruiting-future-cyber-soldiers/.

20. Miranda Summers Lowe, "The Gradual Shift to an Operational Reserve: Reserve Component Mobilizations in the 1990s," *Military Review* 99, no. 3 (May–June 2019): 119–126, https://www.armyupress.army.mil/Portals/7/military-review/Archives/English/MJ-19/Summers-Lowe-Reserve-1990s.pdf; David R. Segal and Lawrence J. Korb, "Manning and Financing the Twenty-First-Century All-Volunteer Force," in *The Modern American Military*, ed. David M. Kennedy (Oxford: Oxford University Press, 2013), 111–134, esp. 123–128; Danielle DeSimone, "Reserve and National Guard Members Signed Up to Serve Part-Time; But They're Deploying More than Ever Before," USO, October 23, 2020, https://www.uso.org/stories/2870-reserve-and-national-guard-members-signed-up-to-serve-part-time-but-theyre-deploying-more-than-ever-before; Jacquelyn Schneider, "Moving beyond Total Force: Building a True Strategic Reserve," War on the Rocks, November 2, 2020, https://warontherocks.com/2020/11/moving-beyond-total-force-building-a-true-strategic-reserve/; Alex Horton, "Pandemic and Unrest Fuel the Biggest National Guard Mobilization since World War II," *Washington Post*, December 24, 2020, https://www.washingtonpost.com/national-security/2020/12/24/national-guard-response/.

21. Phillip Carter, "Final Draft: Forty Years after the End of Conscription, Can We Fix the All-Volunteer Force?" *Foreign Policy*, January 28, 2013, https://foreignpolicy.com/2013/01/28/final-draft/; Karl W. Eikenberry, "Reassessing the All-Volunteer Force," in Kennedy, *Modern American Military*, 213–239, esp. 217; Geoff Lamear, "Repealing the AUMF Is Biden's Opportunity to End the 'Forever Wars,'" *The Hill*, February 11, 2021, https://thehill.com/opinion/national-security/538387-repealing-the-aumf-is-bidens-opportunity-to-end-the-forever-wars.

22. Corinne Dillon, Amber Hall, and Adriana Balsamo-Gallina, "Why the Military Is Still the Most Trusted Institution in America," *The Takeaway*, New York Public Radio, September 27, 2016, https://www.wnycstudios.org/podcasts/takeaway/segments/why-military-still-most-trusted-institution-america; C. Todd Lopez, "Commission Begins 90-Day Look into Sexual Assault in the Military," U.S. Department of Defense News, March 24, 2021, https://www.defense.gov/Explore/News/Article/Article/2548632/commission-begins-90-day-look-into-sexual-assault-in-military/; Luis Martinez and J. P. Keenan, "The Military Is Concerned about Extremism in Its Ranks?: Here's What to Know," ABC News, April 28, 2021, https://abcnews.go.com/US/military-concerned-extremism-ranks/story?id=77119201.

23. Michael Runney and Charles Allen, "An All-Volunteer Force for Long-Term Success," *Military Review* 95, no. 6 (November–December 2015): 92–100, esp. 97; Tyler Pager and Natasha Bertrand, "White House Shifts from Middle East Quagmires to a Showdown with China," *Politico*, January 28, 2021, https://www.politico.com/news/2021/01/28/biden-china-foreign-policy-463674; Joseph R. Biden Jr., "Interim National Security Strategic Guidance," March 2021, https://www.whitehouse.gov/wp-content/uploads/2021/03/NSC-1v2.pdf; Daniel S. Hoadley and Kelley M. Sayler, "Artificial Intelligence and National Security," Congressional Research Service, November 10, 2020, https://fas.org/sgp/crs/natsec/R45178.pdf.

24. Simone Williams, "Civil-Military Relations: Increasing Awareness and Reducing the Gap," *New Perspectives in Foreign Policy*, no. 17 (Spring 2019): 54–57; Mark Thompson, "An Army Apart: The Widening Military-Civilian Gap," *Time*, November 10, 2011, https://nation.time.com/2011/11/10/an-army-apart-the-widening-military-civilian-gap/; Jim Garamone, "DOD Official Cites Widening Military-Civilian Gap," U.S. Department of Defense News, May 16, 2019, https://www.defense.gov/Explore/News/Article/Article/1850344/dod-official-cites-widening-military-civilian-gap/; Nathalie Grogan, "The All-Volunteer Force: Civil-Military Relations Hit Home—and Abroad," Center for a New American Strategy, September 17, 2020, https://www.cnas.org/publications/commentary/the-all-volunteer-force-civil-military-relations-hit-home-and-abroad.

Chronology

September 16, 1940	President Franklin D. Roosevelt signed the Selective Training and Service Act of 1940
October 16, 1940	First peacetime registration for the Selective Service System held
July 1, 1941	Second peacetime registration for the Selective Service System held
July 31, 1941	President Roosevelt appointed Lewis B. Hershey director of the Selective Service System
December 5, 1942	Executive Order 9279 terminated voluntary enlistment in the armed forces
May 9, 1945	President Harry S. Truman signed bill to extend the Selective Training and Service Act to May 15, 1946
August 29, 1945	Executive Order 9605 restored voluntary enlistments in the armed forces for registrants in the age group acceptable for induction
October 6, 1945	President Truman signed Public Law 190, 79th Congress, to stimulate voluntary enlistment in the army and navy through immediate and deferred monetary and other benefits
March 31, 1947	Selective Service Act expired
June 24, 1948	Selective Service resumed
June 19, 1951	President Truman signed the Universal Military Training and Service Act
1955	Congress renewed the draft
1959	Congress renewed the draft
1963	Congress renewed the draft
July 1, 1967	Congress changed the Universal Military Training and Service Act to the Military Selective Service Act of 1967
November 8, 1967	Congress repealed restrictions on the percentage of women in American military service
October 17, 1968	Presidential candidate Richard M. Nixon's radio address announced his intention to end the draft and transition the military to an AVF

March 27, 1969	President Nixon created the President's Commission on an All-Volunteer Armed Force, colloquially known as the Gates Commission
May 15, 1969	Gates Commission held its first meeting
February 20, 1970	Gates Commission issued its final report
June 30, 1973	Induction authority for the draft expired
July 1, 1973	Advent of the AVF
June 25, 1981	*Rostker v. Goldberg* decided that male-only registration for the draft was constitutional
January 24, 2013	Secretary of Defense Leon Panetta removed restrictions on women serving in combat
November 10, 2014	Chief Warrant Officer 5 Ralph E. Rigby, the last continuously serving draftee, retired
December 3, 2015	Secretary of Defense Ashton B. Carter opened all military occupational specialties to women
January 23, 2019	National Commission on Military, National, and Public Service released its interim report
February 22, 2019	U.S. District Court, Southern District of Texas, Houston Division ruled that an all-male draft would be unconstitutional
March 25, 2020	National Commission on Military, National, and Public Service released its final report
July 1, 2023	Fiftieth anniversary of the AVF

About the Contributors

Beth Bailey is Foundation Distinguished Professor at the University of Kansas, where she directs the Center for Military, War, and Society Studies. She currently chairs the Department of the Army Historical Advisory Subcommittee and coedits the Cambridge University Press series Military, War, and Society in the Modern United States. Her military history publications include *An Army Afire: How the U.S. Army Confronted Its Racial Crisis in the Vietnam Era* (Chapel Hill: University of North Carolina Press, 2023) and *America's Army: Making the All-Volunteer Force* (Cambridge, MA: Belknap Press of Harvard University Press, 2009) as well as the coedited works *Managing Sex in the U.S. Military: Gender, Identity, and Behavior* (Lincoln: University of Nebraska Press, 2022); *Understanding the U.S. Wars in Iraq and Afghanistan* (New York: New York University Press, 2015); and *Beyond Pearl Harbor: A Pacific History* (Lawrence: University Press of Kansas, 2019). She holds an Andrew Carnegie Fellowship from 2022 to 2024, and her research has been supported by the National Endowment for the Humanities, the Woodrow Wilson International Center for Scholars, and the American Council of Learned Societies. Bailey is a member of the Society of American Historians and, in 2022, received the Society for Military History's Samuel Eliot Morison Award for contributions to the field of military history.

Mark F. Cancian is a senior adviser with the CSIS International Security Program. He joined CSIS in April 2015 from the Office of Management and Budget, where he spent more than seven years as chief of the Force Structure and Investment Division, working on such issues as DOD budget strategy, war funding, and procurement programs, as well as nuclear-weapons development and nonproliferation activities in the Department of Energy. Previously, he worked on force structure and acquisition issues in the Office of the Secretary of Defense and ran research and executive programs at Harvard University's Kennedy School of Government. Cancian retired as a colonel after spending over three decades in the U.S. Marine Corps, active and reserve, serving as an infantry, artillery, and civil-affairs officer and on overseas tours in Vietnam, Desert Storm, and Iraq (twice). Since 2000, he has been an adjunct faculty member at the Johns Hopkins School of Advanced International Studies, where he teaches a course on the connection between policy and analysis. A prolific author, he has published over forty articles on military operations, acquisitions, budgets, and strategy and has received numerous writing awards. He graduated with high honors (magna cum laude) from Harvard College and with highest honors (Baker Scholar) from Harvard Business School.

Titus Firmin is a captain in the Kansas Army National Guard and has served since 2012, when he enlisted as an infantryman. He graduated from Rutgers University with a BA degree in history and earned his MA degree from the University of New Orleans. He has collaborated on several public military history projects with the Louisiana National Guard Museum, Humanities Kansas, Defense POW/MIA Accounting Agency, and the National World War II Museum. He is currently a PhD candidate in history at the University of Kansas. His dissertation examines how U.S. Army leaders managed problems that intersected with racial discrimination and civil-military relations since World War II.

Michael Gibbs is clinical professor of economics at the University of Chicago Booth School of Business and studies the economics of human resources and organizational design. He is coauthor of *Personnel Economics in Practice*, 3d ed. (Hoboken, NJ: Wiley, 2014), which has been translated into Chinese, Japanese, Korean, Bulgarian, and Spanish. Gibbs has published research in the *Journal of Political Economy—Microeconomics, Quarterly Journal of Economics, Review of Economics and Statistics, Industrial and Labor Relations Review*, and *Accounting Review*, among other journals. He is a research fellow of the Center for the Study of Labor in Bonn, Germany, and the Institute for Compensation Studies. From 2012 to 2015, he was faculty director of Chicago Booth's Executive MBA Program. In 2007, he received the Notable Contribution to Management Accounting Literature Award from the American Accounting Association and has received several Hillel Einhorn Excellence in Teaching Awards from Chicago Booth. Gibbs earned bachelor's, master's, and doctoral degrees in economics from the University of Chicago.

David M. Kennedy is the Donald J. McLachlan Professor of History, emeritus, at Stanford University and Pulitzer Prize–winning author of *Freedom from Fear: The American People in Depression and War, 1929–1945* (Oxford: Oxford University Press, 1999). Reflecting his interdisciplinary training in American studies, which combined the fields of history, literature, and economics, Kennedy's scholarship is notable for its integration of economic and cultural analysis with social and political history. His book, *Birth Control in America: The Career of Margaret Sanger* (New Haven, CT: Yale University Press, 1970), embraces the medical, legal, political, and religious dimensions of the subject and helped pioneer the emerging field of women's history. *Over Here: The First World War and American Society* (Oxford: Oxford University Press, 1980) uses the history of U.S. involvement in World War I to analyze the American political system, economy, and culture in the early twentieth century.

Major General Dennis Laich retired from the U.S. Army in 2006 after more than thirty-five years of service, the last fourteen in command positions. His last assignment was commander of the 94th Regional Readiness Command at Fort Devans, Massachusetts, in charge of all Army Reserve forces in the six New England states. Laich has served in Iraq, Kuwait, Germany, the Netherlands, and Honduras. His military awards include the Defense Distinguished Service Medal and Legion of Merit. A graduate of the Army War College, Command and General Staff College, and National Security Management Program, Laich holds a bachelor's degree from Lafayette College and two master's degrees and has completed postgraduate studies at the Kennedy School of Government at Harvard University. He currently serves as the executive director of the All-Volunteer Force Forum and director of the Patriots Program at Ohio Dominican University. Laich is the author of *Skin in the Game: Poor Kids and Patriots* (Bloomington, IN: iUniverse, 2013).

Adrian R. Lewis is the David B. Pittaway Professor of Military History at the University of Kansas, Lawrence. He has researched and written extensively on war, military affairs, and the armed forces of the United States for over twenty years. Lewis's publications include *The American Culture of War: The History of U.S. Military Force from World War II to Operation Enduring Freedom*, now in its third edition, published in 2018; *Omaha Beach: A Flawed Victory*, published in 2001 and still considered the best analysis of Allied amphibious-warfare doctrine in the European theater of operations; and numerous book chapters and articles, most recently "Defeat in Afghanistan: Lessons Ignored, the Deeper Lesson: The American Culture of War," *The Korean Journal of Security Affairs* 26, no. 2 (December 2021). Professor Lewis has taught at the U.S. Military Academy, West Point; the University of California, Berkeley, where he served as professor of military science and chair; and the University of North Texas, Denton, where he served as the chair of the Department of History. Lewis earned his BA in political science at the University of California, Berkeley; MA in history from the University of Michigan, Ann

Arbor; MBA from Southern Illinois University, Edwardsville; and PhD in history from the University of Chicago. Professor Lewis is a retired soldier. He served with the 2/1 Infantry and 2/23 Infantry, 9th Infantry Division, and the 2/75 Infantry (Ranger). He has served in Korea, Alaska, Panama, and Germany.

Jennifer Mittelstadt is professor of history at Rutgers University. She studies the twentieth-century United States, with broad interests in the state and social policy, politics, gender, social movements, the military and militarization, and foreign policy. Mittelstadt is the author of *From Welfare to Workfare: The Unintended Consequences of Liberal Reform, 1945– 1964* (Chapel Hill: University of North Carolina, 2005) and *The Rise of the Military Welfare State* (Cambridge, MA: Harvard University Press, 2015) as well as coauthor and coeditor (with Mark Wilson) of *The Military and the Market* (Philadelphia: University of Pennsylvania Press, 2022). Her work has been supported by the John Simon Guggenheim Foundation, the Dorothy and Lewis Cullman Center of the New York Public Library, and the Woodrow Wilson Center. She also served as the Harold K. Johnson Chair in Military History at the U.S. Army War College. She is series editor of Power, Politics, and the World for the University of Pennsylvania Press and is currently writing a history of grassroots participation in U.S. foreign policy in the twentieth century.

Timothy J. Perri is professor emeritus of economics at Appalachian State University, where he taught for nearly forty years and in 2016 won the Student Government Award for Outstanding Professor in the Walker College of Business. Prior to this, Perri taught at the Ohio State University at Mansfield. His research interests include the economics of conscription and labor economics, and he has published more than thirty articles in refereed journals, including "Can a Draft Induce More Human Capital Investment in the Military?," *Economics Bulletin* 33, no. 2 (April 2013): 905–913; "The Evolution of Military Conscription in the United States," *Independent Review* 17, no. 3 (Winter 2013): 429–439; "Deferments and the Relative Cost of Conscription," *B. E. Journal of Economic Analysis and Policy: Topics* 10, no. 1 (December 2010), https://doi.org/10.2202/1935 -1682.2644; and "The Economics of U.S. Civil War Conscription," *American Law and Economics Review* 10, no. 2 (Fall 2008): 424–453.

Major General Jeffrey E. Phillips, U.S. Army (retired), serves 45,000 members as the executive director of the Reserve Organization of America, a congressionally chartered association, founded in 1922, that promotes a strong national defense and advocates for readiness throughout the military reserves and National Guard. Commissioned in 1979 as a second lieutenant of armor and later command of an M-1 Abrams tank company in the 2d Armored Division, during his thirty-seven years in the army, Phillips has served in Afghanistan, the Balkans, Egypt, Honduras, Israel, Iraq, and Germany as well as in the United States. In 2001, he was appointed by President George W. Bush as the deputy assistant secretary for public affairs and White House liaison for the Department of Veterans Affairs. He has worked in the House of Representatives as a communications and a subcommittee staff director, then later formed and managed a national sales team in a publicly held medical-manufacturing firm. Among his awards and decorations are the Army Distinguished Service Medal, two Legion of Merit medals, two Bronze Stars, and an Army Parachutist Badge. Phillips shares the 1988 Nobel Peace Prize for service with the U.N. Truce Supervision Organization.

Amy J. Rutenberg is an associate professor of history at Iowa State University, where she specializes in U.S. history at the intersection of war and gender. She is the author of *Rough Draft: Cold War Military Manpower Policy and the Origins of Vietnam-Era Draft Resistance* (Ithaca, NY: Cornell University Press, 2019). She received her PhD degree from the University of Maryland and her EdM degree from the Harvard Graduate School of Education. Rutenberg currently serves on the Board of Trustees for the Society for Military History. She is working on a book on the effects of peace activism on the all-volunteer force and editing an essay collection on conscription in transnational context. Her work has appeared in *Cold War History*, the *New York Times*, and *The Atlantic*.

William A. Taylor is the Lee Drain Endowed University Professor of Global Security Studies and previous department chair in the Kay Bailey Hutchison Center for Security Studies at Angelo State University in San Angelo, Texas. He is the editor for two book series, Studies in Civil-Military Relations, with the University Press of Kansas, and Studies in Marine Corps History and Amphibious Warfare, with the Naval Institute Press. He is the author or editor of six other books, including *Peace, War, and Partnership: Congress and the Military since World War II* (College Station: Texas A&M University Press, 2023); *The Advent of the All-Volunteer Force: Protecting Free Society* (New York: Routledge, 2023); *George C. Marshall and the Early Cold War: Policy, Politics, and Society* (Norman: University of Oklahoma Press, 2020); *Contemporary Security Issues in Africa* (Santa Barbara, CA: Praeger, 2019); *Military Service and American Democracy: From World War II to the Iraq and Afghanistan Wars* (Lawrence: University Press of Kansas, 2016); and *Every Citizen a Soldier: The Campaign for Universal Military Training after World War II* (College Station: Texas A&M University Press, 2014), which won the Crader Family Book Prize Honorable Mention in 2015. He also has contributed to twenty-four other books and has published more than ninety-five reference articles and book reviews. Taylor has won eighteen national fellowships and research grants as well as the 2022 Texas Tech University System Chancellor's Council Distinguished Teaching Award, the 2021 Angelo State University President's Award for Faculty Excellence in Teaching, the 2019 Angelo State University President's Award for Faculty Excellence in Leadership/Service, the 2016 Texas Tech University System Chancellor's Council Distinguished Research Award, and the 2016 Angelo State University President's Award for Faculty Excellence in Research/Creative Endeavor. His books are housed in more than 1,900 libraries throughout the United States and in more than fifty-five countries around the world.

Marybeth P. Ulrich is the Gen. Maxwell D. Taylor Chair of the Profession of Arms and professor of government at the U.S. Army War College. She previously taught in the Department of Political Science at the U.S. Air Force Academy. Her active-duty air force career spanned fifteen years, and she logged more than 1,900 hours in Strategic Air Command as a navigator on KC-135Q refueling planes. Her research focuses on strategic studies, especially civil-military relations; national-security democratization; and professionalism. Her publications include *Democratizing Communist Militaries: The Cases of the Czech and Russian Armed Forces* (Ann Arbor: University of Michigan Press, 2000) and numerous journal articles and book chapters. Ulrich retired from the Air Force Reserve as a colonel and has served as the reserve air attaché to the Russian Federation and the Czech Republic. She has served as NATO Defense Education and Enhancement Program faculty in Moldova, Ukraine, Kazakhstan, and the Baltic states. She received a PhD degree in political science from the University of Illinois and a bachelor's degree from the U.S. Air Force Academy, where she was a distinguished graduate in the Class of 1984. Ulrich is a life member of the Council on Foreign Relations.

Kara Dixon Vuic is the LCpl. Benjamin W. Schmidt Professor of War, Conflict, and Society in Twentieth-Century America at Texas Christian University and the author of *The Girls Next Door: Bringing the Home Front to the Front Lines* (Cambridge, MA: Harvard University Press, 2019), which won the Tonous and Warda Johns Family Book Award from the American Historical Association–Pacific Coast Branch and the Captain Richard Lukaszewicz Memorial Book Award from the U.S. Military History Group. Her first book, *Officer, Nurse, Woman: The Army Nurse Corps in the Vietnam War* (Baltimore: Johns Hopkins University Press, 2010), won the Lavinia L. Dock Book Award from the American Association for the History of Nursing and was a finalist for the Army Historical Foundation Distinguished Writing Award. She also edited *The Routledge Handbook on Gender, War, and the U.S. Military* (London: Routledge, 2017), coedited the collection *Managing Sex in the U.S. Military: Gender, Identity, and Behavior* (University of Nebraska Press, 2022), and is coeditor (with Richard Fogarty) of the University of Nebraska Press's book series Studies in War, Society, and the Military. She is currently working on a book project called "Drafting Women."

Lawrence B. Wilkerson was Distinguished Visiting Professor of Government and Public Policy at the College of William & Mary in Williamsburg, Virginia, where he taught for sixteen years (2006–2021). Previously, while serving in the U.S. Army for thirty-one years, he taught at the Naval War College in Newport, Rhode Island, and the Marine Corps War College in Quantico, Virginia. Wilkerson has held senior positions outside teaching, including in the military as special assistant to Chairman of the Joint Chiefs of Staff General Colin L. Powell and in civilian life as chief of staff to Secretary of State Powell.

Other Books by William A. Taylor

Peace, War, and Partnership, ed.
The Advent of the All-Volunteer Force
George C. Marshall and the Early Cold War, ed.
Contemporary Security Issues in Africa
Military Service and American Democracy
Every Citizen a Soldier

Index

Page numbers in *italics* refer to figures and illustrations. Page numbers followed by *n* refer to notes followed by the note number.